THEORY AND PRACTICE
OF EARLY READING
Volume 1

THEORY AND PRACTICE
OF EARLY READING
Volume 1

Edited by   **LAUREN B. RESNICK**
University of Pittsburgh

PHYLLIS A. WEAVER
Harvard University

LEA
LAWRENCE ERLBAUM ASSOCIATES, PUBLISHERS
1979   Hillsdale, New Jersey

Lawrence Erlbaum Associates, Inc., Publishers
365 Broadway
Hillsdale, New Jersey 07642

Library of Congress Cataloging in Publication Data

Main entry under title:
Theory and practice of early reading.

Based on papers presented at a series of three
conferences held at the Learning Research and Develop-
ment Center, University of Pittsburgh in 1976.
   Bibliography: v. 1, p.
   Includes index.
   CONTENTS: v. 1. Research issues.
   1. Reading (Elementary)   2. Reading readiness
3. Children—Language.   4. Reading—Remedial teaching.
I. Resnick, Lauren B.   II. Weaver, Phyllis A.
LB1573.T46   372.4   79-22322
ISBN 0-89859-003-5

Printed in the United States of America

Contents

    Some Facts and Some Opinions
    Isabel L. Beck and Karen K. Block   **279**

    Definition of Reading: Program Scope and Materials   281
    Relationships Between Program Content Units
       and School Grades   282
    Flow of Instruction   283
    Letter–Sound Correspondences   287
    Sight Word Instruction   300
    The Development of Comprehension   302
    Summary and Conclusions   307
    Appendix A:
       Material Resources in the Ginn and Palo Alto Programs   309
    Appendix B:
       Procedures Used to Transform Content Units to
       Relative Proportion of Time Spent in Those Units
       for the First Two Grades   310
    Appendix C:
       An Abstracted Description of the 10 Short *i* Exercises
       in Level 3 of Ginn   312
    Appendix D:
       An Abstracted Description of the Sequence
       for Teaching Short *i* in Book 2 of Palo Alto   315

PART IV: DISCUSSION

12. **Concerning the Marriage of Research and Practice**
    in Beginning Reading Instruction
    Walter Kintsch   **319**

    Research or Intuition and Experience   320
    Reading Research   322
    The Need for a Theory   324
    Status of Reading Research   328

13. **Applying Theories and Theorizing about Applications**
    Michael I. Posner   **331**

    A View of Application and Theory   331
    Developmental and Processing Stages   332
    Nature of Codes   336
    Cognitive Control   337
    Individual Differences   339
    Program Design   340

Preface

Concern for the pedagogy of reading is almost as old as the history of the written word. Yet never before the present century has reading instruction commanded so much attention on the part of so many. A society that aspires to universal literacy must necessarily be fascinated with the question of how people read and how they learn to read. When everyone must be literate, problems that once could be solved by attrition and dropping out must now be solved by instruction. Not only those who learn easily but those who are hard to teach and even those who are reluctant to learn must be taught. Every resource, theoretical and practical, must be brought to bear on the problem of reading instruction.

These volumes explore the range and depth of our theoretical and practical knowledge about early reading instruction. Contributors—psychologists, linguists, instructional designers, reading and special education experts— were asked to address three questions: (1) What is the nature of skilled reading? (2) How is reading skill acquired? (3) What do the nature of skilled reading and the process of acquiring reading skill jointly suggest for reading instruction? In this context, issues such as the centrality of decoding in early reading, "stages" in learning to read, the role of "automatic" word recognition in reading comprehension, the role of oral language in acquiring reading skill, the effect of cultural and linguistic differences on reading acquisition and performance, and the nature of individual differences in learning to read are addressed and debated. Several major instructional programs are analyzed, and there is considerable discussion of the possible and appropriate role of theory and experimental research in guiding the course of reading instruction. Taken together, the chapters of these three volumes suggest clearly where reading research and practice stand with respect to the key questions of skilled performance, acquisition sequences, and early instruction. Accordingly, these volumes should be of interest to reading educators, psychologists, and other theorists of reading.

Many of the chapters in these volumes are based on papers that were presented and discussed at a series of three conferences held at the Learning Research and Development Center, University of Pittsburgh, in 1976. The conferences were supported by the National Institute of Education as part of the Compensatory Education Evaluation Study. Organization of volumes is by conference, with discussion chapters appearing at the end of each volume. The thematic content of each volume and of the series as a whole is outlined in some detail in the introductory chapter.

We gratefully acknowledge those many individuals who assisted in planning and conducting the conferences and preparing these volumes. Cathlene Hardaway and Barbara Haky Viccari assisted in many details of planning and running the conferences; they and Carol Evans had responsibility for many aspects related to preparing these volumes. Shirley Tucker prepared the subject indexes to the three volumes. Charles Teggatz was technical editor for most chapters in the three volumes; his substantive suggestions and editoral assistance were invaluable. During a major part of the preparation of these volumes, one of us (Lauren Resnick) was a fellow at the Center for Advanced Study in the Behavioral Sciences, Palo Alto, California, supported in part by a grant from the Spencer Foundation. This support is gratefully acknowledged.

LAUREN B. RESNICK
PHYLLIS A. WEAVER

THEORY AND PRACTICE
OF EARLY READING
Volume 1

The Theory and
Practice of
Early Reading:
An Introduction

Phyllis A. Weaver
Harvard University

Lauren B. Resnick
University of Pittsburgh

> *There is a kind of idle theory which is antithetical to practice;*
> *but genuinely scientific theory falls within practice as the agency*
> *of its expansion and its direction to new possibilities.*
> John Dewey (1932)

Never before the present century has reading instruction commanded so much attention on the part of so many. The sources of this concern and attention lie in a combination of social and scientific developments that set the context in which these volumes and the positions on reading taken in them can best be understood and evaluated. In the social sphere, standards of literacy have been rising during the course of the past century. Virtually everyone is now expected to become literate, and the criteria for assessing literacy are more stringent today than at any previous time. The result is increased public concern for reading and increased attention to reading on the part of educators. In the scientific sphere, meanwhile, there has been a continuing press to apply scientific knowledge to practical affairs, with the result that attention has been directed most to those aspects of educational practice about which science has the most to say. Together, these social and scientific developments have shaped both the extent and the direction of current work on reading, work that is reported and debated in these volumes. In this chapter, we begin by considering how theory and practice in reading instruction have been influenced by these forces. We then outline the specific issues that are dominant in today's debates about early reading; these issues are directly addressed in the chapters of these volumes.

THE SOCIAL PRESS FOR LITERACY

The Expectation of Universal Literacy

A short story by Somerset Maugham helps to illustrate the ways in which social perceptions of literacy have changed. "The Verger"(Maugham, 1937) is about a man, Albert Edward Foreman, who has held the position of verger in a fashionable church (St. Peter's, Neville Square) for many years. He is illiterate, a fact that has just been discovered by the current vicar and churchwardens. The discovery leads to a request for the verger's resignation, although all involved freely admit that he performs his duties quite acceptably. Nevertheless, they find it inappropriate for a man who cannot read or write to be their verger:

> "It's the most amazing thing I ever heard," cried the [warden]. "Do you mean to say that you've been verger of this church for sixteen years and never learned to read or write?"
> "I went into service when I was twelve, sir. The cook in the first place tried to teach me once, but I didn't seem to 'ave the knack for it, and then what with one thing and another I never seemed to 'ave the time. I've never really found the want of it. I think a lot of these young fellows waste a rare lot of time readin' when they might be doin' something useful."

The story relates how the verger, faced with the need to earn a living in some new way, opens a tabacconist's shop, then a second, then several more. Eventually he owns a string of shops, and he is making weekly bank deposits so large that his holdings total over thirty thousand pounds. Noting this, a bank officer suggests that the funds might better be invested and offers to make out a list of securities so that all the verger-turned-businessman would need to do is to sign the necessary papers:

> "I could do that all right," said Albert uncertainly. "But 'ow should I know what I was signin'?"
> "I suppose you can read," said the manager a trifle sharply.
> Mr. Foreman gave him a disarming smile.
> "Well, sir, that's just it. I can't. I know it sounds funny like, but there it is, I can't read or write, only me name, an' I only learnt to do that when I went into business."
> The manager was so surprised that he jumped up from his chair.
> "That's the most extraordinary thing I ever heard."
> "You see, it's like this, sir, I never 'ad the opportunity until it was too late and then some'ow I wouldn't. I got obstinate like."
> The manager stared at him as though he were a prehistoric monster.
> "And do you mean to say that you've built up this important business and amassed a fortune of thirty thousand pounds without being able to read or

write? Good God, man, what would you be now if you had been able to?"
"I can tell you that, sir," said Mr. Foreman, a little smile on his still aristocratic features. "I'd be verger of St. Peter's, Neville Square."

The story's ironic ending helps to illustrate the profound ways in which society's demands for literacy have changed. The story takes place in a time when an expectation of widespread literacy was just developing. The astonishment of both church and bank officials serves to highlight the expectation. Both groups seem to believe that literacy is required for satisfactory performance of the work in question; in fact, the deepest source of their astonishment is not that Albert Edward cannot read or write but that he has been performing his jobs successfully in spite of being illiterate. Albert Edward's experiences might serve to demonstrate to these people that literacy is not essential to successful performance, at least in many jobs and social functions. But that is not their interpretation. The church officials, offering the excuse of a possible accident in the church, treat literacy, even that of the verger, as a necessary status symbol for members of their organization. The bank official assumes that Albert Edward might have succeeded even more brilliantly had he been literate. Albert Edward, however, understands that his success does not depend on literacy and seems also to recognize that his inability to read is not linked to intelligence but to the accidents of birth in a period in which opportunity and expectation for learning to read were tied to social class.

Maugham wrote "The Verger" in the 1930s, an ironic commentary on an already changing scene in which formal credentials of literacy were beginning to replace functional performance and inherited status as a criterion for access to certain positions. The shifts Maugham noted fifty years ago are all the more marked now. Moreover, it is unlikely that Albert Edward today could be successful as a tabacconist. Opportunities for small business have shrunk, and even these depend heavily on obtaining credit and negotiating other formalities that require at least minimum literacy. Furthermore, it is unlikely that Albert Edward today would be so serenely accepting of his state of illiteracy, juding himself neither incompetent nor lazy for being unable to read.

The Rising Criteria for Literacy

At the same time as we have expected more people to be literate, our criteria for literacy have been rising, placing double pressures on the instructional system. Our definitions of reading competence have changed markedly over the past century, and neither our methods of teaching nor our understanding of the reading process has caught up with our social aspirations. Reviewing the history of literacy standards in Western Europe and America, Resnick and Resnick (1977) noted that until well into the present century, knowing "how to read" meant being able to recognize and respond to highly familiar texts, such as those of catechisms or other religious or civil tracts. Given this criterion, teaching reading meant teaching people to translate printed words into spoken ones—that is, to read aloud. During the 19th century, an able reader—according to the definition used in most schools—was one who could give a good public rendition of a text, declaiming it with appropriate phrasing and emphasis. Although readers undoubtedly needed to grasp at least the gist of what they were reading to achieve such a performance, there is little evidence that schools were expected to *teach* anything having to do with the comprehension of written texts. In fact, there is evidence to the contrary, suggesting that most schools explicitly understood their reading instruction mandate to end with the development of fluent oral reading skill. A description of the pedagogical aims and practices of a well-known Scottish school, drawn from an American teachers' journal of 1831, highlights this understanding (from Mathews, 1966):

> English reading, according to the prevailing notion, consists of nothing more than the power of giving utterance to certain sounds, on the perception of certain figures; and the measure of progress and excellence is the facility and continuous fluency with which those sounds succeed each other from the mouth of the learner. If the child gathers any knowledge from the book before him, beyond that of color, form, and position of the letters, it is to his own sagacity he is indebted for it, and not to his teacher [p. 55].

It is only during the present century that reading for the purpose of gaining information has become a virtually universal goal, an expectation applied in ordinary elementary schools to the entire population of students. This shift in the criteria for literacy has direct bearing on the state of our knowledge regarding reading instruction. To the extent that reading instruction is concerned with the ability to declaim print, it has a long history of pedagogical thought and effort on which to draw. Over several centuries, considerable ingenuity and thoughtfulness have been brought to bear on the problem (see Mathews, 1966, for a review), and there is a great deal of richness and depth in past discussions both of how people manage to translate print to sound and how this skill can best be taught. However, insofar as reading instruction is concerned with the process of drawing meaning from print, it has only a brief history of scientific work to draw on; and there is little richness in the range of instructional practices that have been tried. As a result, there is comparatively little in the way of empirical evidence to support competing conceptions of the nature of skilled comprehension or of how it develops. This difference in historical depth accounts in great part for the difference in how much we are able to say about decoding texts and understanding them—a difference that will become apparent to the readers of these volumes. It also suggests why professionals and scientists concerned with reading are in a position to make some meaningful prescriptive judgments about how people learn and use alphabetic codes but are able to say relatively little, with assurance, about how they develop and enhance their ability to comprehend written text.

THE FOCUS ON EARLY READING

It is in recognition of the differential state of scientific knowledge about decoding and comprehension that we chose to limit the focus of these volumes to early reading. Early reading has often been defined as learning the code, being able to recognize words, or translating print to sound. As we have just suggested, this is a definition with considerable historical tradition: Learning the code *was* learning to read for many centuries. As a result, we know more about how people use the code during both beginning and skilled stages of reading than we do about how they use the semantic or syntactic aspects of texts. If there is a part of the total process of becoming literate in which science and professional practice have an opportunity to interact fruitfully at this time, it is with respect to learning the code. A great deal of research has been conducted on recognizing printed words and translating them into oral language, and a significant amount is known about the processes involved in word recognition and how to teach this aspect of reading to young children. Research provides some knowledge of the relations between word recognition and comprehension, although this knowledge is still limited. Moreover, far less is known about the processes involved in constructing meaning from written or spoken language, and very little is known about how to facilitate the development of these processes in young learners. In fact, the study of natural language processes as part of reading is only now emerging as a major focus of scholarly research.

Code and Meaning

A decision to focus on early reading and thus on learning the code, however well justified in terms of our past history and current knowledge, immediately and inevitably raises the question of whether the equation of early reading and code learning is necessary and proper. The question is central in these volumes, for by no means all of our authors agree that the code should be central to the definition of reading or in research on reading instruction. Concern about the relationship between code and meaning is not new to reading pedagogy. In fact, our present views with respect to the roles of code and meaning in reading instruction can be understood best in light of a dialectic relation in which code and meaning emphases successively challenge, and thereby refine, one another.

Challenge to the code emphasis began in this country in the 19th century and gathered force toward the end of that century as the progressive education movement began to emphasize function and meaning over drill and stylized performance in education. But it was probably not until after World War I that reading comprehension, rather than oral reading, became a central concern of reading pedagogy. Two factors seem to have influenced the direction of this shift. One was the increasing recognition that large numbers of people who had been to school and could read certain texts aloud, although haltingly, could not gather meaning from print. This recognition was given impetus by the World War I army testing program in which about 25% of recruits were insufficiently literate to take the written form of the test (Army Alpha) used to assign men to training and jobs in the army. The other factor was the findings of early research on reading processes. Psychologists such as Cattell (1886), Huey (1908/1968), and Buswell (1920) found that people read in units at least as large as words and that meaningful phrases were the most common units of processing.

Around 1920, the combination of the emphasis on comprehension of text as the goal of reading instruction and the finding that attention to meaningful units rather than to letters and sounds characterized the reading of skilled individuals led to a radical change in reading pedagogy. Reading educators argued that if extraction of meaning is the goal of instruction and the strategy of skilled readers, then the focus from the very outset of reading instruction should be on meaning. This was to be accomplished by teaching children to recognize words as wholes, thereby allowing them—very early in their reading experience—to read sentences and stories about characters and topics of interest to them.

To make this new pedagogy work, new instructional materials were needed. If words were to be learned and read as wholes, ignoring the alphabetic principle, only a limited vocabulary could be taught. From this need grew the idea and practice of "basal readers," graded series of books in which a few words at a time are introduced and extensively reviewed in story contexts. Accompanying the readers were detailed suggestions to teachers for how to teach children to read them. The basal approach with words chosen for their relatively high frequency of occurrence rather than for their spelling-to-sound regularity, gradually replaced most of the older approaches. By the 1950s, it was the established way to teach reading. Virtually all teachers were trained in basal approaches and knew how to manage classes using such approaches. Massive publishing efforts made it possible for schools and teachers to buy varied, attractive, and complete "systems" for teaching reading, all based on the controlled vocabulary, sight recognition principle. A new "establishment" was clearly in place.[1]

Inevitably, reactions to this new orthodoxy developed. Challenges to sight-word methods began to be heard in both scholarly and lay circles in the 1950s and early 1960s (see, e.g., Flesch, 1955; Fries, 1962). In 1967 Chall published a book reviewing research evidence on early reading instruction and concluded that code approaches were generally superior to whole-word and other meaning-oriented approaches in the earliest years of instruction. However, those who advocated a reemphasis on the code in the 1950s and 1960s were not suggesting a return to alphabetic drills stripped of meaning; instead, they were proposing programs of direct code instruction in the context of meaningful reading material. The proposed new code emphasis, in other words, would be systematically refined to incorporate some of the more successful and appealing aspects of basal-style instruction.

In a sense, these volumes are a reexamination of issues considered by Chall a decade ago. Somewhat modified basal reading approaches are still dominant in today's instructional practice, and they are even less favorably viewed by our contributors than they were by Chall. In both theoretical and practical chapters, there is more attention paid to aspects of teaching, learning, and using the code than to comprehending written language. Yet an interest in meaning is not absent. Indeed, a number of the contributors to these volumes express concern that in a return to code approaches to teaching reading, the heart of reading may again be lost. But most of those proposing meaning-oriented initial instruction are not suggesting that the code be abandoned in a return to a 1930s style of basal readers. Instead, emerging theories of how people understand language and how language functions in social communication are being used to refine views of what a new meaning-oriented approach to early reading instruction might become. It is in this general context of debate that a number of specific issues about the nature of reading and of early reading instruction are addressed by the contributors to these volumes. We outline next some of the major themes to be found in the chapters that follow.

THE ISSUES

In inviting contributions to these volumes, we asked each author to consider three sets of questions:

---

[1]In earlier times the terms *basal* and *whole word* were used synonymously, whereas today basal reading series may stress code as well as meaning.

1. What is the nature of skilled reading; that is, what is the goal of reading instruction?
2. How is reading skill acquired? What are the "stages" or steps in competence in the process of going from being a nonreader to being a skilled reader, and how does one pass from one stage to the next?
3. What do the nature of skilled reading and the process of acquiring reading skill jointly suggest for reading instruction?

To answer these questions, we brought together theorists and practitioners, some who were almost exclusively concerned with documenting the nature of skilled reading and some who were largely concerned with reading acquisition and development. We defined our task as relating what is known about skilled reading performance to what is being learned about the development of that performance capability. In so doing, our hope was to shed some light on instruction. What is needed for improving reading instruction is not only a description of skilled performance but also a theory of *propaedeutics*—a theory that does not assume that processes performed early in learning will directly match those performed later but instead, suggests what kind of early preparatory instruction will help people learn subsequent more complex capabilities.

Few of the chapters in these volumes, considered individually, draw explicit connections between the three questions of skilled performance, acquisition sequences, and instruction. Yet taken together, these volumes suggest clearly where reading research and practice stand with respect to these questions. Attention to the questions emerges in the context of a number of specific issues raised by the authors, and we outline some of them here. Table 1.1 depicts these issues, the viewpoints related to them, and which contributors address the various issues. The headings in the table match those in the discussion that follows here. Therefore, the table is useful both as a summary of our discussion and as a guide to the volumes for readers with particular interests.

The Centrality of Decoding to Early Reading

Should beginning reading instruction emphasize the relationship between sounds and graphic symbols, or should it stress getting meaning from print? Although an emphasis on one aspect of reading does not necessarily exclude the other, the question of balance between them has occupied educators and researchers since at least the beginning of the 20th century. Individuals who address this issue tend to take one of several positions that vary along a continuum from: (a) learning to decode (i.e., using knowledge of phoneme-grapheme correspondences to recognize words) *is* early reading; to (b) learning to decode (through phonics instruction or some similar approach) is important because it helps develop sensitivity to orthographic regularity (i.e., recurrent spelling patterns), which is important in the transition from early to skilled reading; to (c) learning to decode is at best incidental to becoming literate and at worst, may interfere with acquiring reading skill. We examine each position briefly.

Early Reading Is Decoding. At one end of the continuum are those who contend that reading is, to use Liberman and Shankweiler's (Vol. 2) term, *parasitic* on spoken language. That is, learning to read is viewed as learning to map graphic symbols onto speech. Once this skill is learned, the established processes of understanding spoken language "take over." This position is represented centrally in the chapters by Liberman and Shankweiler and by Perfetti and Lesgold (Vol. 1). Liberman and Shankweiler propose that children need to be taught the alphabetic principle and skills of phonemic segmentation before they are taught to read. They suggest specific strategies and sequences of instruction that include preparing children for phonemic analysis and teaching them to associate the shape of the letter with its name and sound.

Perfetti and Lesgold contend that comprehension in reading depends on highly skilled generation and manipulation of language codes. They argue that even in skilled reading, there is a form of phonological encoding, albeit an abbreviated one, that precedes comprehension; and they recommend that decoding expertise should be the basic goal of early reading instruction. They offer suggestions for developing coding skills that include games and computer-assisted instruction.

Several other chapters suggest the importance of a code emphasis in early reading instruction or discuss commercially available programs with such an emphasis. Among them are the chapters by Beck and Block and by Chall in Volume 1, by Bartlett and by Fletcher in Volume 2, and by Popp, Wallach and Wallach, and Williams in Volume 3.

Reading and Orthographic Regularity. A less extreme position regarding the role of decoding suggests that although skilled reading may not involve phonological recoding, it involves attention to recurring letter patterns in written language. Furthermore, because direct code instruction necessarily involves attention to this orthographic detail, learning to decode helps develop the awareness of orthographic regularity that is necessary for skilled reading. This position is developed in detail by Venezky and Massaro (Vol. 1). They advocate an early phonics emphasis for both traditional reasons (e.g., it allows independence for beginning readers) and because it provides a vehicle for developing awareness of orthographic regularity. That is, phonics programs introduce almost all the orthographic patterns and do so "by

TABLE 1.1

	VOLUME 1														
	Chall	Perfetti – Lesgold	Venezky – Massaro	Fisher	Goodman – Goodman	Frederiksen	Shuy	Sticht	Bateman	Holland	Beck – Block	Kintsch	Posner	Samuels	Gordon
		WORD RECOG			LANGUAGE				INSTR			DISCUSSION			
Centrality of Decoding															
Early reading is decoding	●	●									●				
Reading and orthographic regularity			●												
Decoding not central					●	●									
Nature of Skilled Reading															
Bottom-up or top-down		●	●	●	●	●	●	●						●	
Direct or mediated access		●	●		●	●									
Automaticity		●												●	
Word recognition			●												
Units of processing				●											
Lexical knowledge		●			●										
Reading and Language															
Oral language transfers to written		●						●			●				
Functional language emphasis					●		●								
Richness and variety in reading materials											●				
Factors Interfering with Learning to Read															
Cultural and linguistic differences								●							●
Individual differences				●					●						
Acquiring Reading Competence															
Developmental theory and research	●												●		
Reading instruction and reading acquisition										●	●				
Assessing reading progress						●		●							
Teacher as an instructional variable					●		●		●		●				
Time engaged in reading										●	●				
Relations Between Theory and Practice												●	●		●

● = This topic is discussed or emphasized in the chapter

VOLUME 2 / VOLUME 3

VOLUME 2

LANGUAGE AND READING	F. Smith, Chomsky, E. Smith – Kleiman, Juola et. al., Liberman – Shankweiler
INSTRUCTION	Rosner, Clay, Calfee – Drum, Johnson, Bartlett, Fletcher
DISCUSSION	Venezky, White, Gordon, Resnick

VOLUME 3

PROCESSES OF READING	LaBerge, Gregg – Farnham-Diggory, McConkie, Danks – Fears
LANG DIFF & READ	Simons, Natalicio
INSTRUCTION	Guthrie–Martuza–Seifert, Williams, Wallach – Wallach, Popp
DISCUSSION	Trabasso, Cazden, Glaser, Carroll – Walton, Resnick

F. Smith	Chomsky	E. Smith – Kleiman	Juola et. al.	Liberman – Shankweiler	Rosner	Clay	Calfee – Drum	Johnson	Bartlett	Fletcher	Venezky	White	Gordon	Resnick	LaBerge	Gregg – Farnham-Diggory	McConkie	Danks – Fears	Simons	Natalicio	Guthrie–Martuza–Seifert	Williams	Wallach – Wallach	Popp	Trabasso	Cazden	Glaser	Carroll – Walton	Resnick
				●					●	●				●								●	●	●				●	●
		●																										●	
●														●			●												
●	●														●													●	
●	●	●																●										●	●
		●													●													●	
		●	●															●											
															●		●												
	●														●														
				●	●									●														●	
●													●	●	●											●			
						●			●	●				●										●				●	
													●	●			●	●					●		●				
				●	●			●	●	●				●								●						●	●
	●		●	●											●	●												●	●
									●	●				●										●				●	●
							●						●					●								●	●		
						●	●												●	●					●	●			
									●	●				●							●		●						
												●	●	●											●			●	●

procedures that give overt attention to the relevant spelling units for orthographic regularity." Thus, phonics instruction helps develop skills that are required for obtaining information from written text. A similar position is held by Juola, Schadler, Chabot, McCaughey, and Wait (Vol. 2), who discuss the development of visual search strategies and their relation to word recognition. In this context they suggest that although phonemic encoding plays a minor role in skilled reading, phonic knowledge and knowledge of English orthography are important for developing reading skill.

Decoding Is Not Central to Reading.   At the far end of the continuum is the position that decoding is secondary, even in early reading, to the task of getting meaning from print. Goodman and Goodman (Vol. 1) hold this position in its most extreme form. They suggest that written language is an alternative form of linguistic communication and like spoken language, can and should be learned in the context of its functional uses. Therefore, if appropriate experiences occur or are arranged, there is no need for explicit decoding instruction. Not only is there no need for it, Goodman and Goodman argue, but providing such instruction can actually interfere with the natural extension of general language skills to understanding the printed form. They offer suggestions for alternative learning experiences designed to promote the development of children's knowledge of language functions and to facilitate reading acquisition.

Smith (Vol. 2) also questions the value of instruction in decoding. He argues that reading is not guided by letter-by-letter or even word-by-word analysis; instead, it begins in the head with a prediction of meaning and ends with selective attention to only parts of the written text. He characterizes this as an "inside-out" process and says that children learn to read by "making sense" of written language. Therefore, he views decoding letters and combining them into words as the most difficult way to learn to read, because it does not match the processes of skilled performance. A focus on decoding, he argues, does not make sense to children and is therefore a hindrance to learning. Danks and Fears (Vol. 3) review some of the research that might provide evidence on the question of whether a hypothesis about meaning always precedes attention to the written text; they conclude that this depends on an interaction between the capability of the reader, the difficulty of the text, and the reader's purpose. The suggestion is that decoding skills are needed in at least some "skilled" reading performances.

The position held by Frederiksen (Vol. 1) reflects this sense of variability in the reading process. He contends that the primary goal in early reading instruction should be to teach children to comprehend written discourse in the same way that they comprehend oral discourse. However, because reading does involve attention to graphemic information, teaching the code is a necessary subgoal of instruction. Nevertheless, Frederiksen recommends that if achieving efficiency in the subgoal interferes with the primary goal of comprehension, then inefficiency in decoding must be tolerated.

The Nature of Skilled Reading

Many chapters in these volumes focus on the issue of how skilled readers process written discourse. Several aspects of the nature of skilled reading processes are discussed, including: (a) whether discourse processing is controlled in a "bottom-up" or "top-down" manner; (b) whether meaning is accessed directly from the graphic display or is mediated by a phonolgical recoding; and (c) what role automaticity of word recognition processes plays.

Bottom-Up or Top-Down?   In a bottom-up processing view of reading, lower level processes (e.g., letter and word recognition) are thought to occur prior to and independent of higher level processes. First words are recognized, then a syntactic processing occurs, and finally a semantic interpretation is made based on the sentence syntax. Furthermore, these processes are controlled by textual input; word recognition precedes comprehension of meaning. By contrast, in a top-down conception, reading is not controlled exclusively by the textual input; instead, higher level cognitive processes (e.g., making inferences) control the system, and lower processes are called into play only as they are needed. Hypotheses regarding the meaning of the text are generated from prior knowledge of the topic, knowledge of the specific textual content, and a minimal syntactic parsing and sampling of visual cues. According to the extreme top-down view, comprehension of meaning precedes recognition of words, and complete encoding of separate words may not occur at all. (See Frederiksen, Vol. 1, for a more detailed discussion of these concepts.)

Although most researchers would not characterize skilled reading as an exclusively bottom-up or top-down process, the authors who discuss this issue tend to do so with one or the other "direction" predominating.[2] Smith and Kleiman (Vol. 2) are the main proponents of reading as predominantly a bottom-up process. Several other authors imply a bottom-up view in the context of discussions of other aspects of reading (see the chapters by Sticht,

---

[2]It is noteworthy that when these volumes went to press, views about this issue had already changed. The nature of this change is captured by Adams and Collins (1977) in their schema theoretic account of reading. They suggest and attribute to Rumelhart (in press) that "top-down and bottom-up processing should be occurring at all levels of analysis simultaneously.... Bottom-up processing insures that the reader will be sensitive to information that is novel or that does not fit his on-going hypotheses about the content of the text; top-down processes help him to resolve ambiguities or to select between alternative possible interpretations of the incoming data [p. 9]."

Perfetti and Lesgold, and Fisher in Vol. 1). The chapters by Frederiksen (Vol. 1) and by Smith (Vol. 2) discuss skilled reading as a top-down controlled process ("inside-out" in Smith's terms), and this position is implied in the chapters by Goodman and Goodman and by Shuy in Volume 1.

It is important to note that several authors distinguish between skilled and novice readers in this respect. They view the skilled reading process as one that is controlled from the top down but see the *development* of reading skill proceeding from the bottom up. This position is represented by Samuels, Shuy, Venezky and Massaro (all in Vol. 1), LaBerge (Vol. 3), and to a certain extent by Frederiksen. On the other hand, Goodman and Goodman and Smith view *both* early and skilled reading as a top-down controlled process.

Direct or Mediated Access?   Several chapters address the issue of whether there is phonological recoding during skilled reading. On one side of this issue are those who hold that even in skilled reading, graphic information is recoded into phonological information before meaning is accessed. Viewpoints on this issue are often related to those on the bottom-up versus top-down conception of skilled reading. That is, those who view reading as a bottom-up process usually hold that there is a phonolgical recoding stage, even in skilled reading (e.g., Liberman & Shankweiler; Perfetti & Lesgold); whereas those who view reading as a top-down process tend to believe that meaning is accessed directly (e.g., Frederiksen; Goodman & Goodman; Smith). Exceptions to this correlation can be found in the chapters of Venezky and Massaro and of Smith and Kleiman, both of which propose a generally bottom-up view of the skilled reading process that does not depend on phonological recoding. Danks and Fears, as we have noted, suggest that whether access is direct or mediated depends on the individual reader and the task.

The Role of Automaticity.   One argument often used to support a direct-access-to-meaning view is that skilled reading proceeds at a rate that precludes the possibility of phonological recoding. A common reply to the argument is that in high-speed skilled reading, word recognition or phonological recoding takes place in an automatic fashion. That is, words are recognized rapidly, accurately, and with minimal attentional resources. Therefore, although it appears that meaning is obtained without actually recognizing words or recoding them, it is possible that these recognition processes are present but highly automatized and abbreviated. This position is central to the discussion by Perfetti and Lesgold, and it is supported by LaBerge (Vol. 3) in his chapter on perceptual units in the reading process and by Samuels in his discussion of the chapters in Volume 1.

Other Aspects Related to Skilled Reading. A number of other topics related to skilled reading are considered by various authors. There is now a considerable body of research literature on word (and letter-string) recognition processes in skilled reading. For reviews and discussions of this literature, see the chapters by Smith and Kleiman, Venezky and Massaro, Juola et al., and Danks and Fears. Smith and Kleiman review this literature in the context of an information-processing model of skilled reading, whereas Venezky and Massaro consider it in supporting their claims for the importance of orthographic regularity in word and letter-string recognition. Juola et al. (Vol. 2) review research on "word superiority" (faster and more accurate recognition of real words than of pseudowords that follow the rules of conventional English spelling) in their discussion of the development of visual search performance. And Danks and Fears (Vol. 3) review a selected body of literature on oral reading errors, eye–voice span, and effects of text alteration in their discussion of oral production in a decoding-comprehension model of reading.

The question of perceptual units in reading is discussed in the chapters by McConkie, Fisher, and LaBerge. McConkie (Vol. 3) reports eye-movement research related to the perceptual span in reading; Fisher (Vol. 1) discusses the effects on reading of limited peripheral-visual processing; and LaBerge (Vol. 3) discusses functions of units for perceptual processing, selection of units for specific tasks, and learning of new units.

Finally, the skilled reader makes use of an extensive body of knowledge about words and what they represent during skilled reading. The extent of this network of lexical and semantic knowledge and the effectiveness of strategies for accessing it determine in part the reader's level of proficiency. Issues related to the lexicon and lexical access are explored in the chapters by Frederiksen, Smith and Kleiman, Perfetti and Lesgold, and Gregg and Farnham-Diggory (Vol. 3).

Reading and Language

We have mentioned the question of the relation between reading and general language skills in the course of discussing other issues. As we noted, some authors argue that reading is a matter of translating print to sound and then using established language skills to derive meaning; others argue that understanding written language is a unique process, more than the sum of decoding plus understanding spoken language. Regardless of which position on the nature of the relations between oral language and reading is held, most authors seem to agree that general language competence is essential to reading skill. Differences of opinion arise, however, over when and how language skills should be taught in the context of reading.

One position is that the development of language skills should be promoted in the oral mode while initial reading (coding) skills are being taught. In this way, language skills of increasing complexity can be transferred to the written language form. Sticht (Vol. 1) develops this argument most explicitly and extensively. His "audread" model implies the need for early code teaching and assumes that training in the oral mode will transfer to reading once the learner is past the decoding stage. He defines individuals' reading potentials in terms of the discrepancy between what they can comprehend aurally and what they can comprehend in written form. A similar position on the relation of aural to written comprehension skills is espoused by Beck and Block (Vol. 1), Perfetti and Lesgold, Liberman and Shankweiler, and by Rosner (Vol. 2).

A contrasting position holds that written language is an alternative functional form of language and that skill in using it does not transfer directly from oral competence as a result of learning the code. Instead, children should be taught reading in the context of the various functional modes that are relevant to them. In this way, written language can become a form of communication that is as useful as oral language. The functional language approach to reading is discussed extensively by Goodman and Goodman and by Shuy in Volume 1, and it is implicit in the chapters by Smith (Vol. 2), by Cazden (Vol. 3), and by Simons (Vol. 3). It is worth noting that whereas a functional language emphasis is usually accompanied by an anticode stance in instruction, this negative relation between functional language and code orientations is not a necessary one. Shuy, for example, recognizes a need for direct code teaching while emphasizing functional aspects of language in reading instruction.

A concern for richness of content and form of language within code-oriented instruction characterizes Bartlett's chapter (Vol. 2) comparing the *Distar* and *Open Court* beginning reading programs. Bartlett speculates that literary forms, or genres, can function as cognitive structures, serving to organize verbal information and to aid comprehension and memory. Both reading programs, Bartlett notes, are organized to facilitate code learning, but they provide a different range of literary experience. Bartlett suggests that the relative literary limitation of one of the programs may foster an impoverished kind of literacy. The need for phonics teaching in a semantically rich context is also acknowledged in the other chapters in which instructional programs are analyzed (Beck & Block in Vol. 1, Fletcher in Vol. 2, and Popp in Vol. 3). Similar concerns are expressed by Clay (Vol. 2), who suggests that reading programs that focus only on word attack and have tightly controlled vocabularies may actually be counterproductive to developing independent reading skills. She advocates programs rich in many aspects of language that may support, to use Clay's term, a *self-improving system* of language development.

Factors That Interfere With
Learning to Read

The motivation for extended research in reading, and especially for the present attempt to explore the implications of theory and research for instructional practice, derives from the fact that large numbers of people in our society are not achieving expected standards of literacy. The efforts of many researchers and educators are directed at improving or preventing this situation. Children who fail to learn to read or who do so slowly and with extreme difficulty are therefore a major concern of many of the contributors to these volumes. In discussing those who have difficulty learniing to read, it is possible to distinguish between students who encounter difficulty because the expectations and habits of their social-cultural group do not match those of the schools and students who have difficulty because of individual differences in ability. These groups have overlapping memberships, even in the most elegant and theoretical classifications, and they are often very difficult to distinguish in practice. Despite this, it is important, for purposes of analysis, to consider separately these different sources of reading difficulty.

Cultural and Linguistic Differences.   The chapters that focus explicitly on social-cultural origins of reading difficulty are those by Shuy, Simons, Natalicio (Vol. 3), Wallach and Wallach (Vol. 3), and Gordon (Vols. 1 & 2). Shuy discusses the mismatch between the language that children bring to school and the language used by teachers and in texts. He suggests that for children who are culturally and linguistically different from the majority, the language mismatch is not so much a phonological or grammatical one as it is a mismatch of functional language competence—the ways in which language is used for various communication purposes. Shuy suggests that research in the area of language functions may be the most promising of all for determining causes of reading difficulty and failure.

Simons reviews the literature on phonological and grammatical inter-ference in reading among speakers of a black dialect. Like Shuy, Simons concludes that there is little evidence to suggest that speaking a dialect interferes with comprehending written texts once basic skills have been mastered. However, according to Simons, the evidence on the role of dialect speech in *acquiring* reading skill is inconclusive, and speaking a dialect may indeed interfere. Simons proposes to study the question by examining reading instruction as it actually occurs in the classroom; he describes several studies that examine reading interference and classroom interaction by analyzing videotaped instructional sequences.

Natalicio reviews the existing literature on reading and the bilingual child. Although there is currently considerable pressure among Hispanics and others to teach reading in the child's native language, Natalicio suggests that there is little empirical evidence for such an approach. She calls for more research on bilingualism and second-language learning to resolve what have become largely political arguments regarding the best way to teach reading to bilingual children. Trabasso (Vol. 3), in discussing Natalicio's paper, suggests that parallel teaching of reading in both English and the home language should also be considered, in the spirit of what has been called by Riegel and Freedle (1976) "independent bilingualism." It is not surprising that we know less about the problems of bilingual children than about those of bidialectic children. As Natalicio points out, the recognition of reading problems among bilinguals is relatively new in the United States, and they have only recently gained the attention of researchers.

Gordon (Vol. 2) addresses issues of social-cultural differences and reading from a broader perspective. He discusses compensatory education, characteristics of the groups served by compensatory education, and the effects of various compensatory educational programs. His comments on the teaching and learning of reading are set in this broader context.

Individual Differences.   The chapters by Fisher and by Bateman in Volume 1, by Johnson and by Rosner in Volume 2, and by Wallach and Wallach and by Williams in Volume 3 are concerned primarily with individuals—rather than members of social or ethnic groups—who have difficulty learning to read. Fisher and Johnson focus on individuals who are from a clinical population, those with severe learning or reading disabilities; the other authors focus on individuals whose reading difficulties are less severe and for whom instruction can take place in a regular classroom setting.

Fisher discusses the visual-neurological origins of severe reading disability and describes experiments that show sharply reduced peripheral-visual processing among the severely reading disabled. He discusses the importance of the visual periphery in obtaining information and guiding eye movements, and he suggests that instruction for the severely disabled should compensate for these difficulties. Johnson discusses a variety of factors as possible sources of learning or reading disabilities, and she proposes a systems analysis approach to diagnosis and remediation. By this, she means identifying the various psychosensory systems and processes that are involved in reading and determining which are intact and which are impaired. She stresses that the population of children with learning disabilities is heterogeneous and that children with learning disabilities require individual remedial instruction. Examples of these individual remedial strategies are described in her chapter.

The chapters by Bateman, Rosner, Wallach and Wallach, and Williams are concerned with classroom instructional procedures for the hard to teach, whether they are labeled disabled, retarded, or culturally different. Although there are differences in the approaches recommended, a common thread in these chapters is an assumption that those who have difficulty learning to read require a structured curriculum that attends to the phonemic nature of the language and to the relationship of the phonemic to the graphemic code. Bateman recommends using principles of applied behavioral analysis and task analytic programming. Operationally, according to Bateman, this means direct practice with many trials to ensure acquisition and development of the decoding aspect of reading. She suggests that *Distar* is an exemplary program for teaching beginning reading (but cf. Bartlett, Vol. 2). Wallach and Wallach and Williams report on programs they designed and implemented to teach certain beginning reading skills to children who are at high risk for reading failure. The Wallachs report an apparently successful attempt at teaching phoneme identification and segmentation skills to inner-city children in Chicago. Williams designed and is testing a program with learning disabled children from inner-city neighborhoods in New York City. Like Bateman, she recommends that the cognitive and perceptual skills necessary for reading be taught in the context of reading rather than apart from it. Her program follows a sequence in which segmentation and blending of syllables are taught before segmentation and blending of phonemes. Both the Wallachs' program and Williams', then, teach the kinds of skills Liberman and Shankweiler stress as necessary for learning the code. Rosner, discussing the general problem of teaching poor-prognosis children, outlines the components of an instructional system in which he believes it is possible to match student traits with instruction so as to optimize learning. His suggestions are slated for children he views as hard to teach, but his outline appears to be for an instructional system that would benefit all students.

Acquiring Reading Competence

As we have noted earlier, it is important in discussing reading and reading instruction to distinguish between descriptions of the skilled reading process and accounts of how reading skill is acquired. In reading as in other skills, it is probable that the novice performs differently from the expert. Novice readers probably are not only slower, but they probably also attend to different features of text, perceive text in different-sized units, and bring knowledge that is both less extensive and less well structured to the reading activity. Therefore, for example, the skilled reader may read in phrase or clause units, whereas the novice may attend to every word or even to every letter. Despite growing knowledge of the processes involved in skilled reading, much less is known about the ways in which the reading process changes in the course of its development (see Gibson & Levin, 1975, for a discussion of developmental research related to reading), and there is virtually nothing that can reliably be said about how transitions from one stage of competence to another occur. Several authors in these volumes call for additional developmental research on reading; others have begun such investigations. Still others have analyzed existing early reading programs and offer comments on the sort of literacy skill that may result from different instructional procedures.

Developmental Theory and Research.   In several chapters, preliminary models or schemes of reading and its development are offered. Chall (Vol. 1) offers a theory of the stages of reading development that can serve to organize much of the subsequent discussion in these volumes. The first three of Chall's stages include a prereading stage; a decoding stage, during which the learner acquires the elements of the code; and a confirmation and fluency stage, during which the code is mastered through the reading of largely familiar material. Following these are stages in which the reader focuses primarily on meaning: first reading for learning from one viewpoint, then reading from multiple viewpoints, and finally reading with what Chall terms a "world view." A stage theory of this kind is of potentially great significance for organizing and focusing the debate over the proper role of the code in reading acquisition. It poses the question of *when* rather than *whether* the code should be emphasized, and it also stresses the role of practice on meaningful and familiar texts. Chall clearly places the code emphasis at the beginning of the acquisition process, but her scheme also emphasizes high levels of comprehension as central to the full cycle of reading development. Other authors would order the emphases differently. What is important is that a stage-oriented theory provides a framework for empirical studies that are both developmental in nature and attentive to the instructional environment in which acquisition proceeds (cf. Kintsch, Vol. 1).

Gregg and Farnham-Diggory (Vol. 3) view reading as a special case of information processing and see the processing system as having three major parts: the perceptual system, the semantic system, and the operations and programs for performing reading tasks. Each of these systems develops greater capability with age and experience. They also offer a taxonomy of reading tasks that is arranged along two dimensions: size of unit and number of operations. The authors suggest that as the processing systems mature, tasks involving larger units and more operations can be performed. Trabasso (Vol. 3), in his discussion chapter, calls for more work on such a taxonomy (and suggests some possible modifications), because it contains an implicit developmental model of reading from prereading to skilled levels with a potential focus on task demands. This, he feels, would force researchers to concentrate on the mechanisms by which skills required for reading are *acquired*. That such schemes have begun to be formulated is promising for our eventual understanding of reading acquisition and development.

The chapters by Chall and by Gregg and Farnham-Diggory offer a relatively macroscopic view of the development of reading skill. By contrast, the chapters by LaBerge (Vol. 3), Juola et al., Liberman and Shankweiler, and

Chomsky (Vol. 2) examine aspects of reading acquisition more microscopically. A focus of LaBerge's chapter is on how readers acquire the cognitive structures necessary for recognizing a word, with an emphasis on units of processing. Juola et al.'s chapter examines the appearance and changes over time of visual search strategies in reading and the development of a word superiority effect. Liberman and Shankweiler examine the relation between spoken and written language and describe the phonemic segmentation skills learners need to acquire (on their own or through direct instruction) to be able to map written onto spoken language. Theirs is a developmental theory with explicit implications for instruction. Chomsky offers evidence to support the view that the ability to construct written language (i.e., to write and spell) developmentally precedes the ability to read, at least in some children. She suggests that children can be introduced to reading through a form of creative writing where they are not formally taught spelling but use a spelling system that they themselves invent.

Reading Instruction and Reading Acquisition.   Instructional implications have been considered throughout our discussion of issues in reading. However, a few instructional topics did not lend themselves to discussions in other contexts, and we mention them briefly here. Attention should perhaps first be directed to several chapters that address matters related to reading acquisition in the course of describing and assessing instructional programs. The chapters by Beck and Block and by Holland in Volume 1, by Fletcher and by Bartlett in Volume 2, and by Popp in Volume 3 analyze a number of early reading programs. Each is interspersed with comments on the processes of reading acquisition. These chapters are major sources for information on the current state of the art in American reading instruction and the kinds of questions that skilled analysts are raising about this practice.

Assessing Reading Progress.   Several chapters stress the importance of assessment as an integral component of the reading instructional process. In order to "deliver" instruction at the proper pace and level of difficulty, the teacher must be able to measure every child's progress in an ongoing way and incorporate the results in daily instruction. This is the major focus of the chapter by Calfee and Drum (Vol. 2), who discuss the goals, methods, and criteria for assessment in the context of instruction. Their emphasis is on measurement of specific skills for short-term instructional decisions rather than on long-term placement decisions. The other chapters that include discussion of assessment are those by Frederiksen, Sticht, and Danks and Fears. Frederiksen suggests that a taxonomy of inference types could be used to construct achievement-test items to measure aspects of discourse processing and that the methods he uses for analyzing children's recall of stories could be adapted for classroom instructional decisions. Sticht describes a procedure for assessing the reading potential of adults. The Literacy Assessment Battery measures the "gap" between auding and reading abilities and reveals the degree to which reading problems are indicative of problems with the printed language specifically or of low levels of general language ability. Danks and Fears offer an experimental task that may be applicable to classroom assessment procedures. They propose a hierarchy of processing levels in reading and describe a series of experiments with texts that have been systematically altered or disrupted. By building the disruptions into the text according to the level in the processing hierarchy that one wishes to study, they argue, it is possible to analyze oral reading behavior to determine if the text is processed at least to the level of the disruption.

The Teacher as an Instructional Variable.   The importance of the teacher both as the deliverer of instruction and as a creator of the learning environment is stressed in several chapters. All authors explicitly or implicitly recognize that the quality of instruction depends in great part on the teacher. Those authors whose chapters emphasize the importance of the teacher are Bateman (Vol. 1), Clay and Rosner (Vol. 2), and Simons, Cazden, and Glaser (Vol. 3). Many other chapters discuss the role of the teacher in the context of other topics (e.g., Beck & Block, Goodman & Goodman, Natalicio, and Shuy). A point that can be drawn from all these discussions is that we know more about the reading process and reading instruction than is currently being used. The teacher is of course pivotal in this matter. Bateman, for example, claims that we already know how to teach the decoding aspect of reading. What we need to do is help teachers to apply the proper methods.

Both Simons and Cazden implicate the teacher and the social interactions in the classroom as possible sources of reading difficulty for some children. They describe observational reasearch suggesting that the quality of instruction may vary for different children even within the same classroom. Rosner describes the traits that teachers must have to be able to teach reading effectively to children who are hard to teach. They must be familiar with basic concepts of reading (many are not), able to be precise and repetitive, able to perform in a structured, relatively nondynamic environment, and able to sustain efforts even when progress is slow and results are small.

Clay describes a program of instructional change in New Zealand. She, like Rosner, emphasizes the importance of teachers' knowledge of reading and reading instruction. She refers also to the importance of teachers as sensitive observers of reading progress, suggesting that observation is itself an assessment technique. She includes an interesting account of in-service training designed to make teachers better informed regarding reading theory and research and more able to apply this knowledge to their teaching.

Time Engaged in Reading.   The importance of time spent in direct instruction in reading is touched on in many of the chapters that analyze and compare different reading instructional approaches. These discussions are found in the chapters by Beck and Block; Bartlett; Fletcher; Guthrie, Martuza, and Seifert (Vol. 3); and Popp. The most direct consideration of this issue is found in the chapter by Guthrie et al., who reanalyzed data collected by the Educational Testing Service on compensatory reading programs. Using that data, they examined the impacts of instructional time in reading on reading achievement among middle- and low-socioeconomic-status (SES) groups. They concluded that amount of time spent in formal reading instruction influenced achievement more than the specific approach used to teach reading. Their findings suggest that a large amount of instructional time benefited sixth graders from low-SES groups but not those from middle- and high-SES groups. Findings at the second-grade level suggest that the amount of instructional time in reading affected achievement but that different SES groups were not affected differently. The authors stress that it is not time itself that affects achievement but the specific events that occur during that time, and they conclude with a recommendation that we improve the measures of instructional intensity by quantifying the events that occur among students and teachers.

Holland focuses explicitly on issues related to the quality rather than the quantity of time spent on reading. Proceeding from a behavioral engineering point of view, he suggests the importance of arranging sequences of contingent interrelations among materials and of clear consequences contingent upon students' responses to details of the materials. Resnick's review chapter (Vol. 2) summarizes and evaluates research on engaged time and instructional programs and suggests that for several reasons, decoding approaches to instruction have probably been correlated with high amounts of time engaged in reading and with more tightly engineered instructional programs. She argues that at least until meaning-oriented instruction can be organized to promote heavy engagement in the actual tasks of reading, code approaches to instruction will best serve the needs of hard-to-teach populations.

On the Relations Between
Theory and Practice

We noted earlier that certain chapters—primarily the discussion chapters at the end of each volume—focus on the actual and potential relationships between theory and research on one hand and practice of reading instruction on the other. Other authors also discuss issues of theory and practice relationships in the context of their specific substantive concerns. Belief in the power of scientific pedagogy is far from universal, as a reading of these volumes will amply demonstrate. Practitioners succeed in teaching reading to many children without being informed of or directly influenced by the results of research. And psychologists themselves are not always convinced that current theory and research can improve educational practice. Depending partly on how individuals became interested in the study of reading and partly on their experiences in applying scientific theory and knowledge to social needs and practices, expectations for the relation between theory and practice differ. All agree, however, that drawing instructional implications directly from current laboratory-based experimental findings is extremely difficult.

Of the several discussants, Venezky (Vol. 2) and Kintsch (Vol. 1) are the least optimistic about the possibility of a direct link between laboratory research and classroom practice. Venezky claims that applying theory to practice is not only difficult but at times has actually led to poor instruction. He argues, not for the direct application of laboratory research, but instead for a "separate but equal" discipline of applied research that is grounded in classroom experimentation. Kintsch, on the other hand, sees a need for more, rather than less, interaction between laboratory and classroom. He holds that although work on reading instruction and basic research in reading are both flourishing, the interaction between them is insufficient. Furthermore, he argues that the lack of a serious theory of reading is a main source of the problem: Instruction is based more on intuition than on research, and research often circumvents important instructional issues.

Kintsch directs attention toward increased efforts in the theoretical realm as an eventual basis for scientifically grounded practice. He perhaps would be joined in this judgment by Posner (Vol. 1), who in addition, points out the ways in which theory can limit as well as expand our work in reading instruction. Posner characterizes theory as both a lens and a set of blinders for practitioners and curriculum developers. He suggests that theory tends to magnify those aspects of a problem on which scientists have worked (the lens), making them more understandable. At the same time, the existence of well-elaborated theory tends to reduce attention to other important aspects of a problem on which there has been little work (the blinders). Posner's chapter elaborates this lens–blinders metaphor with reference to specific issues discussed in the papers on which he comments.

Two discussants, Glaser (Vol. 3) and White (Vol. 2), offer more positive views of actual and potential theory–practice relations. Glaser contends that we know enough now from theory and research to produce positive changes in the outcomes of reading instruction. He suggests that although psychological knowledge is imperfect, it can and should be applied, in an artful and heuristic fashion. White goes a step further. Not only does he think that theory and research can and should change practice; he also suggests a scheme for effecting a more successful change. He argues that the traditional approach of researchers conducting experiments in laboratories and then shipping the results to the classroom has not worked. Instead, he proposes that researchers leave the laboratory to conduct their research in classroom settings and allow their hypotheses to be formulated from actual instructional problems. He argues convincingly that his new scheme may be as important for theory as for education.

It is noteworthy that although Glaser, White, and others seem to be generally satisfied with the state of theory with respect to reading instruction, they all point to a need for more elaborated theories of reading acquisition. The discrepancy between theories of skilled reading and those of reading acquisition and development is discussed by Gordon (Vol. 1), Venezky (Vol. 2), and Trabasso (Vol. 3). Regardless of disagreements on other issues, all contributors whose discussion focuses on this topic unite in calling for more research on reading acquisition. The need for this shift in theoretical and research direction is clarified by Trabasso. He notes that current work in cognitive psychology is preoccupied with the description of processes used for engaging in tasks rather than with how the processes required for engaging in them are learned. To remedy this, Trabasso calls for renewed attention to some of the questions of classical learning theory but within the new context of an enriched cognitive psychology. Resnick (Vol. 3) echoes the need in her summary discussion and develops a proposal for the kinds of questions a psychology of reading instruction would need to address and the methods it may require.

General Issues

The final chapters of each of these volumes are discussion chapters. In most of these, commentary is limited to issues raised in the chapters of the volume itself. However, four of the discussion chapters—those by Gordon and Resnick in Volume 2 and those by Carroll and Walton and by Resnick in Volume 3—present a more general set of reflections. These chapters, written after all the other chapters were submitted and discussed, are intended as integrative reviews highlighting particular issues in early reading instruction that were considered in the volumes as a whole. They do not attempt to respond chapter by chapter or point by point to the other contributions; instead, they use the issues raised in all three volumes as points of departure in considering broad concerns of research and practice in reading instruction.

Gordon's integrative chapter (Vol. 2) is concerned with the problem of reading instruction in the context of compensatory education programs. The chapter begins with a discussion of the concept of compensatory education itself—how the concept developed, the assumptions about the poor that surround it, and common conceptions of the children who receive compensatory education. Gordon suggests that these children have too often been grouped together under the label *disadvantaged* and characterized by their differences from the white, middle-class "norm," rather than being seen as individuals, with individual strengths and weaknesses. He proposes that it is these individual characteristics, and not group labels, that should be taken into account in the design of instruction for all populations. Against this background, Gordon discusses various chapters in the volumes with respect to their implications for compensatory reading programs.

Resnick's integrative chapter in Volume 2 represents an effort to distill from the many specific points of view presented in these volumes the major competing positions on the nature of reading and appropriate reading instruction. She identifies two major views of the nature of reading—reading as translation of print to sound and reading as an autonomous language process. These two positions, Resnick points out, lead to different prescriptions for reading instruction: Adherents of the reading-as-translation view prescribe early and systematic instruction on the alphabetic code; supporters of the reading-as-autonomous-process view prescribe early attention to functional and meaningful use of written language. After reviewing empirical research on instructional program effects, Resnick picks code-oriented instruction for the early years of reading, but cautions that this will not "solve" the reading problem. She goes on to suggest the kinds of research and development that are needed for more successful instruction in comprehension and the functional aspects of reading.

Carroll and Walton's chapter in Volume 3 reviews previous attempts at organizing knowledge about early reading, and discusses these volumes as part of this series of efforts to solve the reading problem. The chapter contains an extensive discussion of the positions and points of view expressed in the chapters of these volumes. This discussion is organized into two major sections: (1) conceptions of the nature of reading, and (2) how well early reading instruction as it is currently conducted reflects theory and knowledge about learning to read. The section on the nature of reading includes detailed analyses of particular points of view expressed in the various chapters of these volumes. It is thus an excellent guide to the often confusing and tangled arguments on topics such as the centrality of decoding, top-down versus bottom-up processing, direct versus mediated word access, and the role of language skills in becoming a good reader. The section on instruction includes a detailed discussion of beginning reading programs, which both comments on and extends the discussion of curriculum and pedagogy presented in various chapters. Throughout their integrative chapter, Carroll and Walton take definite positions on controversial instructional questions.

Finally, Resnick's chapter in Volume 3 addresses the questions of whether and how theory and basic research can contribute to practical pedagogy in reading. Resnick first considers some of the reasons that most basic research in reading has not been as helpful to practice as might be wished. She then proposes a variety of research questions and research methods that she believes would make future reading research both more useful in instructional design and better science in its own right. The result of such research, she suggests, would be a psychology of reading focused directly on instruction, a psychology centrally concerned with processes of acquisition and with the role of intervention (i.e., instruction) in these processes.

REFERENCES

Adams, M. J., & Collins, A. *A schema-theoretic view of reading* (Tech. Rep. No. 32). Urbana, Ill.: Center for the Study of Reading, 1977.

Buswell, G. T. An experimental study of eye–voice span in reading. *Supplementary Educational Monographs,* No. 17. Chicago: University of Chicago, 1920.

Cattell, J. M. The time it takes to see and name objects. *Mind,* 1886, *11,* 63–65.

Chall, J. S. *Learning to read: The great debate.* New York: McGraw-Hill, 1967.

Flesch, R. *Why Johnny can't read, and what you can do about it.* New York: Harper, 1955.

Fries, C. C. *Linguistics and reading.* New York: Holt, Rinehart & Winston, 1962.

Gibson, E. J., & Levin, H. *The psychology of reading.* Cambridge, Mass.: MIT Press, 1975.

Huey, E. B. *The psychology and pedagogy of reading.* New York: Macmillan, 1908. Republished by the MIT Press, Cambridge, Mass., 1968.

Mathews, M. *Teaching to read: Historically considered.* Chicago: University of Chicago Press, 1966.

Maugham, W. S. The verger. In *Cosmopolitans.* New York: Doubleday, Doran, 1937.

Resnick, D. P., & Resnick, L. B. The nature of literacy: An historical exploration. *Harvard Educational Review,* 1977, *47*(3), 370–385.

Riegel, K., & Freedle, R. Bilingualism. In D. Harrison & T. Trabasso (Eds.), *Black English: A seminar.* Hillsdale, N.J.: Lawrence Erlbaum Associates, 1976.

Rumelhart, D. E. Toward an interactive model of reading. In S. Dornic (Ed.), *Attention & performance VI.* Hillsdale, N.J.: Lawrence Erlbaum Associates, 1977.

WORD RECOGNITION

1 The Great Debate: Ten Years Later, With a Modest Proposal for Reading Stages

Jeanne S. Chall
Harvard University

This chapter has a dual purpose. In the first part I present some of my thoughts on the effects on reading theory and practice of *Learning to Read: The Great Debate* (Chall, 1967), the Carnegie Corporation supported study published 10 years ago. In the second part I present my preliminary thoughts on a scheme of reading stages*—a developmental scheme that I have been working on over the past several years. It is my hope that it may prove useful in understanding the reading process, how it develops, and how it is affected by environmental factors. It may also help to explain the periodic controversies we seem subject to in the theories and practice of early reading.

The beginnings of the reading stages scheme were presented in *The Great Debate*. Indeed, as I stated then, I could make no sense of the conflicting results of comparisons of beginning reading methods without hypothesizing developmental changes in reading by age and grade of pupils for the different components of reading—oral reading, silent reading comprehension, word meaning, and so on. Thus, although some methods seemed to produce an immediate, early advantage in some components of reading, other methods seemed to be more effective when comparisons were made at a later date. My explanation for this was that essentially the facts of beginning reading fitted a developmental theory better than a single-process theory. That is, the analysis of the results of the school and laboratory experiments, as well as the clinical findings, seemed to indicate that the first task in learning to read was learning the relation between sounds and letters—decoding. The second task was reading for content and meaning. These results conflicted with the single-process theory, prominent during the early 1960s, which viewed beginning and more mature reading as essentially the same. Thus meaningful reading was to be emphasized from the start.

---

*See Chall, J. S. *Stages of Reading Development*. New York: McGraw-Hill, in press, for a fuller treatment.

THE GREAT DEBATE: TEN YEARS LATER

I am concerned primarily with the impact of the findings and recommendations on the major issue studied—the effectiveness of an emphasis on
decoding rather than on meaning—for beginning reading instruction. The
impact of the other related issues studied (the effect of knowing the alphabet
and sounds on reading achievement, early versus later reading, content of
readers, testing of pupils, grading of materials, and research in beginning
reading) are referred to, if at all, in passing.

Before proceeding, I should like to say that I approached this assignment
with a little less than unalloyed joy. How can one be objective about the
impact of one's work? Is it possible to be objective about the impact of a book
that became, according to the publishing industry, a best seller in education in
a few months and the subject of educational conferences and symposia
(Burrows, 1968; Versacci & Larrick, 1968)? At the same time, it was reviewed
with a little less than delight by some recognized reading scholars but
glowingly by equally recognized scholars somewhat outside the field. The
controversy has now died down, and *The Great Debate* has become one of the
required readings for graduate students in reading and language arts and for
undergraduates preparing to be teachers, and it is included in the professional
book collections of most elementary schools.

I hope these remarks will not be judged as signs of glaring immodesty. Yet it
does seem important to mention that in the 10 years since publication of *The
Great Debate* its basic recommendations, even its terminology, have become
part of the theory and practice of beginning reading to such an extent that the
attributions are now omitted in most journal articles. The issue itself has
become so much a part of the scene that it is not uncommon to find articles in
recent issues of *The Reading Teacher* proclaiming that there is more to
reading than decoding and meaning and that there is more to a reading
program than whether it has a code-emphasis or a meaning-emphasis. I do
not, of course, imply a cause-and-effect relationship; *The Great Debate* was
part of a trend in research, curriculum development, and classroom practice.

The impact of the book seemed to be first among users of research
knowledge—authors and publishers of basal reading programs, producers of
software for programmed instruction and for multimedia programs, and
authors and publishers of reading tests. Another group that gave it early
attention was the researchers. During the late 1960s and early 1970s there
were probably few grant proposals for research in reading that did not cite it.
It was often used to support the statement that, although the research in
reading was less than satisfying, it could be improved with the funding of the
project under consideration. It played a more active role in the rationale and,
I believe, the planning of the U.S. Office of Education's (USOE) Targeted
Research Studies in Reading (Corder, 1971; Davis, 1971). Although some of

the widely used research and development (R&D) reading programs were started earlier, or at about the same time, I believe that the book had an impact on the more recent programs. Generally, the programs developed in the late 1960s and early 1970s focused on a code-emphasis for beginning reading. The book's impact on teacher education came later, but it came. One of the effects was more extensive sections on decoding in new textbooks on the teaching of reading and in revisions of older, standard textbooks. Another effect was the inclusion of descriptions of different methods and approaches to beginning reading in textbooks on methods of teaching reading and in textbooks devoted solely to different approaches to beginning reading. Generally, the strong consensus for a single-process, meaning-emphasis approach to early reading was broken.

Where Are We Now on Issues in The Great Debate?

My finding on the issue of code-emphasis versus meaning-emphasis was that in spite of the shortcomings of the individual research studies, if one examined them developmentally, the code-emphasis programs produced the better results, at least through Grade 3. With many qualifications and reservations, I recommended a change from a meaning- to a code-emphasis for beginning reading programs. Ten years later, code-emphasis beginning reading programs seem to be predominant among commercially published reading programs. They are also the style for beginning reading programs produced by the major R&D centers.[1]

Popp's (1975) analysis of beginning reading programs published since 1967 found, in general, a stronger decoding emphasis than in earlier programs. That is, the first-grade basal reading series published in the late 1950s and early 1960s taught consonant sounds and blends, and perhaps consonant digraphs. Popp found that first-grade reading programs published in the late 1960s and early 1970s taught all these and vowels, vowels digraphs, diphthongs, vowels controlled by *r, l,* and *w,* and high-frequency compound words. This does not, of course, mean that meaning-emphasis programs have disappeared. There are still strong proponents of meaning-emphasis beginning reading programs. One of these proponents, Goodman (1969), who also is one of several authors of the most popular meaning-emphasis reading

---

[1]Although some of these R&D reading programs predated *The Great Debate,* it is interesting that many depend on heavy decoding in their initial instruction—*Wisconsin Design for Reading Skill Development* (Wisconsin Research and Development Center for Cognitive Learning, 1971), the *Pre-reading Skills Program* (Venezky, Pittelman, & Kamm, 1974), *Individually Prescribed Instruction* (Learning Research and Development Center, 19), and SWRL's *Beginning Reading Program* (Southwest Regional Laboratory for Educational Research and Development, 1972).

program, the Scott, Foresman *Reading Unlimited*, emphasizes the meaning aspect of beginning reading:

> Instead of word attack skills, sight vocabularies, and word perception, the program must be designed to build comprehension strategies.... Children learning to read should see words always as units of larger, meaningful units. In that way they can use the correspondences between oral and written English within the semantic and syntactic contexts [p. 32].

Although the 1971 Scott, Foresman program has a strong meaning-emphasis, it provides some instruction in decoding. However, as Popp observed, this may not be readily apparent because exercises that most reading programs classify as decoding exercises are indexed under comprehension in the Scott, Foresman program. Thus "letter–sound relationship cues" are listed there under "comprehension strategies."

The almost universal acceptance of decoding as a major objective for the primary grades is seen as well in recently revised standardized reading achievement tests. The 1971 revisions of the Metropolitan Achievement Tests, Primary I and II, each have a subtest called "Word Analysis" added to the traditional subtests designed to measure word meanings and reading comprehension of earlier editions.

Perhaps the greatest impact of *The Great Debate* was on "Sesame Street" and "The Electric Company." Both of these shows, produced by Children's Television Workshop, accepted, after much discussion and deliberation by advisory committees, decoding as a major focus for teaching beginning reading.[2] Millions of preschoolers and children in the primary grades have learned the names of the letters, the relation of letters to sounds, and how they are combined to form words. The popularity of these shows (about seven million children watch "Sesame Street" and about five million watch "The Electric Company,") and their wide use in schools, particularly "The Electric Company," helped in turn to legitimize this practice among parents and teachers.

It also seems to me to be a tenable hypothesis that these shows, particularly "Sesame Street," put an end, for the time being at least, to another controversy current during the 1960s: whether it is better to give earlier or later reading instruction. It would seem that the results of early reading instruction given on "Sesame Street" and "The Electric Company," which millions of parents saw, were satisfying enough to be accepted by them. This in turn affected the schools. With the exception of some Piagetian theorists (e.g., Elkind, Larson, & Van Doorninck, 1965; Furth & Wachs, 1974), there

---

[2]The present author has been on the Advisory Board since 1968.

seem to be few serious proponents of later reading instruction at the present time.

I cannot emphasize enough that changes in educational practice do not come from one research report alone. Indeed, there was another research in the late 1960s that contributed to the general ferment and to the impact of *The Great Debate*. The 27 USOE First Grade Cooperative Reading Studies (Bond & Dykstra, 1967) comparing various methods in the first grade (many were continued in the second grade and somewhat fewer through the third) drew similar conclusions, although there was much difference of opinion on this (Staufffer, 1966).[3] One of the findings of The Coordinating Center (Bond & Dykstra, 1967) was that basal reading programs supplemented by separate phonics programs produced better results in reading at the end of first grade. There was some loss in the advantage at the end of second grade, and the few studies that continued till the end of third grade seemed to find few if any differences at that point. However, after a reanalysis of the data, Dykstra (1968), one of the project coordinators, found an advantage for the code-emphasis methods through second grade. In a later report, he concluded even more strongly for the efficacy of a code-emphasis, compared to a meaning-emphasis, in beginning reading (Dykstra, 1974):

> We can summarize the results of sixty years of research dealing with beginning reading instruction by stating that early systematic instruction in phonics provides the child with the skills necessary to become an independent reader at an earlier age than is likely if phonics instruction is delayed and less systematic. As a consequence of his early success in "learning to read," the child can more quickly go about the job of "reading to learn" [p. 397].

Would my conclusion regarding the benefits of code-emphasis be the same today—after 10 more years of research? I would tend to say yes, since I do not see any viable data to disconfirm it. The review by Corder (1971), one of the USOE Targeted Research Studies in Reading, included comparisons of reading programs published since 1967, as well as those covered in *The Great Debate*. Using the Gephart procedure (1970) to decide whether to include a study, Corder's overall conclusion was that there can be no conclusion: "It is clear that the present body of literature is too incomplete, too fragmented, and too often conducted and reported on too general a level to be very useful [p. 137]." Admittedly, my criteria for including and excluding research in *The Great Debate* were not as strict as Corder's. I was perhaps more motivated by

---

[3]Some interpreters focused on the large differences within methods, concluding that the teacher was the most essential factor. This observation was interesting because only one of the 27 studies (Chall & Feldmann, 1966) studied the direct effect of the teacher.

a desire to make rational the basis for practical decisions in beginning reading instruction than by a desire to evaluate the nature of the research design. If one's task is to help those who must make the practical decisions, then one hesitates to conclude that we should wait another generation or two for better research. One does the best with what one has. It should be noted that the review by Dykstra (1974), which included studies completed after those analyzed in *The Great Debate*, also concluded in favor of a code-emphasis beginning.

With regard to the possibility that an initial gain is gradually lost, the following hypotheses raised in *The Great Debate* (Chall, 1967) still seem appropriate today:

> Whether an initial code emphasis keeps its advantage in the middle and upper elementary grades, and later, depends on how reading is taught in these grades: how much the reading program stresses language and vocabulary growth and provides sufficiently challenging reading materials. If the reading programs are not challenging enough in these respects, the early advantages will probably be dissipated [p. 138].

A MODEST PROPOSAL FOR READING STAGES

With the issue of the dissipation of early advantages, I come to the second part of the chapter—a brief introduction to a scheme of developmental stages of reading.

My current thinking and my work for the past several years have been concerned with this scheme, which to a certain extent picks up where I left off in *The Great Debate* and in a later paper (Chall, 1969). As I found then that I could understand the conflicting results of earlier studies only by hypothesizing a developmental model of reading, so now I find that the scheme can help to answer some additional crucial questions. The first is the persistent finding that early advantages in reading scores, because of improvements in method or other changes, do not seem to persist (Bond & Dykstra, 1967; Corder, 1971). With a greater understanding of how reading changes with chronological age and maturity of skill and of the kind of practice that would be needed with these changes, it may be possible to find viable explanations for this finding.

The second body of data that I hope this scheme will be able to explain is the strong association of reading test scores with family background factors. Knowledge about this association has existed for decades, but it took on new importance with the publication of the Coleman report (1966) and the more recent International Association for the Evaluation of Educational Achievement (IEA) study of reading comprehension in 15 countries (Thorndike, 1973). This relation is so strong that once it is included in a factor analysis, it is difficult to find a significant relationship for any other factors, particularly school factors. The potency of general background factors appears to be even stronger in the IEA reading study (Thorndike, 1973) where it was found that "differences are so large that by the standards of the developed countries, 14-year-olds in developing countries seem almost illiterate [p. 177]." A developmental model of reading might help to explain the influence of nonschool, as well as school, factors at various points in children's lives and in the development of their reading skills.

The following pages present a brief introduction to reading stages, a brief delineation of the reading stages, and suggestions regarding the values of the stages for research, instruction, and evaluation, and for understanding the reading process and how reading develops.

Introduction to Reading Stages

Although I tend not to refer to the reading stages as a theory, I do hope the proposed stages will lead to questions and hypotheses that can be either confirmed or disconfirmed. I am hopeful, too, that the scheme can help to predict and control achievement in reading. I feel more comfortable about calling it a model and even better about calling the stages a scheme—a scheme for arranging and interpreting facts from basic and applied research and from the wisdom of experience in the classroom and clinic, and for planning new research. The focus of the scheme is on what goes on in the individual and in the environment to bring the reader through the various reading stages to maturity. My major concern is with how reading develops, how it evolves from its primitive beginnings to its most mature forms. How, in essence, do readers change as they proceed from the *Cat in the Hat* to the financial page of the *New York Times*?

The scheme is frankly macroscopic, but it is hoped that it will permit a connection with microscopic data and views. It does not hope to explain what happens during a second or a minute of reading. Such a conceptualization of reading is similar to classic germ theory in biology and medicine. My scheme is closer to a public health model. Although many diseases do come from germs and viruses, the public health model assumes that many diseases can be prevented and alleviated by providing healthful, benevolent environments. I will not dwell on whether the "germ" or "public health" model will prove to be more useful for the theory and practice of reading. I will say only that environmental factors are only recently gaining attention in studies of the effects on achievement of teacher–pupil interaction (Chall & Feldmann, 1966) and of different classroom organizations (Bloom, 1976; Stallings, 1975; White, Day, Freeman, Hantman, & Messenger, 1973).

The presentation to follow is only a brief introduction. Because of space limitations, findings of relevant research on reading stages cannot be presented, nor can the related work of Piaget and other developmentalists be included.

Background of the Scheme

As will become clearer later, I owe much to the work of Piaget—to his theory of stages and to his stages of cognitive development (Inhelder & Piaget, 1958; Piaget, 1970). I also owe a debt to Wolff's (1960) comparison of Piaget's developmental theories with those of Freud and psychoanalysis. With regard to the advanced reading stages, the greatest influence came from Perry's (1970) study of advanced intellectual and ethical development in the college years. Although all the above were influential, my major focus from the beginning was specifically on the development of reading. My work on readability (Chall, 1958) and my work with Dale (Dale & Chall, 1948a, b, 1956) were strong influences, as was my more than 25 years of experience as a clinician diagnosing and teaching children and young people with severe reading disability. The unsolved problems I found while researching for *Learning to Read: The Great Debate* became the most recent impetus.

Generally, although the present scheme was launched by Piaget's stages and by Wolff's analysis, my objective has not been to confirm or disconfirm the applicability of Piaget's general cognitive theories to reading. Instead, I have sought in his work and in the work of other developmentalists ideas and methods for developing a scheme that would be of value for understanding reading. Following are some of the hypotheses I have generated:

1.   There are stages in reading, similar to Piaget's stages of cognitive development, that have a definite structure, that differ from one another in characteristic qualitative ways, and that generally follow a hierarchical progression.

2.   Reading is, at all stages, a form of problem solving in which readers adapt to their environment (as per Piaget) through the processes of assimilation and accommodation.

3.   Individuals progress through the stages by interacting with their environment—the home, school, larger community, and culture.

4.   Measures of having reached a given reading stage will add a further, useful dimension to standardized norm-referenced testing, as well as to criterion-referenced testing. Such measures will add to a theoretical understanding of how reading develops and to the technology for effecting intensified improvement for those who need it.

5.   The successive stages mean that the readers are doing "different" things in relation to printed matter at each stage, although the term *reading* is used to describe each of these stages. In line with the underlying differences in readers'

methods of problem solving as they proceed through the stages, differences should show up in such classic measures as eye movement fixations and regressions, eye–voice span, rate of silent and oral reading, mastery of phonic elements and generalizations, relative efficiency of oral and silent reading comprehension, and so on.

6.   The successive stages are characterized by growth in the ability to read language of greater complexity, rarity, technicality, and abstractness, and by changes in how such printed language is viewed and used.

7.   The successive stages are characterized by the extent to which prior knowledge is needed to read and understand materials. The more advanced the reading stage, the more the reader needs to know about the world and about the topic on which he or she is reading.

8.   At each stage, readers show characteristics that, if continued too long, may prevent the development of the next stage. Thus, if the accuracy and analysis (and synthesis) needed during the decoding stage are not succeeded by reading experiences that require a faster pace and a greater reliance on context (Stage 2—Confirmation), there may be a holding on to the success of the earlier stage. Similarly, if the child is not challenged with the demands of accuracy in gaining new information, as required by Stage 3, he or she may persist in the less accurate, more contextual reading of Stage 2.

9.   Reading has an affective component. The child's attitudes toward reading are related to those of his or her family, culture, and school. At certain points in the development of reading, full engagement with the content and with the reading process are required. Thus energy, daring, and courage are also some of the aspects of developmental changes.

The Stages

The stages of the developmental scheme are presented in this section. The ages and grades given for the different stages are to be considered approximations, or hypotheses, based on typical current educational practices and achievements. Some individuals may achieve a level of reading characterized here as Stage 3 at age 6. Others may not achieve it until age 12 or later. How many reach Stage 5 with current educational practices is not known, but that more sensitive and systematic instruction can help bring it about in many more than is presently the case seems strongly possible (Bloom, 1976).

Only a brief presentation of the Prereading Stage will be given to permit a fuller treatment of the reading stages—Stage 1 to 5. In reality, some of the more advanced aspects of the Prereading Stage overlap with early aspects of Stage 1. One of the characteristics of Stage 1 is the child's becoming conscious of what was acquired incidentally during the Prereading Stage.

   Stage 0. Prereading Stage—Preschool to Kindergarten: Birth to Age 6.[4] The Prereading Stage perhaps covers a greater period of time and probably undergoes a greater series of changes than any of the other stages.[5] From birth until the beginning of formal education most children living in a literate culture with an alphabetic writing system accumulate a fund of knowledge about letters, words, and books. They also develop visual, visual-motor, and auditory perceptual skills needed for tasks in beginning reading, Stage 1. The children grow in their control over aspects of language—the syntactic and semantic, as well as the metalinguistic. That is, they know that spoken words may be segmented, that the parts may be added to designated parts of other words, that some parts of words sound the same (rhyme and alliteration), and that word parts and sounds can be blended (synthesized) to form whole words.

   There has been considerable interest in and investigation of the Prereading Stage during the past decade (Clay, 1966, 1975; Durkin, 1966; Jansky & de Hirsch, 1972; Soderbergh, 1971; Bissex, 1976). These investigators have identified the reading and writing activities engaged in by preschoolers, the children's problem-solving strategies, and the concepts of reading and writing they hold during their different phases of development on the way to beginning reading. It is widely reported that preschoolers today can discriminate and name most of the letters of the alphabet.[6] They can write (print) their names and some letters that are dictated. Many children at this age have also interiorized the universal features of writing and can, when presented with various approximations to writing, select one that most resembles writing (Lavine, 1973). Some can recognize common signs or brand names on packages and on TV and words in favorite books. Many 3-year-olds can pretend they can read a book, and they reveal knowledge of essential concepts of reading: holding the book right-side up, referring with a glance or finger(s) to the words on the page while "saying" the words, using the pictures for demonstration and elaboration, and turning the pages one at a time.

   Extensive research on reading readiness and on early prediction and prevention of reading failure (Chall, 1967; de Hirsch & Jansky, 1966; Durkin, 1966, 1974–1975; Gates & Bond, 1936; Jansky & de Hirsch, 1972) has demonstrated that the various abilities, knowledge, and skills acquired during the Prereading Stage are substantially related to success with reading at Stage 1. Although there is some disagreement among investigators as to whether

---

   [4]An earlier version of this chapter referred to the existence of the Prereading Stage but did not elaborate. I was convinced of the need for the additional detail presented here by Posner's discussion of it and other chapters in this volume.

   [5]I am indebted for this observation to Bissex (1976), who studied the reading and spelling development of her son from ages 3 to 8.

   [6]This was not so 40–50 years ago. Gates (1937) found less extensive knowledge of letters and sounds.

individual characteristics or environment and experience are the more powerful in developing prereading skills and abilities, most agree that both are involved and that an interactional model will prove to be the most fruitful for understanding and for effecting change (Feldman, 1976).

Stage 1. Initial Reading or Decoding Stage—Grades 1–2. Ages 6–7. The essential aspect of Stage 1 is learning the arbitrary set of letters and associating these with the corresponding parts of spoken words. In this stage children and adults interiorize cognitive knowledge about reading such as what the letters are for, how to know that *bun* is not *bug*, and how to know when they have made a mistake. This stage has been referred to pejoratively as a "guessing and memory game," or as "grunting and groaning," "mumbling and bumbling," or "barking at print," depending on whether the prevailing methodology for beginning reading instruction is a sight or a phonic approach. The qualitative change that occurs at the end of this stage is the insight gained about the nature of the spelling system of the particular alphabetic language used.[7]

The transition from Stage 1 to Stage 2 is most vividly illustrated by Sartre's (1964) memory of how he taught himself to read. He recalls persisting and struggling with a favorite book. Determined to read it himself, he was "grunting" and sounding the syllables for hours, until—with what seemed to be a flash of insight—he could read! He let out a roar and shouted for all to hear that he could read.

In a sense it is as if the child has recapitulated historically the early fumblings of the discovery of alphabetic writing and the equal, if not greater, intellectual feat of discovering that the spoken word is made up of a finite number of sounds. The work of Liberman and his associates (Liberman, Cooper, Shankweiler, & Studdert-Kennedy, 1967) makes this feat seem even greater. Since it is difficult to hear the same sounds when they are in different positions in a word on in different contexts (i.e., following vowels or consonants), a capacity for abstraction seems to be important even for Stage 1.

This great discovery—usually accomplished with relief and joy, but also occasionally with tears (Bissex, 1976)—comes with more or less drama to most of us who become literate. It is a familiar one to teachers of the primary grades, to remedial reading teachers, and to parents. On the surface the child's reading does not seem to be very different, although it may be a little more fluent. On the usual tests of oral and silent reading, the scores may be the same. But the reader's understanding of reading has taken on a new structure. Therefore, new tests to capture this change are necessary.

---

[7]The insights might well be different for ideographic languages (Maraini, 1973).

There are phases within Stage 1, which Biemiller's (1970) study of first graders' reading errors seems to bear out. Among first-grade children who were taught by a sight-method emphasis, Biemiller found changes in oral reading errors that coincided with increasing ability in reading. Biemiller's first phase was characterized by word substitution errors, most of which were semantically and syntactically adequate. The second phase was characterized by an increase in nonresponding and by more errors that had a graphic resemblance to the printed word, with a loss of some of the semantic acceptability. In the third phase, there was a continued concern with graphic exactness but also a return to greater semantic acceptability. All children seemed to move through these phases in the same order. The better readers progressed through them faster. The least proficient readers persisted in making the first type of error—substitution on the basis of meaning and syntax. It was only when the children appeared to let go of the "meaning" substitutions and worked instead on what the word looked and sounded like that they made substantial progress.

The Biemiller findings seem to run counter to the psycholinguistic theories of Smith (1971) and Goodman (1969). If one applied their theories to the Biemiller data, would children in the second phase be rated as being lower in ability since they were more "glued" to the print than to the meaning? Would Smith and Goodman consider Biemiller's first phase to be more advanced since the children made errors that were more semantically oriented? Indeed, Biemiller concluded that the second phase, in which there is greater concern for graphic accuracy, is necessary for the transition to the seemingly easy, smooth reading in the third phase.

From still another point of view, it would seem that the children in Biemiller's first phase were still engaging in a kind of pseudoreading—the "reading" common among preschoolers who retell a familiar story with the aid of a picture box, recognizing an occasional word to help them remember the story. The nature of the errors in the first phase suggests that the print has only a minimal effect on reading in that phase. Reading for these beginning first graders is an "inside out" activity (see F. Smith's chapter in Volume 2), which appears to be very much like what mature readers do. They bring more to the printed page, than they take from it, as Dale (1967) has been emphasizing for many years. In a sense readers in this phase and mature readers seem to behave in a similar manner toward print: They do not stick closely to it. Yet mature readers can stick to the print if they want to or need to. Going beyond it is a conscious choice for them, one based on knowledge. Young children in the first phase of reading have no choice. They must supply their own words because they do not know enough about how to get the author's words from the printed page. To advance, to build up the skill for making choices, beginners have to let go of their pseudomaturity. They have to engage, at least temporarily, in what appears to be less mature reading behavior—becoming glued to the print—in order to reach the real maturity later. They have to know enough about the print in order to leave the print.[8]

Stage 2. Confirmation, Fluency, Ungluing from Print—Grades 2-3. Ages 7-8.[9] Essentially, reading in Stage 2 is a consolidation of what was learned in Stage 1 through reading what is familiar and already known. And by reading familiar stories, fluency is gained. At this stage, reading is not for learning which comes later in Stage 3. Stage 2 reading is not for gaining new information but for confirming what is already known to the reader. Since the content of what is read is basically familiar, the reader's attention can be concentrated on the printed words, usually the most common, high-frequency words. Also, with the basic decoding skills and insights interiorized in Stage 1, advantage can be taken of what is said in the story and book, matching it to one's knowledge and language. Although some additional, more complex phonic elements and generalizations are learned during Stage 2 and even later, it appears that what most children learn in Stage 2 is to use their decoding knowledge, the redundancies of the language, and the redundancies of the stories read. They gain courage and skill in using context and thus gain fluency and speed.

Relevant data regarding the reality of Stage 2 comes from the strong predictiveness of the reading achievement test scores at the end of Grade 3, as compared with those at the end of Grades 1 and 2 (Kraus, 1973). Kraus, who also referred to Bloom's (1964) data, found that by Grade 3, if a pupil scores significantly below the norms on achievement tests and does not receive special help, he or she will continue to experience failure throughout the school years.

The reality of Stage 2 may also be seen in the effects of adult literacy campaigns. A tenable hypothesis would be that Stage 2 is the main failing point of most adult literacy campaigns. The literacy campaigns here and in Third World countries indicate that although most adults can get through Stage 1, they begin to falter at Stage 2. Reading a newspaper or a phamphlet containing new agricultural information, which requires at least Stage 3 reading, will be difficult or impossible for most. The following explanation

---

[8]This may be similar to the seeming maturity of young children's art work. Their finger paintings resemble those of Jackson Pollack, and their drawings may smack of Miro. Yet can the children's works be considered works of art? Should the children be discouraged from their later struggles with seemingly awkward horses and stereotyped houses? Perhaps reading, too, must go from what seems like a finished, rounded act at the beginning to what seems more halting and dull in order to reach the maturity of choice and the finished, rounded act.

[9]It is possible that Stage 2 continues throughout one's life and is characterized among adults by reading popular fiction, magazines, mysteries, and some parts of the daily newspaper—reading from which one does not learn much that is new or exacting but that is confirming and satisfying.

may prove useful. After the literacy classes complete their Stage 1 programs, there are not enough readable materials available, material that is familiar in its use of language and content, for the new literates to gain the fluency of Stage 2. Nor is there usually a compelling need to keep on reading.

What kind of environment fosters the development of Stage 2? Essentially, it would require an opportunity for reading many familiar books—familiar because the stories are familiar, the subjects are familiar, or the structure is familiar, as in fairy tales or folktales. (At one time the Bible and religious tracts were familiar.) Familiarity with the language patterns of these books also helps. Generally, the greater the amount of practice and the greater the immersion, the greater the chance of developing the fluency with print that is necessary for the new difficulty to come—the acquisition of new ideas in Stage 3.

For children of low socioeconomic status (SES), although a discrepancy is reported from the Prereading Stage on, the gap seems to widen at Stage 2.[10] The child whose parents cannot afford to buy books or whose own patterns of recreation and work do not include borrowing books and magazines from a public library loses needed time for practice. If the parents do not read regularly to the child, development of language may be slower (Chomsky, 1972). Even more important, the child loses out on the emotionally confirming responses that books and reading matter bring.

Stage 3. Reading for Learning the New–From One Viewpoint—Grades 4–8(?). Ages 9–13(?).   When readers enter Stage 3, they begin to read for knowledge, for information—mainly for what is new—but usually what is new from only one viewpoint. In a sense, entering Stage 3 fits the traditional conception of the difference between primary and later schooling: In the primary grades children learn to read; in the higher grades they read to learn. During Stages 1 and 2, what is learned concerns more the relating of print to speech than the relating of print to ideas. Very little new information is learned about the world from reading before Stage 3; more is learned from listening and watching. It is with the beginning of Stage 3 that reading begins to compete with these other means of knowing. However, at the beginning of Stage 3, learning from print is still less efficient than learning from listening and watching. It is hypothesized that by the end of Stage 3 the efficiency of reading may equal and begin to surpass that of the other means of gaining new information, particularly listening (see Sticht's chapter, this volume).

---

[10]SES is used here and throughout the chapter to refer to the usual kinds of experiences children are exposed to in homes classified by the different socioeconomic levels. I do not mean the income of the family but the overall experiences, particulary the experiences relating to reading and literacy (Bloom, 1976).

Stage 3 reading is also characterized by the growing importance of prior knowledge.[11] The need to know some of the new, if more is to be learned from reading, becomes greater. Readers need to bring knowledge and experience to their reading if they are to learn from it (Chall, 1947, 1950). They also need to learn a process—how to find information in a paragraph, chapter, or book, and how to go about efficiently finding what one is looking for.

It is significant that in traditional schools, the fourth grade, age 9, was the time for starting the study of the so-called subject areas—history, geography, and natural science. The curriculum in the first three grades included the language arts and math. The content subjects were not included until children had mastered enough of the literacy skills to deal with the books necessary for learning about times and places and ideas removed from their direct experience.

The findings from the readability research of the past fifty years seem to fit the proposed stage (Chall, 1958; Klare, 1974–1975). Stage 3 fits the data on and the experiences with the distinctions between primary level reading materials and materials at fourth-grade readability level and above. The materials at fourth-grade level and higher begin to go beyond the elemental, common experiences of the unschooled or barely schooled. To write even the simplest information materials—materials that present ideas that the reader does not already have—a readability level of at least Grade 4 is usually required. Materials at Grade 4 readability level begin to contain more unfamiliar, "bookish" words that are usually learned in school or from books. (Such words may be learned from TV but probably only from the public service programs.) Thus, while the learner is in the decoding (Stage 1) and confirming (Stage 2) stages, the task is to master the print; with Stage 3 the task becomes the mastering of ideas. Because this is a task quite different from, and more difficult than, those of Stages 1 and 2, it can be mastered only in a limited way. That is, I propose that for most children, Stage 3 reading means learning how to learn from reading, but essentially from only one point of view.

Given the one-viewpoint aspect of Stage 3, the reading in that stage is essentially for facts, for concepts, for how to do things. If there is any reading for nuance and variety of viewpoint, it is probably in the reading of fiction. One may hypothesize that the time taken to progress from Stage 3 to Stage 4 relates to the time it takes to acquire knowledge in the many areas needed to read and understand the multiple viewpoints encountered in Stage 4.

---

[11]I appreciate the highlighting of this point by Kintsch in his discussion of an earlier version of this chapter, particularly since it has, for a long time, been a tested generalization in the teaching of reading and in the testing of readability. (See Kintsch, this volume & Chall 1947, 1950.)

Stage 4. Multiple Viewpoints—High School, Ages 14-18.   The essential characteristic of reading in Stage 4 is that it involves dealing with more than one point of view. For example, in contrast to an elementary school textbook on American history, which presupposes Stage 3 reading, the textbook at the high school level requires dealing with a variety of viewpoints. Compared to the textbooks in the lower grades, the increased weight and length of high school textbooks no doubt can be accounted for by greater depth of treatment and greater variety in points of view. Stage 4 reading may be essentially an ability to deal with layers of facts and concepts added on to those acquired earlier. These other viewpoints can be acquired, however, because the simpler viewpoints were acquired earlier. Without the single viewpoint of Stage 3, the multiple viewpoints of Stage 4 would be difficult to acquire.

How is Stage 4 acquired? Mostly, it is acquired through formal education—the assignments in the various school textbooks, original and other sources, and reference works in the physical, biological, and social sciences—through reading of more mature fiction, and through the free reading of books, newspapers, and magazines. In dealing with more than one set of facts, various theories, and multiple viewpoints, as in Stage 4, practice is acquired in learning ever-more-difficult concepts and in learning how to acquire new concepts and new points of view through reading.

Stage 5. A World View—College, Ages 18 and Above.   Stage 5, the most mature stage, I take from Perry's (1970) study of intellectual development during the college years. He contrasted a quantitative approach to knowledge (Stage 4) with a more qualitative approach:

> In our reports, the most difficult instructional moment for the students—and perhaps therefore for the teachers as well—seems to occur at the transition from the conception of knowledge as a quantitative accretion of discrete rightnesses (including the discrete rightnesses of multiplicity in which everyone has a right to his own opinion) to the conception of knowledge as the qualitative assessment of contextual observations and relationships... [p. 210].

When Stage 5 is reached, one has learned to read as much or as little of a book as one needs to for one's purpose, starting at the end, the middle, or the beginning. A reader at Stage 5 knows what not to read, as well as what to read. To reach this stage is to be able to use selectively the printed material in those areas of knowledge central to one's concern.

Whether all people can reach Stage 5 reading, even at the end of four years of college, is open to study. There is some evidence, however, that more college students reach this qualitative stage earlier than they did in previous generations (Perry, 1970).

Succession of the Reading Stages

It is hypothesized that each stage presupposes skills acquired in the previous stage, generally subsumes these in some form, and is subsumed by the next stage. It is assumed that Stage 1, the decoding stage, is built on the skills, attitudes, and knowledge developed in the Prereading Stage. This does not mean that a child cannot learn to read without the full range of prereading skills and abilities. Beginning reading programs where children did not have these skills have succeeded through modifications of the program (Gates, 1937). However, the existing literature on readiness does indicate that achievement on prereading factors is a good predictor of early reading achievement, at least through the end of Grade 2 (Stage 1) (Bond & Dykstra, 1967; de Hirsch & Jansky, 1966; Durkin, 1966; Jansky & de Hirsch, 1972).

Stage 1, in turn, appears to be a necessary condition for Stage 2 because scores on decoding tests have a positive and significant correlation with scores on oral and silent reading tests (Chall, 1967, 1978a; Walmsley, 1976). Since these standardized reading tests cannot restrict themselves to the use of only those words and phonic elements taught specifically in each child's reading program, it is a tenable hypothesis that mastery of Stage 1, particularly the ability to identify words not directly taught, is necessary for proficiency in Stage 2.

Although Stage 1 becomes subsumed by Stage 2, decoding does not stop altogether.[12] The learning and use of correspondences between spoken and written words continues in Stage 2 and other stages. Correspondences are used for new proper names and for new words not immediately recognized and, in fact, continues during Stages 3, 4, and 5. In Stage 5, particularly, decoding is used for reading foreign names, new technical words, and new alphabetic foreign languages. Indeed, it would seem that a Stage 1 type of reading was needed to break the code of the Rosetta Stone—although probably all who tried did most of their other reading on a Stage 5 level. It is also a tenable hypothesis that typical literacy behavior does not stay at one stage only. Those who read at Stage 5 for study and work may relax with a mystery at Stage 2. Although the general character of reading changes with each succeeding stage, the abilities of previous stages remain for use in situations that require them.

Stage 3, the first stage of reading to learn, presupposes the ability to use context and the fluency in reading that are acquired in Stage 2. Without these characteristics, the reading of materials with new concepts, names, and facts

---

[12]The need for making explicit the fact that decoding probably does not stop at the end of Stage 1 was made apparent by Posner's discussion of an earlier version of this chapter. (See Posner, this volume.)

would not be possible. Only when the fundamental decoding skills are mastered (Stage 1) and fluency has become habitual (Stage 2) can reading be used as a tool for learning, even when the new information is relatively straightforward and unencumbered by a variety of viewpoints and subtleties. Since Stage 3 reading requires accurate attention to facts and details, the decoding skills acquired at Stage 1 are still used. And since it requires confidence to move ahead even if a word or idea is not gotten immediately, Stage 3 makes use of Stage 2 fluency.

In a similar manner, Stage 4 subsumes Stage 3, and Stage 5 subsumes Stage 4. Knowing one viewpoint of a subject or topic must be developed so that a multiple viewpoint can be developed. From a multiple viewpoint a world viewpoint may be achieved.

Values of a Reading Stage Theory

For Research. A stage theory might help to prevent some of the persistent controversies that occur in the field of reading research and practice. The research in reading seems to be particularly subject to misunderstandings. It is not uncommon for investigators to disagree over the meaning of *reading*, when each is concerned with a different stage of its development. The proposed stages might help clarify what is or is not being studied or discussed.

The reading stages may also help to provide a framework for analyzing and synthesizing various models of reading. It would appear that the psycholinguistic theories of reading by F. Smith (1971; Volume 2, this series) and the Goodmans (see the chapter by Goodman and Goodman in this volume) start with Stage 2. There appears to be no provision for a decoding stage (Stage 1) and also little concern for the kind of accuracy required in technical and scientific reading (Stage 3 and beyond). Indeed, it is often suggested in their theories that decoding retards reading for meaning and that relying on context for recognition of words and meanings is the ideal reading strategy at all times. To a great extent the theories of Smith and the Goodmans, when applied to beginning reading, resemble the sight and sentence methods of the past and the language experience method of the present. According to these models, there is only one reading process—reading for meaning—which is essentially the same at the beginning level and at the highly skilled level.

Stage theory may add to our knowledge of what happens as the individual learns to read at an ever-increasing level of maturity. Although we use only one word—*reading*—for what happens at the various stages, important quantitative and qualitative changes take place. Measures of quantitative changes already exist—the standardized reading tests for measuring the abilities of readers and the readability formulas for measuring the difficulty of the reading materials. The standardized reading tests are similar to existing measures of mental ability in that they measure growth in maturity in terms of ages or grades. Such quantitative estimates have their value in that they can help to effect a match between reading materials and readers. They also help to determine whether progress has been made from year to year.

What such tests do not provide, however, is information for the researcher, teacher, or clinician about the specific aspects and components of reading that have been mastered and those yet to be acquired. As is the case with most intelligence tests, no provision is made for translating the scores into qualitative descriptions of the reading process that suggest the necessary next steps for instruction and practice. This is particularly important in providing for the millions who have serious reading problems. It would help to know, for example, what an eighth-grade reading level on a standardized reading test means when it is achieved by a fourth grader, an eighth grader, a twelfth grader, a college freshman, or an adult seeking a high school equivalency certificate. Does such a score indicate mastery of decoding, fluency, and reading for facts and concepts? At what level? Tests of these different qualities would help us in research and in practice.

For Instruction. Reading stages can contribute to a better understanding of how reading is acquired and how the total environment, as well as the school environment and instruction, may be optimized for pupils at the different stages. Thus it would appear that children who enter first grade and are at the beginning of Stage 1 should have more specific and systematic instruction than those who have made some inroads into decoding.[13] This is because the relations between sounds and letters, elementary decoding skills, are usually not discovered by the learner but require instruction. Toward the end of the decoding stage, the knowledge and skills acquired are usually sufficient to become self-generative. That is, further growth can be achieved with practice on one's own.[14]

The degree of direct teaching at Stage 2 would be relatively less than at Stage 1, but there would be a need to encourage wide reading. The classroom would need to contain many books that are easy, familiar, and interesting enough to invite reading, and to provide the time and the atmosphere to read them.

---

[13]Many children entering Grade 1 are past Stage 1 and well into Stage 2 because of "Sesame Street" and "The Electric Company" and the general acceptance by parents of the efficacy of early reading.

[14]There are, of course, children who invent their own spelling systems and who teach themselves to write and read (Chomsky, 1976, Volume 2 of this series; Durkin, 1966; Read, 1971). These children are exposed to much "literate" stimulation and receive a great deal of reinforcement for these activities. These conditions are not met in most homes in the United States.

If Stage 3 has been characterized properly, then the focus of reading instruction in the middle grades should be on textbooks, reference works, and other sources in various subject areas. One may ask whether the recent extension of reading instruction to the later elementary grades and even to the high school has been misdirected. That is, could some of the recently reported declines in reading achievement scores at the higher grades possibly be attributed to the fact that during the reading instruction periods, the "reading reading" periods, mostly fiction is read, whereas the development of Stage 3 abilities requires exactness in reading and recalling names, places, and ideas of factual materials? Such exactness is not needed for reading most fiction, and if only fiction is read, it may not be developed.

A qualitative, developmental way of looking at reading may provide a useful set of questions to ask, particularly about the failure points. For example, we may ask why there has been a consistent failure point reported for Grade 4 or 5, the point of transition between Stages 2 and 3. The appropriateness of challenges and instructional strategies for effecting a transition to the next stage could be questioned. Thus, the concept of proper match or challenge, a concept used often in the 1930s, might gain a fresh look.

The importance of an appropriate match for reading instruction has been accepted for years. Most methods textbooks propose three levels for each pupil—an independent level for easy reading, an instructional level for sufficient challenge, and a frustration level that is too difficult. Although specifications are provided for determining whether given material is appropriate for independent reading or for instruction, there is little hard data as to whether the independent level does in fact lead to more comfortable independent reading and whether the instructional level does in fact lead to more learning. There is some work by Bormuth (1975) that attempts to determine the amounts of information acquired at different readability levels. There is also an early study by Gates (1930) on the ratio of "new" to "running words" in first-grade reading materials that leads to optimal learning for children of different levels of intelligence. It is significant that few, if any, such studies have been done since that of Gates.

The records of the production of reading programs by R&D centers should provide some of the necessary data, especially for Stage 1.[15] Most of the current empirical data are relevant mainly to Stage 1 and perhaps to the Prereading Stage. Relatively little empirical data are available for Stages 2

---

[15]See Popp (1972, Volume 3 of this series) for information on two of the Pittsburgh Learning Research and Development Center's reading programs; Atkinson, Fletcher, Chetin, & Stauffer (1970) for the computer-aided beginning reading program at Stanford; the SWRL *Beginning Reading Program* (Southwest Regional Laboratory for Educational Research and Development, 1972); *Wisconsin Design for Reading Skill Development* (Wisconsin Research and Development Center for Cognitive Learning, 1971); and *The Pre-reading Skills Program* (Venezky, Pittelman, & Kamm, 1974).

and beyond, with the exception of the data from theoretical and applied studies of readability measurement and cloze techniques and perhaps the miscue data collected by Goodman and his associates (e.g., Goodman & Burke, 1969).

For Evaluation.   Reading stages can help to provide the broad general principles of the development of reading needed to construct meaningful criterion-referenced tests, diagnostic tests, and prescriptive programs. When some test publishers claim to measure the "379" reading comprehension skills needed by fourth graders, one wonders whether some of the current technology designed to help teachers is going to lead to a general state of paralysis. However, tests are needed, and schools at least, if not teachers, seem to be ready for criterion-referenced tests and other tests of mastery. An understanding of what distinguishes reading at the various stages of development would be one of the essentials for selecting and constructing the crucial subtests and items. Norm-referenced tests could also benefit from a better knowledge of the qualitative changes in reading (Auerbach, 1971).

For Studying "Literate" Environments.   Stages can lead to systematic study of the environments in school and at home that foster reading development. Availability of books is recognized as essential for growth in reading. Are books more essential for some stages than for others? A tenable hypothesis is that availability of books is particularly essential for growth at Stage 2 and beyond but less so for Stage 1.

For Studying the Effects of Classroom Environments.   Stages may also be useful in studying the effects of different kinds of classroom structure and organization. One might hypothesize that for Stage 1, in which the children have not already learned letters and sounds and do not have insight into the fact that the two are related, much has to be taught directly and practiced systematically. For children who are learning such things, a more structured learning environment might lead to more definite gains than one in which the children work on their own more and are expected to discover their own generalizations (Stallings, 1975; White, Day, Freeman, Hantman, & Messenger, 1973). However, those first graders who have considerable knowledge and insight about decoding may well make better progress in an open, unstructured learning environment. Generally, however, children (and adults in literacy classes) who are at the beginning of Stage 1 need more structure and direction.

Students in Stage 2 may thrive more in an open and self-regulated environment since enough of the decoding elements and insights have been learned to engage in what appears to approximate "real reading." It can also be hypothesized that Stage 2 strategies, introduced lightly and playfully while the reader is still in Stage 1, would be a useful way to encourage the transition between the stages. Indeed, a "this is ahead of you, it is to come later, but let's try it now with no prejudice" approach is one of the ways to help students make other transitions as well.

A playful tryout of the next stage may encourage the familiarity that contributes to the pupil's confidence and courage. Indeed, much courage and daring are needed, particularly during the transition from Stage 1 to Stage 2. Stage 1 success is assured if the elements and generalizations are learned and applied in a controlled environment with worksheets, workbooks, and very simple stories. However, Stage 2 reading involves selecting books, being unsure of some of the words, getting confused, and being uncertain. The books may be simple, but when all the words in these simple books are added up, they form a load that is in the thousands. At any rate, if the reader goes outside the required text materials, something unexpected may be encountered that requires confidence, courage, and persistence.

Despite the success with reading books during Stage 2, it would seem that some direct instruction may again be needed for Stage 3, in which the emphasis is on acquiring new, exact knowledge. With the acquisition of exact knowledge comes a need for more words and for the ability to learn these from dictionaries, encyclopedias, and other references. It is at this stage that the old, yet new, question arises: Who should do the teaching of reading—the reading teacher or the subject matter teachers?

For Those Who Have Difficulty With Reading. The stages may help us to gain a better understanding of the reading and other educational problems of those who experience persistent difficulties—those who have reading or learning disabilities and those whose retarded reading is attributed to their lower educational, social, economic, or minority status, or to their being bilingual.

With regard to the poor reading performance of children with reading or learning disabilities, it is notable that the basic characteristic of such children is the significant discrepancy between their reading achievement and their mental ability. They do not generally have problems in understanding or producing language. At the risk of oversimplifying the complexity of their problems, one may say that generally their ability to derive meaning from print lags significantly behind their ability to understand by other means. Their difficulty is usually not with understanding ideas and language. If they have difficulty with language, it is with its phonological aspects—sound discrimination, segmentation, blending, and sequencing.

Experience from clinics and classrooms indicates that children with reading or learning disabilities have great difficulty with Stage 1 (decoding) and Stage 2 (fluency). Indeed, the more severe the reading or learning disability, the more there seems to be a problem with decoding and fluency (Chall, 1967). Furthermore, compared to children of their chronological and mental age, the transition from Stage 1 to Stage 2 is more difficult and takes longer for the disabled children. It takes a long time before they are comfortable with even the simplest book. They almost seem glued to the print, or they still guess wildly.

The difficult transition from the decoding (Stage 1) to the confirmation stage (Stage 2) was noted by many of the early investigators of reading disability—Gray, Gates, Orton, and Fernald (see Chall, 1967). This problem continues to be of concern. Samuels and his associates (Samuels, Begy, & Chaur, 1975–1976) have been developing techniques for effecting this transition and moving toward "automaticity."

An overlong stay in Stage 1 is also serious for a child when the rest of the class moves into Stage 3 and he or she cannot cope with Stage 3 reading. Some provision needs to be made for the pupil's continued conceptual and informational development, which in most schools comes primarily from written materials. If this is not provided while the pupil is learning to read on a lower level, deficiencies in cognitive development may ensue, although the original problem was with decoding rather than with the meaning components of reading.

With respect to the poor reading performance found among low SES children, the reading stages scheme suggests that Stage 1 should present the least relative difficulty to low SES children. Although these children may be less ready to read at age 6, with good instruction there should be little difference by the end of Grade 1, because what needs to be learned at this stage is specific, finite, and when learned, self-generative. That is, the learners can use what has been learned to learn on their own and move on to a higher stage. With good teaching and a good program that provides direct teaching and an opportunity for much practice, there should be little diffence among students from various SES levels. Indeed, such claims are being made by the authors and publishers of some of the new, highly programmed reading systems. See, for example, SWRL's Beginning Reading Program (Southwest Regional Laboratory for Educational Research and Development (1972), Distar Reading (Englemann & Bruner, 1969), Stanford Computer Assisted Instruction Program in Initial Reading (Atkinson, Fletcher, Chetin, & Stauffer, 1970), and Action-Reading (Cureton, 1973).

The gap for low SES children, I would hypothesize, begins to widen at about Stage 2, the stage requiring much reading and daring and ease about one's performance, since no teacher checks all reading, as in Stage 1. It would appear from autobiographical and fictional accounts that the most curious and lonely of these children persist in reading through and beyond Stage 2. However, with the advent of television, perhaps even the curious and the lonely may not discover books at this early age, since their needs for entertainment and curiosity are met by TV. Stage 2 cannot be achieved from school readers and workbooks alone. To the extent that the school has great quantities of children's books and makes them available in school and out will low SES children have a chance to achieve as well as the norm (Weber, 1971).

Stage 3 also needs great care. The literary and "bookish" language of textbooks, encyclopedias, and other informational books creates another hurdle. It would seem, therefore, that concepts, vocabulary, and strategies necessary for reading such books need to be taught. Although it may be possible for children with rich and varied literary experiences to move more smoothly from Stage 2 to Stage 3—from the fluent reading of simple children's books to the reading of textbooks for the acquisition of new information—it is less likely that children with more limited literary experiences can do the same without help.

For the less advantaged children to compete favorably with their more privileged peers, they must be helped to proceed through the stages. For success with Stages 3, 4, and 5, they must be helped to systematically improve their knowledge of words, facts, and ideas—knowledge that children of higher SES backgrounds may acquire around the dinner table, from books on the family shelves, from their own collection of books, and from the magazines cluttering the coffee tables. Since the opportunities for such learning may not be provided by most lower SES homes, it is essential that the school provide them during the reading stages when they are most needed.

REFERENCES

Atkinson, R. C., Fletcher, J. D., Chetin, H. C., & Stauffer, C. M. *Instruction in initial reading under computer control: The Stanford project* (Tech. Rep. 158). Stanford: Stanford University, Institute for Mathematical Studies in the Social Sciences, 1970.

Auerbach, I. *An analysis of reading comprehension tests* (U.S. Office of Education Project No. O-A-074). Washington, D. C.: U.S. Government Printing Office, 1971. (ERIC Document Reproduction Service No. ED 052 914)

Biemiller, A. J. The development of the use of graphic and contextual information as children learn to read. *Reading Research Quarterly*, 1970, *6*, 75–96.

Bissex, G. *Do nat dstrb gnvs at wrk: Invented spelling and beginning reading development.* Unpublished qualifying paper, Harvard Graduate School of Education, 1976.

Bloom, B. *Stability and change in human characteristics.* New York: Wiley, 1964.

Bloom, B. *Human characteristics and school learning.* New York: McGraw–Hill, 1976.

Bond, G. L., & Dykstra, R. The cooperative research program in first-grade reading instruction. *Reading Research Quarterly*, 1967, *2*, 5–142.

Bormuth, J. R. Reading literacy: Its definition and assessment. In J. B. Carroll & J. S. Chall (Eds.), *Toward a literate society.* New York: McGraw–Hill, 1975.

Burrows, A. T. (Ed.). *Report on reading conference: Code emphasis or meaning emphasis in reading instruction.* New York: New York University, School of Education, Center for Field Research and Social Services, 1968.

Chall, J. S. The influence of previous knowledge on reading ability. *Educational Research Bulletin*, 1947, *26*, 225–230.

Chall, J. S. How reading and other aids to learning may be coordinated to promote growth in and through reading in grades 4 to 6. In W. S. Gray (Ed.), *Keeping reading programs abreast of the times* (Supplementary *Educational Monograph* No. 72). Chicago: University of Chicago Press, 1950.

Chall, J. S. *Readability: An appraisal of research and application.* Columbus, Ohio: Bureau of Educational Research, 1958.

Chall, J. S. *Learning to read: The great debate.* New York: McGraw–Hill, 1967.

Chall, J. S. Research in linguistics and reading instruction: Implications for further research and practice. *Proceedings of the Thirteenth Annual Convention, International Reading Association* (Pt. 1), 1969, *13*, 560–571. (Reprinted in R. Karlin (Ed.), *Perspectives on elementary reading: Principles and strategies of teaching.* New York: Harcourt Brace Jovanovich, 1973.)

Chall, J. S. *Technical manual: The Roswell–Chall diagnostic reading test of word analysis skills* (Rev. & extended ed.). San Diego, Cal.: Essay Press, 1978. (a)

Chall, J. S. A decade of research on reading and learning disabilities: Implications for the teacher. In S. Jay Samuels (Ed.), *Research implications for teaching reading.* Newark, Delaware: International Reading Association, 1978. (b)

Chall, J. S., & Feldmann, S. First-grade reading: An analysis of the interactions of professed methods, teacher implementation and child background. *Reading Teacher*, 1966, *19*, 569–575.

Chomsky, C. Stages in language development and reading exposure. *Harvard Educational Review*, 1972, *42*, 1–33.

Chomsky, C. Invented spelling in the open classroom. In W. von Raffler–Engel (Ed.), *Child language—1975.* Milford, Conn.: International linguistics Association, 1976.

Clay, M. The reading behaviour of 5-year-old children: A research report. *New Zealand Journal of Educational Studies*, 1966, *2*, 11–31.

Clay, M. *What did I write?* Aukland, New Zealand: Heineman Educational Books, 1975.

Coleman, J. S., with Campbell, E. Q., Hobson, C. J., McPortland, J., Mood, A. M., Weinfeld, F. D., & York, R. L. *Equality of educational opportunity* (National Center for Educational Statistics, HEW Rep. No. OE-38001). Washington, D. C.: U.S. Government Printing Office, 1966.

Corder, R. *The information base for reading* (HEW Final Rep., Project No. 0-9031). Berkeley, Cal.: Educational Testing Service, 1971. (ERIC Document Reproduction Service No. Ed 054 922)

Cureton, G. *Action-reading.* Boston: Allyn & Bacon, 1973.

Dale, E. *Can you give the public what it wants?* New York: Cowles Educational Corp., 1967.

Dale, E., & Chall, J. S. A formula for predicting readability. *Educational Research Bulletin, 27*(January 1948), pp. 11–20. (a)

Dale, E., & Chall, J. S. A formula for predicting readability. *Educational Research Bulletin, 28*(February 1948), pp. 37–54. (b)

Dale, E., & Chall, J. S. Developing readable materials. *Fifty-fifth Yearbook of the National Society for the Study of Education* (Pt. 2), 1956, *55*, 218–250.

Davis, F. B. (Ed.). *The literature of research in reading with emphasis on models* (HEW Final Rep.). Washington, D. C.: U.S. Government Printing Office, 1971. (ERIC Document Reproduction Service No. ED 059 023)

de Hirsch, K., & Jansky, J. *Predicting reading failure.* New York: Harper & Row, 1966.

Durkin, D. *Children who read early.* New York: Columbia University, Teachers College Press, 1966.

Durkin, D. A six-year study of children who learned to read in school at the age of four. *Reading Research Quarterly*, 1974–1975, *10*, 9–61.

Dykstra, R. The effectiveness of code- and meaning-emphasis beginning reading programs. *Reading Teacher*, 1968, *22*, 17–23.

Dykstra, R. Phonics and beginning reading instruction. Cited in Walcutt, C. C., Lamport, J., & McCracken, G., *Teaching reading: A phonic/linguistic approach to developmental reading.* New York: Macmillan, 1974.

Elkind, D., Larson, M., & Van Doorninck, W. Perceptual decentration learning and performance in slow and average readers. *Journal of Educational Psychology*, 1965, *56*, 50–56.

Englemann, S., & Bruner, E. C. *Distar reading.* Chicago: Science Research Associates, 1969.

Feldman, C. Reply to *On meddling* by L. Thomas. Unpublished manuscript, Harvard University, 1976.

Furth, H. G., & Wachs, H. *Thinking goes to school: Piaget's theory and practice.* New York: Oxford University Press, 1974.

Gates, A. I. *Interest and ability in reading.* New York: Macmillan, 1930.

Gates, A. I. The necessary mental age for beginning reading. *Elementary School Journal*, 1937, *37*, 497–508.

Gates, A. I., & Bond, G. L. Reading readiness: A study of factors determining success and failure in beginning reading. *Teachers College Record*, 1936, *37*, 679–685.

Gephart, W. J. The targeted research and development program on reading: A report on the application of the convergence technique. *Reading Research Quarterly*, 1970, *5*, 505–523.

Goodman, K. S. Words and morphemes in reading. In K. S. Goodman & J. Fleming (Eds.), *Psycholinguistics and the teaching of reading.* Newark, Del.: International Reading Association, 1969.

Goodman, K. S., & Burke, C. L. *A study of oral miscues that result in grammatical retransformation* (U.S. Office of Education Final Rep. No. BR-7-E-219). Washington, D. C.: U.S. Government Printing Office, 1969. (ERIC Document Reproduction Service No. ED 039 101)

Inhelder, B., & Piaget, J. *The growth of logical thinking from childhood to adolescence.* New York: Basic Books, 1958.

Jansky, J., & de Hirsch, K. *Preventing reading failure.* New York: Harper & Row, 1972.

Klare, G. R. Assessing readability. *Reading Research Quarterly*, 1974–1975, *10*, 62–102.

Kraus, P. E. *Yesterday's children: A longitudinal study of children from kindergarten into the adult years.* New York: Wiley, 1973.

Lavine, L. O. The development of perception of writing in pre-reading children: A cross-cultural study (Doctoral dissertation, Cornell University, 1972). *Dissertation Abstracts International*, 1973, *33*, 4491B. (University Microfilms No. 73-6657, 133)

Liberman, A. M., Cooper, F. S., Shankweiler, D. P., & Studdert-Kennedy, M. Perception of the speech code. *Psychological Review*, 1967, *74*, 431–461.

Maraini, F. *The persistence of the ideographic script in the Far East: Its competitive values versus the alphabet.* Paper presented at the meeting of the International Congress of Anthropological and Ethnological Sciences, Chicago, August–September 1973.

Perry, W. *Forms of intellectual and ethical development in the college years: A scheme.* New York: Holt, Rinehart and Winston, 1970.

Piaget, J. *Structuralism.* New York: Basic Books, 1970.

Popp, H. M. *Test project for the LRDC beginning reading program "Stepping Stones to Reading."* Pittsburgh: University of Pittsburgh, Learning Research and Development Center, 1972. (Publication No. 1972/18; ERIC Document Reproduction Service No. ED 070 040)

Popp, H. M. Current practices in the teaching of beginning reading. In J. B. Carroll & J. S. Chall (Eds.), *Toward a literate society.* New York: McGraw-Hill, 1975.

Read, C. Pre-school children's knowledge of English phonology. *Harvard Educational Review*, 1971, *41*, 1–34.

Samuels, S. J., Begy, G., & Chaur, C. C. Comparison of word recognition speed and strategies of less skilled and more highly skilled readers. *Reading Research Quarterly*, 1975–1976, *11*, 72–86.

Sartre, J. P. *The words*. New York: George Braziller, 1964.

Smith, F. Understanding reading: A psycholinguistic analysis of reading and learning to read. New York: Holt, Rinehart and Winston, 1971.

Soderberg, R. *Learning in early childhood*. Stockholm, Sweden: Almqvist and Wiksell, 1971.

Southwest Regional Laboratory for Educational Research and Development. *Beginning reading program*. Boston: Ginn, 1972.

Stallings, J. Implementation and child effects of teaching practices in follow through classrooms. *Monographs of the Society for Research in Child Development*, 1975, *40* 7–8 (Serial No. 163).

Stauffer, R. The verdict: Speculative controversy. *Reading Teacher*, 1966, *19*, 563–564; 575.

Thorndike, R. L. *Reading comprehension education in fifteen countries*. New York: Wiley, 1973.

Venezky, R. L., Pittelman, S. D., & Kamm, M. *The pre-reading skills program*. Chicago: Encyclopedia Britannica Educational Corp., 1974.

Versacci, C. J., & Larrick, N. (Eds.). *Highlights of the seventeenth annual reading conference of Lehigh University*. Bethlehem, Pa.: Interstate Printers and Publishers, 1968.

Walmsley, S. A. The criterion-referenced measurement of an early reading behavior (Doctoral dissertation, Harvard Graduate School of Education, 1975). *Dissertation Abstracts International*, 1976, *36*, 7193A–7194A. (University Microfilms No. 76-10, 570, 190)

Weber, G. *Inner-city children can be taught to read: Four successful schools*. Washington, D. C.: Council for Basic Education, Occasional Papers, 1971.

White, S., Day, M. C., Freeman, P. K., Hantman, S. A., & Messenger, K. P. *Federal programs for young children: Review and recommendations. Vol. I: Goals and standards of public programs for children* (HEW Rep. No. DHEW-05-74-101). Washington, D. C.: U.S. Government Printing Office, 1973. (ERIC Document Reproduction Service No. ED 092 230)

Wisconsin Research and Development Center for Cognitive Learning. *Wisconsin design for reading skill development*. Madison: Interpretive Scoring Systems, 1971.

Wolff, P. H. *The developmental psychologies of Jean Piaget and psychoanalysis*. New York: International Universities Press, 1960.

2 Coding and Comprehension in Skilled Reading and Implications for Reading Instruction

Charles A. Perfetti
Alan M. Lesgold
Learning Research and Development Center
University of Pittsburgh

In this chapter we suggest a view of skilled reading that emphasizes an intimate connection between coding and comprehension. Our thesis is that skilled comprehension depends on a highly refined facility for generating and manipulating language codes. This is our basis for suggesting that decoding expertise should be a basic goal in reading instruction.

We would like to place our argument in perspective by outlining a few of our basic assumptions. Although these assumptions are widely shared, they are not without controversy. In any event, they provide a framework through which we view reading and research on reading.

Assumption 1. Skilled Reading can be Partly Understood as a Set of Interrelated Component Processes. These processes can be described within an information-processing framework or within any other framework that is functionally equivalent in its ability to provide insight into component processes and their relationships. There are two corollaries of this assumption:

Assumption 1a. The components of the reading process are not necessarily functionally independent. We tend to agree with those (e.g., Guthrie, 1973) who have concluded that subskills in reading are mutually facilitative rather than independent. One fairly important consequence of this assumption is that skilled readers are superior to unskilled readers in many components of the reading process. This means that a gain in one subskill allows gains in other subskills, that an insufficiently developed subskill may limit the apparent adequacy of other subskills, and that the processes underlying the skills are difficult to study in isolation. Although these processes may seem to be hierarchically organized when viewed from some perspectives, we assume that a lower level process can be affected by a higher level process, and vice versa. For example, knowledge of subject matter and syntactic structure can influence word recognition, and the shape of words in peripheral vision may bias syntactic segmentation.

Assumption 1b. The component processes are isolable in principle although interrelated in practice. Despite Assumption 1a, understanding skilled reading processes does entail analysis of components. Consider an analogy of high-fidelity systems, with overall reading skill being analogous to measurable sound quality and component processes comparable to [hi-fi] components.[1] If any component is defective or if components are mismatched, sound quality suffers. The components can be independently tested and, more important, independently improved. However, improvement of one component may not immediately improve sound quality (but it may increase the potential of the system to benefit from later improvement in other components). For example, an improved cartridge, capable of encoding more high-frequency information, will improve the sound quality only if the other components are capable of handling the information, but not otherwise. Likewise, one might improve the speakers by making them more accurate at high frequencies, but this will improve the sound quality only within the limits of the cartridge. Changing one component affects the functional characteristics of another component by affecting the quality of the signal or, in some cases, by affecting the speed of the operating system (as in speaker damping). The situation in both reading and hi-fi is one of structural independence but functional interdependence. In particular, components of reading may sometimes be testable only in situations outside of "natural" reading, just as for some tests one must take an amplifier to the repairman while the rest of the system is left at home.

Assumption 2. Within the Constraints of Assumption 1, Reading is Highly Flexible. We agree with Gibson and Levin (1975) that an analysis of reading process components, even allowing for their interdependence, does not comprise a complete description of skilled reading. This flexibility is sometimes difficult to describe because it involves strategies and purposes. This difficulty affects only the theoretical status of reading flexibility, not its practical importance.

Assumption 3. The Relationship Between Skilled Reading and Beginning Reading Instruction is Not Straightforward. This is merely a particular manifestation of the more general principle that a theory of instruction is not

---

[1]J. B. Carroll (1977) has used hi-fi imagery for a somewhat different point, suggesting that an indicator of cognitive ability shows the upper limit of language competence, which in turn indicates the upper limit of reading ability.

identical to a theory of competence, nor is one necessarily a subset of the other. At the same time, a theory of performance that can model both skilled and unskilled readers is likely to be a useful subgoal in efforts made toward a theory of instruction.

We return to this assumption in the final section. Now we turn to a sketch of skilled reading processes that stresses the importance of rapid automatic decoding and its effects on comprehension. Assumptions 1 and 2 are particularly relevant to the discussion that follows because we speak there of a limitation on the human information-processing system as a whole—an inadequate processing capacity. Although there are many ways in which capacity can be increased or decreased, we argue that in reading, capacity limitations are largely the result of properties of the decoding process.

The Bottleneck in Comprehension

The capacity for reading comprehension is limited by momentary data-handling requirements. Working memory is thus a potential bottleneck in reading comprehension. Working memory is particularly taxed if it must keep track of partial solutions for heuristic processes that "home in" on decisions in an iterative manner. On the other hand, if some of the components of the reading process are ballistic (i.e., not requiring attention once they are initiated), there will be less working memory congestion. In our view, skilled reading does not imply a larger working memory capacity but, rather, a more effective use of this capacity.

There are several candidates for components in reading that, when not fully developed, could increase the working memory bottleneck. We discuss three: access to long-term memory, speed and automation of decoding, and efficiency of reading strategies. Access to long-term memory is tied to the structure and content of readers' knowledge. Small vocabularies lead to low comprehension, and presumably, so do underpracticed vocabularies or those with low interconnectedness among concepts. One hypothesis is that improving rapid access to word meanings and prior conceptual structures is a means of relieving the bottleneck. Knowing the exact meaning of a word prevents the cognitive load that would otherwise result from having to figure out its meaning from context. It makes comprehension more a recognition task and less a problem-solving task.

The second, related candidate is speed and automation of decoding. When print maps automatically to phonologically referenced words, the decoding requires no monitoring and hence, does not waste limited working memory. This is a good example of two conceptually independent components that are functionally intertwined. Because decoding leads to meaning, affecting the efficiency of print decoding affects the efficiency of meaning access.

The third candidate is processing strategies, particularly those that take advantage of language structure. Skilled readers might acquire and use segmentation and organizing strategies that less-skilled readers lack. One example of this hypothesis is that skilled readers use sentence and clause boundaries to segment the flow of print as well as the flow of speech. A second example is that more knowledge of grammatical and semantic constraints is acquired and used by skilled readers than by less-skilled readers. This, too, has the effect of relieving the bottleneck. Any information-handling procedure that aids in grouping language units accurately has this effect, because it is both a form of chunking and a means of more rapidly converging on a correct sentence parse.

Language-organizing processes of this sort are patently important in reading processes. However, there may be some reasons to doubt whether they are critical sources of reading skill differences beyond their dependency on rapid verbal coding. Elsewhere (Perfetti & Lesgold, 1977), we discuss these reasons in some detail. In the remainder of this chapter, we prefer to focus on coding operations as they relate to reading skill and the comprehension bottleneck.

CODING AND COMPREHENSION

There are a number of important issues in reading and reading instruction that are related to coding. The starting point is that single-word decoding and reading comprehension skill are highly related for children who have already learned decoding. For example, Shankweiler and Liberman (1972) found that reading words in isolation predicted success in reading connected discourse, and Calfee, Venezky, and Chapman (1969) found that accuracy in pronunciation of pseudowords was related to reading skill. Thus measures of word decoding accuracy are related to measures of comprehension. Still, teachers of reading say that there are children who can read all single words on the Wide Range Achievement Test but who fail to comprehend sentences and passages. It is possible that something more than decoding accuracy is involved. However, before we conclude that this something else is not a coding process, consider again the bottleneck problem.

The relationship between coding and comprehension is one of sharing processing resources. It is possible that observed deficiencies in reading comprehension are partly due to unobserved differences in the extent to which decoding uses an excessive share of the resources. Measuring accuracy of word identification will not necessarily uncover this excessive dependence of decoding on conscious decision making. Measuring speed of word identification may.

In a series of studies, Perfetti and Hogaboam (1975b) have found large, consistent differences between skilled and less-skilled readers in the third through fifth grades on measures of coding speed. Table 2.1 shows the basic relationship.

TABLE 2.1
Mean Vocalization Latencies (in sec) for Skilled and Less-Skilled Readers

Groups	High Frequency Words	Low Frequency Words	Pseudowords
Grade 3			
High skill	.95	1.30	1.59
Low skill	1.17	2.38	2.72
Grade 5			
High skill	1.08	1.45	1.48
Low skill	1.25	2.48	2.71

Note. For real words, data are only for words that subjects get correct on a vocabulary test. (Data are based on Perfetti & Hogaboam, 1975a.)

The decoding speed measure was vocalization latency, the time taken to begin vocalizing single words displayed in normal type on a slide projector. The groups were divided by scores on the reading comprehension section of the Metropolitan Achievement Tests (MAT). Not all the letter strings seen by subjects were real words. When nonwords with acceptable English spelling patterns (pseudowords) were used, the speed differences between skilled and less-skilled readers increased. This is an important fact because it argues against the hypothesis that decoding speed differences were due to differential reading experience with the particular words tested. This hypothesis is otherwise very plausible, because it is probably true that a skilled reader, as measured by a comprehension test, has had more reading experience and a better chance to develop holistic word recognition capability. Instead, the Perfetti-Hogaboam data imply the importance of subword components of the coding process.

In a more recent experiment (Hogaboam & Perfetti, in press), the "wordness" factor is again clearly seen, along with the effect of syllable length. In this experiment, entire third- and fourth-grade populations were tested in single-word vocalization. A median split on comprehension measures (based on reading subtests of the Durrell Listening-Reading Series) produced two skill levels that were compared for vocalization speed. Word strings were either real words or pseudowords and were either one syllable or two syllables. They were presented in blocks of trials so that any differences in response time could not be attributed to some orientation reaction to a changing stimulus. The results are shown in Fig. 2.1.

Regardless of grade level, the less-skilled readers were slower than the skilled readers. In addition, there were significant interactions of stimulus type and syllable length with reading skill. There was a greater cost for the less-skilled readers compared with the skilled readers for either an extra syllable or for a pseudoword. In particular, pseudowords took nearly twice as long as real words for less-skilled readers (an extra 1,200 msec), compared

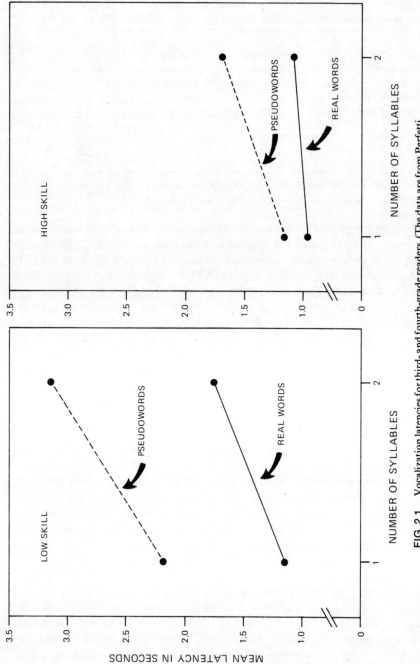

FIG. 2.1.   Vocalization latencies for third- and fourth-grade readers. (The data are from Perfetti and Hogaboam, 1975b.)

with 40% extra time for skilled readers (an extra 400 msec). The cost of a second syllable was about 800 msec (50% increase) for less skilled readers, compared with about 300 msec (about 30% increase) for skilled readers. These data support the earlier results of Perfetti and Hogaboam (1975a) in suggesting a basic coding difference involving units smaller than words. They go further in suggesting that a syllable-at-a-time process is more characteristic of the less-skilled readers than of the skilled readers. The locus of the syllable and stimulus type interaction, of course, could be at the responding stages rather than at one of the recognition stages.

Experiments underway in a word search task could help to clarify whether syllable interactions occur in decoding or response stages. For now, it is at least possible to suggest that not all the difference is a matter of response programming because the differences between decoding speeds for single-syllable stimuli are not confined to measures requiring vocalization. Perfetti and Hogaboam (1975b) found group differences in a task in which two strings or letters were displayed and subjects were required to say whether the strings were the same. Skilled readers made faster decisions although the differences were not as large as in the vocalization task, suggesting that both decoding stage and response stage differences are involved in that latter task.

Coding and Comprehension: Cause and Effect

The empirical phenomenon seems well established: Coding speed and reading achievement are highly related for young readers. What causes what is another issue, and there are plausible arguments both for what we call *the bottleneck hypothesis* and for what we call the *by-product hypothesis*.

The by-product hypothesis claims that measured comprehension (e.g., a reading test score on the MAT) taps a wide range of knowledge and skills, including word recognition, at something other than the level implied so far. According to this hypothesis, recognizing a word need not involve its sound but only its meaning. Further, but less critical, recognition of word meanings is contextual in skilled reading. Measures of isolated word recognition, whether involving phonological codes or not, are irrelevant. However, a correlation will be observed with reading skill, just because skilled readers are practiced readers and the same reading behaviors that lead to high comprehension scores produce facility in word recognition and articulation as a by-product. A variation is that good readers happen to read a lot and that this in turn produces decoding facility.

In contrast, the bottleneck hypothesis claims that being fast at decoding leads to high comprehension. The essential processing assumption is that single-word coding operations are a critical part of reading, even when control of the reading process flows from higher level pragmatic and inferential processes rather than from stimulus components (see Frederiksen, this volume). These coding operations may share the limited capacity processor to varying degrees with other comprehension work—for example, memory for just-read segments, parsing strategies for text, memory for discourse topics, and so on. Fast decoding is more automatic, in the sense of LaBerge and Samuels (1974), and it leaves more resources for fancier comprehension work.

The weak form of this hypothesis does not require that the coding operations include a "phonetic recoding." It merely assumes that phonetic processes, which are necessarily involved in some single-word decoding tasks, are a subtractable part of the total process for the skilled reader. The strong form of the hypothesis does assume that some phonological representation of a letter string is accessed in skilled reading. It does not assume access to any articulatory component, covert or otherwise.

We return to phonetic recoding in a later section of this chapter. For now, the point is that there are two plausible accounts of the close relationship between decoding speed and reading comprehension skill. No evidence is known to us that directly supports one hypothesis over the other. However, one critical test seems possible. The bottleneck hypothesis will be confirmed if it can be shown that independently increasing decoding speed improves comprehension. This seems to be a clear and testable consequence of the bottleneck hypothesis. Unfortunately, the opposite prediction, that is, that independently improving comprehension will increase decoding speed, seems to be untestable and so, in general, does the by-product hypothesis.

Coding at Higher Levels of Skill

The results reported above apply to children who are beyond beginning reading but still in elementary grades and who range in age from 8 to 11 years. Although our emphasis is purposely on this level of reading development, a comment on higher levels of skill is in order. Hunt and his associates (Hunt, 1976; Hunt, Frost, & Lunneborg, 1973) have discovered a number of differences in college students' performances of basic information-processing tasks. Some of these differences are related to verbal aptitude levels measured by college aptitude tests. For example, differences in continuous paired-associate performance and in name matching for letters (Posner & Mitchell, 1967) were found to be related to college verbal aptitude (Hunt et al., 1973). Analogous differences might be expected to relate to more specific measures of reading skill at the college level. Rapid data handling, which Hunt et al. suggest is one of the critical factors distinguishing high verbal aptitude from low, would seem to be particularly important in reading.

The data we have collected suggest that the relationship between coding facility and reading skill is more subtle in adult readers. An unpublished study by Perfetti and Straub investigated the interference of overt decoding on short-term memory performance. The task required subjects to read five digits for later recall and then to perform an interpolated naming task during a retention interval of unpredictable duration (3, 6, or 12 sec). The interpolated naming task required oral reading of a display of English words, a display of pseudowords, or a display of pictures of common objects. Thus all three tasks had a vocalization component, but only two had a print-decoding component.

One result was that reading pseudowords interfered most with digit memory, whereas reading English words and pictures were about equal. Thus for skilled adults, decoding words may interfere with memory no more than decoding pictures. This was true for both the higher skill group and the lower skill group, where the groups were separated by Davis Reading Test scores. However, higher skilled readers did less well than lower skilled readers at the 3-sec interval, equally well at 6 sec, and better than lower skilled at 12 sec. A possible explanation of these data is that at adult skill levels decoding differences are small enough for their effects to be seen only when other processing demands are high, as they are when a digit string has to be retained during 12 sec of decoding. However, the lack of an overall effect in conjunction with the interaction may suggest a strategy difference rather than a simple decoding difference.

A second relevant study is by Lesgold and Danner (1976), who investigated tachistoscopic recognition of letters, numbers, and trigrams. Measures were taken over three stimulus availability conditions ranging from 50 to 125 msec between stimulus and mask onsets. Although this study had other purposes, the relevant data for this discussion are that higher skilled and lower skilled college students, defined by Davis test scores, showed no differences in accuracy or speed of report, either as main effects or in interaction with stimulus type. However, there may well be important coding speed differences that persist through skilled adult reading that can be revealed by measures more sensitive to specific coding operations.

One possibility in this regard is suggested by a study by Jackson and McClelland (1975). For college students separated on comprehension-corrected reading speed, Jackson and McClelland found that single-letter visual thresholds were not related to reading skill. Nor was performance on pairs of letters presented for 200 msec separated by up to 5.9° of visual angle. What was related to reading skill was report of five-word sentences presented for 200 msec and report of eight unrelated letters presented for this same brief duration. Thus, there is evidence from Jackson and McClelland (see also Gilbert, 1959) that skilled readers can report more information from a brief exposure, but there is no evidence that this difference is operating at the level of visual detection. Furthermore, the difference between groups on sentence perception is not eliminated by a forced-choice procedure in which there is only a single-letter difference between two semantically and syntactically acceptable alternatives (e.g., *Kevin [fired, hired] a new worker*). This fact argues against the possibility that skilled reading is a matter of superior guessing, and the fact that differences are found for groups of unrelated letters suggests that something more basic than use of linguistic structure is involved.

We take the data of Jackson and McClelland (1975) to suggest that differences between adult readers will be found just when the task demands the reader to process a segment of text—either a bunch of letters or a phrase—very rapidly. When demands on processing are light, there will not be differences. By comparison with Jackson and McClelland, the Lesgold and Danner (1976) experiment may involve lower processing demands in general, and the Perfetti and Straub (unpublished) experiment may make differential processing demands only at long intervals (or perhaps not at all).

Coding and Meaning Access

The usual purpose of reading, as someone always reminds us, is to obtain not sound but meaning from print. Coding tasks such as we have been discussing are not particularly interesting from this point of view. However, in terms of the bottleneck hypothesis, two distinct possibilities for the effects of coding in comprehension are implied: One possibility is that the speed of access to phonological information affects comprehension, and the other is that semantic access speed affects comprehension. Semantic access may often require phonological decoding (i.e., semantic information is accessible through a phonologically indexed lexical entry), but in principle it need not. We will ignore the phonological question and simply consider two levels of coding, referred to as *phonological decoding* and *semantic decoding* for convenience. The first question we consider is whether semantic decoding comes automatically with phonological decoding. The second is whether it does so for skilled readers but not for less-skilled readers. We have already shown that phonological decoding is more work for less-skilled readers. The question is: Are less-skilled readers doubly disadvantaged by slower semantic decoding?

An experiment carried out by Perfetti, Hogaboam, and Bell is relevant to this issue, and the data are presented here. Single words or pictures were presented to 8- and 10-year-old subjects separated by reading comprehension scores. In one task, the subject had to decide whether a given stimulus matched an orally presented target. For example, just after the experimenter said, "rabbit," a slide would be shown containing a word (in one condition) or a picture (in a second condition). Blocks of eight trials involved the same target, and the subject responded with a button press according to whether the visual stimulus matched the oral stimulus. Nontarget stimuli in this task were in semantic categories different from the target and, therefore, no semantic interference could be involved in this task. The time it takes to

TABLE 2.2
Matching and Categorization Times (in msec) for Fourth-
Grade Subjects *

Group	Pictures	Words
	Matching task	
Low reading skill	831	883
High reading skill	833	838
	Categorization task	
Low reading skill	875	1095
High reading skill	772	939

decide that *dog* is /dawg/ is perhaps the prototypical phonological decoding measure. This can be compared with the time it takes to decide that a picture of a dog is /dawg/.

The other task was categorization. A target semantic category was announced (e.g., "animals") prior to a block of trials. As in the matching task, trials were blocks of pictures or words. We thus have a measure of semantic decoding speed: the time taken to make a verification of a salient superordinate semantic category. If any aspect of meaning "comes free" with phonological decoding, it should be this kind of superordinate information. Table 2.2 shows a summary of the results for "same" judgments on the two tasks for the 10-year-olds.

For purposes of the present discussion, the results suggest that less skilled readers are not different from skilled readers in picture matching and are only 45 msec slower (not significant) in word matching. However, in word categorization, less-skilled readers are 156 msec slower. In fact, less-skilled readers were 103 msec slower in picture categorization. The difference in semantic judgment time apparently does not depend on whether the stimulus is a word. However, this does not mean that semantic processing is free of phonological coding operations. Indeed, Kleiman's work (1975) suggests otherwise. (Kleiman's work is discussed in more detail on page 00.) Our interpretation of this experiment is that lower-level feature matching is adequate in the less-skilled reader but that retrieval of semantic information associated with a word or picture name is slower.[2] In this sense, useful

---

[2]One of the complexities of these data is that the categorization time of less skilled readers greatly benefited from having the matching task precede the categorization task. In fact, only when the categorization task came first was the difference between high- and low-skill readers statistically significant. This would seem to suggest that the differences are in the processes of either retrieving or using conceptual features. After the name itself has been accessed (matching task), the subsequent use of information stored with the name is facilitated.

semantic decoding may not automatically accompany lower-order decoding for less-skilled readers.

Our conclusion here must be very tentative. However, we can suggest possible clarification of the coding process implicated by the bottleneck hypothesis. Phonological decoding is slower in less-skilled readers and so is the use of semantic information. The decoding difficulty is perhaps not so much due to word recognition as it is to word retrieval. This, at least, is implied by the fact that differences due to reading skill are larger when children have to vocalize a word (which includes name retrieval) than when they hear that word prior to its appearance in print and are required to make only a same/different judgment.

The slower semantic processing of the less-skilled reader may be of even greater practical significance, because not everyone agrees that phonological decoding is involved in skilled reading. We know of no controversy concerning the importance of meaning. We emphasize though that we are not dealing here with the simple question of word knowledge. Rather, we are dealing with the more subtle question of rapid access, retrieval, and use of information about word meanings.

There are data that can be interpreted as being at odds with the foregoing account. Golinkoff and Rosinski (1976) presented a picture-naming task to third- and fifth-grade children classifiable as skilled and less-skilled readers. Picture naming is subject to a semantic interference effect, that is, the time to name pictures is longer when words from the same semantic category are printed on the pictures (Rosinski, Golinkoff, & Kukish, 1975). (For example, the word *cow* is printed on a picture of a pig.) However, skilled readers showed an effect no larger than that of unskilled readers. Compared with the control condition in which the printed word did not contradict the picture, both skilled and less-skilled readers were slowed down by the semantic interference condition. Golinkoff and Rosinski (1976) concluded that the relevant semantic information comes automatically, or at least compellingly, with a word stimulus. The data presented here on categorization do not necessarily contradict this, but they do suggest a somewhat different interpretation. In the semantic interference situation, meaning is incidental to the naming task. Provided that the words were very familiar, enough semantic information to interfere with picture naming was automatically retrieved, although perhaps not for younger, less-skilled readers (Ehri, 1976; Pace & Golinkoff, 1976). This low-level semantic information retrieval may typically occur when a reader sees a word, but when the reader has to use the word's meaning, there are differences in the speed of semantic use.

Summary: The Primacy-of-Coding Principle

In summary to this point, we have presented a view of skilled reading that argues for dependencies of comprehension on both automatic phonological decoding and semantic decoding. The evidence in support of this view is unfortunately still indirect, but it is in principle possible to provide more direct evidence. Meanwhile, we offer the principle of the primacy of coding as a necessary part of a more complete model of skilled reading. We turn now to some related issues in reading that are relevant for our argument.

SOME CLASSICAL ISSUES IN READING

There are many issues, both in the psychology of reading and in reading instruction, that predate modern cognitive psychology. Disagreement about some of these issues remains sufficiently widespread to justify books such as this one. We will discuss two of these issues that are of most direct concern to our primacy-of-coding principle: phonological components of reading and the implications of a coding emphasis for reading instruction.

Phonetic Recoding

The term *phonetic recoding* captures the classical flavor of the first issue, cited above. Is meaning obtained from print without recoding the print into some speech-like code? The sides of the argument are direct visual access versus necessary phonetic recoding. There is a weak form and a strong form of each theory, so the dichotomy tends to break down. We would rephrase the issue as: What is the extent of phonological involvement in skilled reading? For example, Goodman's (1970) theory of reading favors visual access in general and Gibson and Levin's (1975) theory requires it at least some of the time, as does Kolers' (1970) theory.

It seems quite sensible to believe that skilled silent reading does not engage much overt speech behavior. For one thing, as Kolers (1970) has pointed out, text can be read faster than it can be spoken. And here is where a basic clarification can be made: A theory of skilled reading that includes complete (even if silent) speech recoding is incorrect. However, a theory in which a partial and vastly shortened reference to phonetic features of words is posited might still be correct. Another perspective is to say that access of word meanings in long-term memory requires or is facilitated by the phonological representation of the word.

What evidence is there for direct access, that is, bypassing the phonological representation? We will not review all the evidence, but we can mention some of the more important and/or most cited results. Recently, Barron (in press) argued for the direct visual access hypothesis and cited several lines of evidence for it (see also Bradshaw, 1975). We examine some of the studies cited by Barron in support of the direct access hypothesis for the purpose of questioning how strongly they support it. Since Barron acknowledged that much of the data are open to other interpretation, we included only what he considered to be the clearest data for the direct access hypothesis, namely, data on lexical decision tasks and semantic judgment tasks.

Lexical Decision.   In a lexical decision task a subject decides whether a string of letters is or is not a real word. The processes involve access to internal word representation and, hence, are potentially relevant for the issue of phonological versus visual entry into lexical memory.

There are data that appear to support phonological access in decision tasks for single words (Rubenstein, Lewis, & Rubenstein, 1971) and for pairs of words (Meyer, Schvaneveldt, & Ruddy, 1974). For example, Meyer et al. presented subjects with pairs of words that were graphemically identical after the initial letter but whose vowels were phonemically distinct—for example, *COUCH* and *TOUCH*. These pairs were compared with words having both graphemic correspondence and phonemic similarity in the vowel—for example, *BRIBE* and *TRIBE*. The results were that pairs like *COUCH-TOUCH* required more time to verify as real words than did pairs like *BRIBE-TRIBE*. Why? Because for *BRIBE-TRIBE*, phonological features activated in the decision process for the first word were available and useful for the second word. In the *COUCH-TOUCH* case, the activated phonetic features for *COUCH* were less useful for, perhaps interfering with, the second decision on *TOUCH*. If information sufficient for lexical decision could be visual, then these two cases should take equal times, and they did not. Moreover, one interpretation of the visual access hypothesis would predict an advantage for graphemically similar pairs like *COUCH-TOUCH* over nonsimilar pairs, for example, *COUCH-BREAK*, but such was not the result of the Meyer et al. experiment. Meyer et al. were quite cautious about their results, suggesting correctly that the occurrence of a phonemic effect but not a visual effect could be due to a processing strategy applicable to lexical decision tasks but not to other reading.

There are two lexical decision experiments, however, that unlike Meyer et al. (1974) are cited to support the visual access hypothesis. Forster and Chambers (1973) gave subjects both naming and lexical decision tasks on the same set of words and pronounceable nonwords (pseudowords). They found that vocalization latency (naming time) was less for real words than for pseudowords, and they found a frequency effect for real words. Furthermore, they found that naming time and lexical decision time were correlated for words but not for pseudowords. According to Barron (in press), these two results indicate that naming occurs after lexical meaning access, because otherwise there would be no differences in naming speed among the three stimulus types. And there was no correlation between naming and decision time for pseudowords because naming time reflects time to "decode" whereas lexical decision time reflects time to find out that a letter string does not have a lexical entry. This line of argument is problematic, however, because the judgment task is to say *yes* for words and *no* for pseudowords. To find a correlation for words but not for pseudowords is to find a correlation for a *yes* response but not for a *no*. Why would the phonetic recoding hypothesis predict anything else? It assumes that skilled readers can apply decoding rules and vocalize well-formed letter strings. It has nothing to say about how long it takes to decide that a letter string is not a word. However, the phonetic recoding hypothesis does predict the positive correlation between naming speed and lexical decision time for words, which is what Forster and Chambers (1973) found. This experiment then is consistent with both our position and Barron's.

Another experiment cited as evidence for direct access is Novik's (1974) demonstration that in a lexical decision task, rejection of nonmeaningful trigrams was faster than rejection of meaningful trigrams like *JFK* or *LSD*. Such differences might merely reflect extra checking time after a preliminary screening in which *JKF* and *LSD* are found to be familiar enough to merit further processing (as in the Atkinson & Juola, 1973, decision model). These differences present no evidence for direct visual access to complete semantic representations.

Semantic Judgment. There are two different types of data based on semantic judgments that support direct visual access, according to Barron (in press). In the experiment by Meyer and Ruddy (1973), subjects were given semantic categories ("Is a kind of fruit") followed by words. Time to decide whether a word belonged to the category was measured. Consistent with a phonological access hypothesis, it took longer to decide that a word like *PAIR* was not a fruit than to decide that a word like *TAIL* was not a fruit. This effect is presumably due to a reduced ability to reject *pair* because of its phonetic connection with *pear*.

However, the visual access hypothesis appears to be supported in data from a second task in which subjects were required to respond with *yes* to words that sounded like a category member. Thus both *PEAR* and *PAIR* qualify for *yes*, *TAIL* for *no*. The critical result is for *TAIL*, which should be equally quickly rejected in both tasks, that is, it neither looks like nor sounds like any member of the fruit category. However, *TAIL* was rejected more rapidly in the first task, where only category instances were targets, than in the second, where category instances and their sound-alikes were targets. This result, according to Barron, supports the visual access hypothesis because direct visual access operates in the first task, leading to a faster rejection of *TAIL* than in the second task, which takes more time because of phonemic recoding. Also important is the result that *PEAR* was faster than *PAIR* in the sound-alike task, thus implicating visual access. Barron assumes that the phonemic model predicts equal latencies for *PEAR* and *PAIR* on the assumption that they have identical phonemic representations. However, these experimental predictions should not be attributed to a serious phonological coding hypothesis. A serious phonological coding hypothesis does not claim that orthographic and graphemic information are not used. Obviously, visual information is the starting point in the process of phonological coding.

PAIR takes longer than *PEAR* because the latter has a quicker convergence of features relevant to the task demands. PEAR "looks" like a fruit and sounds like a fruit. *PAIR* looks like something else. If this is all that direct visual access means, then it has to be true. The longer rejection time for *TAIL* in the second experiment is also easy to explain. All rejection will take longer if rejections are defined by conjunctive criteria, that is, reject *X* if *X* is not a fruit and is not sounded like the name of a fruit. The data do not shed light on the phonemic recoding issue.

There is at least one other study that is informative for this question, and that is one by Baron (1973). In one experiment, Baron gave adult readers a sense–nonsense task in which time to reject nonsense phrases (and accept meaningful phrases) was measured. Two kinds of nonsense were of interest: phrases such as (1) *I am kill* and (2) *It's knot so*. Baron required phonological coding to predict that (2) should require more time to reject than (1) because (2) "sounds *ok*" and an extra analysis is required to detect its lack of sense. By contrast, the visual access hypothesis predicts no difference because both are rejectable on nonphonetic bases. The results were no difference, as predicted by visual access. However, it must again be noted that the phonological coding hypothesis does not require that graphemic information become useless just because phonological coding occurs. Both graphemic information (as well as other visual information) and phonological information have roles in access of the word or phrase representations that allow a reader to judge meaning properties of a phrase.

In a second experiment, Baron's subjects had to decide whether a word string sounded as though it made sense. Here the key result is that phrases such as *It's knot so* took longer than phrases such as *Tie the knot* and *It's not so*. This result was taken to support direct visual access over phonetic recoding on the assumption that the phonetic recoding hypothesis predicts no difference here. *It's knot so* and *It's not so* both sound sensible. However, it is not clear that this is the most appropriate assumption for such a task. Instead, one can plausibly assume that any phrase that makes sense sounds as though it makes sense, but that a phrase that does not make sense may or may not sound sensible. The visual analysis of *It's not so* leads to a sensible configuration of word meanings. Therefore, it must sound sensible. *It's knot so* leads to a nonsensible configuration of word meanings. Therefore, a second decision process is engaged: Does it sound like something that makes sense? The nonsense phrase's measured decision time is longer because it takes an extra decision process.

The experiments discussed in this section demonstrate the critical role of visual analysis in reading tasks. However, they cannot be used to build a strong case against phonological coding. They can rule out only the possibility that phonological coding erases graphemic and orthographic information. We have labored over these experiments because they are fairly good experiments and because they are taken as evidence against phonetic recoding during reading.[3] A partial phonological coding process during skilled reading is not inconsistent with evidence of this sort.[4]

Other Reading Tasks.   Part of the issue of phonological coding versus visual access is the relevance of any single-word experimental tasks for real reading. The question is most likely to be raised with respect to the relevance of single-word experiments that may have properties that force phonological coding. The implication is that reading text might be quite another matter. However, the tables can be turned on this argument. The bottleneck hypothesis is that comprehension work shares resources with coding work, unless coding is automatic. But this comprehension work has often been said to have phonetic properties. It is here that the silent inner voice is heard. In other words, whether or not individual word coding is phonologically referenced, there is independent reason to believe that cognitive processing makes heavy use of phonological codes. That is, the work of rearranging and interrelating meanings involves phonological codes.

An experiment by Kleiman (1975) is particularly informative on this point. The basic assumption of Kleiman's experiment is that overt digit shadowing (saying digits as they are heard) interferes with phonetic coding. One can determine the phonological involvement of any reading task by noting the effect of concurrent digit shadowing on task performance. In one of Kleiman's experiments, subjects were required to search five-word sentences for targets based on graphemic (visual), phonemic, or semantic categories, with and without digit shadowing. The decisions were always made on visual

---

[3]More recently, Baron (1977) reported experiments that suggest an important role for phonological processes in access to meaning, even in conditions without severe memory demands.

[4]We should comment on another argument sometimes raised in favor of direct visual access. Because certain languages, such as Chinese, use logographic writing, it is claimed (e.g., Barron, in press; Kolers, 1970) that phonological coding cannot be a general and necessary part of reading, since logographs have semantic value rather than phonetic value. This idea represents a confusion between coding process and the size of the coding unit. Alphabetic languages allow coding to occur in units smaller than the units having semantic value, that is, in units smaller than words. Logographic languages also allow corresponding phonological coding (for native speakers, at least); they differ in not generally allowing symbol–sound correspondence.

displays, so if phonological coding was not advantageous, as it would not be with digit shadowing, visual processes could, in principle, suffice.

Significant effects of shadowing were observed on a phonemic decision task (e.g., to decide that a rhyme of *cream* is present in the sentence *He awakened from the dream*). However, graphemic decisions and category decisions are relatively unaffected. (A graphemic decision is to decide, for example, whether a word with the last three letters of *bury* occurs in the sentence *Yesterday the grand jury adjourned.* A category decision is to decide, for example, whether there is a word from the *game* category in the sentence *Everyone at home played Monopoly.*)

What these three tasks all have in common is that the meaning of the word string, even though it is a complete sentence, can be ignored. A word-by-word search can go on, the data suggest, with little phonological coding, except for the phonemic targets, where phonological coding is required to do the task. The interesting comparison is with the effect of shadowing on judgment of sentence acceptability. Here, all five words of the sentence must be worked on more or less simultaneously. The effect of digit shadowing on this performance was severe, at least equal to its effect on the phonemic task. The implication is that phonological recoding has occurred not on a word-by-word basis but on groups of words or perhaps the whole sentence.

Based on these data and those from analogous decisions—phonemic, graphemic, and semantic decisions—in a single-word procedure, Kleiman (1975) concluded that direct visual access to meaning is possible one word at a time, but once even a short sentence is in mind, phonetic recoding has to take place. Although it is open to question whether digit shadowing is a complete inhibitor of phonetic coding, this study seems to provide the least problematical evidence to date.

In our opinion, Kleiman's study is most important in showing that, as a practical matter, phonological recoding does take place within the limits of immediate comprehension. We believe it is time to accept the cautious principle that most comprehension, even in skilled reading, takes place within a system that uses a language-speech code, in addition to a visual-symbol code. Coding may be fairly abstract, as Gough (1972) has argued, and it certainly is abbreviated rather than complete, as Huey (1908/1968) pointed out. But it is a phonologically referenced process for normal readers under most conditions of reading.

We have emphasized the significance of rapid phonological and semantic optimizing of mental resources during reading. We acknowledge certainly that the causal relation between coding and comprehension has not been firmly established. Furthermore, the degree of phonological involvement in reading remains an active scientific issue. What is important for the present purpose is (1) the strong possibility that fast word coding reflecting "automatic" decoding processes can facilitate comprehension, and (2) the plausibility that reading does involve phonological coding in many situations.

Implications for the Teaching of Reading

Although the exact causal connections between language coding efficiency and reading comprehension are not well established, it is possible to explore some implications of the strong relationship that appears to be present. As suggested above, it may be difficult to prove the direction of causation. Indeed, the question of causal direction may not be the most useful question to ask.

Consider an analogy. Is a mountain climber's heart strong because he climbs mountains, or is his success in climbing due partly to being in good physical condition? In this case, causality runs in both directions—you can't climb without the stamina, but the stamina comes with exercise, only one variety of which is mountain climbing. It would be silly to argue over whether physical stamina causes mountain-climbing success or vice versa. A more useful research problem would ask which aspects of mountain climbing and other activities provide the most effective stamina-building exercises and which aspects of mountain climbing are most dependent on physical stamina.

Pushing our analogy further, we note that only after certain exercise patterns have been shown to produce both practical results (feeling better) and objectively measured results (e.g., lower pulse rate) do people accept that those patterns of activity are better than others. Now that pulse rate and related measures are used both to meter exercise and to judge its results, we are finally seeing an emphasis on heart muscle development rather than on skeletal muscle development. The importance of tying exercise to a measure with theoretical, empirical, and face validity should not be underestimated.

Let us note that cardiopulmonary functioning is not the sole criterion of health. If you have cancer, running won't cure you. However, it is also true that a range of mental and physical problems that otherwise seem to have unrelated etiologies and exotic treatments, will disappear with adequate exercise. Building up basic system functions can result in the curing of disorders that otherwise require specialized treatment.

If we replace mountain climbing with reading and stamina with language coding efficiency, our analogy is made. Several useful questions derive from this analogy. They perhaps can help us to determine where to go next in studying the relationship between verbal coding efficiency and reading achievement. We consider these problems in turn:

1. What constitutes effective verbal coding practice?
2. How can we measure verbal coding efficiency?

3. Who should receive verbal coding practice, and what are the implications of further emphasis on the mechanics of reading?

Practice. We have argued that the verbal coding tasks that poor readers do not perform adequately involve skills basic to reading, suggesting that some children need even more practice in word vocalization, immediate memory for text just read, and similar tasks than they currently receive. There is some evidence (Perfetti & Hogaboam, 1975b) that practice will improve verbal coding performance, at least in vocalization of unfamiliar words. There is also more general evidence that practice produces an increase in speed for simple verbal learning tasks, even after a conventional learning criterion has been achieved (Judd & Glaser, 1969).

More extensive drill and practice may be hard to implement in some classrooms. However, there are ways of doing so. One possibility is computer-assisted drill and practice, individualized to match current coding levels. Alternatively, more natural reading situations could be created that still provide extensive verbal coding practice. (As noted, respectively, by Bartlett and Popp in their chapters in these volumes, the Distar program and the New Reading System do a lot of this.) We consider these alternatives in turn.

Computer-assisted instruction (CAI) was developed initially to provide efficient, palatable, and individualized drill and practice. It was abandoned by educational researchers because it was too expensive and because it proved difficult to move beyond drill to more complex instructional tasks. Although there are now computer programs that can engage in sophisticated tutorial conversations (e.g., Carbonell, 1970a, 1970b; see also Collins, Warnock, & Passafiume, 1975), those programs still require massive computer systems. However, the advent of large-scale circuit integration has brought down the price of computer hardware to the point where drill-and-practice systems are quite feasible.

The classical arguments for computer-monitored drill are still valid (see the papers in Atkinson & Wilson, 1969, for example). The computer can deliver immediate reinforcement, keep good records, and (especially important) record not only what the responses are but also how fast they are made. Finally, it is a relatively unforgiving verbal communications medium in which precision of responding is emphasized. We believe the computer should be reconsidered as a tool for providing verbal coding drill, although we still need to determine what sorts of drill are effective.

The alternative to verbal coding drill is massive practice in everyday text reading. Again, there is the problem of knowing what constitutes effective practice. If we knew that, we could presumably embed the practice in a meaningful, and therefore more rewarding, activity. A second problem is that because of the very inefficiency of beginning readers with text, there is not much in the primary grades curriculum other than existing reading instruction that depends on reading. The medium is "unsafe" for instruction.

However, reading can be made a more basic component of games (as in the New Reading System, Beck, 1977) and other enrichment activities in the school. Consider some of the following forms of competition: How many instruction cards (such as *chance* in *Monopoly*) can you read and execute before the hourglass runs out? Can you rearrange some scrambled words to find out which square to move to? Can you solve a crossword puzzle in 15 minutes? Can you figure out what to feed a pet gerbil by reading a pamphlet about gerbils? All these tasks, once children have learned basic strategies for doing them, provide verbal coding practice that is fun. Successful reading classrooms already include many such activities, but further instructional research is needed to assure that such practice is effective.

There are still only a few studies of what constitutes effective practice, but we think we can learn from them. First of all, speeded word recognition practice, even with short-duration presentations, does not, of itself, exert much influence on recognition speed or on comprehension accuracy (Dahl, 1974, 1975–1976; Samuels, Dahl, & Archwamety, 1974). However, when the emphasis on speeded recognition is augmented by instruction in tactics for recognition, both recognition speed and cloze test performance are improved (Dahl, 1974). Similarly, instruction in specific methods of making sense quickly out of sentences whose words are scrambled (Weaver, 1976) can boost reading comprehension (as measured by cloze performance), as can instructions for producing a complete illustration of a story one has been reading (Lesgold, McCormick, & Golinkoff, 1975, which measured improvement in paraphrase recall of text).

On the other hand, we know of no studies in which practice by poor readers, without further instruction, on a task in which good readers are faster has produced improved reading performance. There are two possible reasons for this. One is that verbal coding speed is only a by-product of reading expertise; the other is that more conscious processing is necessary to recognize words that are not well known than is needed for familiar materials. Specifically, a current model of high-speed recognition (Atkinson & Juola, 1973) argues that the process is highly automated if confidence in the recognition is high, but that extra verbal processing is engaged when recognition is less certain. Perhaps Dahl's ineffective task was so easy that no mental effort was required. Dahl used frequent words, but infrequent words are the major source of good/poor recognition speed difference (Perfetti & Hogaboam, 1975a). Therefore, Dahl may have been giving practice on exactly the material for which practice is least needed.

An alternative view of the role of conscious processing is that it enables the learner to better determine the salient properties of the task and the full range of response components required (Welford, 1976). For example, some tailors have great trouble learning to repair woven fabric. This is not because of a lack of needle-moving dexterity or lack of visual acuity but, rather, because they do not understand the structure of the weave (Belbin, Belbin, & Hill, 1957). Similarly, unconscious practice of specific words may produce no transfer, whereas more attention to the task may result in refinement of additional decoding subskills.

To summarize, we do not know the full range of effective reading practice techniques, but it is likely that practice on responses that are already automated will not be as effective as practice in applying specific rules to (i.e., consciously processing in) decoding and other verbal tasks that are accomplishable but not yet highly automated.

Measuring Verbal Coding Efficiency. It is no accident that reading tests are usually time-limited tests, thus giving weight to speed as well as accuracy. The studies of Perfetti and Hogaboam (1975a, 1975b), Hunt et al. (1973), and others have shown speed of verbal coding to be a good predictor of reading success. It is a better predictor than accuracy of performance, since skill accuracy goes to 100% before skill development is complete (see Judd & Glaser, 1969). For example, one can measure letter-naming accuracy on the first day of first grade and predict reading achievement for a while, but one can measure letter-naming speed throughout the first year and it will continue to be correlated with reading achievement (Speer & Lamb, 1976).

We suggest that there are three levels of skill facility that should be distinguished in measurement of verbal coding ability: inaccurate performance; slow, accurate performance; and automated performance. It is the middle level that may most benefit from practice. When performance is highly automated, practice will not help since no conscious processing is required for performance and no load on processing capacity forces skill refinement. A student who performs inaccurately needs to be taught, not drilled. If there is a place for practice, it is at the intermediate level.

Current methods of testing do not make these distinctions very well. There are speed and accuracy measures available from some tests, but those tests are psychometrically designed so that no one does perfectly. Hence, both accuracy and speed scores represent a mixture of the three stages of expertise. However, the steps one might take to develop a reading achievement test that measures processing efficiency in a useful way are straightforward. They would involve procedures that are alien to the normative achievement testing tradition but not at all alien to experimental psychology.

Let us consider how we would write a testing system for vocabulary. First, we would use the difficulty orderings generated by traditional vocabulary test writers, except that instead of relating the ordinal positions in our word list to grade levels, we would express them in some value-free way. Then we would use one of the traditional procedures of perception research to determine an accuracy threshold, say, the point in the ordering at which there is 90% accuracy in recognizing and defining the words.

Determining an automation threshold is not as straightforward, since the criteria for speed of processing are normative rather than absolute. The likely task would be vocalization latency (Perfetti & Hogaboam, 1975a). The performance of third and fifth graders on frequent words and of good readers in that group on infrequent (for those grades) words is fairly uniform and faster than the performance of poor readers on infrequent words. There is a vocalization speed gap of about 1 sec between the presumably automated and presumably unautomated performances. Thus there is the possiblity that one could produce a chart that said, for example, that recognition of words 1,000–1,200 on the ordered list of words is automated if vocalization time is less than 1.6 sec. Given such a normative chart, one could establish a threshold in the word order below which all words have a probability of, say, 90% of being recognized automatically. The threshold would most probably have to be estimated somehow for each child, since there are overall individual differences in speed of responding.

The same procedure could be applied to comprehension testing. There we would establish thresholds for what level of passage difficulty can be handled at all and also for how far in a difficulty-ordered set of passages one can progress with both fast reading and accurate comprehension. Again, there would be norming problems, but that is also true for standard achievement tests. Material just below the child's accuracy threshold would be the subject of specific instruction, presumably based on task analyses, and material between the accuracy and automation thresholds would be used in specific reading practice tasks. It may turn out that for some levels of reading ability, the reading automation threshold could be established by reference to listening comprehension (see Sticht's chapter in this volume). However, we do not generally believe that poor readers will be adequately efficient in listening comprehension (see Perfetti & Lesgold, 1977), and recent data support our view (Berger, 1975; Lesgold, Curtis, & Roth, 1976).

Although it would be possible to do this sort of testing with paper and pencil, it could be unwieldy. Determining thresholds is a complex, time-consuming process if it is done by hand. One can guess that it would become a domain of the reading specialist, not the regular classroom teacher. This means it will be expensive and, therefore, not done too often nor for "better" students. On the other hand, this sort of testing could be done by a very small micro-processor system using cassettes or other recently developed devices to store text material. A classroom teacher could easily learn to make both instructional and practice prescriptions if all he or she had to do was send children to the computer and interpret two threshold measures produced by the computer.

Who Needs Practice?   One outcome of a testing program such as we have outlined could be the discovery that some students, presumably the better readers for their grade, do not have much of a gap between their accuracy and automation thresholds. This is an empirical matter, and we cannot predict whether this will happen. If it did, it would suggest that not all children need the same amount of reading practice and that some children quickly automate the skills they learn. This would be consistent with work of Royer, Hambleton, and Cadorette (1975), which shows that fast learners who meet the same immediate criterion of fact learning as slow learners have actually learned the material better, as shown in later retention tests.

The problems of providing only some students with extra practice in the coding components of reading are twofold. First, there are morale problems and related difficulties that occur when children or their parents realize that not every child is getting the remedial drill activity. We are not social psychologists; we feel that parents, teachers, students, and other experts will have to deal with the question of individualization of instruction. The second problem deserves more comment.

The disparity in reading achievment in differing schools, districts, and neighborhoods is such that reading curricula are beginning to appear that are targeted at one extreme or the other of the achievement continuum. Although we are heartened to see that programs such as Distar, which are targeted at "compensatory education" populations, emphasize verbal coding facility, we must reiterate a warning posed by Bartlett, volume 2, this series.

Bartlett pointed out, in comparing the Open Court and Distar programs, that although Distar provides many opportunities for verbal coding practice, it does not contain in its earlier levels much emphasis on the thinking components of comprehension. There are literal probe questions to assure that each word has been attended to, but there are less of the "Why do you think..." questions found in programs aimed at easier-to-teach populations. Although Bartlett viewed this point in a somewhat different way, we have to agree that while reading practice can simultaneously strengthen both the lexical/verbal/coding and the cognitive/interpretive skills of reading, any given attempt by the teacher to test for coding will deemphasize inferential processing, and vice versa.

A common solution of a test publisher, when confronted with two incompatible design ideals, is to try to satisfy each for part of the time. Although this may be the only solution in terms of materials design, we believe that extensive verbal coding facility and high-level, well-thought-out understanding of text are twin goals and that neither of them should be diluted. Both goals should weigh constantly on the minds of teachers. If the first is not met, the second is, we believe, impossible. If the second is not met, the first is valueless. Although it may be necessary temporarily to put great emphasis on coding practice, children should never be misled into thinking that reading fast or accurately saying words is their final goal. By providing opportunities to be rewarded for reading for information, teachers can help a child to understand the value of reading. By emphasizing analytic comprehension in everyday listening and visual observation situations, they can get the child ready to make use of the decoding facility that extra practice in reading mechanics may provide.

Summary. In simple terms, we can summarize our argument as follows. There is evidence that general verbal coding facility is substantially correlated with reading achievement. We do not know which causes which. However, the analogy with physical fitness suggests that cause runs in both directions and that instead of trying to find out whether lack of verbal facility causes poor reading or vice versa, a better goal would be to try to specify what sorts of verbal skills practice produce improved verbal facility.

When children cannot do a verbal task, they need to be taught how to do it. However, even after they have learned what to do, they may need to practice to learn it well. Although some normative tests measure speed of decoding as well as the ability to decode, much day-to-day testing of students taps only the low mastery level of correct performance. It now seems worthwhile to experiment with and to learn how to measure higher criteria of mastery for basic verbal coding skills, criteria based not on just doing the job but instead on doing the job well.

ACKNOWLEDGMENTS

Our research was supported by the Learning Research and Development Center, University of Pittsburgh, with contract funds supplied by the National Institute of Education. This and other work of ours benefited from discussions we have had with James Voss and the members of his and our research groups. We gratefully acknowledge the insights and hard work of the co-authors of the studies that we have described in this paper: Mary Curtis, Frederick Danner, Thomas Hogaboam, Steven Roth, and Robert Straub. In addition, we thank Laura Bell, Mary Gallagher, Susan Goldman, Ann Radman, Patricia Schuetz, and Linda Swanson for their assistance. Patricia Graw typed innumerable drafts from our scribbles, and we thank her for patience and expertise.

REFERENCES

Atkinson, R. C., & Juola, J. F. Factors influencing speed and accuracy of word recognition. In S. Kornblum (Ed.), *Attention and performance IV*. New York: Academic Press, 1973.
Atkinson, R. C., & Wilson, H. A. *Computer-assisted instruction*. New York: Academic Press, 1969.

Baron, J. Phonemic stage not necessary for reading. *Quarterly Journal of Experimental Psychology*, 1973, *25*, 241–246.

Baron, J. Mechanisms for pronouncing printed words: Use and acquisition. In D. LaBerge & S. J. Samuels (Eds.), *Basic processes in reading: Perception and comprehension.* Hillsdale, N.J.: Lawrence Erlbaum Associates, 1977.

Barron, R. Access to the lexical meanings of written words. In F. A. Murray (Ed.), *Development of the reading process.* Newark, Del.: International Reading Association, in press.

Beck, I. Comprehension during the acquisition of decoding skills. In J. Guthrie (Ed.), *Cognition, comprehension, and curriculum.* Newark, Del.: International Reading Association, 1977.

Belbin, E., Belbin, R. M., & Hill, F. A comparison between the results of three different methods of operator training. *Ergonomics*, 1957, *1*, 39–50.

Berger, N. S. *An investigation of literal comprehension and organizational processes in good and poor readers.* Unpublished doctoral dissertation, University of Pittsburgh, 1975.

Bradshaw, J. L. Three interrelated problems in reading: A review. *Memory & Cognition*, 1975, *3*, 123–134.

Calfee, R. C., Venezky, R. L., & Chapman, R. S. *Pronunciation of synthetic words with predictable and unpredictable letter–sound correspondences* (Tech. Rep. 71). Madison: Wisconsin Research and Development Center for Cognitive Learning, 1969.

Carbonell, J. R. AI in CAI: An artificial intelligence approach to computer-aided instruction. *IEEE Transactions on Man–Machine Systems*, 1970, *MMS-11*, 190-202. (a)

Carbonell, J. R. *Mixed-initiative man–computer instructional dialogues.* Unpublished doctoral dissertation, MIT., 1970. (b)

Carroll, J. B. Developmental parameters of reading comprehension. In J. Guthrie (Ed.), *Cognition, comprehension, and curriculum.* Newark, Del.: International Reading Association, 1977.

Collins, A. M., Warnock, E. H., & Passafiume, J. J. Analysis and synthesis of tutorial dialogues. In G. H. Bower (Ed.), *The psychology of learning and motivation* (Vol. 9). New York: Academic Press, 1975.

Dahl, P. R. *A mastery based experimental program for teaching high speed word recognition skills.* Unpublished doctoral dissertation, University of Minnesota, 1974.

Dahl, P. R. A mastery based experimental program for teaching high speed word recognition skills. *Reading Research Quarterly*, 1975–1976, *11*, 203–211.

Ehri, L. C. Do words really interfere in naming pictures? *Child Development*, 1976, *47*, 502–505.

Forster, K. I., & Chambers, S. M. Lexical access and naming time. *Journal of Verbal Learning and Verbal Behavior*, 1973, *6*, 627–635.

Gibson, E. J., & Levin, H. *The psychology of reading.* Cambridge, Mass.: MIT Press, 1975.

Gilbert, L. Speed of processing visual stimuli and its relation to reading. *Journal of Educational Psychology*, 1959, *55*, 8–14.

Golinkoff, R. M., & Rosinski, R. R. Decoding, semantic processing, and reading comprehension skill. *Child Development*, 1976, *47*, 252–258.

Goodman, K. S. Reading: A psycholinguistic guessing game. In H. Singer & R. B. Ruddell (Eds.), *Theoretical models and processes of reading.* Newark, Del.: International Reading Association, 1970.

Gough, P. B. One second of reading. In J. F. Kavanagh & I. G. Mattingly (Eds.), *Language by ear and by eye: The relationships between speech and reading.* Cambridge, Mass.: MIT Press, 1972.

Guthrie, J. T. Models of reading and reading disability. *Journal of Educational Psychology*, 1973, *65*, 9–19.

Hogaboam, T., & Perfetti, C. A. Reading skill and the role of verbal experience in decoding. *Journal of Educational Psychology*, in press.

Huey, E. B. *The psychology and pedagogy of reading.* Cambridge, Mass.: MIT Press, 1968. (Originally published, 1908)

Hunt, E. Varieties of cognitive power. In L. B. Resnick (Ed.), *The nature of intelligence.* Hillsdale, N.J.: Lawrence Erlbaum Associates, 1976.

Hunt, E., Frost, N., & Lunneborg, C. L. Individual differences in cognition: A new approach to intelligence. In G. Bower (Ed.), *Advances in learning and motivation* (Vol. 7). New York: Academic Press, 1973.

Jackson, M. D., & McClelland, J. L. Sensory and cognitive determinants of reading speed. *Journal of Verbal Learning and Verbal Behavior,* 1975, *14,* 565–574.

Judd, W. A., & Glaser, R. Response latency as a function of training method, information level, acquisition, and overlearning. *Journal of Educational Psychology Monograph,* 1969, *60,* 4 (Pt. 2).

Kleiman, G. M. Speech recoding in reading. *Journal of Verbal Learning and Verbal Behavior,* 1975, *14,* 323–339.

Kolers, P. Three stages of reading. In H. Levin & J. P. Williams (Eds.), *Basic studies on reading.* New York: Basic Books, 1970.

LaBerge, D., & Samuels, S. J. Toward a theory of automatic information processing in reading. *Cognitive Psychology,* 1974, *6,* 293–323.

Lesgold, A. M., Curtis, M. E., & Roth, S. F. *Reading ability and discourse processing rate.* Manuscript submitted for publication, 1976.

Lesgold, A. M., & Danner, F. *Syllables as visual units in letter-string perception.* Pittsburgh, Pa.: University of Pittsburgh, Learning Research and Development Center, 1976. (Publication No. 1976/11; also, submitted for publication.)

Lesgold, A. M., McCormick, C., & Golinkoff, R. M. Imagery training and children's prose learning. *Journal of Educational Psychology,* 1975, *67,* 663–667.

Meyer, D. E., & Ruddy, M. G. *Lexical memory retrieval based on graphemic and phonemic representations of printed words.* Paper presented at the Psychonomic Society, St. Louis, November 1973.

Meyer, D. E., Schvaneveldt, R. W., & Ruddy, M. G. Functions of graphemic and phonemic codes in visual word-recognition. *Memory & Cognition,* 1974, *2,* 309–321.

Novik, N. Parallel processing in a word-nonword decision task. *Journal of Experimental Psychology,* 1974, *102,* 1015–1020.

Pace, A. J., & Golinkoff, R. M. *The relationship between word difficulty and access of single-word meaning.* Paper presented at the meeting of the American Educational Research Association, San Francisco, April 1976.

Perfetti, C. A., & Hogaboam, T. The relationship between single word decoding and reading comprehension skill. *Journal of Educational Psychology,* 1975, *67,* 461–469. (a)

Perfetti, C. A., & Hogaboam, T. *The effects of word experience on decoding speeds of skilled and unskilled readers.* Paper presented at the meeting of the Psychonomic Society, Denver, November 1975. (b)

Perfetti, C. A., & Lesgold, A. M. Discourse comprehension and individual differences. In P. Carpenter & M. Just (Eds.), *Cognitive processes in comprehension.* Hillsdale, N.J.: Lawrence Erlbaum Associates, 1977.

Posner, M. I., & Mitchell, R. F. Chronometric analysis of classification. *Psychological Review,* 1967, *74,* 392–409.

Rosinski, R. R., Golinkoff, R. M., & Kukish, K. S. Automatic semantic processing in a picture–word interference task. *Child Development,* 1975, *46,* 247–253.

Royer, J. M., Hambleton, R. K., & Cadorette, L. *Individual differences in the long-term retention of meaningful materials.* Prepublication manuscript, 1975.

Rubenstein, H., Lewis, S. S., & Rubenstein, M. A. Homographic entries in the internal lexicon: Effects of systematicity and relative frequency of meanings. *Journal of Verbal Learning and Verbal Behavior,* 1971, *10,* 57–62.

Samuels, S. J., Dahl, P., & Archwamety, T. Effect of hypothesis/test training on reading skill. *Journal of Educational Psychology*, 1974, *66*, 835–844.

Shankweiler, D., & Liberman, I. Y. Misreading: A search for causes. In J. G. Kavanagh & I. G. Mattingly (Eds.), *Language by ear and by eye: The relationships between speech and reading.* Cambridge, Mass.: MIT Press, 1972.

Speer, O. B., & Lamb, G. First grade reading ability and influency in naming verbal symbols. *Reading Teacher*, 1976, *29*, 6, 572–576.

Weaver, P. Sentence anagram origanizational training and its effect on reading comprehension (Doctoral dissertation, University of Pittsburgh, 1976). *Dissertation Abstracts International*, 1976, *37*, 1312A. (University Microfilms No. 76-20, 188)

Welford, A. T. *Skilled performance: Perceptual and motor skills.* Glenview, Ill.: Scott, Foresman, 1976.

3 The Role of Orthographic Regularity in Word Recognition

Richard L. Venezky
University of Delaware

Dominic W. Massaro
University of Wisconsin

From preclassical Greece to the present day, most literate people in the Western world have been introduced to reading through correspondences of letters and sounds. This approach to beginning reading, now called phonics, was at the core of the ABC method that dominated reading instruction in Europe and England until well into the nineteenth century and in the United States until the early twentieth century (Smith, N. B., 1934/1965). By this method, children learned first the letters with their names and sounds, then various pronounceable (and not so pronounceable) bigrams and trigrams, then simple words, phrases, and sentences. For example, in *The American Primer*, a popular introduction to spelling and reading in use at the beginning of the nineteenth century, children were cycled through items like *bu, bo, ob, ub, yb, ic, ec, uc, yc, kni, kno*, and *knu*, before encountering their first real words.

By the early 1900s, the ABC method had evolved in the United States into an approach similar to that found in modern phonics programs, with deliberate sequencing of letter–sound patterns, separation of pattern words and sight words, and sensible strategies for decoding. *The Beacon Phonetic Chart*, for example, which was copyrighted in 1912, suggests that letter sounds, not letter names, be taught and that blending be done by a process that seems to minimize memory load. There is, so far as we can determine, no major difference between the Beacon method and the more enlightened (and expensive) phonics program offered in the schools today.

The introduction to reading by means of letters and sounds has not been unchallenged, especially in this century. Both silent reading and the whole-word approach have had periods of sovereignty in the last 75 years, but phonics is the standard approach today and is even found in some language experience programs.

TRADITIONAL JUSTIFICATION FOR PHONICS IN BEGINNING READING

But why? Is there evidence to justify this emphasis, or have reading instructors for 2,500 years (or more) followed false gods, as a few still claim they do (Smith, F., 1971)? The standard justification is that decoding (i.e., attaching sounds to letters and then blending the sounds to make a word) serves a number of ends. First, it provides a certain degree of independence for beginning readers. It allows them to translate unfamiliar printed words into phonological forms that may be familiar in their listening lexicon. Without this ability, the child is dependent on a teacher or another reader to confirm word identifications. Completely predictable letter–sound associations are not essential for this process, because, with context as an aid, the child can approximate the correct pronunciation of a word and then adjust it to a phonologically similar word that fits the immediate syntactic and semantic context. This is, in fact, what many beginning readers appear to do when they decode in context.

Second, decoding ability provides an element of self-assurance. Rather than confronting an ever-expanding number of arbitrary associations between words and printed symbol strings, as in Chinese, the child sees a more manageable set of letter–sound associations that can be used to build a large number of words. In addition, successful decoding is, in the early stages of reading, both an attention-keeping and a motivating device.

Whether these justifications for phonics approaches are supported by anything more than appeals to reason is not our concern at present. We are willing to accept that they are plausible, and we believe that the ends are desirable. If, however, these were the only goals of letter–sound teaching, then the current practice of ending phonics instruction at the end of the third year of reading instruction would be justifiable and we would have little more to say about it. After all, the goal of beginning reading instruction is not letter–sound knowledge but rapid word recognition, probably the only major skill unique to reading. Therefore, if letter–sound associations are not used by adults in recognizing words—and we think that they are usually not—then the sooner they are phased out of instruction the better. However, we suggest that a letter–sound emphasis in early reading serves another goal and that validation of this hypothesis could lead to significant changes in both beginning and middle-grade reading instruction.

ORTHOGRAPHIC REGULARITY AND WORD RECOGNITION

The overlooked role letter–sound instruction plays in reading acquisition is in word recognition but not through the direct application of letter–sound associations. As we show shortly, there is a rapidly expanding literature that demonstrates a central role for orthographic regularity in word recognition. By orthographic regularity we mean those features of printed English words that reduce the uncertainty of what letters might be present. Our basic argument is roughly as follows:

1. Rapid word recognition, which is essential for competent reading—oral or silent—depends on internalized (i.e., automatic) strategies that use orthographic regularity.
2. Phonics instruction, because of its emphasis on regular letter–sound associations, draws attention to the orthographically regular features of printed English words. That is, the procedure for analyzing printed words into subunits of pronunciation facilitates acquisition of the patterns that are also orthographically regular.
3. Furthermore, the instructional practice of separating certain (but not all) irregular words, which are learned as wholes, from pattern words, which are learned by analysis–synthesis, helps the reader to avoid generalizing from orthographically irregular sequences.

If we can establish these claims, then certain implications for initial and intermediate reading instruction need to be considered. We delay discussion of these, however, until after we have discussed (1) what orthographic regularity is, (2) how it relates to what is typically taught in phonics instruction, and (3) the evidence for claiming that orthographic regularity is essential to rapid word recognition. Because our discussion of the relationship between orthographic regularity and word recognition is based on a model of the processes involved in word recognition, we describe the model in the next section.

A MODEL OF WORD RECOGNITION PROCESSES

For purposes of the present discussion, we concentrate on the recognition activities that occur during a single eye fixation in reading. The model for describing these activities or processes, however, is part of a more general information-processing model for language processing that has been developed and tested over the past few years (Massaro, 1975). Our concern in presenting this model here is not to justify it over other models of word recognition but to provide a framework within which our hypothesis about word recognition can be explained and tested.

The text in reading is a sequence of letters and spaces that conform to orthographic, syntactic, and semantic constraints defining the written language. The average English reader begins at the top left-hand corner of the page and reads each line from left to right. A reader's eye movements are not continuous but occur in a series of short jumps called *saccades*. The fixation time between eye movements is roughly ten times longer than the movement time itself. An average reading eye movement of from 1° to 2° requires from 20 to 30 msec, whereas fixation time averages 250 msec (Shebilske, 1975; Woodworth, 1938). Initial processing of the visual stimulus must occur during the fixation time between eye movements, because the intensity of the light pattern is too weak and the processing time is too short during the eye movement.

During the eye fixation, the light pattern of the letters is transduced by the visual receptors into a feature detection system that places a set of visual features in preperceptual visual storage (see Fig. 3.1). For purposes of later exposition, we call this initial process *detection*. We describe the features as visual because we assume that there is a direct relationship between the stimulus properties of the letters and the information in preperceptual storage. The passive transduction of feature detection contrasts with the active construction of the following processing stages. There is no exact one-to-one relationship between the input and output of the following processing stages because these later stages actively use information stored in long-term memory in the sequence of transformations.

Given the set of visual features in preperceptual visual storage, the primary recognition process attempts to synthesize these isolated features into a

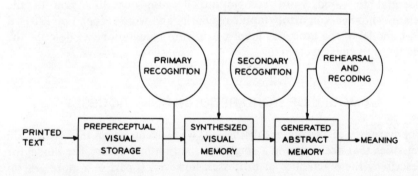

FIG. 3.1.   Flow diagram of processing printed text.

sequence of letters and spaces in synthesized visual memory. To do this, the primary recognition process can use information held in long-term memory, which for the accomplished reader includes a list of features of each letter of the alphabet along with information about the orthographic structure of the language. The primary recognition process uses both visual features and the orthographic structure of the language in its synthesis of the letter strings.

Because there are a limited number of ways that sequences of letters and letter groups can be put together to form English words, the reader's knowledge of this regularity can help to resolve the letters in a string that conforms to the language (Massaro, 1975). This knowledge can also help the reader to resolve the relative spatial positions of the letters once they are recognized (Estes, Allmeyer, & Reder, 1976).

The primary recognition process operates on a number of letters simultaneously (in parallel). The visual features that are read out at each spatial location define a set of possible letters for that position. The recognition process chooses from this candidate set the letter alternative that has the best correspondence in terms of visual features. However, the selection of a "best" correspondence can be facilitated by knowledge of orthographic structure. The primary recognition process, therefore, attempts to use both the visual information in preperceptual storage and knowledge about the structure of legal letter strings. The interaction of these two sources of information is a critical issue in the analysis of word recognition. (We review the most recent literature on the role of orthographic structure in letter and word recognition in a later section of this chapter.)

The primary recognition process transmits a sequence of recognized letters to synthesized visual memory. Figure 3.1 shows that the secondary recognition process transforms this synthesized visual percept into a meaningful form in generated abstract memory. We assume that synthesized visual memory holds a sequence of letters that is operated on by the secondary recognition process that tries to identify a meaningful word. The secondary recognition process makes this transformation by finding the best match between the letter string and a word in the long-term lexicon. Each word in the lexicon contains both perceptual and conceptual codes. The concept recognized is the one whose perceptual code gives the best match and the one most likely to occur in that particular context.

The structure-generated abstract memory corresponds to the short-term or working memory of most information-processing models. Recoding and rehearsal processes build and maintain semantic and syntactic structures at the level of generated abstract memory.

In this model, the role of orthographic structure in word recognition is concentrated in the primary recognition process, and orthographic structure serves to facilitate both the recognition of individual letters and the resolution of relative spatial positions. The use of orthographic structure for letter resolution can be viewed in the following manner:

> For letter strings that are not spelled like English words, orthographic structure probably plays no role. Letters are resolved individually, solely on the basis of their visual features, which are carefully evaluated during the primary recognition process. For letter strings that are spelled like words, however, less visual information needs to be processed than in the nonword case because the constraints of English orthography aid the reader in deciding what might be present. If visual information were to arrive over time, with the gross features available before the detailed features (Massaro & Schmuller, 1975), then the reader would be able, by successive sampling, to terminate visual processing when sufficient information is available for each letter decision. If, for example, an initial *th-* has been resolved in a letter string and the features available for the next letter match either *c* or *e*, the reader might accept *e* without waiting for further visual information, because initial *thc-* is irregular whereas initial *the-* is not.[1]

To test the validity of this model, we must first define orthographic regularity.

DEFINING ORTHOGRAPHIC REGULARITY

A page of printed English looks quite different from a page of printed Hebrew or a page of printed Finnish, even to a person who understands none of these languages. English and Hebrew have no overlap in symbol repertoires, whereas English and Finnish have a large, but not 100%, overlap. (Finnish uses the letters *c, f, q, w, x,* and *z* only in a small number of loan words, and English has no equivalent for Finnish *ä* and *ö*.) Experienced readers of Hebrew texts expect Hebrew letters, readers of Finnish texts expect Finnish letters, and readers of English texts expect English letters.

We presume that, in addition to these differences in symbol repertoires, readers are aware of other characteristics of their written language. Table 1 shows several sentences from Finnish and English first-grade readers in which all nonblanks have been replaced by *X*'s. Because of the difference between average word length in Finnish and English, the identification of the English sample should be obvious. How refined this sense of average length is has not been explored so far as we know. Could an English reader, for example,

---

[1]We have greatly simplified the recognition processes in this description, leaving out for purposes of explication the complexities of what are probably asynchronous, partially overlapping processes. More detailed explanations of these can be found in Turvey (1973) and Massaro (1975).

TABLE 3.1
Differences Between Average Word Length in Finnish and English

Sample A	Sample B
XXXXX XX XXXXXXXXXX XXXXXXXX. XX XX XXXX XXXXXXX XXXXXXXX, XXXXX XXXXX XX XXXXXX XXXXXX XXXX. XXXXX XXXXX XXXXXXXXXXX XXXXXXXX.	XXX XXXX XX XX XXX XXXX. XXX XXXXX XXX XXXXXXXX XXX XXX. XXX XXX XXXXXXX XXXX XXXXX XXXX XXXX XXXX XXXXXX XXXX.

distinguish English from French and German samples composed as in Table 3.1?

A third language-dependent feature of texts is the distribution of word lengths that normally occur in any text. All natural languages have evolved lexicons that contain two groups of words: a relatively small, closed set of function words, which serve primarily (but not entirely) to signal word relationships (i.e., syntax), and an open-ended set of context words that serve primarily to signal meanings (Hockett, 1958). The function words are heavily used, tend to change relatively slowly over time, and tend to be (according to Zipf, 1935) relatively short in phonological and, therefore, alphabetic length. The content words, in contrast, have a wide distribution of frequency of occurrence, change more rapidly over time than the function words, and vary from short to quite long. Real texts are characterized by distinctive distributions of word lengths, depending on the manner in which function words are realized in print. In Hebrew, for example, the definite article, the coordinating conjunction "and," and most prepositions are prefixed to content words, thus reducing the number of short, printed words relative to most European languages.

But the most important characteristics of orthographic regularity for studying word recognition are not those that characterize sequences of words but those that define the allowable patterns of letters within single words. Two entirely different approaches have been taken in describing this regularity. The first method, described as *probabilistic*, uses word tokens sampled from real texts to define probabilities of occurrence for single letters, bigrams, trigrams, and so on. From these data, various types of approximations to English words are generated. For example, Hirata and Bryden (1971) generated tables of zero- to fourth-order approximations to English that have been used in studies of orthographic regularity by, among others, Lefton and Spragins (1974) and Lefton, Spragins, and Byrnes (1973). Mason (1975), on the other hand, generated pseudowords from the single-letter frequency counts published by Mayzner and Tresselt (1965). These differed from the Hirata and Bryden (1971) data in that letter position and word length were considered by the former, but not the latter.

The second method, called *rule-governed*, is based on studies of the English orthography (e.g., Hockett, 1963; Venezky, 1967, 1970). Rules define which letters or letter sequences are allowed (or not allowed) in which positions or graphemic contexts. Although no comprehensive set of such rules exists, reasonable approximations to rules can be drawn from Venezky (1967, 1970). This approach to defining orthographic regularity has been used extensively by Gibson and her colleagues (e.g., Gibson, Osser, & Pick, 1963) and by many others (e.g., Baron, 1977; Thomas, 1968) in studies of word recognition.

Since both methods for defining orthographic regularity are commonly used in experimental studies, and since each implies a different approach to instruction, we consider them in detail.

Probabilistic Approaches

The earliest approach to generating English pseudowords was suggested by Shannon (1948) and used by Miller, Bruner, and Postman (1954) and by Wallach (1963) in studies of word recall. A zero-order approximation to English was generated by selecting each letter for a string randomly, giving equal weight to each letter. A first-order approximation resulted from the same procedure but with the letters weighted by their frequency of occurrence in English texts. For higher orders, an ith-order approximation was generated by selecting an initial string of length $i - 1$. Then a sample text was scanned linearly for that string. Once the string was found, the next letter in sequence was added to the string, the first letter was removed, and the process was repeated until a desired number of letters (including the initial $i - 1$) were selected.

This scheme tends to generate highly regular pseudowords at the higher order approximations, especially if the last letter drawn for each word is always selected from the last position in an English word.[2] Miller et al. (1954) used this restriction in generating eight-letter words that were fourth-order approximations to English (e.g., *mossiant, oneticul, preveral, favorial, aphyster*). Wallach (1963), however, employed six-letter pseudowords by truncating those published by Miller et al., thus occasionally risking non-English endings (e.g., *mossia, onetic, everal, iorial, aphyst*).

Shannon (1951) also suggested a parlor game technique for generating pseudowords. The first person constructed a word by adding letters to an initial string. The first letter added was retained, the first letter of the starting string was dropped, and the process was repeated with another person. Although Shannon assumed that letter frequencies in the resulting strings

---

[2]In the Shannon (1951) system, all 26 letters of the alphabet plus space were used, so positional constraints were guaranteed for second-order and higher approximations to English.

would approximate those of English texts, Attneave (1953) showed that college students often misjudge the relative frequencies of individual letters.

In contrast to these sequential dependency schemes are the correlational approaches that use letter and letter-string frequency tables to produce pseudowords with controlled bigram and trigram counts. Anisfeld (1964), for example, suggested that the Gibson, Pick, Osser, and Hammond (1962) results could be explained by differences in summed bigram frequencies based on the Underwood and Schulz (1960) tables. But a later study (Gibson, Shurcliff, & Yonas, 1970) showed that summed bigram and trigram frequencies were not good predictors of recognition scores on pronounceable and unpronounceable pseudowords.

Underwood and Schulz (1960) generated bigram and trigram frequencies from 2,080 words sampled from Thorndike and Lorge (1944) and weighted with respect to their frequency of occurrence. These counts are based on overall frequency of occurrence (tokens), rather than word types (the number of different words contributing to the sample), and summed over all occurring word lengths and serial positions. Failure to account for word length provides obvious problems in describing orthographic regularity. For example, the trigram *ght* occurs relatively often summed over all word lengths but does not occur in three- or four-letter words.

Summed bigram or trigram frequencies without regard for serial position are also inadequate for a description of orthographic regularity.[3] For example, the bigram *ck* is legal at the end but not at the beginning of a word. It is unlikely, however, that this difference can be accounted for in summed bigram frequencies, because *k* plus vowel is as likely as vowel plus *c*. This allows *ckad* to be as "legal" as *dack*. (Summed trigram frequencies can handle the positional contraints on *ck* quite well but cannot handle positional constraints on trigrams such as *dge* and *tch*.)

The objections to not including word length and serial position in assigning frequencies to bigrams can be overcome by using the Mayzner and Tresselt (1965) tables, which give bigram frequencies for each word position in words of from three to seven letters in length. However, both orthographically regular and orthographically irregular strings can be generated with either high or low bigram counts. Shown in Table 3.2 are two lists of words with their bigram counts. Notice that although the words in the first column are orthographically regular by the rules given in the next section of this chapter, they have extremely low bigram counts. Similarly, the irregular strings in the second column have relatively high bigram counts. Similar but less striking

---

[3]Gibson and Levin (1975, pp. 207–211) distinguish between correlation approaches such as the Underwood and Schulz (1960) and the conditional redundancy approaches, which consider positional constraints. However, this dichotomy does not apply to the positional probability approach, which is discussed shortly.

TABLE 3.2
Bigram Counts for Orthographically Regular and
Irregular Strings

Regular		Irregular	
bipon	17[a]	thrsm	417
slevs	21	thrse	565
slevy	30	sthse	341
eddop	2	eaich	297
edaby	0	whrst	378
dufip	0	hoier	407

Source. Based on Mayzner and Tresselt (1965).
[a]The count of 17 for *bipon,* for example, is the sum of the counts (for 5-letter words) for *bi* in positions 1 and 2, *ip* in positions 2 and 3, and so on.

demonstrations can be made of pseudowords generated by controlling trigram frequencies.

Letter and letter-string frequency tables have also been used to generate approximations to English without regard to summed bigram and trigram frequencies. Hirata and Bryden (1971), for example, generated ten-letter strings for orders of approximation to English from zero to four, using the Mayzner and Tresselt (1965) and Mayzner, Tresselt, and Wolin (1965a, 1965b) tables of single letter, bigram, trigram, and tetragram frequencies. The algorithms used for generating these strings did not use positional information; nevertheless, they guaranteed orthographic regularity for fourth-order strings, except for word endings and word beginnings. Lefton et al. (1973) and others have used these lists in developmental studies of guessing missing letters in pseudowords.

A totally different probabilistic approach is represented by Mason (1975), who used the Mayzner and Tresselt (1965) single-letter tables to generate words with high and low positional frequencies. A word has a high positional frequency count if the letters for that word are in positions in which they are frequently found in words of the same length in texts. Mason (1975) found that positional frequency was a good predictor of letter search speeds in pseudowords. However, her test items confound positional frequency and orthographic regularity, with the pseudowords high in positional frequency tending to be orthographically regular and those low in positional frequency irregular. For example, one of the highest possible positional frequency counts for a four-letter string occurs for *THET* (3,794); nearly as high is an orthographically irregular string, *THRT* (3,421); and an orthographically regular word *JUFF* has a count of only 371. Thus if orthographic regularity relates to recognition ease, positional frequency counts are inadequate for defining it. Since both regular and irregular pseudowords can be generated with both high and low positional frequencies, the relative contributions of the two variables to Mason's task could be examined.

Rule-Governed Approaches

In contrast to probabilistic approaches, rule-governed approaches are based on generalizations about the underlying patterns of English orthography and, therefore, might generate some sequences that do not occur in real words and reject some that do. In addition, rule-governed approaches are based on word types, whereas probabilistic approaches are based on word tokens. In rule-governed approaches the actual frequency of occurrence of a word in texts is not considered. This bias appears to be one of convenience rather than overt decision, resulting from the use of word types in the major studies of English orthography. (Some attempts have been made to evaluate the relative contributions of word types and word tokens in the generalization of letter–sound patterns, but the results have been inconclusive (see Johnson, D. D., 1970; Johnson & Venezky, 1975).

Restrictions on letter sequences in English words derive from two primary sources: graphemic conventions and phonological constraints. The first source is a 1,400-year accumulation of scribal practices, printing conventions, lexicographers' selections, and occasional accidents that somehow became codified as part of the present orthographic system. The second source is the phonology of English, which by its own constraints on sound sequences places restrictions on letter patterns.

Graphemic Conventions.   English graphemic conventions apply primarily to sequences of the same letter and to positions in which letters and letter sequences may occur within words. No letter can be tripled in an English word, and only 16 letters can be doubled (geminated). Those that cannot be doubled include *a, h, i, j, k, q, u, w, x* and *y*. Exceptions to this latter constraint are few (excluding proper nouns and recent borrowings), for example, *aardvark, skiing,* and *trekked.* The letter *v* rarely doubles, but several exceptions are well estabished in the language (e.g. *flivver, savvy, navvy*). Those letters that can double do so only in medial and final word positions. This pattern has fewer than a dozen exceptions (e.g., *llama, eel, oodles, ooze*), not counting technical terms beginning with the combining form *oo-*.

These patterns and their exceptions bring us to the question of how we establish a pattern or rule. Of the 100,000 or so word entries in common desk dictionaries, perhaps from 15 to 20 begin with geminated letters. Does 99.98% regularity establish a pattern? For the present, we will dodge this issue by claiming that the patterns of regularity presented here are only potential patterns suggested as a basis for psychological studies. Their derivation, however, is based entirely on either frequency or graphemic environment, without precise definition of what frequencies are rule-producing, except that types rather than tokens are counted.

A second constraint on doubled consonants is that they do not (with a few exceptions) occur after vowel digraphs. A pseudoword like *louff* would be irregular, or at least more irregular than words like *louf* and *luff*. The three geminate replacements *tch* (*chch*), *dg* (*gg* = /ĵ/), and *ck* (*cc* or *kk*) obey the same rules as geminates: They do not occur initially or after digraph vowels. Thus *tchan, dgerp, heeck,* and *lautch* are irregular.

Some single letters also have positional constraints in English words. The letter *q* must always be followed by *u; j, u,* and *v* do not occur in word final position: and *k* does not occur finally after a single-letter vowel. (A few exceptions exist for *u,* including *you* and *thou,* and there is one for *k: trek.*) By this restriction, pronounceable pseudowords such as *baj, blou, mek, and sliv* are irregular.

Further restrictions can be found for vowel sequences, especially digraph vowels ending in *i* and *y,* but these are less consistent than the constraints mentioned above.

Phonological Conventions. Because of a series of sound changes that began during the Old English period, most noun inflectional endings coalesced into what is presumed to have been an unstressed, neutral vowel (/ə/), which was spelled with the letter *e.* By the time this vowel became silent, other sound changes had lengthened the vowel in a preceding syllable, so that the final *e,* although unpronounced, became a marker for distinguishing vowel quantity. Thus the pairs *man–mane* and *bit–bite* arose. The consequence of these changes, plus other conventions such as the use of a suffix *s* for noun plural and third person singular in the present indicative forms of verbs, is a highly uneven distribution of letters in different word positions. This distribution is further augmented by the frequent use of common prefixes and suffixes as word-forming elements (e.g., *co-, pre-, -ing, -ed*). This feature, which is summarized by Mayzner and Tresselt (1965) for words with from three to seven letters, reflects both phonological and scribal variables.

A different set of constraints results from the restrictions of sound sequences in English. For example, certain consonant sequences do not occur in word initial position (e.g., *ds-*), and certain others do not occur in word final position (e.g., *-sd, -fd, -pg*). Notice also that although / wh-/ is an illegal phonological sequence for English, *wh-* is an orthographically regular spelling. The earlier spelling, *hw-* was reversed by eleventh- and twelfth-century scribes to minimize graphic confusions. Whorf (1956) attempted to summarize these constraints for English monosyllabic words.

Unpronounceable consonant sequences from other languages or from earlier periods in the history of English often retain their original spellings, even when the sound sequences are altered to conform to Modern English. Spellings such as *write, psychology, hymn*, and *lamb* are representative of this group. (However, some forms that appear to belong in this group result from scribal pedantry, e.g., *ptarmigan, thumb, crumb*.)

Other orthographic constraints based on phonological conventions could be listed, but they are of less importance than those already described. One implication of the constraints described above is that different degrees of regularity are possible. For example, *flab, kip*, and *petch* are pronounceable and orthographically regular; *cootch, lev*, and *goff* are pronounceable but (mildly) irregular; *ckab, baaaf*, and *lixx* are pronounceable (?) but more irregular; and, finally, *wksliy, tchfole, and xxx* are unpronounceable and highly irregular.

ORTHOGRAPHIC REGULARITY AND PHONICS INSTRUCTION

If the psychological reality of orthographic regularity is based on probabilistic information derived from token counts, then phonics instruction is only marginally helpful at best, for helping children internalize this structure. Because letter–sound associations presented in phonics programs are selected on the basis of word types and not word tokens, such programs could even have a negative influence by, for example, teaching certain high-frequency words that have irregular correspondences as sight words. Probabilistic information requires continual exposure to normal texts. The tightly controlled vocabularies of the primary readers and the emphasis in phonics instruction on regularly spelled words probably leads to probability generalizations that differ in some instances quite markedly from those published by Mayzner and Tresselt (1965) or Hirata and Bryden (1971).

If, however, the psychological reality of orthographic regularity derives from rule-governed information, then the relationship between some of the potential sources of rule-governed orthographic regularity summarized above and the patterns taught in phonics programs becomes important. The units typically stressed in phonics programs are the simple (i.e., single-letter) vowel patterns, the digraph vowels (*ee, ea, ow*, etc.), sequences such as *wh-, qu-, dge*, and *tch*, the common (and not so common) initial and final consonant clusters, and the common prefixes and suffixes—all of which play a role in rule-governed regularity. What are not introduced overtly are any of the patterns that require the absence of spelling (e.g., the nondoubling of *x*). Exactly how these patterns might be taught is not obvious however. Contrasting legal with illegal spellings might be counterproductive in that it would expose students to irregular strings which they might then incorrectly use in generalizations on regularity.

Equal in importance to which patterns are introduced is the manner of introduction, which depends (in the better programs) on inductive rather than deductive reasoning. A spelling such as *ee* is usually introduced alone (with its most common pronunciation) and then in a group of words divided by position. Thus *see, thee, free*, and *bee* might be grouped, then *seek, beet, seed*, and so on, with the *ee* emphasized by underlining or color.

A second presentation procedure that tends to emphasize orthographic regularity centers on what some phonics programs call phonograms— common vowel–consonant or consonant–vowel sequences that are productive for word building. Early in many programs the *-an* family is introduced: *fan, tan, man, van*, and so on. In addition to emphasizing particular letter–sound patterns, this practice induces a segmentation strategy that may transfer directly to word recognition.

Finally, the isolation of some irregular forms such as *debt, thou, is* and *was*, that are taught as sight words, probably reduces the opportunity for generalizing their spellings as regular. But notice that many other sight words, which are irregular from a letter–sound view (*what, wash*, and *from*), are not orthographically irregular. What effect this has on the reader's sense of orthographic regularity is not clear. The differences between orthographic regularity and letter–sound regularity should not be overlooked. Orthographically irregular strings such as *hek, ssilf*, and *lowtch* are pronounceable (and regularly so), whereas orthographically regular words such as *triple, colonel, eighth, business*, and *arced* have irregular letter–sound associations.

The point to be stressed here, however, is that a logical phonics program introduces almost all the orthographic patterns that can be exemplified positively and introduces them by procedures that give overt attention to the relevant spelling units for orthographic regularity.

WORD RECOGNITION

In this section we review a number of experiments that involve the recognition of letters, nonwords, and words and show the role orthographic regularity plays in the recognition processes.[4] By *recognition* we mean the resolution of the visual information in order to perform the experimental task. Since

---

[4]Orthographic regularity should not be confused, as it often is, with spelling-to-sound regularity. The latter means that there is a regular (i.e., predictable) association between the spelling of the language and the way it is pronounced. The more regular relationships between spelling and sound have led a number of researchers to postulate that reading a word involves first recoding it to speech at some level and then accessing meaning on the basis of this speech code (Gough, 1972). However, it is unlikely that the spelling-to-sound correspondences could facilitate visual processing because the letters would have to be recognized before their sounds would be available.

experimental tasks differ to the extent that they require different degrees of resolution on the part of the subject, the number of processes involved in recognition will vary accordingly. The nature of the task must be accounted for both in the analysis of the results and in the implications that are drawn for theory. It is somewhat disappointing that some researchers have failed to be concerned with the processes involved in tasks such as searching for a target letter in a letter string, reporting component letters, pronouncing a letter string, or determining whether a particular letter string is a word. The different levels of processing in these tasks are clarified somewhat by distinguishing between detection, primary recognition, and secondary recognition (shown in Fig. 3.1).

An example of a study that failed to account for the psychological processes in the task is that of N. F. Johnson (1975). In one of his experiments subjects were given a test word every 10 sec and asked to classify it as either the same as or different from a target word. For example, for the target word *block*, the subjects saw a list of five-letter words and had to classify each word as the same as or different from *block* by hitting one of two buttons. In the letter target condition, the subjects again saw a series of five-letter test words, but now they were asked to respond according to whether each test word contained a particular target letter. The reaction times were shorter for the target word than for the target letter condition, leading Johnson to conclude that words are identified as whole patterns, suppressing the identification of their component letters.

Johnson's results do not show that words are processed as whole patterns when the nature of the task is made apparent. Subjects in the word condition had to decide whether a five-letter string of letters was the same as a five-letter string of letters in memory. Subjects in the letter condition had to decide whether any of five letters in the string was the same as the target letter in memory. Accordingly, the critical difference between the two conditions is probably not in word versus letter targets but in having same-length or different-length target and test items. Because (in our model) letters in a sequence can be processed in parallel, subjects can make a relatively direct comparison between the target and test words in the target word condition. Subjects in the word condition could have adopted a very liberal criterion of sameness. Johnson chose his words randomly; thus, there was a low probability that a test word on different trials would have even one letter in the same position as a letter in the target word. If even one or two test letters had been the same as the corresponding target letters, the subject could have initiated a "same" response before the processing of the test item was complete. Similarly, a difference of one or two letters would have been sufficient to initiate a "different" response. In the target letter condition, however, the target letter had to be compared to each of the five letters in the test word. Therefore, each of the test letters had to be processed sufficiently to determine whether it was the same as or different from the target letter. Subjects in this condition could not terminate their processing until they found the target letter or determined that all the test letters were different from the target letter. The additional processing required in the target letter condition relative to that required in the target word condition can account for the longer reaction times in the target letter condition, even though letters were the unit of analysis in both conditions. Accordingly, Johnson's conclusion that a word is processed as whole, suppressing recognition of its component letters, is not warranted by his experimental results.

In contrast to Johnson's idea that processing a word conceals its component letters, a number of investigators have assumed that a target letter would be found more quickly in a word than in a random letter string. In general, it is assumed that the time to find a target letter should be an inverse function of the conformity of the letter string to the orthographic structure of the language. The implicit assumption in this research is that the visual resolution of a sequence of letters will occur faster when the letters conform to the orthography of the language than when they do not. Letter search is dependent on letter resolution and, therefore, should reflect the time it takes to resolve letter sequences. Subjects appear to be able to perform a Neisser (1964) search task for a given target letter more rapidly if they search through a list of words than if they search through a list of random strings (Krueger, 1970; Novik & Katz, 1971).

Mason (1975) used a target search task to study the contribution of one aspect of orthographic regularity. Good and poor sixth-grade readers searched through six-letter strings for the presence or absence of a target letter. Words and nonwords were used, and the nonwords differed in the degree of orthographic structure as defined by positional frequency. As we explained earlier, the positional frequency of a letter in a letter string is the frequency of occurrence of that letter in the same position in words of the same length sampled from common texts. Given this definition, a letter string can be given a summed positional frequency that represents the sum of the positional frequency of all the letters in the string. Mason tested the idea that search time for a letter should be an inverse function of the summed positional frequency of the letter string. The implicit model of the letter search task is that the subjects must first recognize the letters in a string and then compare these letters to the target letter. Differences in the search times for a given target letter in different letter strings should reflect differences in the time required to recognize the letters of the strings. Mason found that good readers were faster (on both "yes" and "no" trials) on strings with high positional frequencies than on strings with low positional frequencies. Poor readers showed no difference. The results support the idea that the time needed to resolve (recognize) the letters in a string is influenced by the likelihood of letters occurring in their most common positions.

Although summed positional frequency appears to account for the recognition times in Mason's study, we do not believe it is the critical variable that defines orthographic regularity. Consider some of the arrangements of the letters that make up the word *person*, which has a summed positional frequncy of 1,141, based on the Mayzner and Tresselt (1965) single-letter table. The string *pornes* contains the same letters in different positions and has a count of 1,858. The string *enspro* has a count of 383. Looking at these nonwords, we see that *pornes* is spelled like an English word and therefore should be relatively easy to recognize, whereas *enspro* violates what we know about English spelling and should therefore be relatively difficult to recognize. Table 3.3 lists some other letter strings used by Mason. The letters have been rearranged to yield strings with almost equal summed positional frequencies but with differing orthographic regularities. We are currently testing the prediction that the orthographic regularity as defined by graphemic rules and not as defined by the summed positional frequencies will influence recognition times when these variables are independently varied in a target search task.

There is a growing research literature that supports the idea that visual recognition of letter strings can be facilitated by orthographic regularity rather than by spelling-to-sound regularity or word meaning. Baron and Thurston (1973) found that visual recognition is as good for pseudowords that obey orthographic rules as it is for real words. Baron (1975) carried out a series of experiments showing that orthographic regularity, but not phonemic quality or meaningfulness, has an effect on visual information-processing tasks. The time taken to decide whether two strings of letters were visually identical was not longer when the strings were pseudowords instead of words, but it was longer when the strings violated orthographic regularity. Homophone word pairs did not require more time in this task than did nonhomophonic words. Meaningfulness did not facilitate search for a target letter in a letter string, although orthographic regularity decreased search time.

TABLE 3.3
Letter Strings of Similar Positional Frequency that Are
Either Orthographically Regular or Irregular

Regular[a]		Irregular[a]	
girbed	(1,721)	grbied	(1,690)
pirons	(1,409)	sopinr	(1,409)
filtes	(1,750)	flties	(1,775)
citred	(1,861)	tcried	(1,886)
hougen	(1,399)	nhoueg	(1,409)

Note. Based on Mason (1975).
[a]The numbers in parentheses give the summed positional frequency for letter strings.

In contrast to Baron's (1975) and Baron and Thurston's (1973) findings, Manelis (1974) found significant differences between real words and pseudowords in a Reicher (1969) task. Overall, a letter in a word was reported about 5% more often than a letter in a pseudoword. However, that difference could have been due to differences in orthographic regularity, not wordness per se. Although Manelis found no effect of bigram and trigram frequency in a post hoc analysis, the analysis in our section on probabilistic approaches shows that these measures are not good indexes of regularity. It remains to be seen if our interpretation can account for the observed differences in the Manelis study.

We believe that there is substantial evidence to argue that word meaning does not influence the initial visual resolution of letter strings (Baron, 1975; Baron & Thurston, 1973; Massaro, 1975). One implication of this is that there is nothing visually unique about a sequence of letters that spell a word beyond that accounted for by orthographic regularity. The perceptual equivalence between words and pseudowords argues that words do not have supraletter features that allow the words to be recognized without resolution of at least some of the letters or letter features. Many teachers and psychologists believe that words can be recognized on the basis of overall shape or configuration without resolution of the component letters (Johnson, N. F., 1975; Miller, 1972). If words can be recognized as wholes, then orthographic regularity would play a very minor role, if any, in word recognition. If words are recognized on the basis of supraletter features, there would be no chance for orthographic regularity to help resolve the component letters.

However, there is now good evidence against the hypothesis that words can be recognized on the basis of supraletter features. The most straightforward analysis was performed by Groff (1975), who examined the shapes of high-frequency words taken from school books. The shape was defined by drawing a contour around the letters so that, for example, *elephant* would be ⌐elephant⌐. Only 20% of the 283 words sampled were represented by a unique shape. The author rightly concluded that the small number of words that can be represented by a unique shape precludes the use of this cue for accurate word recognition.

There is also experimental evidence against the idea of word recognition based on supraletter features. Thompson and Massaro (1973) and Massaro (1973) found that a letter likely to be confused with another letter was just as likely to be confused in word presentations as in single-letter presentations. If recognition of words involved the use of features other than those contained in the component letters, there should have been different degrees of letter confusability in letter and word presentations.

McClelland (1976) presented four-letter words, pseudowords, or unrelated strings in either the same case or in mixed upper and lower case. (The letters alternated in case in the mixed case condition.) The results showed that the recognition of a letter was equally disrupted by mixing the cases of letters in both words and pseudowords. Mixing letter cases did not disrupt recognition of letters in the unrelated letter strings. If readers used whole word shape or configuration cues in word recognition, mixing letter cases should have disrupted recognition of words more than of pseudowords. The results support the idea that legal spelling patterns are functional at an intermediate stage of visual recognition and that letters alternating in case can disrupt the resolution of these patterns. Given that the unrelated strings did not have legal spelling patterns, alternating letter case did not disrupt processing of the letters.

Baron (1976) asked observers to pronounce regular words and exception words. Regular words were defined as words that obey the rules of spelling-to-sound correspondence in English (see Venezky, 1970); exceptions were defined as words that do not follow the rules. The regular words were chosen from those that are less frequent in the language to eliminate the pronunciation differences between regular words and exceptions. The words were presented in upper, lower, or mixed cases. The idea was that exception words should be more dependent on a whole-word mechanism than regular words and that upper-case letters are less appropriate for this whole-word mechanism. Therefore, if words are recognized as wholes, and exceptions more so than regular words, we would expect an interaction between upper and lower case and regular versus exception words. No interaction was found, however, and this result argues against the whole word mechanism.

Other evidence against the whole word idea and in support of orthographic regularity has been recorded by Brooks (1974), who translated real English words into an artificial alphabet and asked subjects to learn the real-word responses to the words presented in the artificial alphabet. The same subjects were also asked to learn stimuli that had the stimuli and responses re-paired so that the new alphabet would not be a useful guide to pronunciation. Figure 3.2 lists the alphabets and the stimuli and responses used in the experiment. Note that in the orthographic condition each of the artificial letters corresponds to an English letter. In the paired-associate condition, the stimuli are re-paired with the responses so that the orthographic regularity is lost. If subjects learn to process words as wholes without regard to the orthographic regularity of the letters, then we would expect that the speed of reading the paired-associate stimuli should be the same as that of reading the orthographic stimuli. If a whole word analysis is used, the orthographic structure is useless. In contrast, if letter processing mediates word processing, we would expect that the orthographic structure would facilitate reading performance.

Subjects were asked to read aloud lists of six items as fast as possible without error. Although the paired-associate list was initially read faster than the orthographic list, the asymptotic reading times of highly practiced

STIMULI	RESPONSES		STIMULI	RESPONSES	
	Orthographic	Paired-associate		Orthographic	Paired-associate
ПU()C	NAPE	SEAT	ПUΛ∞	PENT	TANS
ПU()III	NAPS	PANE	ПUV∞	PEAT	SANE
IIIXU−	SEAT	NAPE	IVΛU	SANE	PEAT
()UIII−	PAST	SETS	∞VПU	TAPE	SAPS
()UПX	PANE	NAPS	∞VΛI	TANS	PENT
III)C−III	SETS	PAST	IVПI	SAPS	TAPE

FIG. 3.2. Stimuli used by Baron (From "Mechanisms for pronouncing printed words: Use and acquisition" by J. Baron. In D. LaBerge & S. J. Samuels (Eds.), *Basic Processes in Readiing: Perception and Comprehension.* Hillsdale, N.J.: Lawrence Erlbaum Associates, 1977. Copyright 1977 by Lawrence Erlbaum Associates, Inc. Reprinted by permission.)

subjects were significantly faster for the orthographic than for the paired-associate condition. In a second experiment, the component letters were concatenated to form glyphic patterns, making it difficult to recognize the component letters. Even though the glyphic calligraphy was read faster than the words made up of discrete letters, the orthographic patterns were still read faster than the paired-associate patterns at asymptote. Although these results come from a novel paradigm, they support the conclusions of the other research we have reviewed. Words are not recognized as holistic units; letter analysis and the use of orthographic structure must mediate their recognition.

SUMMARY

There is now sufficient experimental evidence to argue that some kind of orthographic regularity facilitates the perception of letter strings. We have set out to determine the nature of this regularity and hope eventually to obtain substantial evidence for constructing a model of the reader's knowledge of orthographic regularity.

In concluding, we return to our concern for phonics instruction, which we expressed earlier in this chapter. If rapid word recognition is essential for competent reading and if orthographic regularity is important for recognition then reading instruction must ensure that students acquire an awareness of orthographic regularity. This awareness might occur simply from exposure to reading, regardless of reading ability. On the other hand, some readers, because of inefficient recognition strategies, might not acquire a sense of orthographic regularity or they might do so only after considerable remedial attention. We suspect that a full sense of orthographic regularity does not develop until at least the middle grades for some readers and, perhaps, much later for others. These are, of course, speculations that can be tested experimentally. We are, nevertheless, no longer willing to agree, as we once did, with Chall's (1967) statement:

> Once the pupil has learned to recognize in print the words he knows (because they are part of his speaking and listening vocabulary), any additional work on decoding is a sheer waste of time [p. 307].

REFERENCES

Anisfeld, M. A. Comment on "The role of grapheme–phoneme correspondence in the perception of words." *American Journal of Psychology*, 1964, *77*, 320–326.

Attneave, F. Psychological probability as a function of experimental frequency. *Journal of Experimental Psychology*, 1953, *46*, 81–86.

Baron, J. Successive stages in word recognition. In P. M. A. Rabbitt & S. Dornic (Eds.), *Attention and performance V*. New York: Academic Press, 1975.

Baron, J. Mechanisms for pronouncing printed words: Use and acquisition. In D. LaBerge & S. J. Samuels (Eds.), *Basic processes in reading: Perception and comprehension*. Hillsdale, N.J.: Lawrence Erlbaum Associates, 1977.

Baron, J., & Thurston, I. An analysis of the word-superiority effect. *Cognitive Psychology*, 1973, *4*, 207–228.

Brooks, L. *Visual pattern in fluent word identification*. Paper presented at the Conference on Reading, Brooklyn, N.Y., 1974.

Chall, J. *Learning to read: The great debate*. New York: McGraw–Hill, 1967.

Estes, W. K., Allmeyer, D. H., & Reder, S. M. Serial position functions for letter identification at brief and extended exposure durations. *Perception and Psychophysics*, 1976, *19*, 1–15.

Gibson, E. J., & Levin, H. *The psychology of reading*, Cambridge, Mass.: MIT Press, 1975.

Gibson, E. J., Osser, H., & Pick, A. D. A study of the development of grapheme–phoneme correspondences. *Journal of Verbal Learning and Verbal Behavior*, 1963, *2*, 142–146.

Gibson, E. J., Pick, A., Osser, H., & Hammond, M. The role of grapheme–phoneme correspondence in the perception of words. *American Journal of Psychology*, 1962, *75*, 554–570.

Gibson, E. J., Shurcliff, A., & Yonas, A. Utilization of spelling patterns by deaf and hearing subjects. In H. Levin & J. P. Williams (Eds.), *Basic studies on reading*. New York: Basic Books, 1970.

Gough, P. B. One second of reading. In J. F. Kavanagh & I. G. Mattingly (Eds.), *Language by ear and by eye: The relationships between speech and reading*. Cambridge, Mass.: MIT Press, 1972.

Groff, P. Research in brief: Shapes as cues to word recognition. *Visible Language*, 1975, *9*, 67–71.

Hirata, K., & Bryden, M. Tables of letter sequences varying in order of approximation to English. *Psychonomic Science*, 1971, *25*, 322–324.

Hockett, C. F. *A course in modern linguistics*. New York: Macmillan, 1958.

Hockett, C. F. Analysis of English spelling. In H. Levin, E. J. Gibson, A. L. Baldwin, J. J. Gibson, C. F. Hockett, H. N. Riccinti, & G. J. Suci (Eds.), *A basic research program on reading* (Cooperative Research Project No. 639). Ithaca, N.Y.: Cornell University and U. S. Office of Education, 1963.

Johnson, D. D. *Factors related to the pronunciation of vowel clusters* (Tech. Rep. 149). Madison: Wisconsin Research and Development Center for Cognitive Learning, 1970.

Johnson, D. D., & Venezky, R. L. Models for predicting how adults pronounce vowel digraph spellings in unfamiliar words (Tech. Rep. 346). Madison: Wisconsin Research and Development Center for Cognitive Learning, 1975.

Johnson, N. F. On the function of letters in word identification: Some data and a preliminary model. *Journal of Verbal Learning and Verbal Behavior*, 1975, *14*, 17–29.

Krueger, L. E. Search time in a redundant visual display. *Journal of Experimental Psychology*, 1970, *83*, 391–399.

Lefton, L. A., & Spragins, A. B. Orthographic structure and reading experience affect the transfer from iconic to short-term memory. *Journal of Experimental Psychology*, 1974, *103*, 775–781.

Lefton, L. A., Spragins, A. B., & Byrnes, J. English orthography: Relation to reading experience. *Bulletin of the Psychonomic Society*, 1973, *2*, 281–282.

Manelis, L. The effect of meaningfulness in tachistoscopic word perception. *Perception and Psychophysics*, 1974, *16*, 183–192.

Mason, M. Reading ability and letter search time: Effects of orthographic structure defined by single-letter positional frequency. *Journal of Experimental Psychology*, 1975, *104*, 146–166.

Massaro, D. W. Perception of letters, words, and nonwords. *Journal of Experimental Psychology*, 1973, *100*, 349–353.

Massaro, D. W. (Ed.). *Understanding language: An information-processing analysis of speech perception, reading, and psycholinguistics*. New York: Academic Press, 1975.

Massaro, D. W., & Schmuller, J. Visual features, perceptual storage, and processing time in reading. In D. W. Massaro (Ed.), *Understanding language: An information-processing analysis of speech perception, reading, and psycholinguistics*. New York: Academic Press, 1975.

Mayzner, M. S., & Tresselt, M. E. Tables of single-letter and bigram frequency counts for various word-length and letter-position combinations. *Psychonomic Monograph Supplements*, 1965, *1* (No. 2).

Mayzner, M. S., Tresselt, M. E., & Wolin, B. R. Tables of tetragram frequency counts for various word-length and letter-position combinations. *Psychonomic Monograph Supplements*, 1965, *1* (4, Whole No. 4). (a)

Mayzner, M. S., Tresselt, M. E., & Wolin, B. R. Tables of trigram frequency counts for various word-length and letter-position combinations. *Psychonomic Monograph Supplements*, 1965, *1* (3, Whole No. 3). (b)

McClelland, J. L. Preliminary letter identification in the perception of words and nonwords. *Journal of Experimental Psychology: Human Perception and Performance*, 1976, *2*, 80–101.

Miller, G. A., Bruner, J. S., & Postman, L. Familiarity of letter sequences and tachistoscopic identification. *Journal of General Psychology*, 1954, *5*, 129–139.

Miller, W. H. *The first R: Elementary reading today*. New York: Holt, Rinehart, and Winston, 1972.

Neisser, U. Visual search. *Scientific American*, June 1964, *210*, 94–102.

Novik, N., & Katy, L. High-speed visual scanning of words and non-words. *Journal of Experimental Psychology*, 1971, *91*, 350–353.

Reicher, G. M. Perceptual recognition as a function of meaningfulness of stimulus material. *Journal of Experimental Psychology*, 1969, *81*, 275–280.

Shannon, C. E. A mathematical theory of communication. *Bell System Technical Journal*, 1948, *27*, 379–423; 622–656.

Shannon, C. E. Prediction and entropy of printed English. *Bell System Technical Journal*, 1951, *30*, 50–64.

Shebilske, W. Reading eye movements from an information-processing point of view. In D. W. Massaro (Ed.), *Understanding language: An information processing analysis of speech perception, reading, and psycholinguistics*. New York: Academic Press, 1975.

Smith, F. *Understanding reading*. New York: Holt, Rinehart, and Winston, 1971.

Smith, N. B. *American reading instruction*. Newark, Del.: International Reading Association, 1965. (Originally published, 1934).

Thomas, H. Children's tachistoscopic recognition of words and pseudowords varying in pronounceability and consonant–vowel sequence. *Journal of Experimental Psychology*, 1968, *77*, 511–513.

Thompson, M. C., & Massaro, D. W. Visual information and redundancy in reading. *Journal of Experimental Psychology*, 1973, *98*, 49–54.

Thorndike, E. L., & Lorge, I. *The teacher's word book of 30,000 words*. New York: Columbia University, Teachers College, 1944.

Turvey, M. T. On peripheral and central processes in vision: Inferences from an information-processing analysis of masking with patterned stimuli. *Psychological Review*, 1973, *80*, 1–52.

Underwood, B. J., & Schulz, R. W. *Meaningfulness and verbal learning*. New York: Lippincott, 1960.

Venezky, R. L. English orthography: Its graphical structure and its relation to sound. *Reading Research Quarterly*, 1967, *2*, 75–106.

Venezky, R. L. *The structure of English orthography*. The Hague: Mouton & Co., 1970.

Wallach, M. A. Perceptual recognition of approximations to English in relation to spelling achievement. *Journal of Educational Psychology*, 1963, *54*, 57–62.

Whorf, B. L. *Language, thought, and reality*. Compiled by J. B. Carroll. Cambridge, Mass.: MIT Press, 1956.

Woodworth, R. S. *Experimental psychology*. New York: Holt, Rinehart and Winston, 1938.

Zipf, G. K. *The psycho-biology of language*, New York: Houghton Mifflin, 1935.

4
Dysfunctions in Reading Disability: There's More than Meets the Eye

Dennis F. Fisher
*U.S. Army Human Engineering Laboratory,
Behavioral Research Directorate*

Over the past decade there has been a resurgence of research in psychology directed toward reading. Unfortunately, the plethora of research efforts has led us to a theoretical morass in which any one theory provides, at best only a partial explanation of the reading process. For this reason, I attempt in this chapter to combine a rather simple model (Hochberg, 1970) with a much more complex model (LaBerge & Samuels, 1974) in order to show that by accepting them as complements, we have a means of describing basic reading processes as well as a means of identifying possible loci of dysfunctions apparent in disability.

In this chapter I describe some basic pattern-analyzing functions that occur during reading. These functions deal mainly with the analysis of typographical factors such as word shape, spacing, and orientation, but they are shown to interact with contextual variables. Although doubts have been expressed about whether these functions are what reading is all about, my own research efforts and those of Lefton, Smith, Kolers, McConkie, and Rayner should allay those doubts.

The data to be described concern reading and search speed, including eye movement dynamics that have been collected developmentally, with disabled readers and with adults alone. These data will be discussed in terms of the support they provide to a model of reading based on Hochberg's notions of peripheral and cognitive search guidance and LaBerge and Samuel's notion of automaticity. In addition, a case will be made for describing reading disability in relation to the model, particularly to dysfunction at the peripheral retinal processing level and at a more cognitive grapheme–phoneme transformation level.

TYPOGRAPHY—IMPLICATIONS FOR
DUAL PROCESSING

A few years ago, I became intrigued by two research efforts that examined the effects of typographical manipulations on reading speed. In the first of these (Hochberg, 1970; Hochberg, Levin, & Frail, 1966), children were asked to read mutilated text, for example, spaces between the words were filled with X's and $\&$'s. These symbols were added to eliminate word boundaries or spacing cues. The results were reported as indicating that the absence of word boundary cues interfered with reading fluency in the older children (fifth and sixth graders) but had little or no effect on the younger children's (first and second graders) reading speed or oral reading errors. The data were interpreted as indicating that the older children were processing rather large units of information that require word boundaries for differentiation, whereas the younger children were reading in a more elementary fashion (letter-by-letter or word-by-word) which requires fewer word boundary cues. It was hypothesized that the older children were at a "disadvantage" because they were developing more fluent and efficient skills through the use of the periphery and that the mutilated word boundary cues interfered with their strategy. Younger children were still bound to foveal processing, and therefore it did not matter to them that the boundary information was missing. A recent experiment (Fisher & Montanary, 1977) replicated and extended Hochberg's findings. Hochberg required both second and fifth graders to read second-grade paragraphs, and the primary changes in performance were restricted to fifth graders. Fisher and Montanary's extension required second and fifth graders to read both second- and fifth-grade paragraphs. The data indicated that both contextual level and typographical mutilation contributed to decreased reading speed, which was interpreted as supporting the notion of a greater dependence on peripheral processing with age. Second graders do use their peripheral vision when reading but to a lesser extent than do fifth graders. Additional theoretical notions expressed by Hochberg have been subsequently confirmed by other research efforts from my laboratory.

The second source of intriguing information came from the data reported by Smith (1969) and Smith, Lott, and Cronnell (1969), who used both reading and multiple-target search tasks to assess effects of word shape on reading and search efficiency. Their manipulations included altering letter size and type case within words. When all the letters of words were in the upper case, little difference was found in either reading speed or target search efficiency. However, when the upper and lower cases were alternated and when letter size was varied, reading speed decreased by over 20% and target search efficiency was reduced by 10%. The authors interpreted these data rather narrowly in terms of feature discriminability and claimed that recognition involves attending to sets of features and not simply to the shape of the word. Futhermore, they claimed that unfamiliarity with the mutilated word form should not adversely affect word identification unless discrimination of the features within the word is impaired.

In subsequent research, Coltheart and Freeman (1974) found even greater decrements in recognition performance when words mutilated typographically in the same ways that Smith's stimuli had been mutilated were exposed tachistoscopically. I hope to make the case later that one of the reasons for the greater decrement with tachistoscopic exposures is that subjects could not benefit in any way from a peripheral retinal prescreening of the words to be recognized. Further verification of word shape influences have been described by Rayner (1976) and Rayner and Hagelberg (1976).

The Role of Peripheral Processing

Having identified two types of typographical cues, word boundary and word shape, that affect normal reading efficiency, I hypothesized (Fisher, 1973) that the primary disruption caused when these cues are mutilated came at the peripheral visual processing level and hoped to find some interactive effects between the cues. The initial assessments of these two cues were made with adults who were asked to read paragraphs that typed in normal case, all upper case, or alternating upper and lower case. Additional manipulations were made on word boundaries: normal spacing; spaces filled with @'s or +'s, depending on the size of the letters; and no spaces at all, that is, all the letters run together. These two kinds of manipulations were combined factorially for a total of nine typographical combinations.

The data indicated that when word shape or word boundary information was disrupted, reading speed decreased. When both cues were mutilated (e.g., alternating case and no space), reading speed was reduced to less than 33% of normal. The fastest reading speeds were achieved only when word shape (i.e., capitals and alternating case) was changed and where word boundary information was available, and then decrements appeared in the range of 10%, confirming Smith's (1969) data on these conditions.

It was possible that these results were confounded with effects of comprehension demands. To get a "pure" indication of possible peripheral visual activity, a visual search task was adopted in which subjects were asked to find a critical word embedded in the paragraph. Fortunately, even though search performance was up to three times faster than reading, the general form of the performance curves mimicked the reading performance curves, indicating the appropriateness of the task as a tool for measuring peripheral to foveal processing strategies.

As part of the verification of a peripheral to foveal retinal processing strategy, I invoked a Mackworth (1965) "tunnel vision" hypothesis.

According to this hypothesis, as the peripheral visual field becomes more complex, there is a restriction or a construction in the amount of information available during fixation. I assumed, then, with the manipulations just described, that as the typography became more mutilated, less information per unit area would be processed. I expected that as the periphery was rendered dysfunctional, eye movements would occur more frequently and the information taken in during a fixation would decrease and be strictly foveal. Further, I assumed that the reduced comprehension demands of the search task would reduce the load of peripheral retinal processing, and I therefore expected to find larger saccades of shorter duration, indicating that larger sections of text were being per fixation while searching them while reading. This was what occurred.

Table 4.1 summarizes the eye movement scan path data for two typographical variations recorded during reading and search and shown in Fig. 4.1 and 4.2. Line discontinuities indicate pause at fixation locations. Fewer fixations located farther apart characterize reading and search of normal text (Fig. 4.1), whereas many fixations occur closer together while reading and searching severely mutilated typography (Fig. 4.2). Additionally, tasks demands such as comprehension are high when reading and low when searching for the single-word targets. Task demands can be assessed by comparing the right (search) and left (reading) portions of the figures. These data indicate that both typographical factors and comprehension demands affect the rate and amount of information processed per unit time, and they verify peripheral and foveal processing.

To investigate the developmental progression of peripheral and foveal processing, eye movements of third and fifth graders and adults were monitored while they read and searched text with case and space manipulations (Spragins, Lefton, & Fisher, 1976). The results indicated that over grade levels, about twice as many characters are processed per fixation during search as during reading and that increases in the size of the perceptual

TABLE 4.1
Eye Movement Data Summary for Scan-Path Records in Figures 4.1 and 4.2

Measure	Normal Case—Normal Space		Alternating Case—No Space	
	Reading	Search	Reading	Search
Rate (words/min)	180	256	36	148
Fixation duration (msec)	266	260	417	310
Words (read or searched)	66	47	116	59
Words per fixation	1.05	1.9	.27	1.00
Spaces (read or searched)	351	270	511	260
Spaces per fixation	5.6	10.8	1.2	4.4

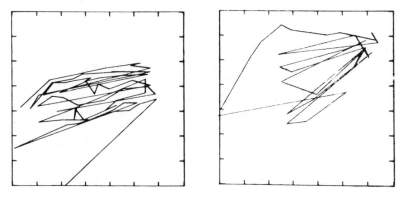

FIG. 4.1.   Eye movement scan path recordings of a subject reading (left) and searching (right) paragraphs with normal type and normal space.

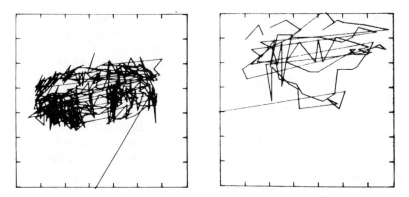

FIG. 4.2.   Eye movement scan path recordings of a subject reading (left) and searching (right) paragraphs with alternating case and no space.

span occur with experience. Fisher and Lefton (1976) found that when subjects at similar grade levels were asked to read these mutilations, differences between reading paragraphs with normal type and normal space and paragraphs with alternating case and no space increased directly with grade level. In other words, reading and search performance for the early readers was quite similar for both normal and mutilated paragraphs, whereas there were large differences, similar to those described by Fisher (1975), for the adults.

Reading Competence and Peripheral Processing

With experience, there seems to be an increasing dependence on the periphery to aid in the expansion of the perceptual span and to detect cues about where a subsequent eye movement should land. Early readers do not have these peripheral facilitating processing strategies and therefore must basically rely on a foveal, word-by-word, or even letter-by-letter, processing strategy. The Fisher and Lefton (1976) behavioral data were confirmed by the Spragins et al. (1976) eye movement data. Additionally, the latter data were interpreted as indicating that although development leads to increases in the size of the perceptual span, adults have a processing repertoire that allows them to resort to a word-by-word strategy when the task demands it. That is when reading the severe mutilations of no space and alternating case, the accomplished adult readers reverted to a more elemental word-by-word or letter-by-letter processing strategy, as reflected in their reading speeds and eye movement patterns, which were the same as those of inexperienced early readers.

Lefton and Haber (1974) demonstrated that as letters were presented at varied distances from fixation (i.e., 0° to 4°, or the spatial equivalent of 16 letters), reaction times for judging whether the letters were the same or different increased. Fisher and Lefton (1976) used a similar task to test the hypothesis that with development there is an increase in the dependency/ facility with which the periphery extracts information from the visual array. It was expected that the more peripherally eccentric letters would be reacted to faster in direct relationship to increasing age, but that this same relationship should also be reflected in overall reaction time (i.e., the younger the child, the slower the time). Both expectancies were confirmed, and support was found for the notion of increased dependency with development.

Implications about peripheral retinal involvement are not new, but they generally have gone without substantial notice. Poulton (1962), Mackworth (1965), and others, including Woodworth (1938), have demonstrated a substantial "tunnel vision effect" when the periphery is active and subjected to various manipulations of textual density. Tinker (1951) showed the relationship of reading speed to typographical features and contextual difficulty. The implications of those studies are that the effective perceptual span or peripheral retinal involvement may be totally subjective and sensitive to task demands and memory load.

Two experiments, variously reported by McConkie and Rayner (1973, 1975), Rayner (1975a, 1975b), and Rayner and McConkie (1976), sought to determine the degree to which reading efficiency is dependent on parafoveal or peripheral input. Both studies used eye movement monitoring, with text displayed on cathode ray tubes. The text was mutilated in such ways as to change critical word location (CWL) by changing the initial, final, and interior letters affecting word shape and identification at various locations away from fixation. With adults, the experimenters found that by changing typography around CWL at certain specifiable distances from fixation, semantic interpretation of the word was available from 1 to 6 character spaces from the fixation, whereas cues such as word shape and initial final letters were available from 7 to 12 spaces, or a maximum of from 4° to 5°.

Discussions of their findings by Rayner and McConkie tend to minimize the parafoveal involvement in efficient reading. They prefer a direct perception interpretation, or one in which fixations are spent primarily determining the nature of the text within the fixated region rather than hypothesizing what is coming next and directing subsequent eye movements. In short, Rayner and McConkie claimed that the information gotten from the periphery is of no predictive value.

McConkie and Rayner's primary argument is that word recognition functions are left up to processing at the fovea centralis, which is equal to approximately 1° to 2° of visual angle. They claim that normal peripheral involvement in reading processes directly mimics the falloff of the acuity function. That is, at 1°, 28', acuity is 75% of fixation; at 2°, 45', it is reduced to 45% and at 6°, 30', it is reduced to 25% of foveal fixation acuity (Taylor, 1965). I find little to disagree with in these figures or the imposed 5° limitation (the equivalent of about 20 letter spaces), except that an important distinction is being overlooked—the distinction between visual peripheral acuity and functional peripheral acuity. That is, the semantic and syntactic extraction may enable the reader to acquire global cues from the text, such as word boundaries and shapes, over an area that functionally exceeds the bounds established by psychophysical measures of peripheral visual acuity. The following three findings are evidence of this. The first comes from McConkie and Rayner (1973) themselves. Overall, their data indicated that the window size (distance from fixation to CWL) effects continue to facilitate reading efficiency to 45 characters (the equivalent of about 10 words). They interpreted the data as being artifacts of the experimental technique (i.e., CRT display changes) rather than as being effects of changes in the width of the field of attention. Second, using another variable window technique, Poulton (1962) indicated that reading speed decreased substantially when the window size was reduced from 14 to 5 words, substantially more than the rigid estimates of 12 to 14 letter spaces provided by McConkie and Rayner. Third, data reported by Lukiesh and Moss (1942) showed that the perceptual span is not necessarily related to acuity measures. That is, they found that the span remained relatively constant (at about 8 characters) as the type size was changed from 4 points (1 point = .0138 inches) to 18 points—a retinal image change of from 1° to 4.5° in linear visual angle.

Hochberg (1976) has also taken issue with McConkie and Rayner's interpretation of their data. Uncomfortable with the notion of simultaneous peripheral and foveal word recognition processes (a notion examined in more detail later), Hochberg used the span estimates of McConkie and Rayner and interpreted their data as indicating that peripheral processing of word shape helps the skilled reader to identify message strings of up to 12 to 14 characters long as a unit but only if they are highly redundant speech units. The four letters that are discerned foveally plus what is discerned peripherally aid in integrating distinctive features that assist, through preprocessing, recognition of the string as a unit.

I believe that Hochberg's description is a good approximation to what occurs when we read. The involvement of different strategies depends on the type of material being read and the contextual demands present in what we read. However, I believe McConkie and Rayner's estimate of 12 to 14 characters is too restrictive to account for contributions from peripheral preprocessing to normal reading.

The Encoding of Typographical Features

Another set of typographical manipulations has been described by Kolers and his associates. Emphasizing the importance of typography Kolers (1974, 1976) pointed out that, contrary to previous intuitions, 2 to 3 weeks (and even 1 year) after reading a passage people still remember and recognize its typographical characteristics. Kolers and Ostry (1974) showed that the typographical information normally assumed not to be part of the normal memory processes was retained for up to 4 weeks and that the typography aided semantic memory.

Kolers and Perkins (1969) examined reading speed and naming errors using a series of eight geometrical transformations of typography, including sentences left to right, sentences right to left, letters within words (left to right, right to left), and vertical inversions. From this work they arrived at a hierarchy of processing or pattern-analyzing difficulty. Kolers (1975b) went on to show that the combination of typographical or graphemic information and the linguistic features embedded in the textual material aided in the retention of meaningful information contained in the text. In that study he showed that reading typographical manipulations increased in efficiency (speed and comprehension) with practice on that typography. The study basically sought to discriminate between the semantic and graphemic encoding processes as single or mutual facilitators in the recognition of sentences. The data were interpreted as indicating that semantic components of textual material facilitated only short-term memory processes, whereas the graphemic encoding or pattern analysis process facilitated long-term memory processes. Graphemic, phonemic, and semantic processing were considered to be basically complementary.

In summary, a case has been made for the importance of typographical considerations on efficient reading processes, peripheral-retinal processing in effecting efficient reading performance, and the complementary nature of typographical (graphemic) and semantic processes.

MODELS: THE WHOLE IS EQUAL TO MORE THAN
THE SUM OF THE COMPLEMENTARY PARTS

Hochberg (1970) and Hochberg and Brooks (1970) described a rather simple two-stage model of reading. The first stage is peripheral search guidance (PSG) which was hypothesized to be a process activated during eye movements and tuned to pick up contours (physical cues and features) in the periphery. Information about important cues and features is then sent to a higher processing unit, cognitive search guidance (CSG), for integration and meaning extraction. As meaning increases the PSG mechanism interrogates larger areas of text. It is simply not the responsibility of PSG to handle contextual information beyond the point of feature discrimination of such elements as word boundary and word shape. It is likely that once these peripheral cues can no longer be discriminated, as is the case with mutilated word boundary and word shape, PSG is rendered dysfunctional, and search and reading become totally foveal activities. Thus foveal processing strategy is demonstrated by early reading performance and advanced reading performance with mutilated text.

Hochberg (1976) recently extended his original attentional model of reading to include the notion of implicit speech. In essence, he has become highly critical of traditional measures of parafoveal processing which are based on subjective reports, because he claims it may be the function of the visual periphery to "constrain the effects of subsequent foveal fixation (and not primarily to permit recognition on the basis of peripheral vision alone)[p. 401]." What he proposed and what I am advocating is that the peripheral processing amounts to a prescreening of the visual textual input. Hochberg went on to claim that the subjects' eye movements while reading are clearly being guided "solely" by peripheral indications of where they should look next and that the periphery is responsible only for picking up the grossest type of visual information. That is, the main function of peripheral viewing is to direct the eye to subsequent locations and, when the eye reaches that location, to provide a second view of important elements (which Hochberg considers to be speech strings). The complementary aspects of the PSG and CSG mechanisms aid the reader in changing strategies depending on typographical considerations, contextual constraints, and task demands.

LaBerge and Samuels (1974) also proposed an attentional model of reading. The model depends on stage analyses. According to the model, reading begins with decoding graphemic information and ends with interpretation of the contextual material. Initially, emphasis moves from feature detectors, to letter codes, to spelling pattern analyses, and eventually to a visual word-code analysis. In essence, the model proposes that with increasing exposure to graphemic information, attention may be directed to subsequent higher levels of processing, such as storing meaning, whereas the initial stages, no longer requiring attention, are operating automatically. That is, as normal readers experience more and more graphemic information, they become more sensitive to word shape and spelling pattern shape, and the processing of this visual verbal information becomes more automatic. Less attention is then necessarily dedicated to graphemic decoding skills, allowing higher-order processing stages to recoup more of the attentional capacity. However, if unfamiliar patterns are encountered, the attentional mechanisms can be redirected back to some more elemental stage (e.g., the feature detector or letter code stage) so that higher-order processing may be accomplished, even if at a slower rate, rather than be stymied by uninterpreted graphemic input (a reversion not unlike that described by Fisher, 1975, and Fisher and Lefton, 1976). For the disabled reader, breaking the graphemic code may represent an enormous task that keeps attention from ever being directed totally to higher-order processing.

Justifiably concerned with the unitizing of visual information, LaBerge and Samuels (1974) proposed that it takes place either within the visual system or at the phonological encoding level:

> For the experienced reader, the particular location used is optional. If he is reading easy material at a fast pace, he may select as visual units words or even word groups; if he is reading difficult material at a slow pace, he may select spelling patterns and unitize these into word units at the phonological level [p. 306].

For the accomplished reader, once the graphemic information is successfully processed by the initial visual memory system, it passes on to phonological memory for specific phonological encoding, then to episodic memory and response systems for either higher order interpretations or output.

I now describe in more detail the complementary nature of the Hochberg ideas of PSG and CSG and LaBerge and Samuels' idea of automaticity. Figure 4.3 shows the initial visual memory system in LaBerge and Samuels' model, with processing progressions from feature detectors, to letter codes, to spelling pattern codes, to visual word codes. At the left of the figure has been added what I consider to be a critical first stage in processing visual verbal information. This stage includes information flow from the peripheral retina to foveal processing. The peripheral input is at a "preawareness" level, but it is critical to gross cue screening and the subsequent determination of eye movement sequences. Once the peripheral information is brought into the fovea, feature detectors and attentional mechanisms take over. This is an important aspect of the PSG and CSG oculomotor control loop.

A more complete processing chain is represented in Figure 4.4. In this figure the same peripheral to foveal processing flow is shown. At the first fixation, visual memory and phonological memory systems are activated, which then put the CSG mechanism into operation. This CSG mechanism

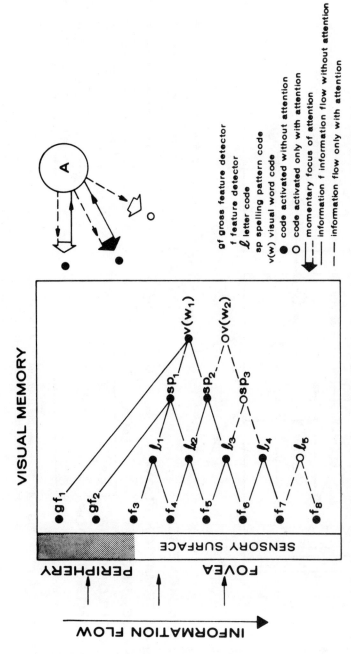

FIG. 4.3.   Model of the initial processing stage during reading incorporating peripheral retinal involvement and the first stages of automaticity. (Portions of this figure courtesy of LaBerge and Samuels, 1974.)

gf gross feature detector
f   feature detector
ℓ   letter code
sp spelling pattern code
v(w) visual word code
●   code activated without attention
○   code activated only with attention
➤   momentary focus of attention
      information f information flow without attention
      information flow only with attention

120

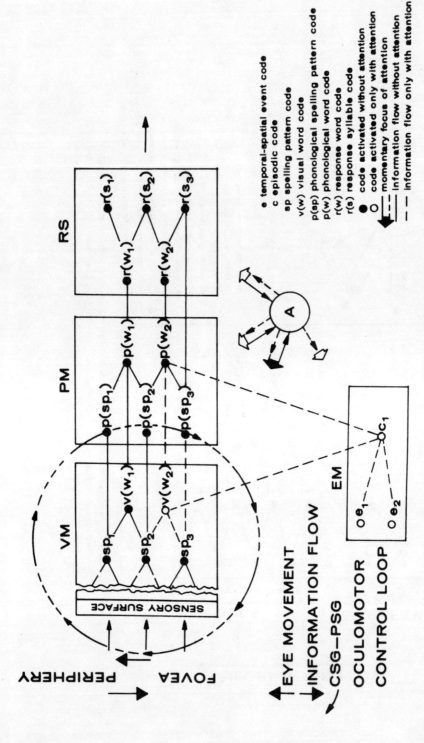

FIG. 4.4. More complete attentional model of informative processing during reading. Model incorporates eye movement sequencing and complementary PSG and CSG systems into an automatic processing sequence. (Portions of this figure courtesy of LaBerge and Samuels, 1974.)

fulfills two necessary functions: The first is to establish basic meaning, and the second is to provide PSG with clues to highly probable word shape and word length information that may appear farther along a line of text. Operationally, we see that with more difficult material (e.g., a chemistry textbook) there is a shrinking of the functional field of view and of eye movement travel extent. When comprehension demands are minimized, as in a search task, there is an overall expansion of the functional field of view and of eye movement travel extent. Developmentally, there are increases in size of the perceptual span and in the distance eye movements travel. These changes may well be interpreted as indicating that a greater use of PSG develops directly with the reader's ability to direct attention away from graphemic codes and, consequently, deal with larger portions of text, facilitating automaticity still further.

In short, I believe that an understanding of the complementary nature of PSG, CSG, and automaticity is critical to an understanding of the basic reading processes. I propose that prediction and hypothesis testing are aided in normal readers by the preprocessing of the periphery. These preprocessing capabilities become more proficient through exposure because less attention must be directed to decoding. That is, phonological and visual memory systems increasingly interact more efficiently, reducing the foveal processing load and enhancing peripheral retinal processing and automaticity. Without peripheral retinal involvement, unitization is encumbered and provides a likely first source of difficulty in reading disabilities. The second source of breakdown is at the grapheme–phoneme transformation point, where it is likely that the disabled reader's CSG mechanism functions improperly. The PSG system of dyslexics may remain constrained or in a state of "functional tunnel vision." These constraints put a heavy load on foveal and phonological processes, resulting in little or no feedback from CSG to PSG. Consequently, there is word-by-word reading, with many regressive eye movements (indicative of memory overload).

LET'S READ: IMPLICATIONS FOR PREPROCESSING AND AUTOMATICITY

In this section of the chapter I provide an analysis of how task, context, and typography affect peripheral retinal processing, how that processing subsequently affects efficient and rapid information search (as must occur during reading), and how automaticity develops with experience. The relationship of input variables, experiential factors, and other characteristics of the reader as a dynamic information processor are described.

Reading is accomplished as follows. The initial word in the text is fixated, with from 14 to 45 additional letters being available to the right of fixation, most at less than optimal clarity, through peripheral retinal processing. The individual then makes a second fixation based on the identification of information taken in during the first fixation and localization of additional cues picked up from the periphery. Meanwhile, the initial, foveally fixated word has been attended to and has passed from the early visual system, hopefully intact as a unit, to the visual cortex and to phonological/ articulatory language transformation areas. A previous fixation may have indicated that a "meaningful" word or at least a long one would appear subsequently in the text, and it is fixated next. That new and seemingly interesting shape, located about one or two words away from the center of the initial fixation, may not have provided very much meaningful information because of acuity constraints. However, because of its size and shape, it allowed for an ever so slight amount of preprocessing even across 2, 3 or more fixations. Increasing amounts of preprocessing occur as more meaning is established. Subsequent fixations are then directed by higher-order process-ing and peripheral retinal information, which then serves to guide the oculomotor system (see Fig. 4.4). The accuracy of eye movements and their angular extent and fixation duration are determined by experience, attention, and level of automaticity.

An eye fixation duration during reading may last from approximately 250 msec to as long as 400 msec, depending on experience and text difficulty. An eye movement take approximatley 20 to 40 msec to execute and is most likely to terminate at a location previewed on a prior fixation by the periphery. Fully 50 msec prior to the beginning of that movement, the muscles of the eye begin to tighten and prepare for the movement itself. This muscle tightening, or shearing, along with smearing and masking, forces the receptors to discard the information in the visual array. Similarly, after the eye movement another 50 msec are required for the receptors to recover. Iconic storage preserves visual information for about 250 msec. Iconic storage is not an isolated or laboratory process but one that function during reading to preserve the image while the shearing forces render the reader functionally blind (Latour, 1962; Volkman, 1962, 1976). Of the original 250 msec fixation duration, only about 150 msec dedicated to picking up visual information.

With the normal perceptual span of about 1.1 words, or about 6 to 8 letters, the entire 150 msec is not needed for information processing. According to Sperling (1960, 1963, 1967), after some initial starting time, only about 10 msec per item is needed on an item-by-item basis (assuming that unitization is not taking place here). Because of response limitations, only 4 to 6 items are reportable out of an available 12 or 16-item array. Looking at normal masking functions, maximum "maskability" occurs at about 100 msec and then levels off. Therefore, there are 50 to 75 msec left of potential processing time, which may well be dedicated to integration or to peripheral retinal processing.

Additional time may be available depending on the amount of attention dedicated to decoding, representing the automaticity level achieved by the reader. That is, it is possible that processing words as wholes takes place in a very brief time period at the foveal level, consequently providing more time for the periphery to act on subsequent information. Although many investigations employed tachistoscopic displays that present information in isolation and require activities somewhat removed from reading under normal circumstances, experiments (e.g., Lefton, 1973) have shown that with experience there is an increasing sensitivity to subsequent levels of approximation to English. This increasing sensitivity can be thought of as enhancing predictability and perceptual span. In other words, priority changes occur as the reader becomes more familiar with printed text and automaticity increases.

In summary, I have discussed the peripheral to foveal processing sequence, automaticity, and the grapheme to phoneme transformation stage. The last is important in acquiring and integrating meaning, as well as in completing the circuit between the PSG and CSG mechanisms. This final "main way station" is critical. For the normal reader, it is probably located in the left temporal hemisphere, particularly interconnecting at Broca's area and Wernicke's area. It is there, in the language areas, that graphemes are transformed into phonemes and subsequently transformed into meaning devoid of syntactic constraint. Meaning is constructed of bits and pieces of the visual array through complementary loop processing of the peripheral and foveal input systems. As more meaning is constructed out of successful grapheme to phoneme transformations, the periphery is free, due to fewer attentional constraints, to examine larger regions of text.

I find the LaBerge–Samuels analysis of visual memory, phonological memory, episodic memory, and semantic memory to be acceptable. I also believe, however, that any model of reading is inadequate that excludes peripheral and foveal involvement in the recognition process and the shift in priority given to each that occurs with experience. I therefore hypothesize that the Hochberg and the LaBerge–Samuels models are complementary. There is time during a normal fixation–eye movement sequence for all the normal word recognition processes to analyze words on the basis of familiarity, transitional probability, feature discriminability, and semantic and syntactic assessments. By degrading textual material by removing spaces or by other typographic mutilations, the peripheral perceptual span can be reduced in normal readers. Under such conditions, readers adopt a letter-by-letter processing strategy that mimics that used by first- and second-grade readers. In the rest of this chapter I maintain that disabled readers always mimic first- and second-grade readers, not in foveal input processing, but primarily in dysfunctioning peripheral retinal processing and in grapheme to phoneme transformation.

CHARACTERISTICS OF READING DISABILITY: TWO LEVELS OF DYSFUNCTION?

Disabled readers are taken to be individuals who show no uncorrected visual anomalies, no severe emotional instability, no intellectual deficit, and no gross neurological dysfunction. They appear to be normal in every way and may possess special artistic or musical ability. They lack one very important skill, however, and that is the ability to read. Using the ideas discussed and developed earlier, I will try to arrive at a way of describing basic reading processes and identifying possible loci of dysfunctions in reading disability. The peripheral retinal level and the phonological level at which graphemes are transformed to phonemes will be heavily emphasized. I believe there are four areas of primary concern: language sensitivity, perceptual deficit, peripheral involvement, and pattern-analyzing processes.

Language Sensitivity

Guthrie (1973a) found that even though disabled readers may demonstrate inferior syntactic processing and comprehension skill, the inferiority may be a product of an inadequate early stage of processing, for example, decoding. Closer scrutiny of syntactic processing (Guthrie, 1973b) revealed no differences between normal and disabled readers on the use of nouns, verbs, modifiers, or functors. Kolers (1975a) examined the nature of pattern-analyzing ability in good and poor readers. Using good and poor readers who differed by about 5 years in reading grade level, he found that the predominant errors made in reading normal and reversed text were substitutional in nature, that the substitutions were in the same form–class, and that these accounted for 60% of all errors. However, both groups made a high percentage of these substitution errors (75% for poor readers and 79% for good readers). From these data, Kolers countered the hypothesis that reading disability results from attending too closely to the graphemic structure at the sacrifice of semantic information. These data showed the opposite to be true. That is, Kolers found that it was the good reader rather than the poor reader who was more sensitive to features of the typography, whereas both groups maintained a high degree of semantic sensitivity.

A language sensitivity deficit of another kind has been described by Shallice and Warrington (1975), Richardson (1975) and Newcomb and Marshall (1973). All have described case studies in which the disabled reader was unable to process abstract words nearly as efficiently as concrete words. These findings were interpreted as indicating a conceptual or cognitive deficiency that makes it very difficult for the disabled reader to place a meaningful tag on abstract words with no associated image. Young normal readers might well be expected to have such deficits in formal operations. Yet the previously listed case studies found this deficit in adult dyslexics, and Satz, Rardin, and Ross (1971) found it in 8- to 11-year-old dyslexics.

Perceptual Deficit

Until recently, the cause of reading deficiency has been attributed to general visual perceptual deficits in form orientation and spatial discrimination (Frostig, 1968; Orton, 1937) and, with few exceptions (e.g., Benton, 1962), left unchallenged. Stanley, Kaplan, and Poole (1975) examined spatial transformations in normal and disabled readers and failed to find any visual spatial deficit. In fact, Kerschner (1975b) pointed out that deficits reported as perceptual and remediated through perceptual motor training and Frostig-type techniques are likely to be unrelated to reading. Larsen and Hammill (1975) went further and found no correspondence between perceptual deficit and reading ability. Likewise, Downing (1973) questioned the existence of a perceptual deficit and reasoned that the primary processing deficit was in higher cognitive processes, primarily in the ability to recognize and interpret grapheme–phoneme correspondences.

Velluntino, Steger, and Kandel (1972) were also interested in examining the perceptual deficit hypothesis and failed to verify it. Their data suggested a grapheme–phoneme correspondence problem. Poor readers copied as well as normal readers but tended to make more errors in reading than in copying. The authors' contention was that the visual system was adeqaute but that the integration of the visual information was poor:

> It is our contention that poor readers are able to process visual representations as well as normals but find it difficult to integrate and/or retrieve the verbal equivalents of such input. We are of the opinion that "perceptual" errors which do occur in word recognition are more than likely a manifestation rather than the basic cause of reading disorder [p. 113].

It is intriguing that after 25 years or more of assumption, perceptual deficits related to reading disability can no longer be identified. Generally overlooked, however, were iconic storage characteristics of disabled readers. Although children have been found to exhibit iconic storage exceeding the 250 msec duration of adults (Gummerman & Gray, 1972), one contention is that an even longer icon is evidenced by disabled readers, which causes inefficient processing into short-term memory (Stanley & Hall, 1973). One way to investigate iconic storage is to examine performance on a task in which processing time is limited (to 250 msec or less) by a random pattern mask. If performance in the no-mask condition proves to be far superior to performance in the mask condition, there might be one indication of inefficient perceptual processing.

Fisher and Frankfurter (1977) made just such a comparison of disabled readers with normal readers of the same age and with younger children of the same reading level on a backward masking task. They were presented 4 by 4 matrices in which 2, 4, or 6 letters appeared for 200 msec. The experiment was designed to examine location and identification capabilities, as well as iconic processing efficiency, by comparing mask and no-mask performance. In all cases, the disabled readers performed at or above the level of the control groups, and differences between mask and no-mask performance were greater for the control groups than for disabled readers. Granted, the task was not reading, but it did allow for an assessment of two vital attack skills: localization and identification.

It may be that the disabled readers outperformed their matched counterparts because they were thoroughly familiar with and could easily identify single letters, and that was what the task required, whereas the normal readers were advancing away from letters to words. In addition, the stimuli were all presented within the region of foveal viewing—less than 2.5° of visual angle. Had the matrix been much larger or had it contained trigrams or larger words that required higher-order processing at the grapheme–phoneme level, we might have obtained a substantially different outcome.

Peripheral Retinal Processing

The previously described data of Fisher (1973, 1975), Fisher and Lefton (1976), Lefton and Fisher (1976), Spragins, Lefton, and Fisher (1976), and McConkie and Rayner (1975) indicated the degree to which peripheral retinal involvement was hypothesized to affect reading performance. Others have also hinted at this processing function. Kerschner (1975a) reviewed laterality functions in good and poor readers. He touched lightly on data showing that poor readers were as accurate as good readers in identifying foveally presented stimuli. However, when presentation was restricted to one hemisphere (specifically, presented to the right visual field), retarded readers performed more poorly than normal readers. Although he did not report how far into the periphery he examined, I believe his findings are in accord with a peripheral retinal processing decrement interpretation. Similar results were noted by Marcel and Rajan (1975), who spread stimuli out to 3° on either side of fixation and found that good and poor reader differences were apparent in the right visual field only.

Bradshaw (1974, 1975) discussed some very interesting points related to the connection between contextual complexity and peripheral retinal involvement. He expressed the view that semantic information may be availabe from words beyond the one currently being fixated, and that although it is low level, it enhances visual verbal processing. Marcel (1974) also examined the effective visual field and the use of context in fast and slow readers and similarly concluded that a more effective and efficient use of context tends to enlarge the effective visual field.

This expansion may come about in two ways: first, by "priming," or early sampling or preprocessing, which reduces the overall load on visual recognition processes (preprocessing enhances automaticity), and second, by using the reduced load to process more material faster or by redirecting attention to other reading tasks such as meaning extraction.

One final point. Mickish (1974) examined first-grade children for word boundary awareness by running words together and having the children mark off word boundaries. Her data provided evidence that first graders "had little idea of what words are.... as subjects became better readers, they were better at marking word boundaries [p. 19]." These data may be taken as additional evidence for undeveloped peripheral retinal processing capability in early readers, with similar effects being highly likely in older disabled readers as evidence of dysfunctional peripheral processing. In short, as the processing load increases, the perceptual span decreases. If this were the case for the disabled reader, there would be an increasing load on memory because all the information must be taken in through the fovea if the periphery is dysfunctional. With total foveal processing, as shown in Table 4.1, the eye movements would be close together, very frequent, and involve many regressions. This is exactly what Zangwill and Blakemore (1972) found.

Pattern Analyzing Functions

A primary aspect of pattern analyzing occurs at the grapheme to phoneme encoding stage. Baron and McKillop (1975) were concerned with the breakdown in two processing strategies. The first of these is strictly visual and is analogous to the peripheral processing stage described earlier. The second is the grapheme to phoneme encoding strategy. Reading disability was attributed to a breakdown in either or both of these strategies.

Kolers (1975a) examined performance of good and poor readers while they were reading normal and reversed text. He found that both good and poor readers performed about equally well on tests involving language use and grammar but that the poor readers were markedly retarded in aspects of graphemic analysis (pattern-analyzing functions). In all cases involving unfamiliar *rN* transformations (i.e., right to left letter orientation in text that was read left to right), poor readers did worse. Moreover, poor readers gained little information between pattern-analyzing familiarization stages and pattern recognition stages. Because the memory of poor readers for semantic usage was little impaired, the ability to anayze words incorporated in unfamiliar typographic patterns was considered to be the locus of the reading disability. Kolers (1975a) interpreted these data as indicating "that the poor reader is not impaired at the linguistic or semantic level *nor at the peripheral optical level* but at the graphemic pattern-analyzing level [p. 290, italics added]." I am in basic agreement with Kolers except for one issue—his exclusion of the peripheral optical level. He has never tested it.

Staller and Sekuler (1975) used the Kolers transformations in a letter-naming task and found that both normal and disabled readers performed at the same level in naming letters that were individually spaced and reverse oriented (*rN*—right to left letters that were read left to right). However, when the letters were normally oriented, the normal readers did better than the disabled readers. The authors accounted for these letter data primarily on the basis that the normal reader gained access to the letters from peripheral cues, whereas the disabled reader did not. With unfamiliar orientation, the periphery provided little assistance to either group. (It should be noted that in previously described naming tasks, no difference appeared between normal and disabled readers in simple graphemic identification.)

In general, Kolers (Kolers & Perkins, 1975) discounted the necessity for stimulus generalization, tuned detectors, and preprocessing stages. In fact, in the case of *rM* transformations (left to right letters that were read right to left), the reader reading leftward would read a word such as *not* or *saw* in the familiar rightward direction (not or saw) rather than in the prescribed leftward direction (*ton* or *was*). Reversal errors of this type are often attributed to errors in selective attention, such as inappropriate switching mechanisms. Kolers and Perkins took issue with this point of view and interpreted them as slips from the nonstandard orientation to another. They concluded (1975): "These kinds of phenomena are seen as cases in which a familiar and well-inculcated form of the pattern analysis runs off in an almost wholly automatic way, taking precedence over the less familiar and less practiced skill [p. 264]."

Summary

This large body of data indicates that the primary source of disability in dyslexia is at some neurological input transformation location, probably Broca's area where visual graphemic information is transformed or encoded into its phonemic counterpart. The second source of disability is at the peripheral retinal processing level. It is at these two primary points of dysfunction that instructional and remedial practices should be concentrated. I believe, furthermore, that dysfunction at these two locations are exemplified by two distinct behavioral characteristics: dyslexia and hyperlexia. That is, the dyslexic is an individual who cannot read but who can understand, whereas the hyperlexic, as described by Mehegan and Driefuss (1972), is one who can read very proficiently at a very early age but who has little or no comprehension capability. The former probably results from very low-level peripheral processing and mediocre language area processing, whereas the latter reflects an intact peripheral processing system and a dysfunctional semantic extraction system. To describe etiology is quite another matter and may include organismic responses to, for example, perinatal events (Balow, Rubin, & Rosen, 1976).

INSTRUCTION AND REMEDIATION

My interpretation of this large body of data as providing evidence for dual-process dysfunction attributes the primary site for dysfunctioning to be at the grapheme–phoneme transformation point (neurologically, at Broca's or Wernicke's area). It should be noted that all the evidence indicates that disabled readers have at their disposal all the immediate perceptual processing and memory available to normal readers. This is especially important because it indicates that the functions of this area may be particularly susceptible to compensatory instructional activity. Such activity may include practice and overpractice on grapheme–phoneme correspondence activities and other word-related skills. This practice is a necessity in order to approach automaticity. Given the potential of disabled readers, they will then have at their grasp the opportunity to build a very large repertoire of words and grapheme–phoneme recognition skills. However, because of the second dysfunction proposed, these skills must strictly operate on foveal input, without the benefit of normal preprocessing.

I have hypothesized that the second site of dysfunction in the disabled reader is at the peripheral retinal processing level. It is not dysfunctional in the sense of acuity, but it is dysfunctional in the sense that information in the periphery is not brought into awareness. This dysfunction, then, forces the reader to be dependent primarily on foveal input.

Many have expressed cautions against using eye movement recordings to diagnose a disabled reader (e.g., Bond & Tinker, 1973), and I concur. Such use of eye movement measures is foolhardy. However, once the diagnosis has been made on the basis of other behavioral inventories, patterns similar to those reported by Zangwill and Blakemore (1972) might be found. That is, eye movements of disabled readers tend to be very short in angular extent, have relatively long fixation times, and show many regressions. The closeness of the fixations might be attributed to the lack of peripheral guidance of subsequent eye movements, the long duration might be attributed to the inability to integrate the graphemic pattern into its phonemic counterpart, and the many regressions might be attributed to the overload on memory necessitated by processing many small pieces of information. The second of these characteristics might be altered through compensatory training activity. However, the first prohibits disabled readers from ever becoming accomplished readers. The expansion of the nonfunctional visual periphery is highly unlikely, and therefore disabled readers must remain disabled. They will never acquire effective, efficient reading skills because they are limited by an elemental, word-by-word reading strategy caused by strictly foveal input. However, by increasing their repertoire of words (sight vocabulary) and the efficiency of their word recognition skills, they should approach the level of automated processing that would at least allow them to move down a line of print quickly. Some disabled readers reportedly "read" up to 200 words a minute.

Reorientation and Instructional Implications

I believe that before procedures for instructional remediation can be defined, a problem must be solved and a shift in emphasis must be accomplished. The problem is that of defining and describing the specific learning disability. Glenn (1975) recently described "the myth of the learning disabled child." He claimed that one of the principal problems in labeling a child as learning disabled is the unawareness of mixed symptoms. The literature is replete with descriptions of learning disabilities that generally refer to children who have difficulty understanding or using spoken or written language. Some samples of the terms used to describe a learning disabled child are: *dyslexic, educationally handicapped, emotionally disturbed, learning disabled, minimal brain damaged, organic brain syndrome, perceptually handicapped, specific learning disability, specific reading disability*, or nearly any term but *mentally retarded, gifted*, or *normal*. Any and all of these and others have been used synonymously and discriminatorily. Of 500 "learning disabled children" Glenn found 67% with visual perceptual difficulties, 65% with anxiety syndrome, 44% with mixed laterality, 39% with poor concentration, 31% with low frustration tolerance, 27% with hyperactivity, 22% with speech disorders, 21% with hypoactivity, 21% with withdrawal, and 12% with aggressiveness. And none of these possible symptoms include cognitive disorders.

I advocate a shift in importance or emphasis from the perceptual to the cognitive—in other words, from input processing to integration. The only evidence of dysfunctional perceptual processing is that of dysfunctional peripheral retinal processing. Expansion of the perceptual span or training enhancement of the right visual field input to the left hemisphere is basically impossible and impractical. It is therefore imperative that concentration be shifted to the direct enhancement of language-based skills.

I would like to summarize what has been described here and previously (Fisher, 1976) and, at the same time, make some projections about what might be incorporated in instructional procedures, while expressing some related concerns.

1. Disabled readers know the letters and can locate them.

2. When two graphemes are put together, disabled readers have difficulty generating the appropriate phonemic representation (e.g., /ba/ for *bar*).

3. With appropriate practice, disabled readers will learn appropriate grapheme–phoneme correspondences and will be able to say appropriate letter names and blends. Additional problems are presented when disabled readers encounter new and infrequent words, especially when a one-to-one grapheme–phoneme correspondence does not exist. Emphases on such correspondences and, perhaps more important, on orthographics (see the Venezky and Massaro chapter in this volume) are critical.

4. When subsequent stages of "proficiency" are attained—through phonics reinforcement and repetition—disabled readers will still be processing text word-by-word, an elementary processing strategy. This may be due to a dysfunctional peripheral visual processing strategy that exhibits itself in inappropriate attack skills (e.g., making many eye movements with fixations of long duration).

5. The truly dyslexic or reading disabled child, as opposed to a slow reading child, will never learn to read in the sense of exhibiting the efficient left to right information flow evidenced in normal reading adults. Compensatory instructional activities in decoding and increasing the vocabulary repertoire using words in isolation are appropriate, especially since such activity may enable disabled readers to become more "automatic" in word recognition and allow them to eventually move across a line of print, word-by-word, at up to about 200 wpm. Glenn (1975) also called for a relearning of the specifics of the disorder so as to make the child competent, but he maintained that such a call is overly ambitious, idealistic, and consequently naive.

6. If disabled readers are to attain even this degree of proficiency, we must get rid of diagram, block, and form training and three-dimensional feature discrimation—tactile and visual—and invoke an intense remediation program of phonics, including advanced grapheme–phoneme correspon-dence, letter strings, and words in both auditory and visual modalities. Glenn (1975) criticized Frostig's Developmental Test of Visual Perception, the Illinois Test of Psycholinguistic Abilities, and other similar tests. It is not only that these tests measure different things (low intercorrelations), but they measure behavior that is probably unrelated to reading behavior or learning disabilities. Reorienting is imperative! It must be done at the classroom level. Teachers must discard perceptual-motor and physical programs and provide children with instruction in language-centered programs such as phonics and other direct approaches to language-based skill acquisition.

7. What is needed is more than a descriptive, gobbledegook-based analysis of specific dyslexia and learning disorders. It must be understood that dyslexia cannot be cured—the brain will not stand for that. But the brain is

susceptible to compensatory training that will allow the dyslexic to process visual verbal information.

8. From educators of children with special problems there seems to be an overwhelming cry for corrective procedures. These teachers and reading specialists seek appropriate tools for providing compensatory reading instruction. The majority of the tools now available are either inappropriate and a waste of time or not tested fully (Miller, 1976, c.f. Bateman, this volume). What is needed is a tool directed toward basic language acquisition skills. To be optimal, the tools should be easily administered and not time consuming.

9. With such great concern for the disabled reader, what about accomplished, skilled early-reading children? What are they doing right, even with so much less effort devoted to them? Another point in favor of reorientation!

10. Question the concept of "perceptually handicapped." If the children are perceptually handicapped, how is it that they often show high degrees of artistic ability, both graphic and musical?

11. Beware! In describing learning and reading disabilities, it is often common to describe the cause of disability by attacking the symptoms. This is not enough, however. For over 50 years we have acquired little understanding of the reading process and have from 40% to 50% of school-age children reading below grade level, 10% of whom are boys who are severely disabled readers.

12. Question the two-stage peripheral to foveal notion and its analogous peripheral to cognitive process stream and automaticity. If it doesn't work, discard it and move on. If it works, use it!

REFERENCES

Balow, B., Rubin, R., & Rosen, M. J. Perinatal events as precursors of reading disability. *Reading Research Quarterly*, 1976, *11*, 36–71.

Baron, J., & McKillop, B. J. Individual differences in speed of phonemic analysis, visual analysis, and reading. *Acta Psychologica*, 1975, *39*, 91–96.

Benton, A. Dyslexia in relation to form perception and directional sense. In J. Money (Ed.), *Reading disability: Progress and research needs in dyslexia*. Baltimore: Johns Hopkins University Press, 1962.

Bond, G. L., & Tinker, M. A. *Reading difficulties: Their diagnosis and correction* (3rd ed.). Englewood Cliffs, N.J.: Prentice-Hall, 1973.

Bradshaw, J. L. Peripherally presented and unreported words may bias the perceived meaning of a centrally fixated homograph. *Journal of Experimental Psychology*, 1974, *103*, 1200–1202.

Bradshaw, J. L. Three interrelated problems in reading: A review. *Memory & Cognition*, 1975, *3*, 123–134.

Coltheart, M., & Freeman, R. Case alternatives impairs word identification. *Bulletin of the Psychonomic Society*, 1974, *3*, 102–104.

Downing, J. Cognitive factors in dyslexia. *Child Psychiatry and Human Development*, 1973, *4*, 115–120.

Fisher, D. F. *Reading as visual search: A look at processes.* Unpublished doctoral dissertation, University of Rochester, 1973.

Fisher, D. F. Reading and visual search. *Memory & Cognition*, 1975, *3*, 188–196.

Fisher, D. F. Perceptual processes in learning. *Proceedings of the Seventh Annual Western Washington State College Symposium on Learning*, 1976, *7*, 5–31.

Fisher, D. F., & Frankfurter, A. Normal and disabled readers can locate and identify letters: Where is the perceptual deficit? *Journal of Reading Behavior*, 1977, *9*, 31–43.

Fisher, D. F., & Lefton, L. A. Peripheral information extraction: A developmental examination. *Journal of Experimental Child Psychology*, 1976, *21*, 77–93.

Fisher, D. F., & Montanary, W. E. Spatial and contextual factors in beginning reading: Evidence for PSG–CSG complements to developing automaticity? *Memory & Cognition*, 1977, *5*, 247–251.

Frostig, M. Visual modality, research and practice. In H. K. Smith (Ed.), *Perception and reading*. Newark, Del.: International Reading Association, 1968.

Glenn, H. W. *The myth of the learning disabled child. Elementary School Journal*, 1975, *75*, 357–361.

Gummerman, K., & Gray, C. R. Age, iconic storage, and visual information processing. *Journal of Experimental Child Psychology*, 1972, *13*, 165–170.

Guthrie, J. T. Models of reading and reading disability. *Journal of Educational Psychology*, 1973, *65*, 9–18. (a)

Guthrie, J. T. Reading comprehension and syntactic responses in good and poor readers. *Journal of Educational Psychology*, 1973, *65*, 294–299. (b)

Hochberg, J. Components of literacy: Speculation and exploratory research. In H. Levin & J. P. Williams (Eds.), *Basic studies on reading*. New York: Basic Books, 1970.

Hochberg, J. Toward a speech–plan eye-movement model of reading. In R. A. Monty & J. W. Senders (Eds.), *Eye movements and psychological processes*. Hillsdale, N.J.: Lawrence Erlbaum Associates, 1976.

Hochberg, J., & Brooks, V. Reading as intentional behavior. In H. Singer & R. Ruddell (Eds.), *Theoretical models and process of reading*. Newark, Del.: International Reading Association, 1970.

Hochberg, J., Levin, H., & Frail, C. *Studies of oral reading: VII. How interword spaces affect reading*. Unpublished report, Cornell University, 1966.

Kerschner, J. R. Reading and laterality revisited. *Journal of Special Education*, 1975, *9*, 269–279. (a)

Kerschner, J. R. Visual-spatial organization and reading: Support for a cognitive-development interpretation. *Journal of Learning Disabilities*, 1975, *8*, 9–16. (b)

Kolers, P. A. Remembering trivia. *Language and Speech*, 1974, *17*, 324–336.

Kolers, P. A. Pattern-analyzing disability in poor readers. *Development Psychology*, 1975, *11*, 282–290. (a)

Kolers, P. A. Specificity of operations in sentence recognition. *Cognitive Psychology*, 1975, *7*, 289–306. (b)

Kolers, P. A. Reading a year later. *Journal of Experimental Psychology: Human Learning and Memory*, 1976, *2*, 554–565.

Kolers, P. A., & Ostry, D. J. Time course of loss of information regarding pattern analyzing operations. *Journal of Verbal Learning and Verbal Behavior*, 1974, *13*, 599–612.

Kolers, P. A., & Perkins, D. N. Orientation of letters and errors and their recognition. *Perception and Psychophysics*, 1969, *5*, 265–270.

Kolers, P. A., & Perkins, D. N. Spatial and ordinal components of form perception and literacy. *Cognitive Psychology*, 1975, *7*, 228–267.

LaBerge, D., & Samuels, S. J. Toward a theory of automatic information processing in reading. *Cognitive Psychology*, 1974, *6*, 293–323.

Larsen, S. C., & Hammill, D. C. The relationship of selected visual perceptual abilities to school learning. *Journal of Special Education*, 1975, *9*, 281–291.

Latour, P. L. Visual threshold during eye movements. *Vision Research*, 1962, *2*, 261–262.

Lefton, L. A. Guessing and the order of approximation effect. *Journal of Experimental Psychology*, 1973, *101*, 401–403.

Lefton, L. A., & Fisher, D. F. Information extraction during visual search: A developmental progression. *Journal of Experimental Child Psychology*, 1976, *22*, 346–361.

Lefton, L. A., & Haber, R. N. Information extraction from different retinal locations. *Journal of Experimental Psychology*, 1974, *102*, 975–980.

Lukiesh, M., & Moss, F. *Reading as a visual task.* New York: Von Nostrand, 1942.

Mackworth, N. H. Visual noise causes tunnel vision. *Psychonomic Science*, 1965, *3*, 67–68.

Marcel, T. The effective visual field and the use of context in fast and slow readers of two ages. *British Journal of Psychology*, 1974, *65*, 479–492.

Marcel, T., & Rajan, P. Lateral specialization for recognition of words and faces in good and poor readers. *Neuropsychologia*, 1975, *13*, 487–497.

McConkie, G. W., & Rayner, K. *The span of the effective stimulus during fixations in reading.* Paper presented at the meeting of the American Educational Research Association, New Orleans, February, 1973.

McConkie, G. W., & Rayner, K. The span of the effective stimulus during a fixation in reading. *Perception and Psychophysics*, 1975, *17*, 578–586.

Mehegan, C. C., & Driefuss, F. E. Hyperlexia. *Neurology*, 1972, *22*, 1105–1111.

Mickish, V. Childrens' perceptions of written word boundaries. *Journal of Reading Behavior*, 1974, *6*, 19–22.

Miller, W. H. *Reading correction kit.* West Nyack, N.Y.: The Center for Applied Research in Education (Prentice-Hall), 1976.

Newcomb, F., & Marshall, J. C. Stages in recovery from dyslexia following a left cerebral abcess. *Cortex*, 1973, 329–332.

Orton, S. T. *Reading, writing and speech problems in children.* New York: Norton, 1937.

Poulton, E. C. Peripheral vision, refractories, and eye movements in fast oral reading. *British Journal of Psychology*, 1962, *53*, 409–419.

Rayner, K. Parafoveal identification during a fixation in reading. *Acta Psychologica*, 1975, *39*, 271–282. (a)

Rayner, K. The perceptual span and peripheral cues in reading. *Cognitive Psychology*, 1975, *7*, 65–81. (b)

Rayner, K. Develomental changes in word recognition strategies. *Journal of Educational Psychology*, 1976, *68*, 323–329.

Rayner, K., & Hagelberg, E. M. Word recognition cues for beginning and skilled readers. *Journal of Experimental Child Psychology*, 1976, *20*, 444–455.

Rayner, K., & McConkie, G. W. What guides a reader's eye movements? *Vision Research*, 1976, *16*, 829–837.

Richardson, J. T. E. Further evidence on the effect of word imageability in dyslexia. *Quarterly Journal of Experimental Psychology*, 1975, *27*, 445–449.

Satz, P., Rardin, D., & Ross, J. An evaluation of a theory of specific developmental dyslexia. *Child Development*, 1971, *42*, 2009–2021.

Shallice, T., & Warrington, E. K. Word recognition in a phonemic dyslexic patient. *Quarterly Journal of Experimental Psychology*, 1975, *27*, 187–199.

Smith, F. Uses of featural dependencies across letters in the visual identification of words. *Journal of Verbal Learning and Verbal Behavior*, 1969, *8*, 215–218.

Smith, F., Lott, D., & Cronnell, B. The effect of type size and case alternation of word identification. *American Journal of Psychology*, 1969, *82*, 248–253.

Sperling, G. The information available in brief visual presentation. *Psychological Monographs*, 1960, *74*(11, Whole No. 498).

Sperling, G. A model for visual memory tasks. *Human Factors*, 1963, *5*, 19–31.

Sperling, G. Successive approximation to a model for short-term memory. *Acta Psychologica*, 1967, *27*, 285–292.

Spragins, A. B., Lefton, L. A., & Fisher, D. F. Eye movements while reading and searching spatially transformed text: A developmental examinatin, *Memory & Cognition*, 1976, *4*, 36–42.

Staller, J., & Sekuler, R. Children read normal and reversed letters: A simple test of reading skill. *Quarterly Journal of Experimental Psychology*, 1975, *27*, 539–550.

Stanley, G., & Hall, R. Short-term visual information processing in dyslexics. *Child Development*, 1973, *44*, 841–844.

Stanley, G., Kaplan, L., & Poole, C. Cognitive and non-verbal perceptual processing in dyslexics. *Journal of General Psychology*, 1975, *93*, 67–73.

Taylor, S. E. Eye movements in reading: Facts and fallacies. *American Educational Research Journal*, 1965, *2*, 187–202.

Tinker, M. A. Fixation pause during reading. *Journal of Educational Research*, 1951, *44*, 471–479.

Velluntino, F. R., Steger, J. A., & Kandel, G. Reading disability: An investigation of the perceptual deficit hypothesis. *Cortex*, 1972, *8*, 106–118.

Volkman, F. C. Vision during voluntary sacadic eye movements. *Journal of the Optical Society of America*, 1962, *52*, 571–578.

Volkman, F. C. Saccadic suppression: A brief review. In R. A. Monty & J. W. Senders (Eds.), *Eye movements and psychological processes*. Hillsdale, N.J.: Lawrence Erlbaum Associates, 1976.

Woodworth, R. S. *Experimental psychology*. New York: Holt, 1938.

Zangwill, O. L., & Blakemore, C. Dyslexia: Reversal of eye movements during reading. *Neuropsychologia*, 1972, *10*, 371–373.

II LANGUAGE

5 Learning to Read Is Natural

Kenneth S. Goodman
Yetta M. Goodman
University of Arizona

When a human society experiences the need for communication over time and space, then written language is developed. Until that time, language is used in face-to-face, here-and-now contexts, and oral/aural language suffices. But when a society is literate, written language is functional for the society, and the members of that society must learn the written form. We believe they learn it and oral/aural language in similar fashions. Written language includes two of the four language processes. Reading is the receptive and writing is the productive form.

Children are born into a family, a community, and a society in which language is used. Children are born dependent. Furthermore, humans are social animals; they need to interact linguistically and to communicate in order to survive and to participate. Because of this need, almost all children develop language easily and naturally. They do so within the "noisy" situations in which they interact with parents, siblings, and others. Strongly motivated by the need to understand and be understood, they sort out and relate language to nonlanguage, acquire control of symbol and rule systems, use appropriate language for appropriate purposes, build an impressive, even precocious, repertoire of utterances, and become able both to understand and produce language they have never heard before.

Their language moves rapidly toward the familiolect and dialect that surrounds them, so rapidly that some scholars have come to view language as innate, while others have seen it as an example of conditioning through stimulus and response. Our view is that language is both personal and social invention. Both the individual and the society never lose the ability to create language. We believe, as does Halliday (1975), that function precedes form in language development. The ability to create language makes it possible for individuals to express original thought in original, yet understandable, language and for society to cope with new situations, new circumstances, new insights. It is communicative purpose that motivates language development and moves children toward the language around them.

Children growing up in a literate society begin to encounter written language before they personally experience the need to communicate beyond face-to-face situations. All of them become aware of and able to use written language to some extent. They become aware of books, signs, captions, printed containers, logos, and handwriting in their day-to-day experiences. They recognize stop signs, read cereal boxes, scribble letters, write their names, and follow and join in the reading of familiar stories.

For some children, their awareness of written language and its uses leads so naturally to participation that they are reading and writing, even inventing their own spelling rules, before they or their parents are aware that they are becoming literate. For such children, the process of developing written language parallels that of developing oral language.

Our contention is that acquisition of literacy is an extension of natural language learning for all children. Instruction consistent with this process will facilitate learning. Instruction that does not build on the process of natural language learning will, in some respects, be at cross-purposes with learners' natural tendencies, will neutralize or blunt the force of their language learning strengths, and may become counterproductive. To become literate, learners may then have to overcome barriers placed in their way.

NATURAL LANGUAGE LEARNING

We believe that children learn to read and write in the same way and for the same reason that they learn to speak and listen. That way is to encounter language in use as a vehicle of communicating meaning. The reason is need. Language learning, whether oral or written, is motivated by the need to communicate, to understand and be understood.

Natural, Not Innate

Our view of the development of literacy as natural is not the same as the view held by those who regard language as not learned but innate. Many of those who espouse such a position have tended, reasoning back from the apparent lack of universality in acquisition of literacy, to treat oral language as innate and written language as acquired. Mattingly (1972) summarized such a view:

> The possible forms of natural language are very restricted; its acquisition and
> function are biologically determined. . . . special neural machinery is intricately

linked to the vocal tract and the ear, the output and input devices used by all *normal* human beings for linguistic communication... My view is that... speaking and listening are primary linguistic activities; reading is a secondary and rather special sort of activity that relies critically upon the reader's awareness of these primary activities [p. 133; italics added]."

That leaves Mattingly by his own admission rather surprised "that a substantial number of human beings can also perform linguistic functions by means of the hand and the eye. If we had never observed actual reading or writing we would probably not believe these activities possible [p. 133]."

Mattingly's use of *awareness* in describing reading is a focal point. Oral language is a "synthetic," creative process that is not "in great part deliberately and consciously learned behavior like playing a piano... [p. 139]." "Synthesis of an utterance is one thing; the awareness of the process of synthesis quite another [p. 140]." Mattingly is led then to conclude that reading, unlike speech, requires very deliberate awareness of the linguistic process. This view makes the learning of oral and written language very different. Learning to read is seen, not as natural like learning to listen, but as a deliberate, conscious, academic achievement, dependent on awareness of certain aspects of oral language.

Since we view language as a personal-social invention, we see both oral and written language as learned in the same way. In neither case is the user required by the nature of the task to have a high level of conscious awareness of the units and system. In both cases control over language comes through the preoccupation with communicative use. Awareness of the uses of language is needed, but in neither case is it possible or profitable for the competent language user to be linguistically aware in Mattingly's sense. In reading, as in listening, preoccupation with language itself detracts from meaning and produces inefficient and ineffective language use.

Not a Garden of Print Either

When we use the term *natural learning*, we do not regard the process as an unfolding in an environment free of obstructive intrusions. Teaching children to read is not putting them into a garden of print and leaving them unmolested.

Readers are active participants in communication with unseen writers. They are seekers of meaning, motivated by the need to comprehend, aware of the functions of print, and adaptive to the characteristics of print. The environment for reading development must certainly be rich in print, a literate one. But reading instruction, particularly beginning instruction, has a vital role to play in creating and enhancing the conditions that will bring the reader's natural language-learning competence into play. Children must be among people who talk in order to learn to speak and listen. But that's not enough. Their need to communicate must also be present for learning to take place. This is also the case in acquiring literacy.

Instruction does not teach children to read. Children are in no more need of being taught to read than they are of being taught to listen. What reading instruction does is help children to learn.

This distinction between learning and teaching is a vital one. Helping children learn to read is, as Smith (1973) has put it, "responding to what the child is trying to do [p. 95]." That's possible, given children's language competence, language-learning competence, and the social function of written language. Teaching children to read has often meant simplifying and fractionating reading into sequenced component skills to be learned and used. With the focus on learning, the teacher must understand and deal with language and language learning. The learners keep their minds on meaning; they learn language through using it to communicate meaning. With the focus on teaching, both teachers and learners are dealing with language, often in abstract bits and pieces. The need of the learners for making sense may help them to use their language-learning competence to circumvent such instruction. But that demonstrates how we have tended, as Smith (1973) has said, to find easy ways to make learning to read hard.

Halliday (1973) has stated aa position we can agree with:

> There is no doubt that many of our problems in literacy education are of our own making; not just ourselves as individuals, or even educators as a profession, but ourselves as a whole—society, if you like. In part the problems stem from our cultural attitudes to language. We take language all too solemnly—and yet not seriously enough. If we (and this includes teachers) can learn to be a lot more serious about language, and at the same time a great deal less solemn about it (on both sides of the Atlantic, in our different ways), then we might be more ready to recognize linguistic success for what it is when we see it, and so do more to bring it about where it would otherwise fail to appear [p. viii].

We have been solemnly teaching letters, phonics, words, and word attacks, hoping to make children aware of linguistic abstractions, while failing to take seriously their constantly demonstrated competence in using and learning functional language.

THE FUNCTIONS OF LANGUAGE
AND THE DIFFERENCES BETWEEN
ORAL AND WRITTEN LANGUAGE

According to Halliday (1969), "What is common to every use of language is that it is meaningful, contextualized, and in the broadest sense social [p. 26]." Modern linguistics correctly shifted the main focus of linguistic concern from written to oral language several decades ago. It is unfortunate, however, that many linguists began to equate speech with language to such an extent that written language came to be treated as something other than language. Such a view is unscientific since it is largely unexamined and illogical: If written language can perform the functions of language, it must be language. Rather than being surprised that people can perform linguistic functions by means of hand and eye, we must be prepared to abandon a view of language that would make such linguistic reality surprising. Written language in use is also "meaningful, contexualized, and social."

For literate users of language, linguistic effectiveness is expanded and extended. They have alternate language forms, oral and written, that overlap in functions but that have characteristics that make each better suited to performing certain functions than the other. Table 5.1 shows the basic characteristics of the alternate language forms.

Speech lends itself easily to here-and-now, face-to-face uses. Writing is best suited for use over time and space. Certainly the need for extending communication between people separated by time and distance was historically the social, cultural reason for development of literacy. In some early societies, this social need required literacy from only a few people who functioned either as a kind of signal corps or as the archivists of the communities. The Persians used a small corps of literate Hebrew slaves to handle communication across their empire. In other societies, the need for and uses of written language become more pervasive. Religious communities that hold the belief that each individual must share in a body of knowledge stored in printed documents will develop widespread literacy.

TABLE 5.1
Basic Characteristics of Alternate Language Forms

Characteristics	Oral Language	Written Language
Input–output medium	Ear/voice	Eye/hand
Symbolic units	Sounds and sound patterns	Print and print patterns
Display	Over time	Over space
Permanence	Instantly perishable unless electronically recorded	As permanent as desired
Distance limits	Distance between encoder and decoder limited unless amplified or electronically transmitted	Distance between encoder and decoder unlimited
Structure	Phonological surface representation of deep structure and meaning	Orthographic surface representation of deep structure and meaning

Oral language is, of course, the first language form used by most individuals, even in literate societies. This means that for a period of their lives, children will use oral language as the primary means of dealing with all the language functions. Evidence exists, however, that very young children have some awareness and make some use of both the form and function of written language long before their control of oral language has become fully functional.

Our contention is that acquisition and lack of acquisition of literacy can be explained in terms of the internalization of the social-personal functions of written language by children. Let's start with a simple example: Children in a developing nation go off to a village or boarding school where they are taught basic literacy, among other things. The functions of written language they encounter in school may have no parallels in their homes. Instruction may deal with the mechanics of reading and writing and not even attempt to establish need or linguistic function. Instruction, literacy, and materials may even be in an unknown language. Success in initial acquisition of literacy will certainly be limited in any sense. If any mechanical skill is achieved, it is unlikely to become functional. Furthermore, when the pupils leave school, there will be little or no use to be made of written language. The village culture is one with little use for print. Literacy is not required because the functions have not been culturally sustained or personally internalized. Since there are strong patterns in many countries of early school drop out before the third or fourth grade, progress in developing literacy is unlikely.

Halliday (1969) has presented a view of children's models of language that we wish to apply to written language. In his view children create a model of each function, a "positive impression of... what language is and what it is for [p. 28]." Halliday stated that "the child knows what language is because he knows what language does [p. 27]" Children in literate societies use written language to various degrees and for various social or personal purposes. Halliday says that these functions appear in approximate order, and he believes that they develop before children learn the adult language. In building initial literacy it is important to understand that function precedes form in language development and that children have acquired all functions before they go to school. Halliday's functions of language and the sequence in which children become aware of them are as follows (1975, p. 244):

Instrumental: I want
Regulatory: Do as I tell you
Interactional: Me and you
Personal: Here I come
Heuristic: Tell me why
Imaginative: Let's pretend
Informative: I've got something to tell you

The extent to which children become aware of each function in written language depends on which ones are most commonly served by print and which continue to be best served by speech in their cultures and communities.

The people who write the advertising copy for the Saturday morning TV cartoon shows work hard at establishing the *I want* function so that millions of preschoolers will be able to spot the Count Chocula box and say, "I want Count Chocula."

Children in literate societies are aware early of the regulatory function. For example, they become aware of the function of stop signs quickly. When a 6-year-old was asked why she thought it was important to read, she said, "You might be out driving. And you might want to park. And there might be a sign that says 'No Parking.' And a man might come out and say, 'Can't you read?'"

Letter and note writing represent the interactional function of language. Many children become aware of letters, enjoy receiving them, dictate letters to be sent to grandparents, and begin to play at writing or actually produce letters. Parents often leave notes for children.

At this point it should be noticed that the interactional function illustrates important differences between the oral and written forms of language in use. Conversation is oral interaction. Usually, it is strongly situationally supported. Speaker and listener are together, responses are quick, and topics usually relate to the situational context itself. Pointing, facial expressions, and body movements support successful communication. Interacting through print is not situationally supported (the context is more abstract). Telephone use also lacks situational support; the extension of oral interaction to telephone conversation causes children to refine and extend the function. But telephones provide immediate response, whereas written letters result in delayed responses. Another difference between oral and written interaction is that the writer, the partner in communication with the reader, is most often unseen and unknown. The young reader may be aware of the message but not its source. This difference also shows in other written language. Signs tell you to "keep off the grass." Who wrote and put them there may not be something children have considered. Children may be no more concerned with who puts stories in books than they are with who puts milk in bottles. In fact, the message may appear to come from the language itself (or from its context in the case of signs).

Some children may become aware of the personal function of written language earlier than others. They may be in a very egocentric stage when they become aware that they have their own written names. This written representation of self becomes a way of identifying what is "mine." One of our graduate students recently reported an experience of a 10-year-old fifth grader who was considered learning disabled. Reading is so far from having a personal function for him that he encountered the name *Miguel* four times in a story before he recognized it as his own name. Then he was amazed to find it in print. On the other hand, a 3-year-old, asked to write his own name, scrawled an *A*. "That's Ali," he said. Then he drew a picture with an *A* discernible in its center and said, "That's Ali on his bike." His graphic name was his image.

If Halliday is right about the sequence in development of language functions, then it is interesting that the last three—heuristic, imaginative, and informative—are the functions for which written language is most heavily used in literate societies. As language functions are extended beyond immediate concerns, needs, and interactions of children to exploration of the real world, the world of ideas, and the world of what might be, language expands, takes on new textures, and begins to transcend the immediate contexts in which it occurs. Similarly, the language of children expands to serve their needs as they become fully interactive with their communities.

Halliday (1969) suggested that the informative (or representational) function of language, which is the abstract use of language to talk about ideas, may be the only function of language that adults articulate, but that it is a "very inadequate model from the point of view of the child [p. 33]." He indicated that if our concept of language is to be helpful to children, it must be exhaustive. It must take into account all the things language can do for children. In reading, that means using street signs, buying favorite toys and foods, finding favorite TV programs, writing and reading notes from parents left under magnetic markers on the refrigerator, reading stories that expand the creative and fanciful world of play, using books to discover how to make a sock puppet, or reading a recipe from the box to find out how to make marshmallow Rice Krispy crunch.

Readers in our society who are the readers who do read, as opposed to the readers who can read, use reading for all its varied purposes. We must focus more and more attention on how written language is used in society, because it is through the relevant use of language that children learn it. They learn it because it has meaning and purpose for them. Written language, too, can then fit into Halliday's statement that what is common to every use of language is that it is meaningful, contextualized, and social.

WHEN AND HOW DOES READING BEGIN?

Reading begins when children respond to meaningful printed symbols in a situational context with which they are familiar. The onset of this process probably goes as unnoticed as the time when children begin listening. Yet there is lots of evidence in the literature that suggests that children develop some kind of print awareness at a very early age without formal instruction.

Smith (1976) makes several points relating to the onset of reading:

> The first is that children probably begin to read from the moment they become aware of print in any meaningful way, and the second is that the roots of reading are discernible whenever children strive to make sense of print before they are able to recognize many of the actual words. . . .
>
> Third, not only are the formal mechanics of reading unnecessary in these initial stages, they may well be a hindrance. It is the ability of children to make sense. . . that will enable them to make use of the mechanics. . . . Fourth, words do not need to be in sentences to be meaningful, they just have to be in a meaningful context. . . [pp. 297–299].

The awareness of print seems to develop as children learn to categorize the large amount of print information surrounding them in a literate society. As they drive down a highway, walk down a street or through a shopping center, or watch television, they are bombarded with print. Children learn to organize their world and make sense out of it. When printed language is part of that world, they use that aspect of the environment if it is functional and significant to their life and culture. Gibson (1970) reported on 4-year-old children who not only could "separate pictures from writing and scribbles. . . [but who could also] separate scribbles from writing [p. 137]."

After becoming aware of print as being different from other graphic information, children begin to assign meaning to the print in their environment. Ylisto (1968) studied preschoolers who, with no formal instruction, responded to signs in a situational context. Ylisto concluded, "In reading as the child interacts in a print culture his awareness and recognition of printed word symbols become more and more autonomous. He abstracts the printed word symbol from the contextual setting, classifies and orders it and systematizes or assimiliates it in a language system he knows [p. 35]"

Our current pilot research substantiates this movement from learning to read printed symbols in familiar situational contexts toward more reliance on language contexts. Children from age 3 on are asked to respond to common signs in their environment. Certain signs are recognized in the situational context only. The logo *Circle K Market* may be recognized when the family drives by the store, but the same logo may not be recognized on a matchbook cover. However, certain logos such as those of McDonald's and Coca Cola are recognized as long as the print retains its distinctive form, even when away from the golden arches or the sexy bottle.

Children's responses to signs suggest that they are more concerned with the meaning of the graphic unit than with the representation of the name itself. When some children see *Chicken and Stars* in white block letters similar to those printed on the can, they will say, "That's Campbell Soup"; and they respond to the Campbell logo the same way. One 3-year-old called signs of

Burger Chef, Burger King, and McDonald's all McDonald's. But when the child was shown the sign of a local hamburger place that was more distinctly a sit-down, as opposed to a take-out, place, the child said, "That's a restaurant." Children categorize using associations other than significant graphic features to read. One 2½-year-old says *mother* when she sees the words *Myna* and *Mother*. Myna is her mother's name. Her father's name is Mark. When *Myna, Mark, Daddy*, and *Mother* are all presented to her, she interchanges *Daddy* and *Mark* but never confuses *Mark* with *Mother* or *Myna*. In the beginning of reading, children may relate a concept of meaning to a graphic unit and not be concerned with an exact oral representation. It is not surprising, therefore, when a kindergartner responds to each grapic alternative of his name by saying, "That says Jimmy," whether the name is written *Jimmy, Jim, James*, or *James Jones, Junior*.

Just as oral language meanings are developed and used in ongoing everyday experiences, so written language is learned through functional use. Clay (1972a) studied 5-year-old entrants to New Zealand's schools. She suggested that children are print aware when they ask, "What's that say?" in response to a TV advertisement, or when, in telling a story from a picture storybook, they might sigh and say, "I can't read all the words but I know what they say [p. 28]." She described children who are reading a book, obviously not following the print, but using a book-like pattern such as "Once upon a time..." or "Mother said, 'Do you want a piece of cake?'" Instead of the familiar "Reading is Talk Written Down," these children indicate that "Books Talk in a Special Way" (Clay, 1972a, p. 29).

As children respond to written language in its contextual setting, they begin to respond to significant features and may even use metalinguistic terminology to suggest their developing rule structures. In our own pilot research, for example, one child named Roberta suggested, "Revco has the same face as my name." But for the most part, children use language. They become interested in signs that help them to control their lives. The Men, Boys, and Señores signs are all important signs to learn to read. Exit signs are important, and many preschoolers respond to them appropriately (although a doctor's son at age 4 responded to one by saying, "I know that's not *X-ray*").

Read and others have made us aware of the children who seem to be developing rules of written language through their invented spellings. According to Read (1975):

> Certain pre-school children print messages, employing an orthography that is partly of their own invention. They represent English words with the standard alphabet and are thus compelled to classify distinct phones in some way. They do so according to articulatory features, making judgements of similarity that are quite different from those that most parents or teachers might make [p. 329].

Clay (1972a) suggested her own model of beginning reading and how children begin to develop rules about written languages:

Beginning reading is a communication system in a formative stage. At first the child is producing a message from his oral language experience and a context of past associations. He verifies it as probable or improbable in terms of these past experiences and changes the response if the check produces uncertainty.

At some time during the first year at school visual perception begins to provide cues but for a long period these are piecemeal, unreliable and unstable. This is largely because the child must learn where and how to attend to print [pp. 161–162].

Clay (1976) suggested that they way children view the significance and function of written language in their own particular culture may provide the basis for success in reading. She studied Pakeha,* Maori, and Samoan children in New Zealand. Statistics indicated that "the English language skills did not relate closely to progress in reading. While every Samoan group had the poorest average scores on each language test at every age, the Maoris had the poorest reading averages [p. 337]." She suggested these reasons: The Maoris had little contact with printed material prior to entry into school and had few opportunities to learn concepts about print. The Samoan children do not have homes filled with books, but their culture provides oral Bible reading in the home. A Sunday School teacher reported (Clay, 1976) that "...four year old Samoan children who came to Sunday School all want to write. They take the pencils and paper and write [p. 341]." This teacher described back-home relatives involved in selling various crafts at the market place to tourists on Boat Day. While working, they are "reading their mail from New Zealand and frantically writing their answers so that the boat which only stays a few hours can take the letters back to New Zealand... Children would see high value placed on written messages [p. 341]." Clay (1976) said:

The Samoan child, who speaks two langauges, who is introduced to a book and to written messages in his home, who is urged to participate fully in schooling and is generally supported by a proud ethnic group with firm child-rearing practices, manages to progress well in the early years of his school without handicap from his low scores on oral English tests [p. 341].

Readers know how to use written language long before they can talk about it. Downing and Oliver (1974), Clay (1975), and Read (1975) have all reported that 5- and 6-year-old children cannot respond appropriately with terms such as *word, letter,* and *number.* However, it is important to consider that the ability to apply the labels may follow the grasp of the concepts.

---

*European.

HOW BEGINNERS DIFFER
FROM PROFICIENT READERS

In our research on the reading process in readers with widely different levels of proficiency we (Goodman & Burke, 1973) reached certain key conclusions:

1. There is only one reading process. Readers may differ in the control of this process but not in the process they use.

2. Nonproficient readers show problems in getting it all together. They tend to bog down in preoccupation with letters and words and lose meaning.

3. The major difference among readers of varying proficiency is their ability to comprehend what they read.

4. Older, nonproficient readers seem to have acquired a nonfunctional skill. They can produce phonic matches or near-misses for words. They can handle short phrases. But they don't get much sense from what they read and seem not to expect sense.

In fact, it appears that a gap develops for some children between the skills of reading and any useful function of language. So much focus has been placed on form and those functions explored through reading have been so removed from the functional needs of the learner that reading becomes a school subject, not a useful language process. Even when some degree of functional reading competence is achieved through such instruction, it often leaves people with so strong a distaste for reading that they read only what they must, particularly avoiding literature and educational materials, the most common school-related written language.

Beginners may follow four basic paths in moving into literacy:

1. They may move forward from the natural beginning they have made, gaining flexibility and control of the process as they expand the functions of written language they control.

2. They may be distracted from function by instruction and come to regard reading as an essentially nonfunctional, nonlinguistic school activity.

3. They may, themselves, bring their natural growth and school instruction together, choosing from instruction that which facilitates learning.

4. They may develop functional literacy outside school, while developing a school behavior that is nonfunctional but which satisfies school and teacher demands.

The key to these different results lies in reader's perceptions of the functions of reading, the extent to which reading is functional in their culture, the extent to which instruction is facilitative, building on natural development, and the extent to which school experiences are relevant to the functional needs of the learners.

Beginners have a sense of function that leads to some beginning of literacy before instruction. Shifting their focus to the forms of written language does not make them like proficient readers since the latter never sacrifice function to form, even when they encounter misprints. That people can achieve literacy under less than optimal conditions, even in very unlikely circumstances, is more a tribute to the universal human ability to acquire and use language than it is proof that educators can afford to be unconcerned about building programs that create optimal conditions.

How Does Proficient Reading Work?

Our research (Goodman, 1976) on reading miscues has been primarily concerned with developing and testing against reality a theory and model of proficient reading. We have come to view proficient reading as a process in which readers integrate grapho-phonic, syntactic, and semantic information as they strive to construct meaning. Reading consists of optical, perceptual, syntactic, and semantic cycles, each melting into the next as readers try to get to meaning as efficiently as possible using minimal time and energy. That involves sampling from available cues, predicting syntactic structures and subsequent graphic cues, confirming or disconfirming predictions, correcting when necessary, and accommodating the developing sense as new information is decoded.

Efficiency (using minimal cues) and effectiveness (constructing meaning) depend on the reader's ability to maintain focus on meaning. For that to be true, the material being read must be meaningful, comprehensible, and functional to the reader. We are not surprised by the facility readers develop or by the fact that reading actually becomes more efficient than listening. This difference in efficiency is due, not to a basic distinction in the two receptive processes, but to differences in the conditions of use. Listening need happen only as rapidly as speech is produced; reading has no such constraint, so it happens more rapidly with no loss of comprehension. We could listen as efficiently as we read; we just don't need to.

Proficient reading and listening processes are parallel except for the form of the input, their speed, and the special uses we make of each. Proficient readers do not recode print as speech before decoding it. Why should they depend on a less efficient process, and how could they, given the greater efficiency of reading? It is not their ability to listen but their underlying ability to process language to get to meaning that beginning readers rely on to develop reading competence. The strategies we have described proficient readers as using are already used effectively and efficiently by children beginning to read their native language. Within meaningful, functional use of written language, children naturally, quickly, and easily learn to use these same strategies with the new graphic inputs in the new contexts.

THE NATURAL SEQUENCE:
A THEORY AND SOME PREMISES

We believe that motivation is inseparable from learning. Recognition of function, the need for language, precedes and is a prerequisite for acquisition. The crucial relationships of language with meaning and with the context that makes language meaningful is also vital. Learners build from whole to part and build a sense of form and structure within their functional, meaningful experiences with langauge.

Written language development draws on competence in oral language, since both written and oral language share underlying structures and since, for most learners, oral language competence reaches a high level earlier. As children become literate, the two systems become interactive, and children use each to support the other when they need to.

We believe that it helps educators in understanding the reading process to study what proficient readers do when they read. But it is a serious mistake to create curricula based on artificial skill sequences and hierarchies derived from such studies. To build facilitative instruction, we must understand not only how language processes work but also how and why they are learned. Our research has convinced us that the skills displayed by the proficient reader derive from the meaningful use of written language and that sequential instruction in those skills is as pointless and fruitless as instruction in the skills of a proficient listener would be to teach infants to comprehend speech.

Methodology and Motivating

We take as our principle premise in designing initial reading instruction that our goal is to create conditions that help all students to learn as naturally as some do. In this chapter we focus on instruction for children growing up in a highly literate society. But we must, in passing, reiterate our premise that literacy will not be acquired if the community and society do not use literacy to any significant degree for any significant purpose.

Our initial instructional concerns are twofold: (1) to determine and expand on the literacy learners have already achieved, and (2) to establish and expand children's awareness of the function of literacy.

An old but essential educational premise is that education takes the learners where they are and helps them grow in whatever directions are legitimate for them. That turns out to be essential in building literacy. In the balance of this chapter we explore some in-school activities that school and teachers can include in initial reading instruction. What we propose are elements in a program; it is not yet a full program.

Finding Out What They Can Read. If teachers take children for a walk around the school, the neighborhood, or a supermarket, they can get quick insights into the literacy kids have already attained. With a Polaroid camera, a pictorial record can be brought back to the classroom. The teacher needs only to say, "Show me anything you can read, and I'll take a picture of it." Developing this sense of what children are reading is important for the teacher, but the activity is also important for the kids, who will discover that reading isn't new, it's already part of their experience.

Clay's (1972b) Sand test gets at kids' concepts about print. The tests relate to Clay's concept that careful observation of children is a basic requisite to facilitative instruction. However, noting how children handle books, how they respond to print, and how they relate print to meaning are things teachers can do with or without the test. The teachers must be informed monitors, able to see where the kids are and able to help them to find function in printed language and build competence.

Creating A Literate Environment. The classroom and school must become an environment rich in functional use of written language. That means that there must be lots of written language pupils will need and want to read. It does not mean that every chair, table, or window should be labeled. The uses of written language must be both natural and functional. Furthermore, it will be helpful if the kids are involved in creating the literate environment to give them some sense of where written language comes from. Dictating a set of "Rules for Taking Care of Our Hamster" is an example of this kind of participation.

Work, Play, and Living. Play is the child's equivalent of the work world of the adult. In language development, play forms a valuable adjunct to the real-life experiences of children. They can read real letters, but they can also create a classroom post office that delivers letters and notes between class members. We need to bring back into kindergartens and primary classrooms the stores, kitchens, gas stations, play houses, and other centers for dramatic play.

Reading Something. Language, reading included, is always a means and never an end. Reading is best learned when the learners are using it to get something else: a message, a story, or other needed information. Literacy development, therefore, must be integrated with science, social studies, math, arts, and other concerns of the classroom. In isolation reading becomes nonlanguage and nonfunctional.

TABLE 5.2
Language Functions and Learning Experiences

Function	Experiences and Activities
Instrumental (I want)	Sign-ups for activities or interest centers
	Picture collages with captions: *Things I Want*
	Play stores and gas stations
	Orders for supplies: *Things I Need*
Regulatory (Do as I tell you)	Signs
	Directions
	Rules for care of class pets, plants, materials
	Instructions to make things
Interactional (Me and you)	Message board for notes from teacher to children
	Class post office
	Games involving reading
Personal (Here I come)	Books about self and family with captioned pictures
	Individual language-experience stories
Heuristic (Tell me why)	Question box
	Single concept books
	Science experiments
Imaginative (Let's pretend)	Storytelling
	Picture–story sessions with class participation
	Creative dramatics activities
	Read-along books and records
	Comic strips
Informative (I've got something to tell you)	Message boards and bulletin boards
	Notes to pupils paralleling school messages to parents
	Class newspaper
	Community newspaper and *TV Guide*
	Content textbooks
	Resource books

Reading and Writing. Reading needs to be related constantly to writing. Wherever possible, composition in written language should be related to reading activities.

Using All Functions. Halliday's (1975) seven functions make a good guide for generating learning experiences for initial and continuing reading instruction. Since most forms of writing are almost completely outside a situational context, it is important to begin in school with those situationlly supported functions that children have already begun using: the instrumental, regulatory, and personal.

Teachers

In all that we have said, we see the teacher as making the crucial difference in whether some or all children will learn to read. The teacher's role, in our view, is a complex one. It includes the following.

Kid-Watching.   To build on what kids have learned and to facilitate natural acquisition of reading, teachers must be insightful kid-watchers. They must know what to look for, how to look, and how to interpret what they see. As children progress, teachers must be able to monitor progress, build on strengths, and help them over the hang-ups.

Environment-Arranging.   Teachers must be able to create the literate environment that will facilitate learning. They must constantly be bringing kids in contact with relevant, functional print.

Interacting.   The teachers will be the literate adult using print in functional ways to interact with the learners.

Motivating, Stimulating, and Encouraging.   Teachers have major roles to play in helping children to recognize functional need, stimulating children's interests, and encouraging and responding to their efforts.

SUMMARY

We have argued that learning to read, like learning to listen, is a natural process for children in a literate society. We have argued that instruction facilitates children's development of literacy only if it is based on understanding the following:

1. How language functions in conveying meaning.
2. How communication of meaning functions as the context in which language is used and learned.
3. The subtle differences and similarities of oral and written language in use.
4. The personal and social motivations that lead children to learn or not learn language.
5. The social, cultural factors that make the acquisition of literacy of more or less personal importance to children of differing backgrounds.
6. The natural process by which some children achieve literacy.
7. All children's self-initiation of literacy in literate societies.
8. How programs and environments that enhance children's natural motivations, awareness, experiences, and cultural backgrounds can be created so that reading is learned naturally by all children.
9. The roles teachers must play as guides, monitors, environmental arrangers, and stimulators to facilitate the process.

ACKNOWLEDGMENTS

Some of the research reported in this paper was supported by the United States Office of Education and The National Institute of Education, Department of Health, Education, and Welfare. The opinions expressed do not necessarily reflect the position or policy of the Office of Education or the NIE and no official endoresement should be inferred. Other research was supported by The Center for Expansion of Language and Thinking.

REFERENCES

Clay, M. M. *Reading: The patterning of complex behavior.* Auckland, New Zealand: Heinemann Educational Books, 1972. (a)

Clay, M. M. *Sand—the concepts about print test.* Auckland, New Zealand: Heinemann Educational Books, 1972. (b)

Clay, M. M. *What did I write?* Auckland, New Zealand: Heinemann Educational Books, 1975.

Clay, M. M. Early childhood and cultural diversity in New Zealand. *Reading Teacher*, 1976, *29*, 333–342.

Downing, J., & Oliver, P. The child's conception of a word. *Reading Research Quarterly*, 1974, *4*, 568–582.

Gibson, E. J. The ontogeny of reading. *American Psychologist*, 1970, *25*, 136–143.

Goodman, K. S. Reading: A psycholinguistic guessing game. In H. Singer & R. Ruddell (Eds.), *Theoretical models and processes of reading* (2nd ed.). Newark, Del.: International Reading Association, 1976.

Goodman, K. S., & Burke, C. L. *Theoretically based studies of patterns of miscues in oral reading performance* (U.S. Office of Education Project No. 9-0375). Washington, D. C.: U.S. Government Printing Office, 1973. (ERIC Document Reproduction Service No. ED 079 708)

Halliday, M. A. K. Relevant models of language. *Educational Review*, 1969, *22*, 1–128.

Halliday, M. A. K. Foreword to *Breakthrough to literacy* by D. Mackay, B. Thompson, & P. Schaub. Glendale, Cal.: Bowmar, 1973.

Halliday, M. A. K. Learning how to mean. In E. H. Lenneberg, & E. Lenneberg (Eds.), *Foundations of language development: A multidisciplinary approach* (Vol. 1). New York: Academic Press, 1975.

Mattingly, I. G. Reading, the linguistic process, and linguistic awareness. In J. F. Kavanagh & I. G. Mattingly (Eds.), *Language by ear and by eye: The relationship between speaking and reading*. Cambridge, Mass.: MIT Press, 1972.

Read, C. Lessons to be learned from the pre-school orthographers. In E. H. Lenneberg & E. Lenneberg (Eds.), *Foundations of language development: A multidisciplinary approach* (Vol. 2). New York: Academic Press, 1975.

Smith, F. Twelve easy ways to make learning to read difficult. In F. Smith (Ed.), *Psycholinguistics and reading*. New York: Holt, Rinehart, & Winston, 1973.

Smith, F. Learning to read by reading. *Language Arts*, 1976, *53*, 297–299; 322.

Ylisto, I. P. *An empirical investigation of early reading responses of young children.* Unpublished doctoral dissertation, University of Michigan, 1968.

6 Discourse Comprehension and Early Reading

Carl H. Frederiksen
McGill University

Beginning reading imposes two kinds of demands on a child: to learn to recognize (decode) printed words and to apply already developed oral lanuage comprehension skills to written language. Subsequent reading development involves the acquisition of new comprehension strategies and processes that are specific to the increasingly specialized demands of written school language, that is, to the specialized forms, structures and uses of written language that children encounter in the late elementary grades and beyond. Literacy development thus involves two important transitions, a transition to written language codes in which a child learns to recognize printed words and apply already developed oral comprehension skills to written text, and a transition to literate school discourse in which new comprehension skills develop that are adapted to the progressively increasing cognitive demands of school discourse. The major thesis of this chapter is that to prepare children for the increasing demands school texts make for their comprehension, beginning reading instruction should have a more explicit emphasis on comprehension.

In this chapter I examine early reading from the viewpoint of comprehension theory in an effort to clarify how early reading instruction can enable a child who already is proficient in understanding oral language to transfer this ability to written texts. I begin by briefly characterizing present theories and knowledge about discourse comprehension and then attempt to identify goals for beginning reading instruction that take these theories and knowledge into account. It is argued that the primary objectives of beginning reading instruction should be to help children develop an ability to comprehend written discourse in a manner comparable to their comprehension of oral discourse. Since an ability to decode orthographic information and thus recognize printed words is necessary but not sufficient to enable a child to comprehend written texts, a subgoal to teaching comprehension should be to teach necessary orthographic decoding skills. However, decoding objectives should be clearly subordinated to comprehension objectives in early reading instruction.

In the second part of the paper I describe recent theoretical and methodological developments in our research on children's discourse comprehension that can contribute to knowledge of the process of discourse comprehension in children beginning to read and of the transfer of oral discourse processing skill to the processing of written discourse in early reading. The theoretical development involves (1) a representation of propositional structures that underlie the production and comprehension of discourse, and (2) a preliminary taxonomy of inferences in discourse comprehension. The taxonomy identifies classes of inferential operations that may be applied to propositions given in a discourse to generate new inferred propositions. Since the first component of the theory has been presented elsewhere (Frederiksen, 1975c), this chapter concentrates on the second component—discourse inference.

The methodological development consists of coding procedures that allow one (1) to determine from children's story (or other discourse) recalls what propositions they have recalled from stories, and (2) to investigate the inferences children make in comprehending and retelling stories. Inferences are investigated by comparing those propositions in children's story recalls that are not explicitly represented in a story with those that are explicitly represented in the story. The method provides a detailed account of the kinds and amount of propositional information children acquire from a story and of the inferences they make in comprehending the story. The method provides sensitive indexes of how children process a story during reading or oral discourse comprehension that can be used to compare the two processes.

Finally, I consider how the methods and theory described may contribute to accomplishing the primary goal of comprehension in early reading by enabling us to assess and diagnose differences between children's processing of oral and written discourse and design reading activities and texts that facilitate the development of comprehension in early reading.

THE NATURE OF CHILDREN'S DISCOURSE COMPREHENSION

The conventional way to think about the reading process (and the process of oral language comprehension) is to begin by distinguishing different processing levels associated with different internal representations of graphic (or acoustic) input information. All that is required to establish distinct processing levels is to establish that a linguistic input is represented by means of different abstract internal codes such that each code is distinct from the others and the codes may be generated from one another in sequence. Figure 6.1 summarizes five processing levels associated with four distinct internal codes. Since there is substantial evidence for the existence of each of these internal codes and since each code may be derived from a code earlier in the sequence, the processing levels in Fig. 6.1 may be regarded as given and taken as a point of departure in thinking about the comprehension process.

At the first level, a graphic (or acoustic) input is represented as a set of abstract visual (or acoustic) features. The existence of an abstract feature code has been established by research on visual and auditory information processing (Lindsay & Norman, 1972) and by many experimental studies of, for example, letter and word recognition (Gibson & Levin, 1975; Neisser, 1967). The neural processes that operate on a graphic (or acoustic) input and encode the input information as a set of abstract visual (or auditory) features are referred to collectively as *feature analysis* in Fig. 6.1.

The second processing level involves the generation of an internal information structure consisting of a sequence of surface linguistic units—normally a string of lexical concepts and grammatical morphemes—from the available feature information. The process that generates this abstract language code from a set of graphic (or acoustic) features is referred to as *graphic* (or *acoustic*) *decoding*. Decoding is a complex pattern-recognition process that operates both on the abstract feature code and on an internal lexicon that contains information about words—their pronunciation,

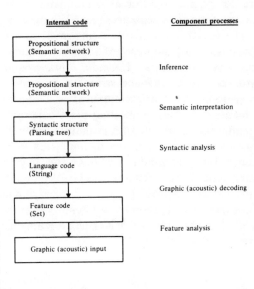

Internal code

Propositional structure
(Semantic network)

Propositional structure
(Semantic network)

Syntactic structure
(Parsing tree)

Language code
(String)

Feature code
(Set)

Graphic (acoustic) input

Component processes

Inference

Semantic interpretation

Syntactic analysis

Graphic (acoustic) decoding

Feature analysis

FIG. 6.1. Processing levels in discourse comprehension. An arrow indicates that an internal data structure, or code, is derived from the data structure immediately below it. The type of data structure is indicated in parentheses.

[The type of data structure is indicated in parentheses.]

orthographic structure, syntactic categories, meaning, and pragmatic uses. Decoding itself may involve additional intermediate internal codes consisting of sequences of units such as phonemes (phonemic code) or orthographic patterns (orthographic code). By far the most attention has been given to decoding processes in research and instructional design related to early reading (Gibson & Levin, 1975). Research issues concerning the nature of the decoding component of discourse comprehension are not the concern of this chapter. They are, however, extensively discussed by others in these volumes (see chapters in this series by Gregg & Farnham-Diggory; Juola; LaBerge; McConkie; Perfetti & Lesgold; Smith & Kleiman; Venezky & Massaro).

The third level involves the generation of an internal representation of the syntactic structure of a language string. Although psycholinguistic research has established beyond a doubt that such a representation occurs, the specific nature of the syntactic representation and of the syntactic component of the comprehension process is an open question. While many psycholinguists in the past have accepted the representation of sentence structure associated with generative transformational grammar as *the* internal representation of sentence structure, the notion that a grammar ought to be "psychologically realistic" has now been accepted by linguists and psycholinguists associated with the generative grammar tradition, leading them to consider alternatives to generative grammar that apper to be more plausible psychologically.[1] Computational approaches to syntax appear to be particulary promising as psycholinguistic models of syntactic processing [e.g., Woods (1970) and Kaplan's (1972) augmented transition netword grammars], especially if they are designed to operate as components of systems that generate semantic interpretations of sentences [e.g., Winograd's (1972) procedural grammar].

The fourth level of processing involves a represenation of the semantic (propositional) "content" of a syntactic unit such as a sentence or clause. At this level, processes of *semantic interpretation* operate on the syntactic structure of a language string to generate a propositional "reading" or interpretation of a grammatical unit consisting of lexical concepts and semantic relations connecting these concepts into semantic networks. The attempt to specify semantic structures for English sentences is a problem that has occupied investigators in linguistics (e.g., Chafe, 1970; Grimes, 1975; Leech, 1969), computational linguistics (e.g., Simmons, 1973), and artificial intelligence (e.g., Schank, 1973; Winograd, 1972). Psychologists have approached the problem as one of specifying the form in which propositional information is represented in memory (Crothers, 1975; Frederiksen, 1975c; Kintsch & van Dijk, 1975; Norman & Rumelhart, 1975). The most interesting attempts to specify models of the process of semantic interpretation have been

---

[1]Conference on "New Approaches to a Realistic Model of Language," Massachusetts Institute of Technology, March 1976. Cosponsored by MIT and the American Telephone and Telegraph Company.

made by computer scientists who have attempted to program computers to answer questions or in other ways to demonstrate an ability to "understand" English sentences (Schank, 1973; Winograd, 1972).

The fifth and highest level of processing operates entirely on propositions, generating new propositions from propositions that are given, for example, from prior discourse, from discourse context, or from previously acquired knowledge about the world. Any such processes will be referred to here as *inferences*. Note that no reference to truth value or conditions of valid inference is implied in this definition of inference. Any proposition that can be generated from one or more given propositions by means of specified operations (discussed later) will be referred to as an *inferred proposition*. Inferential processes in discourse comprehension have become a central topic among workers in the fields of artificial intelligence and computational linguistics who are interested in building "intelligent" language under-standing systems (Collins, 1977; Collins, Warnock, Aiello, & Miller, 1975; Rieger, 1976; Schank & Rieger, 1974; Wilks, 1975; Winograd, 1972). In addition to providing theories of how inference operates in language comprehension, this work makes clear the extent to which inference is involved in the everyday processing of natural language discourse. Furthermore, inferentially related propositions frequently occur in discourse, although the inferential relations may not always be explicitly expressed (Frederiksen, 1977a). The existence of high-level "text macro-structures" involving such inferentially related propositions has been recognized by a number of contributors to the field of discourse analysis (e.g. Crothers, 1975; Kintsch & van Dijk, 1975; Rumelhart, 1975; van Dijk, 1977). This fact and the fact that a host of language-processing problems at the discourse level (e.g., anaphora) require inference for their solution, establish that a discourse comprehension system must embody high-level inferential processes.

Although discourse comprehension certainly involves the processing levels indicated in Fig. 6.1, the most important questions about the nature of discourse processing remain to be answered. What is the form of internal representation or internal code at each processing level? How does each component process operate? How do these component processes interact?. This last question is the key to understanding how the comprehension process operates as a whole. It is the complex interactions among component processes that have posed the greatest theoretical challenge to those attempting to model the comprehension process in any detail (e.g., Winograd, 1972).

Process Interaction and Inference

There are two contrasting conceptions of how different components of the discourse comprehension system interact. In one conception, which may be referred to as the *bottom-up* conception of discourse processing, decoding, syntactic processing, semantic interpretation and inference are conceived of as occurring in sequence. The term *bottom-up* refers to the fact that lower-level processes are thought to occur prior to (and independent of) higher-level processes. In the bottom-up conception, the processes by which a person understands a discourse are controlled by the textual input, that is, word recognition is followed by a more or less automatic parsing of each sentence in an input text followed by semantic interpretation based on sentence syntax followed by inferences required to understand the text.

The bottom-up conception has tended to be predominant in the thinking of many psycholinguists and reading researchers. An emphasis on decoding in early reading instruction makes sense if the comprehension process is essentially bottom-up in its organization. However, attempts to program computers to "understand" language (e.g., to answer questions and carry out English dialogue), have established clearly that language comprehension systems must operate in a more complex fashion than is consistent with a purely bottom-up conception of discourse processing. For example, although Winograd's (1972) computer program to understand natural language is organized around a syntactic parser, it requires semantic and deductive (inferential) routines that interact with the parser in complex ways. Although the parser in Winograd's system calls on these other components when it is necessary to complete syntactic analysis and semantic interpretation (e.g., in determining pronominal reference), his system incorporates the notion that the process of comprehension involves the ability of a language user to combine syntactic, semantic, and inferential procedural knowledge in an interactive fashion to produce a semantic "reading" of sentential inputs. Furthermore, recent linguistic investigations of language structures such as anaphora, conjunction, presupposition, deixis, and implicatures suggest that discourse inferences are routinely required to interpret texts composed of related sentences.

The *top-down* conception represents an alternative conception of discourse processing in which syntactic and interpretive processes are presumed to be under the control of high-level inferential processes. For example, in Schank's (1973, 1974) system, comprehension is regarded as a process of mapping from grammatical and lexical information contained in input sentences to "conceptual dependency networks." A conceptual dependency network is generated inferentially from a (minimal) syntactic parsing of an input sentence, from world knowledge and from knowledge of the context of an utterance. Lexical verbs are transformed or decomposed into primitive "case frames" containing slots that can be filled by lexical concepts from a sentence or other known concepts. By identifying a verb, retrieving its primitive case frame, and assigning concepts from an input sentence or sentence context into "slots" in the frame, the system operates primarily at an inferential level, using lower level components as necessary to "instantiate" the stored frames, thus building up a conceptual dependency network that "fits" the input "data." Thus the system operates primarily in a "top-down" fashion. While no discourse processing system can be entirely top-down or bottom-up in its operation, two aspects of Schank's system, the notion of frame structures and the importance of inference in understanding language, have proved to be extremely powerful ideas (see Minsky, 1975; Schank & Rieger, 1974; Wilks, 1975). The notion of a frame has been extended to units of information much larger than single propositions to include e.g., "scripts" (Schank & Abelson, 1975), plans (Bruce, 1977) and story structures (Rumelhart, 1975; Mandler & Johnson, 1977).

Top-down conceptions of the comprehension process have a history in psychology that goes back to Bartlett's (1932) experiments on constructive memory for text. The notion in constructive theories of discourse comprehension is that in understanding stories or other connected discourse, a person constructs an internal cognitive structure or "schema" that relates the content of a discourse to the person's prior knowledge structure. Notions of frames or scripts in artificial intelligence work may be thought of as specific proposals concerning the nature of the internal memory schemas language users have that enable them to interpret linguistic messages. The constructive view of discourse comprehension is top-down in the sense that the inferences a person makes in understanding language are based on a process of "instantiating" schemas, that is, using prior knowledge structures to interpret new information. In this view, discourse inferences are "driven" by an effort to use prior knowledge to interpret linguistic messages.

The psychological evidence for constructive discourse processing is of two kinds: research on the role of inference in discourse comprehension and research demonstrating that children have prior expectations about the structure of stories that they use in comprehending them. In the first line of investigation, Bransford and Franks (1971) revived Bartlett's constructive approach to discourse comprehension with the demonstration that in understanding sentences subjects generate new information that is not explicit in the input sentences. Furthermore, they do not discriminate between the two kinds of information—that which was explicit in the sentences and that which was inferred. Paris (1975) has extended Bransford and Frank's observations to children showing that children routinely make inferences that extend the meanings encoded in sentences. To explore the role of inference in comprehending multisentence discourse, I investigated inferred propositions present in subjects' discourse recalls and obtained evidence that inferences are generated during comprehension of discourse as well as during recall (Frederiksen, 1975a). Furthermore, to demonstrate the constructive role of inference, I experimentally manipulated contextual factors that ought to control the extent of discourse inference and produced expected contextual effects on extent of inferential processing (Frederiksen, 1975b). There was evidence that most of these inferences were generated during input processing, demonstrating that contextually based goals may influence discourse inferencing. In another study (Frederiksen, 1977a), I established that propositions presented early in a text influence the processing of inferentially related propositions presented later in the text, demonstrating that prior discourse context also may influence the interpretation of later text. The second line of evidence for top-down processing comes from work on story comprehension (Mandler & Johnson, 1977; Stein & Glenn, 1979) that attempts to demonstrate how a reader's (or listener's) prior knowledge of the structure of stories may result in expectations about story structure that influence story comprehension. These studies provide evidence that children have expectations concerning the structure and organization of stories that they use in understanding them.

In summary, discourse comprehension involves both top-down and bottom-up aspects. There is a legitimate controversy over the extent to which the comprehension system is essentially a bottom-up system in which processing activities are controlled principally by the linguistic structures a reader (or listener) encounters; or a top-down system in which processing strategies are controlled principally by the reader (or listener) on the basis of the knowledge he or she brings to the reading (or listening) task—knowledge which may be based on prior discourse or situational context, goals, world knowledge, and expectations about the structure and content of the message being communicated. While research is needed to investigate this interplay of text and knowledge in controlling comprehension, it is clear that discourse comprehension normally involves inferences. These inferences may be based on given textual information, *text-based inferences*, or they may be based on prior knowledge structures, *schema-based inferences*, (Frederiksen, 1977b). Both types of inference are central to the comprehension process providing the means by which textual structures are related to one another and to a language user's prior knowledge.

Variation in the Comprehension Process

The conception of discourse comprehension that has been outlined can provide us with a framework for analyzing how discourse processing may vary from one text or communicative situation to another and from one language user to another. First consider the question of what features of discourse or discourse context are likely to have important effects on discourse comprehension and the likely nature of their effects. Three kinds of effects are possible. First, a particular component process may be affected by features of discourse or context. For example, degrading a visual or auditory message may cause difficulty in decoding the message, complex syntax may cause difficulty in syntactic analysis and sentence interpretation, and unfamiliar text content or context may result in difficulty in making appropriate discourse inferences. Second, conditions affecting a component process also may indirectly affect higher levels of processing. For example, the fact that a degraded sentence is harder to decode may lead to incomplete syntactic analysis, semantic interpretation and inferential integration with other sentences because after the sentence has been decoded, insufficient processing resources remain to complete higher levels of processing. This "limited processing capacity" hypothesis has been frequently suggested as an explanation for differences in the comprehension of readers who differ in their decoding ability (LaBerge & Samuels, 1974; Perfetti & Lesgold, 1977). A third possible kind of effect is on the nature of the interaction among component processes. Encountering a degraded or syntactically complex message may lead a reader (or listener) to adopt a relatively bottom-up (text-based) mode of processing, while reading or listening to a message that deals with a familiar topic or which has a familiar structure and context (e.g. stories) may lead one to adopt a more top-down (schema-based) mode of processing. In fact one would expect that language users develop an ability to adopt relatively more text-based or schema-based controls on their discourse inferences depending on the demand characteristics of particular texts and situations of language use.

These three kinds of processing differences also are possible ways in which individuals may differ. For example a reader who has difficulty decoding printed text may as a result of limited processing capacity fail to completely interpret the meaning of a passage. Or such a reader may revert to bottom-up processing strategies that are atypical of his or her normal comprehension of oral language. Readers who are familiar with the form and content of what they are reading naturally may make appropriate inferences relating a text's content to their prior knowledge and expectations, while readers unfamiliar with the form and content of a text may limit their interpretation to explicit text propositions and text-based inferences. The overwhelming emphasis in research on differences between good and poor readers has been on differences in low-level component processes, especially decoding processes, and on the "limited capacity" explanation of how such differences could be presumed to affect comprehension. Despite the fact that theories of comprehension lead us to expect that individual language users may differ fundamentally in how they approach discourse comprehension and inference, there is very little evidence bearing directly on this possibility. However there is a body of research suggestive of and consistent with this viewpoint. Gibson and Levin (1975) conclude their review of this literature with the following summary:

> Good and poor readers do not necessarily differ in the ability to transform a written word to speech, in other words, in the mechanics of reading. The ability

to use larger units and to make inferences from the text is involved in skilled reading rather than simply the ability to decode, so that skilled decoders who have not learned to organize the text into higher-order groupings may still be poor readers, so far as comprehension is concerned (p. 391).

What this explanation offers is one reason good and poor readers who differ only minimally in decoding ability would be expected to exhibit such striking differences in the ability to comprehend written text.

GOALS FOR BEGINNING READING INSTRUCTION

What, then, is the nature of reading development during the early grades? According to the present view, learning to read involves both acquiring graphic decoding skills and learning to apply the full power of the oral discourse processing system to written text. The problem is that even if beginning reading instruction were able to make children as efficient in graphic decoding as in acoustic decoding, this would be no guarantee that they would process written text as efficiently or in the same manner as oral discourse. In fact, instruction designed to teach decoding skills efficiently may actually have demand characteristics that cause children to approach reading in a relatively bottom-up manner, whether or not they experience difficulty in decoding. Even the seemingly innocuous task of oral reading may bias children to approach reading as a task essentially different from that of comprehending oral language.

The argument for teaching decoding directly is not that children cannot otherwise learn to decode [see Söderberg's (1976) case studies of preschool children learning to decode spontaneously]; it is that there is an increase in efficiency if decoding is taught directly. The premise, which is consistent with a bottom-up conception of discourse processing, is that making children efficient decoders will result automatically in their being able to apply their oral language skills to written text. However, if the increase in efficiency in teaching decoding is bought at the expense of producing children who process written discourse in a manner fundamentally different from the way they process oral discourse, it may not be worth the cost.

Early reading instruction, then, must be oriented toward achieving two objectives:

1. The primary objective of early reading instruction is to enable children to process written discourse in the same manner as oral discourse, applying the same powerful inferential processes that they apply to understand oral language discourse.

2. A subsidiary objective is to enable children to develop efficient processes for decoding written language.

The problem is to design beginning reading instruction to accomplish both goals simultaneously. However, if attainment of the primary goal necessitates some inefficiency with respect to the secondary goal, then that inefficiency should be tolerated.

If beginning reading instruction is to accomplish both objectives, it must be based on an understanding of the inferential processes children have available to them for comprehending oral discourse as they begin to read, of developmental changes that take place in oral discourse processing during the period of early reading, and of changes that take place in the processing of written discourse as children learn to read. It will also require that we have available procedures for assessing how a child processes oral and written discourse differently and whether he or she makes the same kinds of inferences in comprehending oral as written discourse. In the next section some recent theoretical and methodological developments are presented that provide both an approach to describing the inferences children make from oral and written discourse and comparing children's processing of oral and written discourse.

INFERENCE IN CHILDREN'S STORY COMPREHENSION

The preceeding discussion examined the comprehension process in some detail, identifying different processing levels associated with different levels of representation and analysis of language, and contrasting two different kinds of process interaction—bottom-up processing in which comprehension activities at different levels occur in succession and are controlled principally by features of the textual input, and top-down processing in which comprehension is under the control of high level inferential processes that are based on a language user's goals, prior knowledge, and expectations about language events. Discourse inferences were found to be central to the comprehension process, providing the means by which a language user relates the sentences of a discourse to one another and to his prior knowledge structure. Discourse inferences may be text based, occuring primarily in response to discourse features, or they may be schema-based, that is, based on a language user's prior knowledge schemas. The study of discourse inferences therefore is crucial to understanding the comprehension process. In beginning readers who are just learning to decode print and to treat printed text, like oral language discourse, as an object, to be understood, an analysis of discourse inferences can reveal much about the development of comprehension in beginning readers.

The Propositional Structure of Discourse

To approach the topic of discourse inference, we begin with the position argued by Halliday and Hasan (1976) that discourse inferences involve relations among propositions. Put another way, inferential relations between sentences in a discourse relate the propositional content of the sentences, not the particular grammatical forms chosen to express that content. While surface discourse features such as anaphora, conjunction and lexical cohesion (Halliday & Hasan, 1976; Nash-Webber, 1977) may require or invite particular discourse inferences, the inferential relations they signal are at the semantic level and should in many instances be valid in the absence of the surface linguistic cues. For example, two sentences expressing temporally ordered events and connected by the conjunctives *and then* also may be connected causatively. This causative relation would be valid in the absence of the conjunctives.

To describe the processes of semantic interpretation and inference in any detail requires that we first be able to specify the propositional content that is explicit in a discourse. One way to approach the problem of specifying the propositional content of discourse is to consider the other half of the communication process—discourse production. Figure 6.2 presents a conception of the process of discourse production in which a text is viewed as resulting from a series of communicative decisions whereby speakers (or writers) generate discourse from their store of message-relevant conceptual and propositional knowledge. The store of propositional knowledge from which a textual message is derived is referred to as a *message domain*. In the present connection, discourse production involves three levels of decision, each of which determines a different aspect of discourse structure—propositional content, textual organization and cohesion, and sentence structure.

At the first decision level, speakers (or writers) select units of propositional information for explicit incorporation into a discourse. This selection process

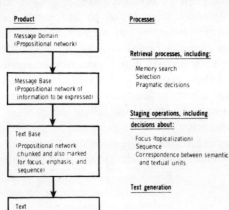

FIG. 6.2. Communicative decisions in discourse production. (From C. H. Frederiksen, Semantic Processing Units in Understanding Text, in R. Freedle (Ed.), *Discourse Production and Comprehension*, Norwood, N.J.: Ablex Publishing Co., 1977a. Copyright 1977a by Ablex Publishing Co. Reprinted by permission.)

reflects pragmatic assumptions speakers (or writers) make about what information they want to communicate, what knowledge they already share with the person being addressed, and the inferential capabilities and likely pragmatic assumptions of the addressee. That propositional knowledge which speakers (or writers) select for explicit incorporation into a message is called a *message base*.

At the second level of decision, speakers (or writers) make staging decisions that determine how the selected units of propositional information are to be organized into discourse, including decisions about sequence, topicalization, reference, and correspondences between semantic units (such as propositions) and grammatical units (such as sentences).[2] Staging decisions provide a means whereby speakers (or writers) can incorporate into a linguistic message a perspective on the content of that message by assigning relative prominence to units of semantic information in the message base. The resulting staged message base is referred to here as a *text base*, indicating that it contains both textual and propositional information.

Finally, speakers (or writers) apply their knowledge of sentence structure to generate sequences of sentences from the text base. Since each of the previous decision levels has involved communicative decisions that successively reduced the amount of free variation in text, most free variation presumably has been eliminated at the level of the text base. Thus the last stage, text generation, involves only the application of grammatical rules appropriate in a speaker's (or writer's) language community to communicate the perspective and message content of the text base. Of course, discourse production occurs in real time with many interactions among component processes.

To illustrate, Fig. 6.3 contains an example of a list of propositions for the following children's story (from Hall, Reder, & Cole, 1975):

The Flower Pot Story

1. This is Michele. She is watering the flowers.
2. Crash! Now Michele thinks that Mother will be mad. She wants to run away.
3. "I'm not mad," says Mother. "I know you didn't mean to do it. Let's clean up the mess."
4. Michele picks up the flowers. She gives them to Mother. "Don't worry," says Mother, "we'll put them in a nice pot."
5. Now the flowers are okay and the mess is all cleaned up. "Come on," says Mother. "Let's go and make some cookies" [p. 630].[3]

---

[2]The term *staging* was suggested by Grimes (1975), who has drawn an analogy between the "staging" of discourse and the "staging" of a theatrical production.

[3]In Hall, Reder, and Cole (1975), the Flower Pot Story was accompanied by pictures illustrating the story. Of course, children's story recall protocols could include semantic information derived from the picture as well as from the text.

```
                    Proposition List - Michele and her Mother

100    (:MICHELE)--AGT@TEM(PRES)@ASPCT(CONT)->('WATER)*--OBJ1->(:FLOWERS)

200    ()--I.PAT->('CRASH)
201    (:MICHELE)--PAT@TEM(PRES)->('THINK)*--THEME2->("202)
202    (:MOTHER)--PAT@TEM(FUT)->()--MAN.EXT1->('MAD)
203    (:MICHELE)--PAT@TEM(PRES)->('WANT)--GOAL2->("204)
204    (:MICHELE)--AGT->('RUN)*┌-SOURCE->("205)
                               └-RESULT->("206)
205    (:MICHELE)--LOC.0,2->(#205)
206    (:MICHELE)--LOC.0,2->(#206)
207    (#205)<-PROX@NEG->(#206)

300    (:MOTHER)--AGT@TEM(PRES)->('SAY)--THEME1->(("301),("302),("305))
301    (:MOTHER)--PAT@NEG@TEM(PRES)->()--MAN.EXT1->('MAD)
302    (:MOTHER)--PAT@TEM(PRES)->('KNOW)--THEME2->("304)
304    (:MICHELE)--AGT->()--RESULT->("200)
305    (:MOTHER)--AGT->('SUGGEST)--THEME1->("306)
306    ((:MOTHER),(:MICHELE))--AGT->('CLEAN)--OBJ1->(:MESS)

400    (:MICHELE)--AGT@TEM(PRES)->('PICK.UF)--OBJ1->(:FLOWERS)
401    (:MICHELE)--AGT@TEM(PRES)->('GIVE)*┌-OBJ1->(:FLOWERS)
                                          └-DAT1->(:MOTHER)
403    (:MOTHER)--AGT@TEM(PRES)->('SAY)--THEME1->(("404),("406))
404    (:MOTHER)--PAT->('WANT)--GOAL2->("405)
405    (:MICHELE)--PAT@NEG->('WORRY)
406    ((:MOTHER),(:MICHELE))--AGT@TEM(FUT)->('PUT)*┌-OBJ1->(:FLOWERS)
                                                    └-RESULT->("407)
407    (:FLOWERS)--LOC.0,3->(:POT.TOK)
408    (:POT.TOK)--EXTO->('NICE)

500    ()--AGT@TEM(PAST)@ASPCT(COMP)->('CLEAN)*--OBJ1->(:MESS)
501    (:FLOWERS)--CAT.ATT->('OK)
502    (:MOTHER)--AGT@TEM(PRES)->('SAY)*┌-THEME1->(("503),("510),("515))
                                        └-LOC.0,0->(#502)
503    (:MOTHER)--PAT->('WANT)--GOAL2->("504)
504    (:MICHELE)--AGT->('MOVE)--RESULT->("505)
505    (:MICHELE)--LOC.0,0->(#505)
506    (#502)<-PROX->(#505)
510    ((:MOTHER),(:MICHELE))--AGT->('MOVE)*┌-SOURCE->("511)
                                            └-RESULT->("513)
511    ((:MOTHER),(:MICHELE))--LOC.0,0->(#511)
512    (#502)<-PROX->(#511)
513    ((:MOTHER),(:MICHELE))--LOC.0,0->(#513)
514    (#511)<-PROX@NEG->(#513)
515    ((:MOTHER),(:MICHELE))--AGT->('MAKE)--RESULT->(:COOKIE)

(:FLOWERS)     ('FLOWER)--DEF->()--NUM1->('PL)
(:MICHELE)     ('MICHELE)--DEF->()--NUMO->('1)
(:MOTHER)      ('MOTHER)--DEF->()--NUMO->('1)
(:MESS)        ('MESS)--DEF->()--NUMO->('1)
(:POT.TOK)     ('POT)--TOK->()--NUMO->('1)
(:COOKIE)      ('COOKIE)--TOK->()--NUM1->('SOME)
```

FIG. 6.3. Propositional network: The Flower Pot Story (Story 1).

Each numbered row in Fig. 6.3 denotes a proposition consisting of a network of concepts (in parentheses) connected by labeled semantic relations (the arrows connecting the concepts); each proposition represents an event or state. For example, Proposition 100 represents the event of *Michele* causing the action *water* affecting the object set *flowers*. The action in Proposition 100 was initiated in the past with continuous aspect, as indicated by the operators TEM (PRES) and ASPCT (CONT) on the AGT relation (each of which is denoted by an @ sign followed by an operator label). A concept may be an object (in which case it is preceded by a colon in the figure) or an action, attribute, degree, location, or time. Objects appear both within propositions and on an object list together with relations that indicate how each object is determined and quantified. For example, *Michele* is definite and quantified singular. Propositions frequently are embedded within other propositions (as indicated by a square bracket in a proposition containing a proposition number). For example, in Proposition 203, *Michele* is the patient of the processive action *want*, which has as a goal the event represented by the embedded Proposition 204. Full details of these network structures for representing propositional knowledge are given in Frederiksen (1975c).

Staging decisions explain why, for example, Sentences 1, rather than some other sentences or sentence, were generated from Proposition 100. This particular staging establishes *Michele* as the main topic of the story and the action as a subsidiary comment. An alternative staging might have been *Michele is watering the flowers* (correspondence between the textual unit sentence and the semantic unit proposition) or *Here are the flowers. They are being watered by Michele* (topicalization of *the flowers*). A detailed theory of staging remains to be developed, but the outlines of a theory have been given by Grimes (1975) and summarized by Clements (1976). Presumably, once staging decisions have been made, a text may be generated by applying grammatical rules that map from propositions plus staging information (the text base) to English sentences. (Notice that in research on discourse comprehension it has been common to confuse aspects of staging with aspects of the propositional message base.)

Suppose that the Flower Pot Story was read to a child (or alternatively, the child read the story), and the child was then asked to recall the story. The child's recall was recorded and transcribed. For example, the following recall protocol was obtained from a four-year-old (Subject 1) in the study by Hall, Reder, and Cole (1975):

A little girl was watering the flowers and then she was... that she was watering the flowers. She... she broke the glass. Don't worry, said Mom, we'll clean up the mess...she won't get mad. She put it in a nice new pot and then she was cleaning up the pot, and that was only a accident also. The flowers are okay, and the mess is all cleaned up.[4]

To determine what information from the propositional structure in Fig. 6.3 was recalled by this child, the child's recall protocol is coded against the propositional data structure, checking off every concept or relation recalled. A detailed account of what propositional information the child has recalled from the story is obtained in this way. Fig. 6.4 presents a list of propositions that were recalled by this child. Notice that in addition to recalling a portion of the story content, this child has included propositions that are related but not identical to propositons in the message base. The attempt to analyze propositions such as these leads directly to a theory of discourse inference.

---

[4]Supplied by Hall, Reder, and Cole.

```
                    Proposition List - Michele and her Mother

                              Subject 1 Recall

   100   (:GIRL)--AGT@TEM(PAST)@ASPCT(CONT)->('WATER)*--OBJ1->(:FLOWERS)

   202   (:MOTHER)--PAT@TEM(FUT)->()--MAN.EXT1->('MAD)

   306   ((:MOTHER),(:MICHELE))--AGT@TEM(FUT)->('CLEAN)*--OBJ1->(:MESS)

   403   (:MOTHER)--AGT@TEM(PAST)->('SAY)--THEME1->("404)
   404   (:MOTHER)--PAT->('WANT)--GOAL2->("405)
   405   (:MICHELE)--PAT@NEG->('WORRY)
   406   (:MOTHER)--AGT@TEM(PAST)->('PUT)*┌-OBJ1->(:FLOWERS)
                                          └-RESULT->("407)
   407   (:FLOWERS)--LOC.0,3->(:POT.TOK)
   408   (:POT.TOK)--EXT0->('NICE)

   500   ()--AGT@TEM(PAST)@ASPCT(COMP)->('CLEAN)*--OBJ1->(:MESS)
   501   (:FLOWERS)--CAT.ATT->('OK)

  (:FLOWERS)       ('FLOWER)--DEF->()--NUM1->('PL)
  (:MOTHER)        ('MOTHER)--DEF->()--NUM0->('1)
  (:MESS)          ('MESS)--DEF->()--NUM0->('1)
  (:POT.TOK)       ('POT)--TOK->()--NUM0->('1)
```

FIG. 6.4.   Propositional network: Subject 1.

Before describing our approach to text-based inference, it will be helpful to characterize further the propositional structures on which inferences are based.[5] A propositional structure consists of a set of concepts connected into networks by labeled binary semantic relations. A relation is defined in terms of a triple consisting of a pair of concept slots and a connecting relation. For example, the relation $() - CAT \rightarrow ()$ connects two object categories so that the object category in the right slot is a subset of the object category in the left slot, for example, $(:BIRDS) - CAT \rightarrow (:CANARIES)$. The two smallest units of semantic information are thus: lexical concepts and relational triples consisting of pairs of concepts connected by semantic relations. All higher-order units of semantic information are composed of relational triples. Higher-order units may occur at several levels of rank or complexity, and they will be described in their order of complexity (see Frederiksen, 1977a).

The next largest semantic unit, an event frame, is analogous to a case frame in Schank's (1973) theory and is composed of a system of relational triples connected to an action and identifying the various participants in the action, its resulting effects, and so on. An example of a resultive event frame is found in Proposition 100. Here the event frame consists of everything except the time (tense and aspect) information. Notice that this is an instance of an incomplete event frame; it represents only that part of the frame that was explicitly expressed in the story. The full event frame is

(:MICHELE)—AGT→ ('WATER)* —OBJ1→ (:FLOWERS)
$\qquad\qquad\qquad\qquad\qquad$—SOURCE→["101]
$\qquad\qquad\qquad\qquad\qquad$—RESULT→["102]

---

[5]The propositional structures are presented in detail in Frederiksen (1975c); the propositional notation and the characteristics of these structures in terms of ranked units are given in Frederiksen (1977a).

where embedded Propsitions 101 and 102 represent the unspecified state of the flowers prior to and after the action *water* has taken place, respectively. Proposition 500 contains an example of an event frame with an unfilled slot—the agent slot. One kind of inferential operation might be to fill this slot with an animate object. Proposition 201 contains an example of a processive event frame:

$$(:\text{MICHELE})—\text{PAT}\rightarrow ('\text{THINK})—\text{THEME2}\rightarrow [\text{"202}]$$

where 202 is an embedded proposition specifying the content or "theme" of the cognitive process *think*.

A proposition is the next largest semantic unit and represents an event or state. An event proposition is composed of an event frame together with additional relations that further identify the event, for example, by specifying the time and location at which the event took place or by further specifying the nature of the action. Examples of stative propositions in the Flower Pot Story are Propositions 205 (locative) and 408 (attributive). Other stative propositions are 206, 407, 501, and 505. All other propositions in the story represent events. Proposition 502 is an example of an event proposition consisting of an event frame containing embedded propositions, a tense operator, and a locative relational triple (a branch in the network occurs at the point indicated by an *).

The two units highest in rank are composed of propositions that are connected, either by algebraic relations or dependency relations, that is, logical, causal, or conditional relations. A unit composed of a pair of propositions connected by an algebraic relation is a relative system. A relative system may specify relative time, location, or comparative information involving attributes of objects or actions. An example of a relative system, in this instance one involving relative location, is given by Proposition 207, which specifies that the location of *Michele* after the action *run* (206) is not the same as her location prior to the action (205). (Here, a # sign is used to indicate an unfilled slot.) The algebraic relation proximity connects slots in 205 and 206 and has the negative operator NEG applied to it. A dependency system consists of a pair of propositions connected by logical, causal, or conditional relations—relations that indicate logical, causal, or conditional dependencies among propositions. No examples of dependency systems occur in the Flower Pot Story, but examples may be found in Frederiksen (1975c).

Classification of Discourse Inferences

Now consider the first sentence in the story recall of Subject 1:

A little girl was watering the flowers and then she was... that she was watering the flowers.

What information has this child recalled from the story? And what inferences has she made from the story to generate this sentence? Figure 6.4 lists the propositions in this child's story recall. Comparing Proposition 100 in Fig. 6.4 with Proposition 100 in Fig. 6.3 shows that the Fig. 6.4 version reproduces some of the information of the Fig. 6.3 version and also includes two alterations of the proposition. First, the object class occurring in the AGT slot, *Michele*, has been replaced with *a little girl*, a less specific class of children. That is, *Michele* refers to a definite little girl, and *a little girl* refers to any token from the class of little girls. Therefore, the object class in the AGT slot in Proposition 100 is a subset of the object class in the child's proposition, and the child's proposition is thus more general than that given in the story. Second, the child has changed the time reference from present to past. Both the changes in the child's text are evidence for inference—processes that operate on given propositions to produce new propositions.

The occurrence of such operations in children's story recalls is evidence for discourse processing at the inferential level. The kind and amount of such text-based inference ought to be indicative of the nature of discourse processing in these children. It is important in this research to determine when inferences are generated: during input as a discourse is understood, or during recall as an aspect of discourse production. Prior research with adults indicates that we can expect inference to be important in both discourse comprehension and discourse production (Frederiksen, 1975a, 1975b, 1977a). Detailed descriptions of children's text-based inferences and of the propositional information they acquire from discourse ought to contribute significantly to describing the processing of both oral and written discourse during the period of early reading and developmental changes in both processes.

The classification of text-based inferences involves examining the relationships between propositions in a child's story recall protocol and propositions in the message base for the story presented to the child. A child's propositions may be classified on the basis of the particular inferential operations that can be applied to propositions in the message base to generate the child's propositions. Since in some instances it may be possible to generate a child's propositions in more than one way from propositions in a message base, the convention will be adopted that in classifying a child's propositions, the fewest possible operations are applied.

Table 6.1 presents a summary of the inference types we have identified thus far. This classification is intended to be exhaustive and is based on considerations of what operations are possible given the nature of propositional structures and on analyses of propositions in children's story recall protocols. Eight major classes of operations on propositions have been identified that operate on different semantic units and/or involve different operations on these units. Major classes of operations are subdivided into more specific categories of inferential operations. The resulting classification

TABLE 6.1
Major Classes of Text-Based Inference

Class of Operations	Units[a]	Inference Types[b]
I. Lexical operations	Lexical concepts, propositions	1. Lexical expansion 2. Lexicalization
II. Identification operations	Objects, actions, states, events	3. Attribute inference 4. Category inference 5. Time inference 6. Locative inference 7. Hasp inference 8. Degree inference
III. Frame operations	Event frames	9. Act inference 10. Case inference 11. Instrumental inference 12. Result inference 13. Source inference 14. Goal inference 15. Theme inference 16. Frame transformation 17. Disembedding operations 18. Embedding operations
IV. Event generation	Event propositions	19. Event inference
V. Macrostructure operations	Propositions	20. Superordinate inference 21. Subordinate inference

VI. Algebraic operations		22. Algebraic inference
		   A. Metric
		   B. Nonmetric

VII. Dependency operations	Dependency systems	23. Causal inference
		24. Conditional inference
		   A. Enablement inference
		   B. Presupposition
		   C. Antecedent inference
		25. Logical inference
		   A. Deductive inference
		   B. Conditional perfection

VIII. Truth–value operations	Propositions	26. Truth–value operations
		   A. Qualification
		   B. Negation

[a]Semantic units to which inferential operations are applied.
[b]See text for definitions and examples of inference types.

consists of 26 inference types (see Table 6.1). In the full classification of text-based inferences, the inference types themselves are further subdivided (Frederiksen, 1977c). The classification is illustrated by examples in what follows.

Lexical Operations.   The first major class of inference, lexical operations, operates at the conceptual level. Two types of operations can occur:

1. Lexical expansion: expanding a lexical concept into one or more propositions.

2. Lexicalization: replacing one or more propositions with a lexical concept.

For example, if in retelling The Flower Pot Story, a child said (1) *Let's clean up the dirt and pieces of flower pot all over the floor* instead of (2) *Let's clean up the mess*, the child would have expanded the lexical concept *mess*. If the child generated (2) from (1), the child would have lexicalized the propositions underlying (1).

Identification Operations. The second major class of inference, identification operations, involves operation on objects, actions, stative propositions, or events that further specify or identify an object, action, state, or event. For example, identifying an object involves providing stative information about the object that distinguishes it from other objects. Six types of identification operations may be distinguished:

3. Attribute inference: specifying an attribute of an object or action.

    3A. Stative attribution:

        Story 1:[6] We'll put them in a nice pot. (Proposition 408)

        Protocol (Subject 1): She put it in a nice *new* pot. (*Pot* is identified by the attribute *new*.)

    3B. Manner attribution:

        Story 2:[7] Now Jimmy's mad.... That makes him feel better. (Proposition 520)

        Protocol (Subject 5): Jimmy was happy. (The attribute *happy* is attributed to the processive action feel in 520.)

4. Category inference: classifying an object or action into a category.

    4A. Story 2: He is buying an ice cream. (Ice cream)

        Protocol (Subject 1): He was buying a popsicles of ice cream. (*Popsicles* is a subset of the category *ice cream*.)

5. Time inference: specifying a time or duration for an event or state.

    5A. PRES → PAST:

        Story 1: She *is* watering the flowers. (Proposition 100)

        Protocol (Subject 1): A little girl *was* watering the flowers.

    5B. TENSELESS → FUT:

        Story 1: Let's clean up the mess. (Proposition 306)

        Protocol (Subject 1): *We'll* clean up the mess.

    5C. ASPCT: COMPLETIVE → CONT:

        Story 1: The mess *is all cleaned up*. (Proposition 500)

        Protocol (Subject 1): She *was cleaning up* the pot.

---

[6]Story 1 is the Flower Pot Story in Hall, Reder, and Cole (1975), Table 1.

[7]Story 2 is the Ice Cream Story in Hall, Reder, and Cole (1975), Table 2.

6.   Locative inference: specifying a location for an event or state.

> Story 1: She (Michele) is watering the flowers. (Proposition 100)
> Protocol: Michele is watering the flowers *on the windowsill.*

7.   Part-structure (HASP) inference: specifying a part of an object, for example, *the flower's blossoms.*

8.   Degree inference: specifying a degree of an attribute.

> Story 1: We'll put them in a nice pot. (Proposition 408)
> Protocol: We'll put them in a *very* nice pot.

Frame Operations.   The third major class of text-based inferences, frame operations, consists of operations on event frames. Ten distinct categories of operations on event frames can be identified that correpond to inference types 9 through 18 in Table 6.1.

9.   Act inference: filling an unfilled action slot in an event frame.

> Story 1: Mother will be mad. (Proposition 202)
> Protocol: Mother will *feel* mad. (The cognitive action *feel* is specified.)

10.   Case inference: filling a case slot in an event frame; specifically, inserting a concept into an agent, instrument, dative, or object slot in a resultive event frame, or into a patient, dative, or object slot in a processive event frame.

> Story 1: Now the mess is all cleaned up (Proposition 500).
> Protocol (Subject 1): *She* (Mother) was cleaning up the pot.
> (An empty AGT slot is filled with *Mother.*)

11.   Instrumental inference: generating a cause of a proposition marked as a result. For example, if Story 1 said: *Mother got mad* (Proposition 202 marked as a result), and a child's recall said *Michele made her mother mad,* the child would have supplied an agent and an action for Proposition 202.

12.   Result inference: generating a proposition indicating the result of an action.

> Story 2: Take half of mine (ice cream). (Proposition 511)
> This is represented as:
> (JIMMY)—AGT → ('TAKE)

$$\begin{array}{l} \text{—OBJ1} \rightarrow \\ (\text{:HALF.ICE.CREAM.B}) \\ \text{—RESULT} \rightarrow [\ ] \end{array}$$

> Protocol (Subject 5): Jimmy, *you* can have *half* of mine.
> The protocol fills the result slot with:
> (:JIMMY)—PAT → ('HAVE)—OBJ2 →
> (:HALF.ICE.CREAM.B)

13.   Source inference: generating a proposition indicating a state existing prior to an action. For example, in the preceding example, a child might say *Jimmy, you don't have any ice cream. Take half of mine.*

14. Goal inference: generating a goal for an action.

Story 1: Michele picks up the flowers. (Proposition 400)

Protocol: Michele picks up the flowers *so her mother won't be mad*. (A goal for the action *pick up* is specified.)

15. Theme inference: generating a theme for a cognitive action.

Story 1: Let's clean up the mess. (Proposition 305)

Michele picks up the flowers (Proposition 400)

Protocol (Subject 3): Let's pick up the flowers. (Proposition 400 is inserted into the theme slot of 305.)

16. Frame transformation: transforming a frame of one type into a frame of another type (see Frederiksen, 1977b, for examples).

17. Disembedding operations: removing a proposition from an event frame in which it is embedded.

Story 1: She (Michele) wants *to run away*. (Proposition 204 embedded in the goal slot of 203.

Protocol (Subject 4): Michele... *did run off*. (Proposition 204 has been removed from the goal slot of Proposition 203.)

18. Embedding operations: inserting a proposition into a slot in an event frame.

Story 2: This is Jimmy. He is buying ice cream. (Proposition 100)

Protocol (Subject 2): Jimmy wanted *to buy ice cream*. (Proposition 100 has been embedded in the goal slot of a generated event, *Jimmy wanted*.)

Event Generation. The fourth major class of inference, event generation, involves generating an event frame into which an object or proposition is inserted. Ten subtypes of event inference (19) occur corresponding to the different slots ("cases") that occur in processive and resultive event frames. Examples of several types of event inference are as follows:

Processive events:

19A. PAT

Protocol (Story 1, Subject 1): She (Michele) broke the glass.

(*Michele* is inserted into the PAT slot of a generated event.)

19B. OBJ2:

Protocol (Story 2, Subject 5): (See example of 12. The generated result contains the concept (*:HALF.ICE.CREAM.B*) in the OBJ2 slot.)

19AB. PAT + OBJ2:

Protocol (Story 1, Subject 3): Said mother, come, *let's have some cookies*. (The generated event contains *Mother* and *Michele* in the PAT slot and *cookies* in the OBJ2 slot.)

Resultive events:

19E.   AGT

Protocol (Story 1, Subject 3): *Michele* broke (the flowers). (An event is generated having an animate object from the text as AGT—*Michele*.)

19G.   OBJ1:

Protocol (Story 2, Subject 1): It (the ice cream) got all broken. (The object *ice cream* is inserted into the OBJ1 slot of a generated event.)

19EG.   AGT + OBJ1:

Protocol (Story 2, Subject 2): *He* (Jimmy) dropped *it* (the ice cream).

Macrostructure Operations.   The fifth major class of text-based inference, macrostructure operations, involves operations on propositions in a text that result in new propositions either more general than (i.e., superordinate to) or more specific than (i.e., subordinate to) the propositions in the message base for the text. Superordinate inference (20) involves replacing a concept occupying a slot in a proposition with a superordinate class of concepts (i.e., a class of concept that includes the concept in the proposition as a subset). Numerous subtypes of superordinate inference can be distinguished on the basis of the type of slot and/or concept operated on. Subordinate inference (21) involves the same operations in reverse; a conceptual class is replaced by a subordinate concept. Again, there are as many subtypes of operations as there are different slots on which to operate. Examples of superordinate inference are:

20B.   AGT:

Story 1: This is Michele. She is watering the flowers.

Protocol (Subject 1): *A little girl* was watering the flowers. (Superordinate object class in AGT slot.)

20B.   OBJ1:

Story 1: She is watering the flowers. (Proposition 100)

Protocol (Subject 5): She was waterin' *the plants.* (Superordinate object class in OBJ1 slot.)

20B.   PAT:

Story 2: (You) come on and fight. (Proposition 420)

Protocol (Subject 1): Let's come on and fight. (Superordinate object class in PAT slot. PAT slot contains both *Jimmy* and *the other boy.*)

Examples of subordinate inference are:

21A.   Subordinate action:

Story 2: I'm gonna beat you up. Come on and fight.

(Proposition 410)
Protocol (Subject 5): Sock (you) *in the head*. Let's fight. (The action is subordinate to *beat up*.)

21B. AGT:
Story 1: We'll put them in a nice pot. (Propositions 406–408)
Protocol (Subject 1): *She* (mother) put it (flowers) in a nice new pot. (Subordinate object class in AGT slot.)

21B. OBJ1:
Story 1: *the mess* is all cleaned up. (Proposition 500)
Protocol (Subject 1): She was cleaning up *the pot*. (Subordinate object class in OBJ1 slot.)

Algebraic Operations. The sixth major class of inference, algebraic operations, involves generating a relative (algebraic) system given a set of relative propositions. For example, if a text specified that two children were naughty, and, in retelling the story, a child produced a comparative statement about how naughty the children were, the child would have made an algebraic inference (22). Algebraic inference may involve metric propositions that specify metric attributes (i.e., attributes having a degree), or they may involve relative object classes or propositions that are nonmetric. Examples of each subtype are:

22A. Connecting metric propositions with algebraic relations, for example, specifying temporal order:
Protocol (Story 1, Subject 1): A little girl was watering the flowers and then she...

22B. Connecting nonmetric relative object classes or propositions:
Protocol (Story 1, Subject 2): her (Michele's) mother. (Kinship relations are examples of nonmetric algebraic relations between relative object classes, i.e., object classes that are defined relative to one another.)

Dependency Operations. Dependency operations, the seventh class of inference, are operations that connect propositions with dependency relations, that is, relations that establish that one proposition is dependent on another proposition—logically, conditionally, or causally (functionally). Three inference types may be identified within this class: causal inference (23), connecting propositions by means of causal relations, thus generating a causal system; conditional inference (24), connecting propositions by means of conditional relations, thus generating a conditional system; and logical inference (25), connecting propositions by means of logical relations, thus generating a logical system. Again, subtypes can be identified for each inference type. Three illustrative examples are:

23. Causal inference:
   23A. Connecting unconnected events with causal relations:
         Protocol (Story 1, Subject 3): Michele was watering the flowers and crashed and broke.... (*Michele* caused Proposition 200.)
   23F. Inchoative:
         Story 1: Michele thinks that mother will *be mad.* (Proposition 202)
         Protocol (Subject 1): She (Mother) won't *get mad.*
24. Conditional inference:
   24A. Specifying antecedent conditions for an event or state:
         Story 1: Now Michele thinks that Mother will be mad. She wants to run away.
         Protocol (Subject 5): She (Michele) thought her mother might be mad. (201, 202) *Then* she *would* run away. (204–207)

Truth–value Operations. Finally, a child may operate on the truth–value of a proposition. Three types of truth–value operations (26) are possible; qualification, negation, and interrogation. Examples of subtypes are:

   26A. Qualification:
         Story 1: Now Michele thinks that Mother will be mad. (Propositions 201 and 202)
         Protocol (Subject 5): She thought her *might* mother be *mad.*
   26B. Negation:
         Story 1: Mother will be mad.
         Protocol (Subject 1): She (Mother) *won't* get mad.

To illustrate the coding of inference types, the analysis of text-based inferences that occur in the story recall protocol given previously is presented in Table 6.2. For each line of text from the child's protocol, the table presents (1) the number(s) of the propositions(s) in the message base most closely matching the proposition produced by the child in that line of text, and (2) the code number (from Table 6.1) of the inference type(s) corresponding to those operations that must be applied to the indicated proposition(s) to derive the child's proposition. This child's protocol is fairly typical of those obtained by Hall et al. (1975) for The Flower Pot Story. Inspection of Table 6.2 confirms, by example, that inference is heavily involved in the everyday processing of natural discourse.

Inference in Young Children

How much inference actually occurs when four-year-old comprehend and retell simple narrative stories? What kinds of inferences occur and how

TABLE 6.2
Classification of Inferences: Subject 1, Story 1

Text from Protocol	Proposition(s)[a]	Inference Types
A little girl[1] was[2] watering the flowers	100	20B (AGT), 5a (PAST)
and then	100	22A (TEM) (ORD)
she broke the glass	100	19E
Don't worry *said* Mom,	403	5A (PAST)
we'll clean up the mess	306	5A (FUT)
she *won't*[1] get[2] mad.	202	26B, 23F
She[1] put[2] it in a nice *new*[3] pot[4]	406–408, (:POT)	21B (AGT), 5A (PAST), 3A, 17D (THEME)
and then	406, 500	22A (TEM) (ORD)
she[1] was[2] cleaning up the *pot*[3]	500	10A, 5A (ASPCT-CONT), 21B (OBJ1)
and that was only a accident also.	302, 303	19A

[a]Proposition(s) in message base most closely matching proposition(s) in subject's protocol.

frequently? Are there important individual and developmental differences in the amount and kinds of inferences children produce? How are discourse inferences affected by the characteristics of a text? Although we do not have answers to all these questions, some preliminary indication of what we can expect to find is provided in Table 6.3, which reports the distribution of inferences for five of the children studied by Hall et al. (1975).

It is apparent from Table 6.3 that many of the possible inference types occur in this sample of children's story recall protocols. Although we need to obtain recall protocols for stories unaccompanied by pictures (because inferred information may be derived from the pictures accompanying the story), the experimental conditions used by Hall et al. (1975) were sufficiently natural for it to be reasonable to suppose that the inferences observed are representative of those that typically would occur in the comprehension of short narrative stories. Of the 26 inference types, 16 occurred in these children's recall protocols, and many different subtypes also occurred. The most frequent class of inferential operations was identifying operations (33 occurrences), followed by event generation (23), macrostructure operations (18), frame operations (14), algebraic operations (11), dependency operations (5), and truth-value operations (2). No lexical operations occurred. Most identifying operations involved time inference, reflecting a strong tendency to shift the time orientation from the present to the past. Event generation is that category of inferences most likely to reflect the effects of pictures. Most of the algebraic inferences involved the temporal ordering of events. Dependency operations were infrequent for these stories, but there is reason to expect this category of inferences to be greater for types of discourse other than simple narrative stories. In answer to the first two questions posed above, there is a substantial amount of inference, and the inferences are distributed over a wide range of inference types.

TABLE 6.3

Frequencies of Inference Types in Five Children's Recalls of Two Stories

Inference Type	Story 1					Story 2					Total
	S1	S2	S3	S4	S5	S1	S2	S3	S4	S5	
Identifying Operations											
3A. Attribute inference: states	1	1	1							1	4
3B. Attribute inference: events										1	1
4A. Category inference: states						1					1
5A. Time inference	5	4	6	2	2	1	3	1		3	27
Frame Operations											
10A. Frame inference	1										1
12A. Result inference									1		1
15. Theme inference			1								1
16D. Frame transformation					1	1					2
17C. Disembedding operations: GOAL			1	1	1						3
17D. Disembedding operations: THEME				1	1						2
18C. Embedding operations: GOAL							1	1			2
18D. Embedding operations: THEME			2								2
Event Generation											
Processive event:											
19A PAT	1	1	1	1	1	1		2			8
19B OBJ2										1	1
19AB PAT + OBJ2			1								1
Resultive event											
19E AGT	1		2			1				3	8
19G OBJI			1			3					4
19EG AGT + OBJI							1				1

(continued)

181

TABLE 6.3 (continued)

Inference Type	Story 1					Story 2					Total
	S1	S2	S3	S4	S5	S1	S2	S3	S4	S5	
Macrostructure Operations											
Superordinate inference:											
20B(AGT). Superordinate agent	1					2		1			4
20B(OBJI). Superordinate object		1	1			1	1		1	1	6
20B(PAT). Superordinate patient						2				1	3
20E. Superordinate result				1							1
Subordinate inference:											
21B(AGT). Subordinate agent	1										1
21B(OBJI). Subordinate object	1					1					2
21A. Subordinate action										1	1
Algebraic Operations											
22A. Metric algebraic operations	2		2			2				3	9
22B. Nonmetric algebraic operations		1			1						2
Dependency Operations											
Causal inference											
23A. Connect unconnected events			1								1
23F. Inchoative							1			1	2
Conditional inference:											
24A. Enablement inference				1	1						2
Truth–Value Operations											
26.A Qualification					1						1
26B. Negation	1										1
Subject totals	17	9	20	7	8	15	7	4	1	18	

What about individual differences? If one looks simply at the total number of inferences produced by individual children for each story, there appear to be very substantial individual differences in the amount of text-based inference. However, there is some instability of these differences across stories. If one looks at the patterns of inference types for individual subjects, there is consistency over subjects for some types (e.g., time inference) and inconsistency for others. The results indicate that a detailed investigation of individual and developmental differences would be extremely fruitful. Finally, there were very substantial story effects, even for two short narrative stories. The strong suggestion is that discourse characteristics will prove to have important effects on text-based inferences. What is needed is an investigation of specific discourse characteristics that produce particular kinds of text-based inferences.

INFERENCE IN EARLY READING

It remains to consider how the developments in the study of children's discourse comprehension reported here can contribute to the design and practice of early reading instruction. There appear to be three principal ways in which this research can benefit the teaching of reading: (1) by establishing explicit objectives for early reading instruction; (2) by providing assessment procedures on which to base instructional decisions; and (3) by providing instructional tasks and procedures teachers can employ in teaching beginning reading.

Objectives need to be established for early reading instruction at many levels. We have already examined the highest level objectives and have seen that researchers' conceptions of the comprehension process have a direct bearing on the establishment of high-level instructional objectives. However, more detailed and specific objectives must be established in order to accomplish the major comprehension objective. Specific objectives can be established on the basis of research that investigates the extent and types of discourse inferences characteristic of children who are highly successful in school tasks and the kinds and amounts of semantic information these children acquire from written texts. Another kind of specific instructional objective is an objective established for an individual child. Such individual objectives could be based on, for example, an analysis of the kinds of semantic information a child acquires from written texts, including information that is inferred, or on comparisons of the kinds of information a child acquires from written and spoken discourse.

The research that has been described can contribute to the development of assessment procedures in two ways. First, the methods that have been described for analyzing children's story recall protocols could be adapted for use in classrooms as an assessment technique, much in the way analysis of oral reading "miscues" is employed as a classroom technique. For example, the methods could be used to compare the information a child acquires in reading to that which he or she acquires from a structurally similar text presented orally. Such a comparison could be of value in making instructional decisions for an individual child. A teacher could establish reading goals for a child consistent with that child's comprehension of oral discourse; or a teacher might identify a child's comprehension problem as a general language problem rather than a problem specific to reading. Second, the classification of inference types could be employed as a basis for systematically constructing achievement test items to assess aspects of discourse processing.

Research on discourse inference in early readers also can contribute directly to improving beginning reading instruction. For example, the study of the inferences beginning readers at different levels of proficiency make from school texts can provide teachers with a basis for interacting with children and texts to lead children to fully grasp the inferential requirements and possibilities of a text. Research comparing school texts in terms of their inferential requirements and possibilities can provide a basis for selecting reading texts and deciding what texts are appropriate for children at different levels of reading or language development. The methods I have described also can be applied to analze the inferences teachers make or require of students when they generate questions from school texts. We are now conducting research that investigates these questions concerning inferencing from school texts (see Frederiksen, 1977c for a description of the methods used and some examples of our results). Finally, the story retelling task I have been employing in my research may be used not only as a research task but also as an instructional task. Discourse recall is natural for children, it is appropriate both for reading and for oral discourse comprehension, it does not necessarily bias a child to process a text in a particular way, and it provides a rich source of information about the way a child processes a text in comprehending it. Furthermore, as research knowledge based on this task accumulates, that knowledge will be directly generalizable to instruction that employs the same or similar tasks.

ACKNOWLEDGMENTS

This research was supported by a grant from the National Science Foundation (number GS-4023). This chapter was written while the author was at the national Institute of Education, Washington, D.C. Any conclusions or other views expressed here are the author's own and do not represent the views of the National Institute of Education or the National Science Foundation.

REFERENCES

Bartlett, F. C. *Remembering*. Cambridge: The University Press, 1932.

Bobrow, D. G., & Norman, D. A. Some principles of memory schemata. In D. Bobrow & A. Collins (Eds.), *Representation and understanding*. New York: Academic Press, 1975.

Bransford, J. D., & Franks, J. J. The abstraction of linguistic ideas. *Cognitive Psychology*, 1971, *2*, 331–350.

Bruce, B. *Plans and social actions* (Technical Report No. 34). Urbana, IL.: University of Illinois, Center for the Study of Reading, 1977.

Chafe, W. *Meaning and the structure of language*. Chicago: University of Chicago Press, 1970.

Clements, P. *Effects of staging on recall from prose*. Unpublished doctoral dissertation, Cornell University, 1976.

Collins, A. Processes in acquiring knowledge. In R. C. Anderson, B. J. Spiro, & W. E. Montague (Eds.), *Schooling and the acquisition of knowledge*. Hillsdale, N.J.: Lawrence Erlbaum Associates, 1977.

Collins, A., Warnock, E. H., Aiello, N., & Miller, M. Reasoning from incomplete knowledge. In D. Bobrow & A. Collins (Eds.), *Representation and understanding: Studies in cognitive science*. New York: Academic Press, 1975.

Crothers, E. J. *Paragraph structure description* (Rep. No. 40). Boulder, Col.: University of Colorado, Institute for the Study of Intellectual Behavior, 1975.

Frederiksen, C. H. Acquisition of semantic information from discourse: Effects of repeated exposures. *Journal of Verbal Learning and Verbal Behavior*, 1975, *14*, 158–169. (a)

Frederiksen, C. H. Effects of context-induced processing operations on semantic information acquired from discourse. *Cognitive Psychology*, 1975, *7*, 139–166. (b)

Frederiksen, C. H. Representing logical and semantic structure of knowledge acquired from discourse. *Cognitive Psychology*, 1975, *7*, 371–458. (c)

Frederiksen, C. H. Semantic processing units in understanding text. In R. Freedle (Ed.), *Discourse production and comprehension, Vol. I*. Norwood, N.J.: Ablex, 1977. (a)

Frederiksen, C. H. Structure and process in discourse production and comprehension. In P. Carpenter & M. Just (Eds.), *Cognitive processes in comprehension*. Hillsdale, N.J.: Lawrence Erlbaum Associates, 1977. (b)

Frederiksen, C. H. Inference and the structure of children's discourse. Paper presented at Society for Research in Child Development, New Orleans, March 17–19, 1977 (c).

Gibson, E. J., & Levin, H. *The psychology of reading*. Cambridge, Mass.: MIT Press, 1975.

Grimes, J. E. *The thread of discourse*. The Hague: Mouton, 1975.

Hall, W., Reder, S., & Cole, M. Story recall in young black and white children: Effects of racial group membership, race of experimenter and dialect. *Developmental Psychology*, 1975, *11*, 628–634.

Halliday, M. A. K., & Hasan, R. *Cohesion in English*. London: Longmans, 1976.

Kaplan, R. M. Augmented transition networks as psychological models of sentence comprehension. *Artificial Intelligence*, 1972, *3*, 77–100.

Kintsch, W., & van Dijk, T. A. Comment on se rappelle et on resume des histoires. *Languages*, 1975, *40*, 18–116.

LaBerge, D., & Samuels, S. J. Toward a theory of automatic information processing in reading. *Cognitive Psychology*, 1974, *6*, 293–323.

Leech, G. *Towards a semantic description of English*. Bloomington, Ind.: Indiana University Press, 1969.

Lindsay, P., & Norman, D. A. *Human information processing*. New York: Academic Press, 1972.

Mandler, J. M., & Johnson, N. S. Remembrance of things parsed: Story structure and recall. *Cognitive Psychology*, 1977, *9*, 111–151.

Minsky, M. A framework for the representation of knowledge. In P. Winston (Ed.), *The psychology of computer vision.* New York: McGraw-Hill, 1975.

Nash-Webber, B. *Inference in an approach to discourse anaphora.* (Technical Report No. 77). Urbana, IL.: University of Illinois, Center for the Study of Reading, 1977.

Neisser, U. *Cognitive psychology.* New York: Appleton-Century-Crofts, 1967.

Norman, D. A., & Rumelhart, D. E. (Eds.), *Explorations in cognition.* San Francisco: Freeman, 1975.

Paris, S. G. Integration and inference in children's comprehension and memory. In F. Restle, R. M. Shiffrin, N. J. Castellan, H. R. Lindman, & D. B. Pisoni (Eds.), *Cognitive theory, Vol. I.* Hillsdale, N. J.: Lawrence Erlbaum Associates, 1975.

Perfetti, C., & Lesgold, A. M. Discourse comprehension and individual differences. In P. Carpenter & M. Just (Eds.), *Cognitive processes in comprehension.* Hillsdale, N. J.: Lawrence Erlbaum Associates, 1977.

Rieger, C. The algorithmic basis of language-related human intelligence. *Georgetown University Round Table on Languages and Linguistics,* 1976.

Rumelhart, D. E. Notes on a schema for stories. In D. Bobrow & A. Collins (Eds.), *Representation and understanding: Studies in cognitive science.* New York: Academic Press, 1975.

Schank, R. Identification of conceptualizations underlying natural language. In R. Schank & K. Colby (Eds.), *Computer models of thought and language.* San Francisco: Freeman, 1973.

Schank, R. C., & Abelson, R. P. Scripts, plans and knowledge. In *Advance Papers of the Fourth International Joint Conference on Artificial Intelligence.* Tbilisi, Georgia, U.S.S.R., 1975.

Schank, R. C., & Rieger, C. J. Inference and the computer understanding of natural language. *Artificial Intelligence,* 1974, *5,* 373–412.

Simmons, R. F. Semantic networks: Their computation and use for understanding English sentences. In R. Schank & K. Colby (Eds.), *Computer models of thought and language.* San Francisco: Freeman, 1973.

Söderberg, R. Learning to read from two and five: Some observations on normal hearing and deaf children. *Georgetown University Round Table on Languages and Linguistics,* 1976.

Stein, N. L., & Glenn, C. G. An analysis of story comprehension in elementary school children. In R. Freedle (Ed.), *Discourse processes: Advances in research and theory, Vol. II.* Norwood, N. J.: Ablex, 1979.

van Dijk, T. A. Macro-structure and cognition. In P. Carpenter & M. Just (Eds.), *Cognitive processes in comprehension.* Hillsdale, N.J.: Lawrence Erlbaum Associates, 1977.

Wilks, Y. A preferential, pattern-seeking, semantics for natural language. *Artificial Intelligence,* 1975, *6,* 53–74.

Winograd, T. Understanding natural language. *Cognitive Psychology,* 1972, *3,* 1–191.

Woods, W. A. Transition network grammars for natural language analysis. *Communications of the ACM,* 1970, *13,* 591–606.

7 The Mismatch of Child Language and School Language: Implications of Beginning Reading Instruction

Roger W. Shuy
Georgetown University
  and
Center for Applied Linguistics

The emotional heat generated by the discussion of the relationship of Vernacular English to spoken English in the reading process has been spectacular, if not enlightening. What was originally postulated as a reasonable hypothesis for serious analysis quickly became a political football, which prevented the very investigation it suggested. The idea was simple enough. Learning theory indicates that people tend to learn what they do know on the basis of what they do not know. That is, we learn new things by building on the common ground of existing knowledge.

Anthropologists have for years espoused this principle of common ground when establishing a cross-cultural relationship. They find similarities between cultures and use these similarities to build future understandings and relationships. Children's literature of good quality also seems to support this principle, at least in practice if not in recognized theoretical stance. A children's poem that is good begins from the child's point of view, not from the adult's. Laura Richards' poem about rain, with the lines, "Pitter, patter falls the rain, gently splashing on my window pane," is written from the adult perspective. Dorothy Aldis' rain poem, on the other hand, seems to be written from the perspective of the child: "The rain is washing all the worms pink and beautiful."

PAST ASSUMPTIONS ABOUT THE MISMATCH OF CHILD LANGUAGE AND SCHOOL LANGUAGE

In the late 1960s, papers appeared by several linguists and educators who challenged the assumptions that reading failure was the result of some sort of genetic handicap or that it occurred in some random or accidental distribution. These authors asserted that the distance between the beginning point of language for children who habitually speak a vernacular and the point at which beginning reading materials are written might be worth examining as the potential cause of reading failure.

Distance

The distance principle of language mismatch is illustrated in Fig. 7.1. Mismatch is determined by measuring differences in phonology, grammar, and functions.

The graphic portrayal of the distance between various types of language use is, of course, more schematic than scientific. It suggests, without scientific quantitative research supporting it, that the sort of written language used in everyday life (C) is measurably different from the spoken language used even by the mainstream population (B); that this written language is even more different from vernaculars (A) of a given speech community (degrees of difference between vernaculars might also be noted); and that the common written language (C) is also different, in the opposite direction, from the sort of written language frequently used for the instruction of beginning readers (D). Those who believe that there is some validity to the suggestion of this figure have hypothesized that all children experience some interference between spoken language and the written materials they are required to read, but that those children whose vernacular spoken language is different from the mainstream spoken language probably have even more difficulty.

Interference

The interference of one language system with another is not a new concept in linguistics. Foreign accents are well known examples. In such cases, the phonology of the mother tongue, modified only slightly if at all, is used for both languages. Likewise, the grammatical patterns of one language system may intrude upon another system. Modification of one system based on the model of another is referred to as interference. Interference may be noted in the production of language, whether written or spoken, and also in the reception of language. In the production of language, interference tends to

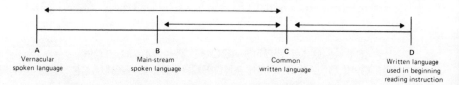

FIG. 7.1. The distance principle of language mismatch. The critical measurement points are phonology, grammar, and functions.

result from the differences between the language systems. In the reception of language, interference may also result from the similarities between the language systems. An educated American may need to be able to hear and understand a number of varieties of American, British, and foreign-accented English (although there is considerably less need to learn to speak them all). Similarly, such receptivity may need to be developed for a number of varieties of literary English: formal, informal, older versions, and slang (although there is considerably less need to learn to compose in all of them).

Treatment Hypotheses

Based on the assumption that differences between children's spoken language and the language used in their instructional materials are at least partially responsible for the fact that so many poor readers are found among speakers of certain vernacular versions of English, several research directions have been projected. At least five treatment hypotheses have been suggested for reducing the mismatch between the Vernacular Black English used by some beginning readers and the language in which their initial reading materials are written (see Shuy, 1972). These hypotheses are:

1. Teach children to speak Standard English and then teach them to read it.
2. Teach teachers about Vernacular Black English so that they will not confuse the use of it with real reading problems (Goodman, 1965).
3. Develop beginning reading materials in Vernacular Black English (Stewart, 1969).
4. Develop beginning reading materials that systematically avoid the mismatch of Vernacular Black English to written Standard English (Seymour, 1973).
5. Make use of the language experience approach.

To date, there has been little research to support, without qualification and question, any one of these approaches. Number 1, the standard, historical approach, has never been proven effective. Some progress is being made on Number 2, but the road has been and will continue to be slow and rocky. Research has been hampered by inordinate negative public reaction to any attempts to implement Number 3. Number 4 has been implemented in only the most indirect fashion to date. Number 5 has been restricted by the average teacher's difficulty in writing exactly what children say rather than what the teacher thinks they say or wishes they would say, although recent progress has helped to neutralize this problem.

Regardless of the apparent inconclusiveness concerning the effectiveness of these approaches, the study of Vernacular English has provided certain benefits to the field of reading. For example, the call by linguists for more realistic and believable language in beginning reading materials has helped to remove some of the stilted language of earlier primers, bringing *D* of Figure 1 a bit closer to *C*. Linguists who study the syntax of Vernacular English and who stress the importance of processing whole language units rather than only letter-sound correspondences have helped to shape current reading instruction along lines consistent with their focus. The linguists' contention that surface-structure oral reading does not necessarily reflect deep-structure comprehension is helping to minimize the importance of supposed misreadings, such as *she go* for *she goes*, by speakers of Vernacular Black English. Some progress is being made in helping teachers to realize that learning to read Standard English is not the same as learning to speak it and that teaching and evaluating both at the same time is confusing for both teachers and students.

PAST RESEARCH IN LANGUAGE MISMATCH IN READING

Although research on the question of language interference has not been lacking, unfortunately much of this research has been misdirected, flawed, or based on the assumption that a methodology is the proper focus of examination. Some of the deficiencies in research grow naturally out of the assumptions of the field of reading, assumptions that are generally unsupported by linguists.

Phonological Mismatch

It has been generally assumed in the field of reading that phonology plays a tremendously important role in early reading. It was only natural, then, that someone would study the potential interference of Vernacular English on learning to read. A case in point is Melmed's (1971) comparison of Black and White third-grade children's ability to discriminate auditorily, to read aloud, and to understand content that contained the major diagnostic phonological features of Vernacular Black English. In a carefully worked out procedure, Melmed concluded that although the Black subjects' auditory discrimination and production of these diagnostic features differed from that of White subjects's, comprehension after both oral and silent reading was the same for both groups. This research, therefore, rejects the hypothesis that phonological interference affects learning to read. As Simons (1973) pointed out, Melmed's study is flawed in several ways. Nevertheless, what is particularly interesting to the linguist is the fact that phonological interference was even suggested. To the linguist, the English spelling system, though complicated, is highly regular. In an article (Shuy, 1968) that appeared at least two years before Melmed's research, I analyzed the potential phonological interference between Verncular Black English and mainstream usage and concluded:

> A careful description of the phonology of Black English speakers will be of more use to teachers than to writers of classroom materials. The arbitrariness of the symbolization process makes it rather unnecessary to recast primers into a graphemic series which delete the *r* in *car* (cah), the *l* in *help* (hep), which substitute voiceless stops for voiced ones in words like *red* (ret), and which show consonant-cluster reductions in words like *just* (jus) and *send* (sen). Urban disadvantaged Negroes should not find it difficult to discover that (jus) is realized in print as *just*. Their grapheme rule would be <st>→/s/ in final position. This is certainly no more unreasonable than other double grapheme relations as single sounds, such as <th>→/Θ/ in *thin* or <mb>→/m/ in *thumb* [p. 122].

The major thrust of the work of linguists who pursued the question of the mismatch of spoken language and beginning reading was to focus on grammatical, not phonological interference. Melmed's research and that of Rystrom (1970), Rentel and Kennedy (1972), and Osterberg (1961) tend to be elaborate rejections of positions never held, at least not by linguists.

Grammatical Mismatch

That some of the research on dialect interference in reading is flawed has been pointed out by Simons (1973) and by Venezky (1970). The usual educational research flaws of sample size and comparability are shared by the study of Schaaf (1971) and Sims (1972), neither of whom had an adequate number of subjects or comparable reading materials across dialects. Both studies focused on grammatical interference rather than on phonological inter-ference, but problems arose when decisions had to be made regarding the adequacy of the language representation in the text. Sociolinguists have been careful to point out that dialect variation is more a continuum than a polarity and that speakers of one dialect may differ from those of another dialect in such minute matters as the frequency of occurrence of a particular feature rather than in its categorical presence or absence.

It is very clear, for example, that copula deletion is a characteristic of Vernacular Black English as it is spoken in New York, Washington, D.C., and Detroit. Certain linguists violently object to this idea, noting that Southern Whites also say *be here* or *you gonna do it*. Of course, those linguists are correct. What they fail to see, however, is that those who posit copula deletion as a characteristic of Vernacular Black English are comparing Southern Whites with Northern Blacks but are, quite to the contrary, concerned about what is considered to be Vernacular Black English in those specific Northern contexts. But even in those contexts we find that speakers of that dialect do not delete every copula. In fact, the frequency of that deletion stratifies quite nicely according to socioeconomic status. Likewise, not all Standard English speakers produce a copula every time one might be expected in their speech, although the frequency is probably very high. An even clearer case is that of multiple negation, which is also said to characterize Vernacular Black English, even though it is quite clear that many Whites also use the form regularly. What, then, does it mean to call a dialect "Vernacular Black English"? Simply that its characteristic grammatical features occur consistently in the continuous, natural speech of Blacks at a much higher frequency than they occur in the speech of Whites of the same socioeconomic status from the same communities. Strangely enough, this sort of finding is still rather new in linguistics and, to some linguists, quite heretical.

This sort of realization has implications for research of the sort required to compare the effects of dialect on reading ability. If we were to construct a comparable set of materials in Vernacular English and mainstream English, just exactly how would we represent this variability? Likewise, if we were to select dialect speakers for experimentation or analysis, exactly what criteria would we use for accurately determining whether people are speakers of the dialect in question? Does one occurrence of the diagnostic feature qualify them? Must we elicit 100 tokens of potential multiple negatives in order to find the 73.6% frequency of occurrence for lower working-class Blacks and 56.3% for lower working-class Whites, as the Detroit research indicates (Shuy, Wolfram, & Riley, 1967)? Johnson and Simons (1973) developed presumably equivalent stories for vernacular and mainstream dialects and presented them to Black third-grade children. No differences were discovered in comprehension, recall, or reading errors, offering no support to the grammatical interference hypothesis. Considerable question remains, however, about the extent to which the 57 subjects were speakers of the dialect under consideration, largely because the minute linguistic analysis required of each subject was not done. Being Black or being lower class (usually judged by correlational evidence of housing patterns) are usually assumed to imply speaking vernacular. Sociolinguists shudder at such assumptions.

Dialect Reading Materials

Efforts to develop beginning reading materials in Vernacular English in order to avoid the mismatch of spoken language to the printed page have been spectacular but less than successful. Based on the assumption that the subject matter should be relevant to the background and experience of the learner, the Chicago Board of Education created its *Psycholinguistics Reading Series—A Bi-Dialectal Approach* (Leaverton, Gladney, & Davis, 1969). Because many urban children speak a dialect of English that varies from the

Standard English spoken in the schools, the program is aimed at avoiding the usual problems faced by these students when learning to read. Instead of attempting to introduce a new pattern of speech at the same time as reading is introduced, the program builds on the language the child brings to the classroom.

The authors wanted to discover what effects the use of children's actual word patterns and grammatical structures would have on the quality of learning in the beginning reading situation. They were also interested in the extent to which use of the dialect would help children to master the same material written in the Standard English form.

The book itself consists of eight units with each story presented in both the children's dialect (everday talk) and Standard English (school talk). The terms in parentheses are used by the authors of the series to avoid making value judgments that might be psychologically damaging to the child.

Leaverton (1973), one of the authors of the series, conducted a study designed to measure the success of the program. The study included two groups of students matched on sex and on scores on the Wechsler Intelligence Scale for Children. The experimental group was given the everyday talk version of the story first. The control group was given the school talk version of the same story. When the teacher judged that half of the experimental group had mastered the everyday talk story, both groups were given word and phrase recognition tests. These tests (Leaverton, 1973) were designed to answer the question, "Will the children learn to read the everyday talk stories quicker than the school talk stories? [p. 119]." Then, when the teacher thought that half of the experimental group was able to read the school talk story orally without mistakes, both groups were given word and phrase recognition tests. These tests were designed to answer the question, "Will learning to read the everyday talk story facilitate the learning of the school talk story? [p. 120]." The word and phrase recognition tests consisted of oral review tests and retention tests. The oral review tests, given after each unit, used the same vocabulary as the unit, although the order was rearranged to alter the meaning of the story. The two groups were compared on total mean errors, errors on verb forms, and time required to read the story. About 4 to 6 months after both groups had completed a unit, they were given word recognition and oral review tests to measure their retention of the materials. Leaverton (1973) concluded that there was a definite trend in favor of the experimental group. The program seemed to be especially successful with boys who scored in the lowest quartile on the reading readiness test given at the beginning of the first grade. Leaverton states that the most significant value of the program "... lies in the influence it has on the attitude and behavior of the teacher toward the children's oral speech [p. 125]." The teacher at no time is to criticize the speech of the children; instead, the teacher is to encourage the children to learn to handle both dialects systematically.

From a linguistic viewpoint, the dialect materials produced by this program suffer from a flaw similar to that of reading materials using the Initial Teaching Alphabet (ITA). One basic claim of ITA is that it reduces the mismatch of sound to spelling by increasing the number of sound symbols and adding supposed consistency to the spelling system. In reality, ITA comes no closer to representing speech than does the regular alphabet. Because ITA texts are in a regularized standard dialect that does not permit regional, social, or individual variation, they fail to reduce the mismatch of spoken to written language. The Chicago dialect readers have also standardized the representation of spoken language, this time by grammatical units rather than by spelling. In the everyday talk versions, for examples, past tenses are categorically realized as zero, when actually such realization is variable. Such variation may or may not need to be represented in the text, but this project and these readers cannot show whether it needs to be represented because the issue of frequency of occurrence was not addressed.

Another celebrated dialect reader project, conducted by Baratz and Stewart (1969), produced materials that more closely approximate actual vernacular dialect than do the Chicago materials, although the variability issue was no better addressed. The project suffered from serious public relations problems growing out of a number of factors, not the least of which was the unwillingness of the public (parent–consumers) to approve of the vernacular in print. There is a mystique about the printed page that argues against any form of representation other than the accepted code. All else is considered to be in the same category as the comic strips and pulp sensationalism. Public reaction to the Baratz and Stewart dialect readers was so intense that the authors' research project was seriously thwarted.

The emotional outburst against the suggestion that vernacular reading materials should be tested has fairly well inhibited any further investigation in this area. This issue is not one that can be researched without real experimentation with real children. Yet despite what educators have been saying for decades about the need for "starting with children where they are," the matter of starting with a child's language where it is has never been accepted. This inconsistency between principle and practice has had more recent visibility in the bilingual education issue, which argues from essentially the same premise: that the child's cognitive growth, reading ability, and self-esteem will be significantly furthered if the child is taught first in the mother tongue. As in the bidialectal situation, the advocates of bilingualism argue that although the nonnative child should learn the mainstream language (English), the mother tongue need not be eradicated in the process, nor need it be demeaned, for it can be used as an effective medium of instruction, particularly at the onset of formal education. Somehow the notion of bilingualism has received more public support than bidialectalism, despite the similarity of claims and promises.

Results of the Treatment and Research

Perhaps it is time to step back and assess exactly what has been accomplished during the past decade of the new awareness of the potential mismatch of child language and school language. As is so often the case, it took several years for a problem born in the classroom to come to the attention of disciplines that could help to clarify and perhaps solve it (psychology, anthropology, linguistics, sociology). And until proper attention could be given to the problem several misdirections were inevitably taken. It is difficult to remember exactly what was considered canon just a few years ago. However, minority children's language was considered unsystematic and haphazard, and the failure of their oral language to match that of their teachers was thought to reflect cognitive deficits in the children. The myths linger on in the minds of some people, but the wide acceptance of deficit, "nonverbality," small vocabulary, parental isolation, noisy environment, and squalid living as the bases for reading problems has been at least somewhat reduced.

Despite all the attacks and counterattacks that have grown out of the study of Vernacular English, a number of useful and important developments have taken place. One of these has been in the field of linguistics. Today, variability has become a crucial issue in language analysis, due, at least partially, to the influence of the study of Vernacular English. Static grammars are suddenly out of favor, even among generative linguists, many of whom believe that syntax cannot be studied apart from its semantic context. In one way, then, the study of Vernacular English has had a significant effect on the development of linguists.

The study of Vernacular English has also begun to open the door to the solution of a number of broader educational problems having to do with linguistic and cultural variability in a much larger context than that suggested by the Vernacular English used by minorities. The discovery that minorities have a wide repertoire of language uses is finally beginning to be seen for what it is—a distinct linguistic advantage. Ignoring for a moment the politics of education, which might argue for eradicating or modifying one or more styles or for building new ones, the existence of such a range of styles is beginning to be viewed as a good and useful thing. The binary, right–wrong classroom paradigm is now subject to question. People use language in a number of contexts, for a number of purposes, to communicate with a number of different people. Variation in language can be viewed as a fantastically complex tool with which degrees of subtlety can be effected, tone can be manipulated, and poetry can be produced. A few years ago, it seems we wanted everyone to talk and write alike. Today, even the most pessimistic observer has to admit that the scene is gradually changing. The study of Vernacular English has helped to bring about this gradual change, and it is clear that even though we are only in the early stages of such change, we might not be even this far along if such studies had not been done.

NEEDED RESEARCH IN THE MISMATCH
OF CHILD LANGUAGE AND SCHOOL LANGUAGE

Part of the problem in assessing the mismatch of child language and school language stems from the fact that only part of the needed research has been completed. However perceptive it may have seemed to study Vernacular English a decade ago, the linguistic analyses that grew out of such studies suffered from a common malady: a lack of comparison between one language system and another.

The Need for Expanded Linguistic Focus

Careful investigations of minority speech in New York, Detroit, Washington, D.C., Los Angeles, and other places revealed useful patterns and systematism. What was lacking, however, was the touchstone for comparison. We ended up knowing a great deal about variable rules for Vernacular English but little or nothing about the corresponding rules for standard speech. We learned about frequency distributions for Vernacular Black English speakers but little about comparable distributions among Standard English speakers, regardless of race.

"Studying Up"

Linguists historically have studied the speech of individuals, the speech of areas (regional dialects), and the speech of large social groups (social dialects), but they have given little or no attention to the discourse of institutions or occupations (e.g., What is it like to talk like a lawyer?). Nader (1969) observed that anthropologists would do well to stop examining only the more exotic cultures of the world and "study up" (not down) in their own society: "...there is a certain urgency to the kind of anthropology that is concerned with power..., for the quality of life and our lives themselves may depend upon the extent to which citizens understand those who shape attitudes and actually control institutional structures [p. 285]." If we are to learn anything useful about what goes wrong in the communication exchange between doctor and patient, for example, we can certainly benefit from examining the speech of both participants. Recent research on that very topic has revealed that the major problem in such communication resides in the physician as well as in the patient (Shuy, 1974).

   Much of the study of the mismatch of child language and school language in the past focused on only one end of the continuum. That is, a great deal of effort went into the study of vernacular spoken language, but practically no attention was given to mainstream spoken language or to the teacher/parent/ adult variety of language. It was as though mainstream children and adults were assumed to speak in a way that was the opposite of that of the vernacular speakers. It has only recently become apparent that it might prove useful to study "effective" speech and to attempt to determine how speakers acquire this thing called "effectiveness."

Studying Effective Language Use

Social, legislative, and judicial pressures are raising questions about effective language use, questions that are crucial to the education of children from homes or communities where English is not the dominant language. Experiences growing out of the *Lau* vs. *Nichols* Supreme Court decision in 1974, the Aspira Consent Decree in New York City in 1975, and various bilingual education bills have revealed a gap in the knowledge base for educational programming. There is no doubt that legislative and judicial actions have provided momentum for education to become more responsive to the needs of children who are linguistically and culturally different from the mainstream. However, sustaining the momentum requires educational technology that remains to be developed.

For example, the Aspira Consent Decree requires that the placement of children in educational programs using English or Spanish as the medium of instruction be determined by their ability to "effectively participate" in the instruction. This legislation precedes by a large margin the technology needed to implement it. No assessment instruments are available that purport to test this ability. There is general consensus among second-language specialists that performance on tests of grammar and phonology is not an accurate predictor of "effective participation" and that functional language competence is a far better index. That is, effective participation in the classroom is more a matter of whether children can seek clarification or get a turn than it is a matter of whether they can distinguish phonologically between *shoes* and *choose* or make proper use of past-tense markers. To develop instruments capable of testing what needs to be tested, there must be available an inventory of the functional language competence demanded in the educational setting at the various age or grade levels.

Studying Functional Language Competence

Functional language competence is the underlying knowledge that enables people to use their language to make utterances in order to accomplish goals and to understand others' utterances in terms of the latter's goals. It includes knowledge of what kinds of goals language can accomplish (the functions of language) and of what utterances are permissable for accomplishing each goal

TABLE 7.1
Some Language Functions, Strategies, and Utterances of Adult
English Speakers

Function	Strategy	Utterance
Giving an order	Performative	I hereby order you to come home.
	Direct imperative	Give Jane some food.
	Wh–imperative	Won't you please buy me some candy?
	Statement	Mr. Jones, I need some more paper.
Promising	Performative	I hereby promise you that I will be home by eleven.
	Future statement	I'll be home by eleven.
	Conditional statement	If you give me a dollar, I'll be home by eleven.
	Questions	Will you let me take care of my own affairs?

(language strategies). Table 7.1 displays a small selection of the functions, strategies, and sample utterances that have been noted for adult English speakers.

This table is in no way complete. There are many more functions, many other strategies for each function, and, of course, many other utterances that could be used for each strategy. More important, the table is incomplete in that the context of each utterance needs to be specified to ensure that the utterance is permissable to accomplish the function. For example, the sentence *If you give me a dollar, I'll be home by eleven* is a promise only if in the context the addressee desires that the speaker come home at that time and only if the speaker believes that a dollar is valuable incentive. It could also be a threat if in the context the addressee desires that the speaker stay away and the speaker either considers receiving money to be inappropriate or does not consider a dollar to be enough of an incentive.

Functional language competence also accounts for knowing what utterances cannot do. For example, in English, the statement *You are a frog* does not work to turn the addressee into a frog. In the United States, at least, uttering the words *I divorce you* does not constitute the completion of divorce, but *I christen you John* does christen a child if uttered by his parents or some religious authority. Likewise, the utterance *You have one minute to get over here* can, if directed to a student by a teacher, function as an order; but if the student says the same thing to the teacher, such a function is, at best, unusual.

This very sketchy and incomplete discussion of some aspects of functional language competence shows that a speaker's underlying knowledge must be extensive and complex. In the literature of linguistics, sociolinguistics, and philosophy, three other terms are also used to refer to functional language competence: *communicative competence, pragmatics of natural language,* and *speech-act competence.* All who have studied language competence agree that language users cannot possibly learn and store in memory all the complexities of functions, strategies, and utterances as item lists, any more than they can store phonological or grammatical features of language as item lists. This knowledge must be learned and stored according to organizational principles. These principles may be considered constitutive rules that, for example, define the conditions under which utterances succeed or fail as promises and that serve to distinguish promises from orders or requests. Similarly, the constitutive rules of football not only account for the successes or failures of particular plays, but they also distinguish football from baseball or soccer.

In terms of the mismatch between child language and school language, a great deal needs to be learned about functional language. It is my opinion that mismatches in this area produce considerably greater interference than anything researched in the past. We have ample evidence that phonological interference is not very important. Grammatical interference, although possibly important, is not nearly so important as functional language interference may prove to be.

Functional Language in the Reading Classroom

Functional language competence is relevant to beginning reading instruction in several ways: It is relevant to teacher education, to the fit between the child's developing functional language competence and the school's curricula and materials, and, more generally, to current issues concerning the education of culturally and linguistically different children.

Teacher Education. To say that more emphasis should be placed on educating teachers about language functions so that they can better understand, appreciate, and diagnose problems in their students is a gross understatement. Various studies have shown that teachers are not adequately trained to diagnose student problems related to language (Shuy, 1970). Reading teachers, in particular, suffer from receiving information only on methods of teaching reading, without knowledge of linguistics, which would enable them to distinguish between a pronunciation problem and a grammatical miscue; without knowledge of psychology, which would enable them to evaluate the gestalt of reading and distinguish it from its component parts; and without knowledge of the cultural aspects of reading, which would enable them to distinguish reading problems from sex-role fulfillment or group-membership pressures.

Knowledge of language functions can help a teacher to interpret apparent misreadings appropriately. The most prominent occasions on which such diagnoses might be made concern comprehension questions. For example, if a teacher makes requests using strategies children have not yet acquired, confusion is apt to result. The meaning of the teacher's utterances, regardless of how well intentioned, must be expressed in both the semantic and pragmatic (functional) meaning system of the children. Teachers receive insufficient information regarding any kind of language competence, and problems arise from a failure to apply information about teachers' and children's functional language competence. The following incident illustrates what can occur when teachers lack this information. This incident was observed by a colleague during an outside free-play activity among 4-year-olds:

> Three boys are in a fairly separate area of the play yard with a teacher observing the action. The first child had brought a very nice glider to school. The rule is that when toys are brought from home they must be shared or left in the child's cubbyhole. The first and the second child are playing freely with the glider. The third child is not playing. Finally the third child sees the glider and goes to retrieve it. The first child runs faster and picks it up quickly. The following conversation ensues:
>
> Third Child:I want a turn. Can I have a turn? I want a turn. Let me have a turn.
>
> First Child: Look, I'd let you have a turn but you dropped it. You'll break it.
>
> Third Child:If you let me have a turn, I'll (pause) be your friend.
>
> First Child: I don't need you to be my friend.

> The teacher then enters the conversation and addresses the first child by name, talking to him about everyone needing friends and about sharing toys. After about five minutes of discussion of these values, she gives him the option of returning the toy to his cubby or letting the third child play with it after the first child tells him some rules about it. Then the following occurs:
>
> First Child: Say you won't drop it and break it.
>
> Third Child:I won't drop it. I won't break it.

The teacher and the observer discussed the incident later. From the teacher's actions and discussion, it became clear that she did not notice that the third child had experienced and exhibited a problem in functional language competence. He was trying to make a promise using a conditional statement strategy and was unable to do so successfully. The first child located the problem—a promise has to involve what the addressee perceives as valuable, and, in this case, the general childhood value of having friends was not specific enough. The first child needed to hear in the promise that the third child would not drop and break the glider. Instead of being rewarded for attempting to assist his peer in developing functional language competence, the child was rebuked for socialization offenses, that is, not sharing and being exclusive in friendships. The third child needed some assistance in developing a new strategy for making prmises. Instead, this need was ignored by the teacher, and he was allowed to play with the glider anyway. The teacher needed some information about language functions and strategies, expected developmental sequences, and teaching strategies that foster development of functional language competence. The teacher also would have benefited from some practice in observing children's language behavior, hypothesizing the causes of certain behavior, and planning, implementing, and evaluating teaching strategies that capitalize on those aspects of the educational setting that encourage the development of functional language competence.

It is not surprising that teachers are not well aware of the significance of developing language functions; they are scarcely aware of the child's developing phonology and grammar. Furthermore, this area of study has only recently become aparent, even to linguists, and research is only beginning.

It appears that competence in language functions, unlike that in phonology and grammar, continues to develop almost throughout one's life. Few adults, for example, ever become proficient in the language function of condoling. For the sake of survival, children learn how to interrupt appropriately rather early. They learn that strategies of interruption are complex and often asymetrical (teachers can interrupt children rather blatantly, but children must develop sophisticated strategies for interrupting teachers). One also learns how to avoid being interrupted, how to get or avoid a turn in talking, how to refuse, how to clarify, how to obfuscate with dignity (see especially the Watergate transcripts). What may be considered rudeness may be only an imperfectly developed set of interruption skills. It seems critical that teachers be able to distinguish among these cases.

Fit Between Functional Language Competence and School Curricula and Materials.   Although base-line normative data on functional language acquisition do not exist, some of the ways in which curricula and materials can conflict with or support the development can be noted. For example, reading primers that use a playground setting depict characters who range in age and status, but their language is often undifferentiated according to age and status. There is an obvious effort to have the setting relate to the child's experience, but the questions asked by the characters, the requests made, or the orders given do not relate to actual elements in the child's experience or to functional language rules related to politeness and the relative status of the addressee and the speaker. Such samples of language give little assistance to children in developing these distinctions and even potentially conflict with their development.

Curricula can also conflict with functional language development. For younger children, a major curriculum objective is to learn cooperative social organization. In an incident in which two children had agreed to a turn-taking arrangement in play, one teacher interpreted an argument, which was actually caused by a violation in turn taking, as the unwillingness of one child to share. This incident illustrates that cooperative social organization, which was the goal of both the curriculum and the children's use of language in their conflict, can be easily misconstrued or too narrowly defined.

Culturally Specific Application.   Much about functional language appears to be culture specific. What needs to be researched are specifics of the functional language competence necessary for effective interaction in an educational setting, and a comparison of the realization of such competence across cultures must be made. For example, what appears to American teachers to be defiance in Vietnamese refugee children (arms folded in front of them) is actually a stance of submissiveness in that culture. We need to know what functional language performance by children is judged to be necessary or desirable by teachers even though it may not be necessary for effective interaction. We need to obtain data on the differences in functional language competence across cultures and languages and on the demands made by the school setting on such functions. Such research has just begun, but it offers a much richer source of explanatory power concerning the mismatch of child language and school language than has heretofore been conceived.

NEEDED RESEARCH IN THE MISMATCH OF
CHILD LANGUAGE AND LEARNING STYLES

I have assumed in this chapter that the mismatch of child language and school language is a critical factor in identifying and remediating much of what is currently called "reading failure." I have also suggested that phonological mismatch is probably not important, that grammatical mismatch is slightly more important (but such a claim is still unsupported by research), and that functional mismatch is probably the most important of all. My assumptions and claims are based on the complex interaction of productive and receptive language on the part of student, teacher, and materials.

Since reading is a language-processing operation, a theory of reading should account for language in the many ways it reveals itself developmentally. In at least one sense of the term, reading can be viewed on a timeframe continuum in which early skills are developed, only to be abandoned as soon as possible for other, more advanced cognitive processes. Reading offers a rather clear example of a mixture of such early behavioral skills, later cognitive strategies, and a potential for cultural interpretation and individual learning style. Elsewhere I have noted the acquisition sequence of the language accesses in reading (Shuy, 1975). By *language accesses*, I mean those units of language (sounds, syllables, morphemes, words, syntactic and semantic units) through which reading (silent or oral) is realized.

Figure 7.2 represents a theory of reading in which the various language accesses to reading (letter–sound correspondences, syllables, etc.) are of different degrees of importance to the process of learning to read at different stages in the acquisition process. For example, letter–sound correspondences seem to be of great importance at the onset of reading (as a behavioral "starting" skill), but they become less critical as a given reader becomes more and more proficient. Good readers do not read letter by letter; they process in larger and larger units, up to and including contextual meaning units. Such a theory argues for early attention to meaning in reading and for realistic meaning contexts at all times (i.e., no study of letters in isolation from meaning units). There has been some disagreement among reputable scholars

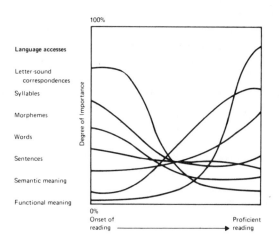

FIG. 7.2.   Language accesses to reading.

on exactly how this attention to meaning and realistic meaning context is to be carried out. Some argue that it is better to start to read whole sentences (e.g., Smith, 1973), because meaning is thought to be most significant at the syntactic level. I have argued (Shuy, 1975) that meaning exists as far down as the morpheme level, and although I agree that it is important to develop materials using language found in realistic language contexts, I disagree with those who would totally abandon decoding. Learning theory has long held that different kinds of learning can take place at different stages of learning. Behavioral, skill-focused learning can be adequate in the early stages of reading but should be replaced as soon as possible by more advanced cognitive strategies involving meaning. For some, this means using sentences. I believe that for typical cooperative children, who will accept the fact that certain dull or odd things must be done in order to get to later more interesting things, almost any reading approach can be successful. Some children may be ready to accept such behavioral (letter–sound type) instruction earlier or later than others. Some sort of diagnostic instrument should be able to predict who such children are. It is likely that one type of prediction will be based on the child's personality more than on the reading tasks or on the language accesses themselves.

Relatively little is known about learning style, despite the rather large amount of attention given it in educational discussion. We know (or think we know) some things about cultural learning styles (e.g., Navajos sit in circles), but we know relatively little about individual, nonsocially determined styles. Some research exists on perceptual styles, and personal experience shows me that in judging a work of art, I see shape before color or detail. It seems reasonable that such perceptual styles might be relevant to learning style as well. The seven language accesses to reading shown in Fig. 7.2 may be explored for evidences of learning style. It is clear that some children have learned to read using only letter–sound correspondence materials. Some children have learned to read when only look–say (whole word) materials are used. Interestingly enough, children who have been taught using only the look–say, whole-word approach have been known to develop letter–sound correspondence abilities (otherwise, they might never have leaned to spell well).

Although a good mainstream reading program has the obligation to provide multilanguage accesses to its general or normal audience, we have no reason to believe that all children will need all the accesses or techniques equally or in the same proportion or, for that matter, at all. It seems reasonable to me that some children's learning styles might involve, for example, a combination of letter–sound correspondences and syntax, completely ignoring the whole-word and syllable accesses. Other children may have similarly idiosyncratic learning styles. This does not mean that a mainstream program is in error for presenting all the accesses. What it suggests, instead, is that it would be efficient if we could determine what combinations of the language accesses best suit the learning styles of each child.

To discuss doing this efficiently, we must first clarify what we mean by efficiency. What I mean by efficiency is getting to the right-hand side of Fig. 7.2 (proficient reading) as soon and as well as possible. This means that I am not very concerned that children who become proficient readers maintain their ability to attend to the component skills that helped to develop the proficiency. I regard letter–sound correspondences, syllables, morphemes, and, to a certain extent, words as components of the gestalt of reading for meaning by means of sentences, paragraphs, pages, or books. As such, letter–sound correspondences are beginning skills, primarily useful as stages in the acquisition of the real skill. The real skill of reading involves getting various kinds of meaning from the printed page.

It is reasonable to believe, for example, that for particular children, the accesses represented in Figure 2 might look like those in Fig. 7.3 and 7.4.

Figures 7.3 and 7.4 suggest that there is much work to be done, not only in the area of general research, but also in the area of assessment of individual children's learning styles, if we are to develop effective mainstream reading programs. The knowledge gained through research and assessment of language mismatch at all levels could provide additional insights into the problem of reading failure.

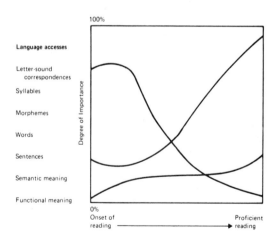

FIG. 7.3.   A possible language accesses configuration.

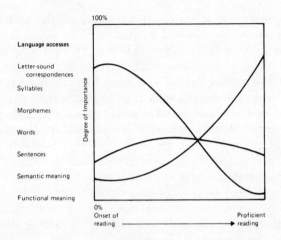

FIG. 7.4.   A possible language accesses configuration.

SUMMARY

This chapter first described the past assumptions about the mismatch of child language and school language, especially as they relate to the distance principle, to language interference, and to various treatment hypotheses. Next, it assessed past research, especially that dealing with phonological and grammatical mismatches of language in reading. The major thrust of the chapter was to suggest that recent developments in linguistic theory and research have opened the area of language functions for investigation and that this area is certainly the most promising of all for determining causes of reading difficulty and failure. Finally, the chapter suggested that a language-based theory of reading can provide the framework for discovering what might be at least one dimension of the elusive search for learning styles. If individualization is to mean anything beyond motivation and attitude, hope is certainly offered by such an analysis.

REFERENCES

Baratz, J. C., & Stewart, W. *Ollie and friends* (Experimental readers). Washington, D.C.: Education Study Center, 1969.

Goodman, K. Dialect barriers to reading comprehension. *Elementary English*, 1965, *42*, 853–860.

Johnson, K. R., & Simons, H. D. *Black children's reading of dialect and standard text* (U.S. Office of Education, Final Rep., Project No. OEC-9-72-011[057]). Washington, D.C.: U.S. Government Printing Office, 1973.

Leaverton, L. Dialectal readers: Rationale, use and value. In J. Laffey & R. Shuy (Eds.), *Language differences: Do they interfere?* Newark, Del.: International Reading Association, 1973.

Leaverton, L., Gladney, M., & Davis, O. *The psycholinguistics reading series—a bidialectal approach.* Chicago: Board of Education, 1969.

Melmed, J. P. *Black English phonology: The question of reading interference* (Monographs of the Language–Behavior Research Laboratory, No. 1). Berkeley: University of California, 1971.

Nadar, L. Up the anthropologist—perspectives gained from studying up. In D. Hymes (Ed.), *Reinventing anthropology.* New York: Random House, 1969.

Osterberg, T. *Bilingualism and the first school language.* Umea, Sweden: Vastenbottens Togckeri AB, 1961.

Rentel, V., & Kennedy, J. Effects of pattern drill on the phonology, syntax and reading achievement of rural Appalachian children. *American Educational Research Journal,* 1972, *9,* 87–100.

Rystrom, R. Dialect training and reading: A further look. *Reading Research Quarterly,* 1970, *5,* 581–599.

Schaaf, E. *A study of black English syntax and reading comprehension.* Unpublished master's thesis, University of California, Berkeley, 1971.

Seymour, D. Neutralizing the effect of the nonstandard dialect. In J. Laffey & R. Shuy (Eds.), *Language differences: Do they interfere?* Newak, Del.: International Reading Association, 1973.

Shuy, R. W. A linguistic background for developing beginning reading materials for black children. In J. Baratz & R. Shuy (Eds.), *Teaching black children to read.* Washington, D.C.: Center for Applied Linguistics, 1968.

Shuy, R. W. Teacher training and urban language problems. In R. Fasold & R. Shuy (Eds.), *Teaching standard English in the inner city.* Washington, D.C.: Center for Applied Linguistics, 1970.

Shuy, R. W. Speech differences and teaching strategies: How different is enough? In R. Hodges & E. Rudorf (Eds.), *Language and learning to read: What teachers need to know about language.* Boston: Houghton Mifflin, 1972.

Shuy, R. W. Communications problems in the cross-cultural medical interview. *Papers of the second annual conferences on psychosematic obstetrics and gynecology,* 1974, *2,* 17–19.

Shuy, R. W. Pragmatics: Still another contribution of linguistics to reading. In S. Smiley & J. Towner (Eds.), *Language and reading.* Bellingham: Western Washington State College Press, 1975.

Shuy, R. W., Wolfram, W., & Riley, W. K. *Field techniques in an urban language study.* Washington, D.C.: Center for Applied Linguistics, 1967.

Simons, H. D. *Black dialect and reading interference: A review and analysis of the research evidence.* Unpublished manuscript, University of California, Berkeley, 1973.

Sims, R. *A psycholinguistic description of miscues created by selected young readers during oral reading of text in black dialect and standard English.* Unpublished doctoral dissertation, Wayne State University, 1972.

Smith, F. Decoding: The great fallacy. In F. Smith (Ed.), *Psycholinguistics and reading.* New York: Holt, Rinehart and Winston, 1973.

Stewart, W. On the use of Negro dialect in the teaching of reading. In J. Baratz & R. Shuy (Eds.), *Teaching black children to read.* Washington, D.C.: Center for Applied Linguistics, 1969.

Venezky, R. L. *Non-standard language and reading* (Working Paper No. 43). Madison: University of Wisconsin, Wisconsin Research and Development Center for Cognitive Learning, 1970.

8 Applications of the Audread Model to Reading Evaluation and Instruction

Thomas G. Sticht
National Institute of Education

This chapter is concerned with the relationship of oral language to written language as presented in the developmental model of auding and reading (the Audread model) presented by Sticht, Beck, Hauke, Kleiman, and James (1974) and by the writings of Fries (1963). Fries made several points that have been further developed in the Audread model:

1. He distinguished meanings from language and language from the stimulus displays used to convey the language. Thus three components are involved in the communication process: meanings or thoughts, language as an internal representation of thoughts, and speech or writing as an external representation of the internal language signals.

2. Reading involves the use of internal language representations of thoughts that are the same as those used earlier in comprehending spoken language. Following Brown (1954), we call the latter process *auding*. Auding developmentally precedes reading, and reading and auding use the same language signals.

3. Auding and reading use the same language system for representing the same thoughts, that is, they share the same meaning system. Thus in learning to read people learn to comprehend by reading what they could previously comprehend by auding.

4. With sufficient practice, readers not only come to comprehend by reading what they previously could comprehend only by auding, but they also become as efficient at developing internal language signals from the written display as they are at deriving internal language signals from speech displays. This occurs as the decoding component of reading becomes automatic.

Fries took for granted that once students develop reading skill, they derive meanings from the printed page comparable to those derived from the spoken word. He focused his attention on the "transfer" skills involved in learning the visual signs for language. Others who have been concerned with various aspects of decoding have also focused on the skills students need to learn the printed language, and considerable debate has centered on this aspect of learning to read. This debate has been documented and discussed thoroughly by Chall (1967).

Work less systematic and less comprehensive than Chall's book on aspects of learning the written "code" has examined the notion that the language signs and systems used in auding and reading are the same and the notion that the meaning systems of auding and reading are the same. Sticht et al. (1974) presented an extensive study of these relationships. This work, developed before the authors had read Fries, integrated many of the ideas expressed by Fries into a developmental model of the language skills of auding and reading.

THE DEVELOPMENTAL MODEL

Briefly, the model states that children are born with certain basic processes for adapting to the world around them. These processes include certain information-processing capacities for acquiring, storing, retrieving, and manipulating information. Through this information-processing capacity, a cognitive content is developed that, in its earlier forms, is prelinguistic. After some time children develop skills for receiving information that represents the cognitive content of others and for representing their own cognitive content to others. This is accomplished through the specialization of the information-processing activities of listening, looking, uttering, and marking. The specialization is one in which these skills are used for the purpose of externally representing one's own thoughts for others to interpret, and for forming internal representations of the external representations of others' thoughts. The specialization of present concern is the representation of thoughts by conventionalized signs (words) and rules for sequencing these signs (syntax) in speaking and auding. Finally, if children are in a literate society, they may acquire the specialized looking and marking skills of reading and writing.

The developmental model also holds that the development of the oracy skills of speaking and auding requires the development of the prelinguistic cognitive content through intellectual activity, which we call *conceptualizing*. In other words, children must have something to think about before the need for a language for sharing thoughts arises. It is important to understand that this early, prelinguistic cognitive content, or knowledge, forms the foundation for the acquisition of new knowledge over the lifetime of the person. Thus any concern for children's acquisition of literacy skills must involve their prelinguistic acquisition of knowledge and their later acquisition of knowledge of and by the oral language.

Finally, the model asserts that literacy skills use a conceptual base (cognitive content, conceptualizing processes, and knowledge) that is the same as that used in auding and speaking and that the literacy skills use signs and rules for sequencing those signs that are the same as those used in the oral language skills for receiving and expressing thoughts. These assertions are based on the developmental sequence; that is, the literacy skills are built on existing oracy skills as the end of the developmental sequence. This does not mean that once literacy skills are acquired, they do not contribute anything new to knowledge or language capability; clearly, they do. What is asserted is that when the literacy skills are initially acquired, they are to be construed as a second way of using the same language system that the child uses in speaking and auding. Presumably, this is what is meant by being able to use language by eye as well as it is used by ear (Kavanagh & Mattingly, 1972).

Hypotheses Derived from the Audread Model

From the Audread model, four hypotheses regarding relationships of auding and reading at the level of meaning outcomes, or "conceptualizations," have been formulated and evaluated. Extensive literature review has supported these hypotheses.

> Hypothesis 1. *Ability to comprehend language by auding ought to surpass ability to comprehend language by reading in the early years of schooling; this gap should close as reading ability is acquired.*

This hypothesis calls attention to the closing of the gap between auding and reading as the latter skill is learned. Literature review suggests that, on the average, it may take as long as 6 to 8 years for students entering first grade to develop the reading process to the point where, as Fries (1963) has stated, it "... is so automatic that the reading is used equally with or even more than live language in the acquiring and developing of experience [p. 132]."

This very fundamental process, the development of reading into an alternative language skill as effective and efficient as auding, has received practically no attention from researchers. Spache (1972) and Durrell and Brassard (1970) have considered this problem and have developed tests to assess differences between auding and reading skills, but to my knowledge no one has conducted studies of how long it typically takes students to learn to read, that is, to become as accurate and efficient in using the printed language as they are in using the spoken language. The development of a test for this purpose for use with adults is described later in this chapter.

Hypothesis 2. *Ability to comprehend language by auding should be predictive of ability to comprehend language by reading when reading is developed beyond the decoding stage.*

If it is true that in learning to read children become capable of comprehending in print what they could comprehend previously by auding, then it follows that those children of high auding ability (i.e., large vocabulary, verbal fluency, and ability to store and retrieve spoken messages accurately and efficiently) will be high in reading ability. The reverse will hold for those of low auding ability.

It is important to keep in mind that this relationship holds after the learning-to-read (decoding) period is complete. Obviously, if no one of a group of auders could read, then the correlation between auding and reading would be zero. The correlation between auding and reading should, and literature review suggests that it does, grow larger with increased years of schooling (at least up to the fourth grade). Loban's (1964) data clearly indicate that students low in oral language skills, including auding, and low on various speech measures become students low in reading skills over the school years. Students high in oral language skills become the more able readers, and the groups grow farther apart over the school years.

Again, there is distressingly little well-designed research related to this hypothesis. The literature reviewed by Sticht et al. (1974) used different tests at different grade levels, and none of the tests was designed for maximal comparability of auding and reading skills. In addition, no longitudinal studies have been conducted to determine relationships between prereading auding skills and reading ability as the latter skill is developed over the school years.

Hypothesis 3. *Training in comprehending by auding should transfer to comprehending by reading when reading is developed beyond the learning-to-decode stage.*

If both auding and reading use the same conceptual base, then concepts added to that base by auding ought to be accessible by reading when the latter skill is developed. The validity of this hypothesis underlies the common teachers' practice of defining new reading words in oral discussions. If there were no transfer from the comprehension of the word and its meanings developed through auding, then it would do no good for teachers to define and discuss words in the oral mode.

Again, there have been few well-designed studies of the transfer from training in comprehending by auding to comprehending by reading. Compensatory education efforts, which have attempted to improve children's oral language and, hence, written language skills, have at times failed to consider that the effects of such training can best be assessed after the decoding skills of reading are acquired. Hence, failure to find such transfer effects may be due to premature evaluation.

Some studies provide training in oral vocabulary and in comprehension tasks in the oral language but then test for the effects of such training on reading comprehension with tests using completely different vocabulary items and content domains. This practice reflects the notion that some "generic comprehension skills" are being developed and fails to recognize that the vocabulary and comprehension tasks performed on specific content domains in the auding training should form the basis for testing following reading training.

This problem emerges at times as the question of a "mismatch" between the student's knowledge formed by experience in the world and by oral language, and the knowledge and language terms used in reading texts. Merely having a student develop skill in sight–sound correspondences so that words in print can be decoded and spoken rapidly (which could be accomplished using nonsense words) does not ensure that the student will comprehend those words. If the words are not in the student's spoken language repertoire, then, unless the words around the target word are in the auding repertoire so that the meaning of the target word can be inferred from context, the student cannot be expected to comprehend the selections as well as those students who know the meaning of the target word. Such problems underlie the current concern that reading materials should reflect the cultural experiences of the students who use them. Also, if education in the oral mode is going to emphasize vocabulary and concepts relevant to a particular minority culture, then the readers these students encounter should also incorporate this language and concept domain for adequate transfer in comprehending by reading.

Of the studies related to this hypothesis that were reviewed by Sticht et al. (1974), those that reported transfer from auding to reading suggested that such transfer was most likely to be indexed when the skills and knowledge of the auding training and measurement tests most closely resembled the skills and knowledge used to measure the effects of such training on reading test performance. Future work should develop programs and tests explicitly designed to assess transfer from auding training to reading.

Hypothesis 4.   *Maximal rates for auding and reading will be comparable after the reading skill is developed beyond the learning-to-decode period.*

If the languaging and conceptualizing skills used in reading are the same as those used in auding, then the rate at which these skills can be performed limits the rate at which both auding and reading can be performed.

Once more, there are only a few adequately designed studies that compare auding and reading rates. One of the earliest and best-designed studies was by

Goldstein (1940), who reported comparable immediate retention comprehension scores for auding and reading over speech rates of from 100 to 322 words per minute (wpm). The best work on this problem that I am aware of is Carver's (1973), who also found comparable performance by auding and reading for rates of from 75 to 450 wpm.

In both the Goldstein and Carver studies, auding and reading scores declined comparably and significantly at the faster rates. Since both of these studies used skilled adult readers (college students), there is no evidence here that reading can be or is performed at exceedingly fast rates (e.g., 1,000 to 10,000 wpm) without significant losses in comprehension (at least as indicated by immediate retention and judgments of information stored). The rates at which languaging and conceptualizing can be performed set limits for both auding and reading.

APPLICATIONS OF THE MODEL OF
AUDING AND READING DEVELOPMENT

From the point of view of Fries (1963) and Sticht et al. (1974), in learning to read people must close the gap between auding and reading, two skills that permit them to comprehend linguistic messages. Two research projects concerned with assessing the language by ear and by eye gap are summarized below.

Reading Talk in the First Grade

Keithly (1974) obtained a measure of the gap between first-grade children's speaking ability and their ability to read their own spoken language when it was presented in written (typed) form. Keithly assumed that children have an understanding of the words and sentences they use in talking. If children's spoken words and sentences are presented in printed form for them to read aloud, an estimate of the extent to which they can read what they can speak can be obtained. By using this procedure, one can index the closing of the speaking–reading gap as decoding skills in reading are acquired.

Keithly studied 48 first-grade children. Samples of spoken languages were obtained during the second and third months of the school year. The children were induced to speak about a family photo brought from home, their personal interests (hobbies, likes, dislikes), their families, exciting experiences, and a series of eight magazine pictures. All conversations were tape recorded and transcribed. After 5 days, each child was asked to read his or her typewritten speech sample and two of the stories dictated by other children (peer stories) to determine how general the child's reading ability was. From

April to June, children were asked to reread their speech and their peers' stories.

The differences between their fall pretest and spring posttest reading scores constituted the major data of interest. These data were based on the percentage correct of the different types of words correctly read aloud by the child. That is, if a word occurred more than once, it was scored only one time, although for credit it had to be correctly read each time it was encountered. On the pretest no child scored 0%, and three children scored 100% correct. The median pretest score was 11.3% correct, and this rose to 84% correct on the posttest, indicating considerable improvement in reading for these children. Generally speaking, there was a high correlation between being able to read one's own words in prose and being able to read the words of one's peers.

Additional data indicated correlation coefficients of more than .50 between children's scores on the Murphy–Durrell Reading Readiness Analysis (Murphy & Durrell, 1965) given at the beginning of school and their scores on the pretest reading of their own speech and their peers' stories. Posttest correlation coefficients between scores for reading the transcriptions of speech and the Cooperative Primary Tests (Cooperative Tests and Services, 1970) were in the area of .80. Finally, it was found that the children's reading of their own speech at the beginning of first grade was slightly better than the Murphy–Durrell Reading Readiness Analysis for predicting end-of-first-grade Cooperative Primary Test scores ($r = .60$, compared to .50 for the Murphy–Durrell), and they were equally accurate in predicting reading of the child's own speech at the posttest session ($r \geq .60$ in both cases).

Although Keithly's study demonstrates that many children succeed considerably in closing the speaking–reading gap in the first year, many others do not make much progress. Of the 40 children for whom pretest and posttest data were available 17 scored 10% or less on the pretest reading of their own story; 3 of these 17 scored less than 10% on the posttest, and 13 scored less than 30% correct on the posttest.

The utility of Keithly's approach to assessing reading has not been fully explored. It is an interesting approach because it has great face validity and because it relates rather nicely to the language experience method, which many teachers and reading specialists favor. Generally in this method students maintain files of words they and their classmates have contributed from their oral language repertoire that they have learned to read. Keithly's approach formalizes the gathering of information about the words students speak and are able to read. The pretest and posttest measures provide a summative measure of achievement, which is compatible with the language experience approach, but which is not obtained simply by accumulating words in a file as they are learned. Future work along these lines should include tests of comprehension because it is not certain that children would be able to comprehend the written text of their own speech at a later date.

Assessing the Auding and Reading Gap in Adults

In the developmental model of auding and reading it is considered that in learning to read people gradually close the gap between their ability to comprehend spoken language and their ability to comprehend printed language. An implication of this hypothesis is that the development of an auding/reading test battery capable of indexing discrepancies between these abilities would be useful in revealing the degree to which reading problems reflect difficulties in handling printed language and in revealing low levels of general language ability. A comparison of auding and reading would help to indicate the nature and extent of a reading problem and provide information on the type of reading training that might be necessary.

The applicability of this concept to identifying remedial training needs and predicting improvement in literacy for adults was explored by Sticht and Beck (1976) in the development of the experimental Literacy Assessment Battery (LAB) for the U.S. Air Force.[1] The population for the LAB are secondary school students and adults who volunteer or are otherwise selected for basic literacy training. Generally, they are students who routinely score at or below the sixth-grade level on a grade-school normed, standardized reading test.

The LAB test was designed to indicate whether a person is unskilled in the use of the printed form of language but of roughly average skill relative to age peers in processing spoken prose materials, or is equally (un)skilled in both forms of language processing. More explicitly, the question of interest is whether a person's ability to read and store printed information for subsequent use in an immediate retention test equals his or her ability to store and retrieve the same information when it is presented in spoken form at rates comparable to that typically used to present printed prose orally.

The LAB was not designed to determine how well people can comprehend spoken language in general or whether they can comprehend spoken language when it is presented in printed form. Instead, the LAB was designed to determine how well a person who cannot read and store information from a printed text of a given difficulty level can process that text when it is presented

---

[1]Two standardized tests currently exist to measure both auding and reading and to provide comparisons between these two abilities for the purpose of identifying individuals with reading potential (i.e., those whose auding performance exceeds their reading performance). These tests, the Diagnostic Reading Scales (Spache, 1972) and the Durrell Listening–Reading Series (Durrell & Brassard, 1970), although developed for and standardized on school children, were examined to investigate various approaches that might be used to measure reading potential of adults.

orally. This approach reflects the primary interest in reading. A further restriction on the design of the LAB is that it was not designed to obtain information on how well a person constructs meanings from texts by a long, arduous reading. Instead, it was designed to determine if the person's processing of information by reading a text is as efficient and accurate as it is by auding the text.

Other decisions that should be facilitated by the LAB include:

1. Given reading potential (auding performance exceeding reading performance), is the person's failure to read well due primarily to lack of knowledge of the content referred to in the message or to deficiency of skill in decoding?

2. Given low scores for both auding and reading of passages, are the person's low scores due primarily to lack of relevant knowledge or to lack of skill in sequentially processing the information in a passage of connected discourse?

Components of the LAB. The LAB is comprised of three tests. A paragraph test was designed to measure the discrepancy between a person's ability to efficiently store and retrieve language information presented as connected prose in spoken or written displays. This test consists of four paragraphs, 150 to 190 words in length, or ninth-grade level in readability as determined by the FORCAST readability formula (Sticht, 1975b). Two of the passages are presented for auding and two for reading. These passages were calibrated to be of equal difficulty. Following each paragraph, 12 constructed-response retention test items calling for near verbatim recall of factual information are administered. These questions, interrogative transformations of paragraph material, were determined to be passage-dependent (i.e., not answerable without having auded or read the passage). The questions following the auding passages are read aloud for auding. The questions following the reading passages are read silently by the student. Time for reading the paragraphs is limited to the time used to present the auding paragraphs. Time for reading the questions (following the removal of each passage) is limited to the time required to read the auding questions aloud.

A vocabulary test was designed to measure the discrepancy between a person's knowledge of word meanings presented by auding and by reading. The vocabulary words were selected from the paragraphs test in an attempt to be somewhat "diagnostic" and to determine whether poor performance on the paragraphs test might reflect lack of knowledge of word meanings. Additionally, however, the vocabulary test provides evidence for whether poor performance on the paragraphs test may be due to the requirement that the person efficiently process information in connected prose format. There is a 14-item, mulitiple-choice vocabulary subtest for each of the four paragraphs test passages. When the vocabulary–reading subtests are given, they are presented for silent reading only. When the vocabulary–auding subtests are given, they are presented both by auding and by reading. Thus the vocabulary–auding subtest is actually a simultaneous auding and reading subtest. This procedure was followed because the vocabulary test was designed to determine whether the person knew the words from the passages, not to assess an auding–reading gap.

Using units of connected discourse, a decoding test was designed to measure the efficiency with which a reading decoding task can be performed. This test represents an attempt to operationally index the degree of automaticity of decoding, as discussed by Fries (1963). With regard to reading, *automaticity* refers to the ability to decode print so efficiently that attention can be directed to the processing of meaning instead of to performing the decoding task.

In the LAB decoding test, the student is required simultaneously to aud and to read passages at four rates of presentation: 100, 150, 200, and 250 wpm. The rates are established by the spoken message; thus the auding message sets the pace for performing the reading task. In each passage a number of mismatches occur between words seen on the page and words heard. Because these mismatch words are syntactically and semantically acceptable substitutes, they are not detectable unless they are both auded and read. The student's task is to circle the mismatch words when he or she encounters thems. The score on the test is the number of correct out of 10 mismatches for each speech rate and the total number of correct for the four speech rates.

Results of a Tryout of the LAB.   The LAB was administered to a group of about 70 men in a minimum security correctional facility in northern California. The Gates–MacGinitie Reading Tests, Survey D (Gates & MacGinitie, 1965) were also administered.

Figure 8.1 presents the results for the LAB paragraphs subtests (auding and reading) and LAB vocabulary subtests (auding and reading) in terms of the percentage correct for men reading at different grade levels as indexed by the Gates–MacGinities tests. As indicated by the paragraphs test, mean auding scores exceeded mean reading scores for men reading at the sixth-grade level and below. A similar finding holds for the vocabulary subtests. These data suggest that it is possible to detect an auding–reading gap using the LAB.

An individual's reading potential (cf. the Diagnostic Reading Scales and the Durrell Listening–Reading Series) is an estimate of the reading grade level a person would have achieved had he read as well as he auded. It is obtained by running a horizontal line from the auding score for a given grade level to the reading curve and then dropping a perpendicular from the reading curve to the abcissa. In the example for the paragraphs test in Fig. 8.1, a person at

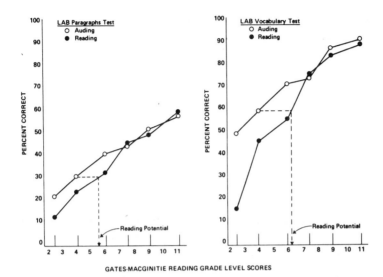

FIG. 8.1.   Mean percent correct for the LAB paragraphs and vocabulary tests as a function of reading ability measured by the Gates–MacGinitie Reading Tests, Survey D.

the fourth-grade level on the Gates–MacGinitie has a reading potential score of 5.5. The data from Fig. 8.1 suggest that even if many of these men were able to comprehend by eye as well as they can by ear, they would still be in need of considerable oracy and literacy training to raise their potential level.

On the LAB decoding test results, mean scores for the 100, 150, 200, and 250 wpm rates were, respectively, 8.1, 7.7, 6.0, and 2.7 correct (out of 10 each), with a total score of 24.7 correct (out of 40 possible). A monotonic decline was obtained as a function of rate of presentation, suggesting that decoding skills can be stressed in this manner to reveal persons possessing more or less automaticity of decoding. The decoding total test score correlated .70 with the Gates–MacGinitie test for speed of reading, suggesting that the decoding test is a valid measure of reading (decoding) speed.

Interpreting LAB Test Profiles.   By converting LAB scores to percentile scores, profiles of paragraphs (reading and reading potential), vocabulary (reading and reading potential), and decoding (total) scores can be constructed. These profiles can be interpreted to aid in making the following decisions: (1) Does this person show reading potential for the paragraphs test? (2) If so, is the reason his reading is not equal to his auding mostly due to lack of relevant vocabulary knowledge of the reading passages? (3) If the vocabulary is known, is the difficulty in reading due to lack of decoding skill or to a particular problem in integrating information from connected discourse for storage and retrieval?

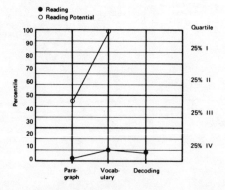

FIG. 8.2.   Profile for the LAB test results of one examinee.

Figure 8.2 presents data for one of the men who took the LAB test. As indicated, he scored in the bottom quarter of people who took the LAB test on all three reading subtests. His auding scores converted to reading potential scores indicate that his potential for paragraphs–reading is around the 50th percentile. If he could read as well as he can aud, he would have been near the group mean score on paragraphs–reading.

The difference between his reading and reading potential scores increases dramatically with the vocabulary test. This, coupled with the very low decoding score, suggests that this person has a true deficit in reading decoding skills. For this reason, he cannot realize his reading potential levels.

Summarily, then, the LAB consists of three interrelated subtests. The paragraphs subtest provides a measure of an individual's auding, reading, and reading potential levels. These are the major data provided by the LAB, and they are intended to facilitate the primary decision of whether a person's ability to read and store information is equal to his or her ability to aud and store information. That is, are the reading level and reading potential equivalent? The vocabulary subtest aims to aid the secondary decision as to whether poor performance on the auding or reading paragraphs subtest reflects low knowledge about the subject matter content, indexed by the knowledge of meanings of words from the paragraphs subtest, or whether such poor performance reflects failure to process language information efficiently when it is presented in connected discourse. The decoding subtest is used to facilitate the secondary decision regarding the outcome of the paragraphs subtest by indicating whether poor performance on the reading paragraphs may result from lack of efficiency in decoding of print to internal language representations.

At the present time the LAB test is an experimental test battery that has had no operational use. Further research is needed to refine the test and properly norm it, and operational research is needed to determine the utility of the test as a basis for making practical instructional decisions.

CONCEPTS FROM THE DEVELOPMENTAL MODEL
OF AUDING AND READING APPLIED
IN AN ADULT LITERACY PROGRAM

A final illustration of how concepts from the Audread model have been used in program development is the work on a functional literacy program (Project FLIT) for the U.S. Army (Sticht, 1975a). In Project FLIT (Functional Literacy) the general concepts of *languaging* and *conceptualizing* provided conceptual guidance for the program development effort.

FLIT required a literacy training program of no more than six weeks duration for personnel reading below the sixth-grade level. There were approximately 100 hours of instructional time available. Because the Army personnel in the FLIT program were supposed to be prepared to deal with Army materials, the program developed job-related, rather than general literacy materials.

The basic material in the FLIT Strand II program consisted of narrative prose passages of about 300 words in length, each of which discussed a major knowledge area for six job fields: clerical, communications, cooks, mechanics, combat, and medic.[2] These passages represented the cognitive content with which the students were to learn to conceptualize and use language. The FLIT program developed conceptualizing and languaging teaching activities to be performed using these core job knowledge passages.

The *languaging* component of FLIT Strand II (Sticht, 1975a) is described as follows:

... deals with language at the level of the individual sentence. Within this broad scope, the focus may highlight different aspects of languaging at different times during the instruction. The three main focal areas are:

1. Focus on individual words. (Meanings of individual words.)
2. Focus on individual words in relation to the total sentence. (The syntactical and semantic fit of a particular word or phrase in a particular sentence.)
3. Focus on the total sentence and on the relationship of its parts to each other. (How the thought units in a sentence work together to build up the complete sentence.)

The languaging segment introduces a new model of sentence structure... It is a "stripped-down" model designed to be simple enough to be learned by learning a small number of "rules," yet comprehensive enough to apply to most sentences which occur in Army training literature [pp. 79–80].

---

[2]Strand I, which provided direct practice in working with reading materials related to jobs, is not discussed here (see Sticht, 1975a).

PARTS OF SENTENCES

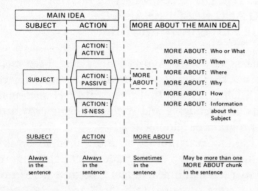

FIG. 8.3. Basic model of sentence structure.

The structure and terminology of the languaging model is based largely on thought units and the kinds of information each thought unit contributes to the complete idea expressed by the sentence (see Fig. 8.3). The most basic structure divides the sentence into the *main idea* and *more about the main idea*. The main idea can be separated into two thought units, the *subject* and the *action*. The action thought unit in a sentence may be one of three kinds: active, passive, or is–ness. (The action is–ness corresponds to a linking or copulative verb.) The thought units that tell more about the main idea may present six different kinds of information, as indicated in Fig. 8.3.

The *conceptualizing* component of FLIT Strand II is based on the idea that thoughts, or conceptualizations, can be represented in different ways. One mode of representation is the *linguistic* mode, which uses speech and writing. This mode has been the focus of the audread model. Additionally, however, people are able to represent thoughts in pictures, or *iconic* displays. Finally, by combining linguistic and iconic modes of representation, special types of displays, *schematics*, may represent conceptualizations. Flow charts, classification tables, graphs, and the like are included in the *schematic* category.

In the FLIT program, students are taught to perform various transformations on the 12 core job reading passages. In some cases, students read the passage and then draw a picture of what the total or a part of the passage is about. In other cases, passages are converted into flow charts or classification tables. Figures 4 and 5 illustrate the types of transformation involved in transforming *linguistic* representations in the form of written prose into *schematic* representations in the form of a classification table (Fig. 8.4) and a flow chart (Fig. 8.5).

In teaching such transformations, teachers lead small group instruction in which the making of a particular type of representation transformation is demonstrated. Guided practice, followed by practice on the 12 job-oriented passages, is then provided. Through this type of activity, the conceptualizing

Types of Bars

Crowbars are used for moving timbers and rocks. They are available in 4 and 5 foot lengths with a diameter of 1 or 1-1/4 inches. Pinch bars are from 12 to 36 inches long and are used for prying out spikes and nails. Pinch bar diameters range from 1/2 to 1 inch depending on their length. Wrecking bars have diameters of 1/2 to 1-1/8 inches and are available in lengths from 12 to 60 inches. They are used for the same things as crowbars. Pry bars are used for prying out gears and bushings. They are 16 inches long and have a diameter of 1-1/16 inches.

Type	Use	Length	Diameter
Crowbar	Moving timbers and rocks	4-5 feet	1 or 1-1/4 inches
Pinch bar	Prying out spikes and nails	12-36 inches	1/2 to 1 inch
Wrecking bar	Moving timbers and rocks	12-60 inches	1/2 to 1-1/8 inches
Pry bar	Prying out gears and bushings	16 inches	1-1/16 inches

FIG. 8.4.   Linguistic to schematic (classification table) transformation.

component (1) focuses on the development of increased reading comprehension skills through teaching various conceptualizing skills, and (2) gives direct instruction to increase job knowledge by using the specially prepared job reading passages as the vehicle for teaching and applying the conceptualizing/comprehension skills.

The evaluation of the FLIT program, including both Strands I and II, was accomplished through pre- and posttesting, using the Metropolitan Achievement Tests, Intermediate Battery (available in a military version known as the United States Armed Forces Institute Intermediate Achievement Tests, USAFI), and specially constructed Job Reading Task Tests (JRTT) made up of material from technical manuals and forms used in the military. For 714 students, entry USAFI scores changed from 5.3 to 6.0, for 7 months' gain in general literacy; JRTT scores changed from 5.2 to 7.3, for 25 months' gain. A comparison of a subset of FLIT students (n = 149) with a group of Air Force (n = 56) and Army (n = 124) students enrolled in remedial reading programs but not receiving job-related reading showed that the FLIT students gained

When a Hand Grenade Is Dropped

When a hand grenade is dropped accidentally after the safety pin is removed, the individual will shout "Grenade." Then he picks up the grenade and throws it into a safe area. He should then get behind any avaliable protective cover until after the grenade explodes. If no protective cover is available, he should assume the prone position until after the explosion.

FIG. 8.5.   Linguistic to schematic (flow chart) transformation.

21 months on the JRTT, whereas the Air Force and Army students gained 5 to 6 months (Sticht, 1975b, p. 136). These results indicate that the direct training using job-related reading materials had a direct effect on the ability to read and use such materials. It further suggests that general literacy training of the very limited type typically provided in manpower training programs does not transfer as rapidly to performance of job reading tasks as does direct, job-related reading training. In terms of the developmental model, the cognitive content relevant to the tasks at hand must be developed, and this can be done rather directly, as in the job-related reading approach, or indirectly, as in general literacy training. It would seem that in order to develop a cognitive content sufficient to include job-specific knowledge and reading skill through general literacy training, a program of long duration would be required.

SUMMARY AND DISCUSSION

In this chapter I have discussed a developmental model of auding and reading that maintains that reading develops on a foundation of language skills acquired in the oral mode by information-processing skills in auding and speaking. These language skills are used to represent one's conceptualizations externally to others (speaking) and to represent internally the external representations of the conceptualizations others produce by speaking (auding). Reading uses the same language and conceptualizing skills and knowledge as are used in auding.

Three probjects based on the Audread model were summarized and discussed:

1. A project to determine the extent to which first-grade children learned to read the words they could speak.
2. A project to assess differences between auding and reading skills in adults.
3. A project of functional job-related literacy training for adults.

Study of these projects to understand how the Audread model has been applied suggests two functions of the model:

1. It suggests important relationships to be studied and exploited for instruction. The first two projects studied the closing of the gap between oral and written language in selected respects, and the third project attempted to produce an instructional program based on interrelations among language and cognitive components in the Audread model.

2. It constrains certain decisions—those relative to content of tests (e.g., use of first-grade children's own stories to ensure that content would be within

their knowledge base) or instruction (use of job-related reading materials to provide a conceptual base for comprehending job-related materials).

Neither the Audread model nor, presumably, any other model of reading processes or language can provide step-by-step procedures or generative rules for educational program development because such development must operate under constraints other than those determined by the model. Limits of time, money, human resources, and so forth will serve to turn the primrose path from theory to practice into a Hampton Court maze where simply avoiding blind alleys may represent progress!

ACKNOWLEDGMENTS

Preparation of this paper has been supported in part by Air Force contract F41609-75-C0014 with the Air Force Human Resources Laboratory/Technical Training Division, Dr. James R. Burkett, Technical Monitor. Special thanks to Maurlaine Jorgenson for transforming my scrambled notes into an attractive manuscript.

The findings and opinions expressed in this report do not necessarily reflect the position or policy of the National Institute of Education or the U.S. Department of Health, Education, and Welfare.

REFERENCES

Brown, D. P. *Auding as the primary language ability.* Unpublished doctoral dissertation, Stanford University, 1954.

Carver, R. P. *Optimal information storage rate for reading prose.* Unpublished manuscript, American Institute for Research, Silver Spring, Md., 1973. (Author now at the University of Missouri, Kansas City.)

Chall, J. *Learning to read: The great debate.* New York: McGraw–Hill, 1967.

Cooperative Tests and Services, *Cooperative primary tests handbook.* Princeton, N.J.: Educational Testing Service, 1970.

Durrell, D., & Brassard, M. *Durrell listening–reading series: Intermediate level.* New York: Harcourt Brace Jovanovich, 1970.

Fries, C. C. *Linguistics and reading.* New York: Holt, Rinehart and Winston, 1963.

Gates, A. I., & MacGinitie, W. H. *Gates–MacGinitie reading tests, Survey D.* New York: Columbia University, Teachers College Press, 1965.

Goldstein, H. *Reading and listening comprehension at various controlled rates.* Unpublished doctoral dissertation, Columbia University, Teachers College, 1940.

Kavanagh, J. F., & Mattingly, I. G. (Eds.). *Language by ear and by eye: The relationship between speech and reading.* Cambridge, Mass.: MIT Press, 1972.

Keithly, G. *The use of a child's own oral language to test reading achievement in first grade.* Unpublished master's thesis, Monterey Institute of Foreign Studies, 1974.

Loban, W. *Language ability: Grades seven, eight, and nine* (Project No. 1131). Berkeley: University of California, 1964.

Murphy, H. A., & Durrell, D. D. *Murphy-Durrell reading readiness analysis.* New York: Harcourt Brace & World, 1965.

Spache, G. D. *Diagnostic reading scales: Revised edition.* Monterey, Cal.: CTB/McGraw-Hill, 1972.

Sticht, T. G. *A program of army functional job reading training: Development, implementation, and delivery systems.* Alexandria, Va.: Human Resources Research Organization, 1975. (a)

Sticht, T. G. (Ed.). *Reading for working.* Alexandria, Va.: Human Resources Research Organization, 1975. (b)

Sticht, T. G., & Beck, L. J. *Experimental literacy assessment battery (LAB)* (AFHRL-TT-76-51). Lowry AFB, Co: Air Force Human Resources Laboratory/Technical Training Division, 1976.

Sticht, T., Beck, L., Hauke, R., Kleiman, G., & James, J. *Auding and reading: A developmental model.* Alexandria, Va.: Human Resources Research Organization, 1974.

III INSTRUCTION

9 Teaching Reading to Learning Disabled and Other Hard-to-Teach Children

Barbara Bateman
University of Oregon

The current organized learning disability movement, replete with journals, conventions, and parent groups, began in the early 1960s. Three distinct approaches to teaching learning disabled children have emerged—the etiological, the diagnostic-remedial, and the task-analytic (Bateman, 1967). The contributions and limitations of each of the three approaches for teaching reading to learning disabled children are reviewed briefly in this chapter, and a fourth approach is proposed. The fourth approach suggests that many learning disabled children have certain characteristics that require very precise and careful teaching of decoding if they are to achieve mastery of beginning reading skills. This fourth approach combines task-analytic programming of reading instruction (e.g., Engelmann & Bruner, 1974; Venezky, 1975) with research on the learning processes of learning disabled children (Hallahan & Kauffman, 1976; Ross, 1976) and proposes that aptitude–treatment interaction is a viable premise on which to rest the combination (Salomon, 1972; Tobias, 1976).

LEARNING DISABILITIES AND READING DISABILITIES

Current texts on learning disabilities necessarily recite two litanies—the phemomenal growth of the field, and the fact that this growth has occurred without an accepted definition of learning disabilities (see Hallahan & Kauffman, 1976; Lerner, 1976; Ross, 1976). Some authors cite several of the more widely known definitions and let the matter rest; others add yet another definition; most point out the circularity and logical inconsistencies implicit in the available definitions.

A major unsettled definitional issue is the role, if any, of central nervous system (CNS) dysfunction in learning problems. Positions range from acceptance of demonstrated CNS dysfunction as a *sine qua non* of learning disabilities (Clements, 1966) to complete rejection of it as irrelevant (Cohen, 1973).

Another unresolved debate centers on the use of a "discrepancy" requirement. Some definitions stipulate a significant discrepancy between cognitive potential and actual educational achievement. The discrepancy concept is, predictably, challenged by those who argue that there is no valid or appropriate way to assess cognitive potential. The strongest support comes from those who would clearly distinguish learning disabilities from mental retardation.

A third difference among definitions centers on etiological exclusions. Many argue that learning disabilities may not be caused primarily by mental retardation or sensory deficits. Some also exclude those children whose learning problems are judged to be due to severe emotional problems, cultural differences, or inadequate instruction. The United States Congress currently uses the definition formulated by the National Advisory Committee on Handicapped Children (1968):

> Children with special learning disabilities exhibit a disorder in one or more of the basic psychological processes involved in understanding or in using spoken or written language. These may be manifested in disorders of listening, thinking, talking, reading, writing, spelling, or arithmetic. They include conditions which have been referred to as perceptual handicaps, brain injury, minimal brain dysfunction, dyslexia, developmental aphasia, etc. They do not include learning problems which are due primarily to visual, hearing or motor handicaps, to mental retardation, emotional disturbance or to environmental deprivation [p. 4].

A committee of the Association for Children with Learning Disabilities recently recommended amending this definition to include children with specific learning disabilities who also have sensory, motor, intellectual, or emotional problems, or who are environmentally disadvantaged (Kirk, 1974). Another dispute is over whether the concept of learning disability necessarily implies a deficiency in academic performance. Few definitions specifically state that it does; yet it is hard to imagine many children who are or should be regarded as learning disabled when their school performance is satisfactory.

Professionals remain unable to agree on a definition, but in practice the overwhelming majority of children labeled as being learning disabled are having difficulty in reading beyond what would be predicted by experienced teachers taking into account such factors as apparent intelligence, home background, and so on. Many also have writing and spelling problems; some are perceived as being hyperactive, as being poorly coordinated, or as having receptive and/or expressive difficulty with spoken language; A few show finger agnosia; and so on. The list of possible accompanying difficulties is nearly endless.

Learning Disabilities Versus Remedial Reading

The question of how, if at all, children with learning disabilities differ from those with reading disabilities is currently being debated (Artley, 1975; Chall, in press; Lerner, 1975). Differences are cited and disputed as to teacher training, terminology, views on etiology, and focus of remediation. As yet, the classroom teacher has few, if any, guidelines for deciding whether Janie, struggling inordinately to learn to read, should be sent to the learning disability or remedial reading teacher. (In fact, evidence is far from clear that either can be counted on to teach Janie to read, but that is not the issue.) Whatever differences there may be in the philosophies and practices of the two disciplines, it seems clear that both are concerned with the same children—those children who are failing to learn to read as rapidly as it seems they should. The label *learning disabled* would not, in all circles, be as readily applied to children with very mild reading problems as would *remedial* or *corrective reader*. With this one minor exception, the terms *learning disabled* and *reading disabled* apply to the same children and are so used here.

One further preliminary observation is vital. As indicated earlier, many would exlude from the category of learning disabled those children who have not had adequate reading instruction. The assumption that instruction is adequate is probably false when it is made regarding conventional whole-word, meaning-emphasis instruction (Otto, 1972; Samuels, 1970). The inadequacy of much current reading instruction is becoming so clear that fewer and fewer are heard to claim that failure to learn to read is but an illusion caused by compulsory attendance, television, or the breakdown of the family. A growing number of educators and special educators now hold that a child's failure to learn to read is, per se, clear and convincing evidence that the instruction was inadequate (e.g., Cohen, 1973; Engelman, 1967b, 1969b). A related position is that even if there might be different or additional etiological factors, the educator is, nonetheless, professionally bound to conceptualize the problem as an instructional one since only instructional variables are under educators' control (e.g., Bateman, 1973; Otto, 1972). Once it has been determined that the child is having difficulty learning to read, the next step is to diagnose the problem and plan intervention. As mentioned at the beginning of this chapter, three approaches have been taken to diagnosis and planning—the etiological, the diagnostic-remedial, and the task-analytic (Bateman, 1967). Each is discussed briefly in the following sections.

THE ETIOLOGICAL APPROACH

The only sure way to prevent a child from learning to read is to preclude all opportunity to make the appropriate associations between written letters and the sounds they represent. Therefore, the only certain cause of reading failure is the absence of incidental or systematic instruction. For every other alleged cause of reading disability, children can be found who are exceptions to the theory. Some brain-injured children read, as do some children with malnutrition, disinterested parents, abnormal electroencephalograms, inadequate lateralization, poor vision, chromosomal aberrations, older sisters who achieve well in school, speech defects, finger agnosia, undescended testicles, hyperactivity, left-handedness, thyroid deficiences, double hair sworls, low IQs, unresolved oedipal conflicts, jagged Illinois Test of Psycholinguistic Abilities profiles, or any other alleged etiological factor. In light of this, those who look for correlates are on safer ground than those who search for causes. But perhaps neither is on the most direct route to solving the educational problem. In one of the most powerful explications of educators' treatment of causes of school faiure, Engelmann (1969b) described how we have sought general rather than specific causes and have failed to concentrate on asking what precisely it is about reading that the child has not been taught. Some formulations of alleged causes of reading failure have educational implications; other do not. Perhaps some of those that do not at the present time will in years to come. The "truth" of any alleged cause is not disputed here; rather, it is urged that educators and program developers examine the utility, for their purposes, of etiological formulations.

A few etiological theories purportedly do lead to teaching strategies. Delacato (1966), for example, included activities designed to establish hemispheric dominance in his program for teaching reading. Other theories do not purport to have such implications. No one argues, for instance, that correlational data on family income and reading achievement should prompt reading teachers to give dollars to parents of children in the lowest reading group. A large number of alleged etiologies do suggest treatment designed to make children more amenable to instruction—for example, correcting visual refractive errors, prescribing Ritalin, or using broad spectrum lighting to replace narrow spectrum artificial lighting. However, none of these replaces reading instruction. [Numerous reviews of the etiology of reading disorders are available, for example, Bannatyne (1966), Blom & Jones (1971), and Westman, Arthur, & Scheidler (1965).]

The relevance-to-teaching position on etiology espoused here is treated at greater length by Bateman (1973), Cohen (1973), Engelmann (1967a, 1969b), and Otto (1972). They and others assert that the etiological classifications most useful to educators are those that specify precisely what the child needs to be taught about reading, for example, short vowel sounds, left-to-right decoding, or sound blending. Opponents object that merely knowing that a child responds to *b* by saying /d/ (and vice versa) about half the time is not sufficient diagnostic information when some children may do so "because" of brain injury, others "because" of inadequate binocular fusion, others "because" of poor motivation, and so on. This objection is premised on the belief that letter discrimination (or phoneme–grapheme correspondence) can or should be taught differently to children who, for different reasons, have not yet learned it. It is this contention that forms the basis of the position that teaching reading to learning disabled children is different from teaching reading to other children. And it is this position that is critically examined in the remainder of this discussion. The source of severe reading disability, excluding original etiological possibilities, may be viewed as inhering in the child, in the instruction, or in a mismatch between child and instruction. Each of these conceptualizations and the instructional techniques deriving from them is examined and evaluated.

THE DIAGNOSTIC-REMEDIAL APPROACH

Several process models, clearly diagnostic-remedial in nature, are presented. Also discussed is Ross's (1976) learning model, perhaps a hybrid of diagnostic-remedial and task-analytic models.

Process Models and Training Approaches

The view that the child has deficiencies that must be remediated has been the majority position in the field of learning disabilities over the past 20 or 30 years. This conceptualization has been known as the diagnostic-remedial approach (Bateman, 1967), prescriptive teaching (Peter, 1965), ability or process training (Ysseldyke & Salvia, 1974), psychometric phrenology (Mann, 1971), and even task analysis (Johnson, D. J., 1967). Typically, approaches based on this view assess the child's cognitive, perceptual, sensory-motor, and other processes by a variety of psychoeducational instruments and ascertain patterns of strong and weak functioning. Often an effort is made to determine which of the deficits observed is "primary." The deficits observed by means of psychoeducational instruments are said to be merely correlated with the academic deficiency, and causality is specifically disavowed (Kirk, 1972). It is, however, interesting that remediation is still planned to overcome or circumvent the correlated deficit, with the implicit hope that such remediation will either alleviate the academic problem or lay a foundation for doing so. This procedure suggests that the belief may still be closer to causality than to mere correlation.

Visual Perceptual, Visual, and Visual-Motor Perceptual Training.   Few programs for the learning disabled have been as extensively researched as has the Frostig visual perceptual training program (Frostig & Horne, 1964). Comprehensive reviews of the research (e.g., Robinson, 1972; Wiederholt & Hammill, 1971) revealed that the Frostig training program does tend to increase scores on the Frostig Developmental Tests of Visual Perception, sometimes increases reading readiness scores, but does not improve reading. Illustrative studies finding no relationship between visual perceptual training and reading are those by Anderson (1972) and Jacobs (1968). Larsen and Hammill's (1975) recent review concluded that research does not support a necessary relationship between reading and visual-motor integration, spatial relations, visual memory, or visual descrimination, as measured by current instruments. One commonly used perceptual test that appears to differentiate reading or learning disabled children from normal readers is the Bender–Gestalt (see, e.g., Keogh, 1965; Larsen, Rogers, & Sowell, 1976). But that test's statistical differentiation holds only for groups of children and, therefore, is of dubious individual predictive or educational value. Furthermore, Koppitz (1975) found that although the Bender distinguished children who were not learning disabled from those who were, it did not differentiate between those learning disabled children who did and did not have reading problems.

A few young children have difficulty learning to name (or give the sound for) letters of the alphabet. Undoubtedly, this fact contributes to the popularity of the view that visual discrimination or perceptual training must be what is needed. But these same children can visually identify hundreds of other objects or events, and as Rozin, Poritsky, and Stotsky (1971) and Harrigan (1976) have demonstrated, even young children with severe reading problems can learn as many as 30 Chinese characters in a few hours. This task clearly requires at least as much visual discrimination or perception as learning English letters. Very young children can usually perceive and discriminate letters (Calfee, Chapman, & Venezky, 1972), so the source of difficulty in naming (or sounding) must be something other than visual perceptual difficulty.

Krippner (1973) and Keogh (1974), in two eminently readable reviews, have examined the controversy surrounding optometric visual and visual perceptual training. Both concluded that the controversy is unresolved and will continue at least until better research is available. As to the relationship between visual perceptual ability and reading, Keogh (1974) astutely observed that good visual perceptual ability may be an outcome of good reading, "that is, as a child learns to read, he develops adequate visual perceptual organization, he masters scanning in a horizontal left–right direction...[p. 227]."

Kephart's (1960) motor perceptual remediation was evaluated in a review of more than 30 studies by Klesius (1972), who found that of 11 studies meeting his criteria for acceptability, more than half did not favor Kephart's procedures. Hammill, Goodman, and Wiederholt (1974) reviewed 76 studies of the Frostig and Kephart programs and concluded that visual and motor perceptual training programs have not demonstrated an effect on academic achievement and that we must question the assumption that perceptual motor inadequacy causes reading problems. (It should be noted that the Frostig and Kephart programs do not use alphabetic symbols.) Delacato's (1966) training method uses motor activities such as creeping and patterning to develop hemispheric dominancy and thus, presumably, improve reading ability. However, independent studies by Anderson (R. W., 1965), Robbins (1966), and O'Donnell (1969) failed to find clear support for the still controversial techniques. Balow (1971) reported that after numerous searches of the literature, he found no scientifically acceptable data that demonstrated special effectiveness for any of the physical, motor, or perceptual programs used in the prevention or correction of reading or other learning disabilities.

Auditory Perceptual Training.   Sabatino (1973) extensively reviewed the development and assessment of auditory perception and intervention efforts, noting that in comparison to visual perception, little information is available. He concluded that research has established a correlational relationship between reading failure and auditory functioning and observed that there is general disagreement as to whether auditory perceptual training or teaching is called for by strengths in auditory perceptual functioning (e.g., Johnson & Myklebust, 1967) or by weaknesses (e.g., Silver & Hagin, 1967b) or is ever indicated at all (Mann, 1970). No studies were reported that clearly demonstrated that auditory perceptual training has a direct effect on reading achievement. Hammill and Larsen's (1974) review found little support in the research literature for the assertions that auditory discrimination, auditory memory, sound blending, or auditory-visual integration as measured is essential to reading. Because 3- or 4-year-olds can accurately repeat words and patterns of sounds, and even infants can differentiate similar syllables (Eimas, Siqueland, Jusczyk, & Vigorito, 1971), we must agree with Rozin and Gleitman's (1977) conclusion that preliterate children have adequate auditory perceptual development for acquiring reading skills and that, except in very rare cases, auditory perceptual training is not important to teaching reading except as teaching reading is per se a form of such training.

Auditory-Visual Integration.   Deficient integration in the sensory systems was proposed by Birch (1962) as causing or being related to reading disability, and the view has been supported by research (e.g., Birch & Belmont, 1964;

Lovell & Gorton, 1968; Zurif & Carson, 1970). However, a possibly stronger view is that the revealed auditory-visual matching deficiencies are caused by verbal labeling problems rather than by cross-model transfer problems (Blank & Bridger, 1966; Blank, Weider, & Bridger, 1968; McGrady & Olson, 1970; Steger, Vellutino, & Meshoulam, 1972; Vellutino, Steger, & Kandel, 1972; cf. Drader, 1975). Direct teaching of grapheme–phoneme correspondences is one visual-auditory integrative activity that is clearly supportable at the present time because it is part of the reading act.

Psycholinguistic Training. The Illinois Test of Psycholinguistic Abilities (ITPA) has been extensively used to diagnose reading problems and to plan remediation for children with reading problems. Apart from possible theoretical weaknesses, severe criticism has been directed at the test's reliability, validity, and factorial structure (e.g., Ysseldyke, 1973; Ysseldyke & Salvia, 1974; cf. Newcomer, Hare, Hammill, & McGettigan, 1975), and it has been suggested that ITPA-based remediation may not be justified (Hammill & Larsen, 1974; Harris, 1976). Carroll (1972) suggested that there may not be a pattern of scores on the ITPA that is characteristic of poor readers. However, a review (Bateman, 1965) of early evidence on the 1961 experimental version of the ITPA showed that poor readers were consistently low in auditory and/or visual sequential memory. Both these tests are at the nonmeaningful, automatic-sequential level of language usage. Poor readers were significantly superior to the ITPA standardization population in visual decoding at the semantic or representational level of language usage (Kass, 1966). These findings, consistent with Rozin and Gleitman's (1977) analysis, suggest that poor readers have difficulty with accessing surface level information, not with accessing meaning.

Summary. Ability or process training has come under severe and growing criticism. However, Bannatyne (1975) has expressed important cautions against uncritically accepting the negative reviews and conclusions regarding possible relationships between these abilities and academic achievement. Ysseldyke and Salvia (1974) have contrasted ability training to task-analytically derived skills training (discussed later) and fault the former for (1) using hypothetical constructs that go beyond observed behaviors and inferring that they are causes of the observed differences, (2) hypothesizing that processes or abilities are essential prerequisites to skills achievement when data show (e.g., Abt Associates, 1976; Bijou, 1970; Cohen, 1969; Haring & Bateman, 1977) that the skills can be taught directly and when only correlational (not causal) data suggest a relationship between process and skill, (3) using diagnostic test instruments of questionable reliability and validity, and (4) assuming aptitude–treatment interactions that have not been shown to exist. Vellutino (1974) has leveled essentially similar criticism specifically at the reading disability field and concluded that (1) there is little support for the theory (or its derivative practices) that views reading disability as caused by visual-spatial confusion stemming from neurological disorders, (2) findings supporting the deficient sensory integration hypothesis are equivocal at best, and (3) much more support is available for the hypothesis that reading disability is associated with verbal learning deficiencies.

At least two essential premises of the diagnostic-remedial approach remain unsupported: (1) that the assumed deficiencies in psychological processes can be reliably and validly assessed, and (2) that remediation of these processes will result in improved academic performance. And yet programs based squarely on these premises continue to flourish and to dominate the field among practitioners, if not among academicians and researchers. Harris (1976) suggested that this situation obtains because research has not had sufficient impact to overcome the three forces he sees as being controlling— the "bandwagon," the "pendulum," and the "zeitgeist" effects. Ultimately, the tide will be turned by the ready availability of more successful approaches. Some are already here.

Attention Deficits

Two recent texts (Hallahan & Kauffman, 1976; Ross, 1976) may signal the beginning of a more data-based approach to teaching learning disabled children (see Hewett, 1974, for related views). Both reflect the movement away from the questionable premises and instrumentation of the diagnostic-remedial approach, and both highlight the probable role of attention deficits in the academic difficulties of the learning disabled child. Ross, however, distinguished attention deficits from hyperactivity and distractibility, whereas Hallahan and Kauffman did not.

The prominent role of attention in perceptual and cognitive development has been recognized and studied by many researchers (e.g., Bandura, 1969; Gibson, 1969; Zeaman & House, 1963), as has the role of attention in the acquisition of reading skills (e.g., Staats, 1968; Staats, Brewer, & Gross, 1970). Ross (1976) and Hallahan and Kauffman (1976) specifically applied theoretical and research contributions on attention and reading to the learning disabled child.

Ross. Ross's (1976) review and analysis of research on learning and learning disabilities led him to conclude that learning disabled children have a developmental delay in sustaining selective attention, a conclusion not inconsistent with observations of others (e.g., Chalfant & Flathouse, 1971; Senf, 1972), but never has it been more systematically and carefully derived and applied to teaching learning disabled children. Although a developmental delay in selective attention is, conceptually, a deficit in the child,

Ross's formulation has been derived from a task analysis of learning and is applied to a simplified hierarchy of reading skills (selective attention → sequential scanning → discrimination → decoding → comprehension) in an effort to extract instructional implications for teaching reading. Ross held that the capacity to inhibit stimuli irrelevant to the task at hand and to focus attention selectively on relevant stimuli develops through interactions of maturation and learning and that many learning disabled children (enough to justify so defining learning disabilities) suffer a delay in its development. He argued convincingly that frequently reported distractibility, hyperactivity, and perceptual-motor integration defects actually may be aspects of the selective attention problem.

Ross suggested several techniques for direct teaching of selective attention to reading. One tactic is to exaggerate the differences between stimuli to be discriminated, making the critical patterns more obvious. Hyman and Cohen (1975) have independently shown the effectiveness of fading the vertical line on b and d to achieve that result successfully. The *Distar* reading program (Engelmann & Bruner, 1974) uses different type styles for b and d for the same purpose (see also Caron, 1968; Koenigsberg, 1973). The evidence is clear that most so-called reversal problems can be prevented by careful teaching and programming, a fact that further supports the contention that learning disabled children do not suffer from visual perceptual problems. Several reading methods commonly recommended for learning disabled children use a sensory-motor component (e.g., Fernald, 1943; Gillingham & Stillman, 1966). Ross suggested that the sensory-motor element may serve merely to focus attention on the all-important shape of the letter being taught rather than to add anything else. Clear empirical evidence supporting the efficacy of sensory-motor reading techniques with learning disabled children is scant, but clinical testimony and case studies attest to their continuing popularity and perceived utility. Another technique Ross recommended is to present the relevant stimulus dimension in a variety of forms. Size, color, brightness, and texture of letters can all be varied while the critical features of shape and position in space remain constant. Such variations also capitalize on the fact that novelty, to a point, enhances attention.

Ross also urged that children who have failed in reading and who have developed an aversion to letters and words may also need systematic extrinsic reinforcement to attend once again to the appropriate stimuli (see, e.g., Engelman, Becker, Carnine, Meyers, Becker, & Johnson, 1975; Heiman, Fischer, & Ross, 1973; Staats & Butterfield, 1965).

Although Ross thoroughly discussed learning disabilities and the teaching of other aspects of reading (e.g., sequential scanning), his unique emphasis was on selective attention. He shared the view, discussed elsewhere, that even young children can be taught to decode consistently in a left–right direction and believed that neither discrimination nor paired-associate learning deficits have been shown to be related causally to reading disorders. He suggested that selective attention deficits could underlie both.

Hallahan and Kauffman.   Hallahan and Kauffman (1976) stopped short of holding that attention deficits are so important as to be a proper part of the definition of learning disabilities, but they did find that the evidence clearly supports the existence of selective attention deficits in many learning disabled children (Hallahan, 1975; Hallahan, Kauffman, & Ball, 1973; Tarver & Hallahan, 1974). They did not find that research supports the frequently advocated reduction of environmental stimuli as an aid to academic achievement. They did, however, recommend the use of color cues to draw attention to the critical features essential to better discriminations and the use of verbal rehearsal and specific instructions for what should be attended to. The majority of their recommendations fall under the rubric of applied behavioral analysis, to be discussed later.

TASK ANALYSIS

In introducing applied behavior analysis, Hallahan and Kauffman (1976) described it as being even more oriented than are diagnostic-remedial approaches to

> the specification and anaysis of molecular units of behavior that are important for learning in school. Those who espouse a behavior modification approach are among the strongest proponents of behavioral assessment or analysis. Interested in the teaching of specific skills to children with specific learning problems, the advocates of behavior modification or applied behavior analysis seek to improve specific behaviors and to determine precisely the teaching procedures that are responsible for the improvement [p. 57].

They further observed that applied behavior analysis is especially useful with learning disabled (and emotionally disturbed and mentally retarded) children because it allows precise measurement, is based on empirical data from the child's own performance, suggests specific remedial methods, facilitates individualization of instruction, and provides continuous evelution of teaching procedures. Applied behavior analysis does not prescribe what specific skills are to be taught, but it can determine the efficiency of any set of skills in reaching an objective. The term *task analysis* is used here to mean the process of determining what specific subskills must be taught. Although there is no necessary implication that educators who use task analysis will also use applied behavioral analysis, the majority do. Applied behavioral analysis is outside the scope of this discussion, except to note that learning disabled children suffer more than most when such analysis is not employed in teaching (as will be discussed later).

Careful analysis of the act of reading, beyond description of possible errors children make, has not been of major concern to the traditional view of reading and learning disabilities. It is as if the basic assumption that children who read poorly must themselves be deficient has precluded serious consideration of the possibility that the reading instruction was inadequate. The fact that the majority of children have learned to read has apparently been accepted as satisfactory evidence that the teaching was appropriate to the nature of the task. Engelmann (1967b) aptly observed that if a child learns to read, the program is credited, but if the child does not learn, the child is faulted.

Many factors have played a part in the emergence of reading and learning disability specialists' interest in an analysis of the reading task. In the field of reading itself there has been the growing awareness that children have been reading less and less well in recent decades (Lerner, 1976; Matthews, 1966) and that the method of teaching does indeed make a difference. No longer do wide intraprogram differences obscure important interprogram differences. The recent reversal of the pendulum in the "methods battle" between the phonics and the whole-word approaches was initially triggered, some believe, by the public outcry in the 1950s over Flesch's (1955) *Why Johnny Can't Read*. Chall's (1967) *Learning to Read: The Great Debate* forced even educators to admit that the controversy was real. More recently, discrepancies have been noted between the data from the U.S. Office of Education Primary Reading Studies (Bond & Dykstra, 1967)—for example, the stellar performance of the Lippincott phonic-linguistic program (Dykstra, 1968)—and the widely publicized impression that method was not found to be an important variable. Most recent, and yet to have its major impact, is the national evaluation of Project Follow-Through in which one task-analytically derived reading program (*Distar*) was so successful that poverty, high-risk, bilingual, and otherwise usually very low-achieving populations taught by *Distar* read at middle-class grade-level norms by the end of the third grade (Abt Associates, 1976). The Right-to-Read program may evidence recognition that method does make a difference and that the more successful methods should be implemented. As yet, lawsuits at only the small claims court level (Diehl, 1975) have been successfully waged against schools for failing to teach children to read, but the day may come very soon when such cases will be successful in higher courts (Stewart, 1971). The success of such cases will depend on many factors, but proof that other methods might have succeeded better than those used will be important (Abel, 1974; Bateman, 1975; Saretsky, 1973). Other factors moving the learning disabilities field toward an anlysis of reading and of teaching methods derived from it include the rapid development and acceptance of behavioral technology in improving instruction and the (not unrelated) current demand that schools become more accountable for communicating their objectives and their actual accomplishments in teaching basic skills.

Della-Piana and Endo (1973) have reviewed three major approaches to the analysis of reading processes: the conceptual (e.g., Hively, 1966), the empirical (e.g., Holmes, 1970), and the experimental (e.g., Gibson, 1970). Treatment of these approaches and many others that could be included is outside the present discussion. Several analyses of the beginning reading process will be briefly examined that are consistent with outcome data on reading programs and that highlight points of particular relevance for teaching reading to those children who, without superb teaching, are likely to encounter undue difficulty in learning to read. Then, after a brief examination of aptitude–treatment interaction, a position will be synthesized, with specific instructional suggestions for how reading should be taught to learning disabled children.

Analyses of Beginning Reading

Venezky.   Venezky (1975) defined prereading skills. These skills are of particular importance to learning disabled children because these children often are initially identified as lacking readiness, that is, they have not yet been effectively taught these skills. According to Venezky (1975), "... we arrive at prereading skills by identifying a complete set of initial reading tasks (objectives) and then defining all of the prerequisite skills for this set of tasks. Then, for a given population of prereaders, those skills which all or almost all members of the population have mastered are eliminated [p. 5]." Subskills are defined by logical analysis of the reading task and by their demonstrated effect on later reading achievement.

Venezky's analysis of sight-word recognition skills revealed three subskills: (1) visual discrimination of letter strings, which in turn requires letter recognition (in which the only problem is orientation), attention to order of letters, and attention to the entire word; (2) association and retention of labels for the letter strings; and (3) retrieval and articulation of labels when the strings are shown. His analysis of decoding revealed five subskills: (1) letter differentiation, (2) association of sound and letter, (3) blending sound, (4) identification of a sound within a word, and (5) sound matching within words.

These subskills were studied in terms of instructional design, and five emerged as the hub of the instructional program: (1) attending to letter order, (2) attending to letter orientation, (3) attending to word detail, (4) sound matching, and (5) sound blending. In designing the experimental teaching program, emphasis was placed on focusing the learner's attention on relevant features of the task, a strategy of the utmost importance and one consistent with Ross's (1976) hypothesis that selective attention deficits are central in learning disabilities. Venezky (1975) noted that many popularly emphasized skills are omitted: letter–name knowledge, fine-motor performance, visual discrimination of objects and shapes, ocular-motor control, and others, Logical analysis reveals that these are similar skills commonly taught or insisted on as playing a vital part in reading readiness or remediation are not part of reading (although they may be correlated with reading, as is family income). Improvement in these skills is not accompanied by improvement in reading, and they may be demonstrated to be present and suffciently developed for reading long before reading instruction is ordinarily attempted.

Engelmann and Bruner (Distar). Engelmann and Bruner's (1974) approach was very similar to Venezky's and, not surprisingly, they obtained a similar result. "We can figure out that skills should be taught before children are introduced to word reading by analyzing a simple word such as *mat* [p. 23]," they said. The skills that they concluded are necessary are (1) symbol identification—recognizing letters and giving correct sounds; (2) sequencing—reading the symbols in the correct order; (3) blending—analyzing a word by sounding it out and then systhesizing the sounds by saying them at normal speed; and (4) rhyming—recognizing similarities among words. *Distar* teaches these four skills to mastery. Symbol identification, the key decoding skill, is taught daily, from the first day of the program. Sequencing is taught in the first 24 lessons, blending in the first 45, and rhyming begins in Lesson 18. In Lesson 37, children begin decoding regular words idependently. Beginning with Lesson 96, techniques for identifying words without sounding them out are begun. Story reading begins in Lesson 40.

Because teaching to mastery and not spending time on material already mastered are essential elements in *Distar* teaching, those children who need more time receive it, and others may skip lessons. *Distar Reading I* emphasizes code cracking but also includes comprehension questions, written exercises, and spelling assignments. *Distar Reading II* (approximately the second year of instruction) places greater emphasis on comprehension and decoding irregular words and teaches letter names. *Distar Reading III* focuses almost entirely on comprehension—teaching children to read for new information and concepts, that is, to read to learn.

That *Distar* is promising for teaching reading to children who without it risk becoming poor readers is obvious. A recent national evaluation of 4-year results of Project Follow-Through in five communities (Abt Associates, 1976) suggested that the Engelmann–Becker direct instruction model (*Distar*) has largely achieved the goal of raising the average achievement of economically disadvantaged children to the level of their middle-class peers. Becker and Engelmann (1973a) reported on over 8,000 economically disadvantaged children from 15 communities—3 that are mostly Native American, 2 Mexican American, 1 Spanish, 8 Black, 3 White, 3 mixed Black and White).

All nonpoor children (approximately 2,000) in these Follow-Through sites were excluded from the analyses. By the end of third grade, the poor children were decoding one standard deviation above the national norm on the Wide Range Achievement Test (WRAT). On the vocabulary and reading comprehension subtests of the Metropolitan Achievement Tests (MAT), they were just slightly below the national norm. However, this MAT performance exceeded the average of all Follow-Through sponsors by .5 standard deviations and also exceeded that of the more advantaged comparison group not in the Follow-Through program. In a fifth-grade and sixth-grade follow-up covariance analysis of 600 *Distar* students, 122 comparisons were made with appropriate comparison subjects. Of these comparisons, 42 were significant at the .05 level (one-tail test), and 40 of those favored *Distar*. The most favorable results were in reading.

Becker, Engelmann, and Thomas (1975) presented data on the below-80 IQ group ($\bar{x}$ = 72) of Follow-Through children. These children gained more than a year on the WRAT reading subtest for each year in the program. Average and above average second graders taught by *Distar* showed almost fifth-grade reading achievement ($\bar{x}$ = 4.7) on the Stanford Achievement Test at the end of second grade (Engelmann & Carnine, 1975). Second-grade Follow-Through children who were not poor read on the average at a 4.5 grade level (on the WRAT), whereas the low-income children read on the average at a 3.7 grade level (Becker & Engelmann, 1973b).

Other Programs.   Another reading program designed from task analysis for children who have difficulty learning to read is *Starter/101* (O'Keefe, 1970). According to O'Keefe (1971), "the program is essentially the product of our task analysis of the process and potential problem of learning to read.... We have delineated, sequenced, and integrated hundreds of specific objectives [p. 55]." The program consists of four-step cycles, each comprised of (1) speaking and understanding words to be read in the fourth step; (2) recognizing, printing, and producing the sound for one letter, both upper and lower cases; (3) combining (blending) sounds; and (4) using learned letter–sounds in new words. Given a range of 22 to 55 hours of instruction, a group of 98 children who had poor school achievement and poor prognoses for reading averaged a seven-month reading gain on the WRAT.

Glass (1971) built a perceptual-conditioning program based on the following assumptions:

1. Decoding and "reading" should be taught separately.
2. Meaning should be made irrelevant to decoding instruction, and this can be done by teaching decoding using only words whose meaning is already known. (Obviously, this can also be done by using nonsense words.)

3. Decoding must be taught without context or picture clues so that only decoding skills can be used.

4. Since syllabication can be accomplished only after a word has been decoded, it should not be part of decoding instruction.

5. Because successful decoders do not consciously use rules, rules should not be taught.

6. Word parts (letter clusters) are the unit to which successful decoders respond.

7. Correct visual and auditory clustering (discrimination of appropriate units of letters and sounds) is vital to decoding.

8. The correct mental set can be conditioned and can cause the decoder to see and respond to the appropriate letter–sound structures.

From this rationale, Glass developed an instructional methodology in which whole words are individually presented and the correct mental set is induced by asking *What letters make_____sound?* and *What sounds do the letters_____make?* The configuration of the whole word is never changed in any way. The decoder is thus perceptually conditioned to see letter clusters that frequently appear in English. Glass argued, as did Rozin and Gleitman (1977), that it is just as easy to learn that three or four letters make a sound cluster as it is to learn that one letter makes a sound. Glass recognized that one cannot necessarily establish from the performance of fluent adult decoders that children should be taught to decode without rules. Nevertheless, he relied on a study by Burton and Glass (1968) which showed that excellent readers in grades two through five also do not use rules. (It should be noted that extrapolation from proficient decoders, even if they are elementary school children to novices may not be justified.)

An interesting program to compare with Glass's is Vail's *Formula Phonics* (1969), which was designed for nonreaders and poor readers of all ages and backgrounds. Vail (1971) wrote, "Certainly middle and upper income Caucasian first-graders who have good attendance patterns, who are not immature, and who do not present atypical learning patterns, will probably...[read] as well, taught by conventional reading methods, as [by] Formula Phonics [p. 111]." However, Vail's concern, like ours, is for the rest of the children. Regular consonant sounds and rules and long and short vowel sounds are "programmed" into pupils as prereading skills, being certain that any incorrectly learned sounds are extinguished. Then regular letter clusters ("pals") are taught. Sounding out words is carefully distinguished from reading. Once "programmed," students read orally from material at their highest level of comprehension. When an unknown word is encountered, the teacher then teaches the use of word–attack skills and phonic units programmed earlier by asking the class a series of questions (the "formula"): Does the word have a suffix, silent letters, "pals," any letters that must change their sounds, and how do you work the remaining vowels? Principles of reinforcement are systematically used. Vail's "pals" and Glass's "clusters" are markedly similar, and "programming" and "conditioning" seems to be related. There is total dissimilarity, however, in the treatment of rules in the two programs.

Other approaches to reaching reading that are consistent with task analysis and/or applied behavioral analysis include the *Monterey Reading Program* (Baker & Gray, 1972), which uses a complex behavioral analysis in monitoring child progress, and the work of Lovitt and Hurlburt (1974) and Haring and Hauck (1969). The application of known principles of learning can also be seen in the construction of certain reading materials such as the *Remedial Reading Drills* (Hegge, Kirk, & Kirk, 1936).

Summary

The programs briefly described in this section have been systematically derived from analyses of reading and/or from behavioral learning principles. None has started from the premise that learning disabled children must be taught unique skills or taught in a unique way, although Glass and Vail use clusters of letters rather than phonemes. Both rely on observed frequency of the clusters, and Glass cites the performance of young, successful decoders as grounds for the larger unit.

Programs such as those cited, most especially *Distar*, illustrate that a reading failure rate of near zero may be achieved by task-analytically derived programs that do not rely on individual diagnoses of children's psychological strengths and weaknesses. The responsibility for teaching all the essential skills in reading is assumed by task-analytically based programs, and no necessary reliance is placed on extra-program training (see Engelmann, 1967b, 1969a).

Not all task-analytically derived programs nor all demonstrably successful programs were included in this brief review. Those discussed were chosen to illustrate task-analytic program derivation and to suggest that some programs are, popular mythology aside, far superior to others in derivation and in outcome data. The same point could have been made, as it has been by many others, by reporting the growing body of research comparing results across programs (e.g., Bliesmer & Yarborough, 1965; Chall, 1967; Gurren & Hughes, 1965). Although this kind of research is fraught with practical problems, it is clear that intensive, systematic decoding programs result in better reading achievement than do other kinds of beginning reading programs. Furthermore, it is just possible that intensive decoding instruction is even more vital for potential low achievers than for their easy-to-teach counterparts, as teachers have long insisted (see Tobias, 1976). Is suggesting that learning disabled children benefit more than other children from systematic decoding instruction tantamount to placing undue reliance on aptitude–treatment interaction? Does research justify such a suggestion? The next section explores the issue of aptitude–treatment interaction in reading instruction.

APTITUDE-TREATMENT INTERACTION

Teachers have long been taught that there is no one way to teach all children—some need one method, others need another. The often unspoken assumption is that somehow we can consistently and accurately identify those children who need technique *A* and those who need *B*. Presumably, the secret of this successful matching is in some set of identifiable characteristics of the children. In this section the success to date of efforts to match learner aptitudes, traits, or characteristics with reading method is examined.

Modality Instruction

Many leading authorities on learning disabilities have recommended that methods of reading instruction should somehow be matched to the child's relative modality patterns. Johnson and Myklebust (1967), Wepman (1964, 1971), and Lerner (1971) all recommended that the teaching of reading be consistent with the child's strong modality (e.g., auditory learners should be taught by phonics). Kirk (1972) recommended direct remediation of the weakness. Rupert (undated) suggested initial teaching to the strengths, with a switch at some unspecified time to the weaknesses. Others have suggested teaching to both, concentrating on strengths in group situations and on weaknesses in private tutoring. Others have advocated using the strengths to improve the weaknesses (Johnson, D. J., 1967). And so on. [See de Hirsch, Jansky, & Langford (1966) and Silver & Hagin (1967a) for slight variations.] This modality-matching advocacy has been so successful that 97% of the teachers of the learning disabled in Illinois who participated in Arter and Jenkins' (1975) recent study were familiar with this modality model, and 95% believed that research supported it. Of the teachers familiar with it, 99% agreed that modality should be a major consideration in devising educational preparations. The model was reported as being used frequently or always by 78% of the teachers.

Arter and Jenkins (1975) reviewed 15 reading studies that (1) assessed modality strengths and weaknesses, (2) designed or used materials that stress various modalities, and (3) attempted to discover modality–instructional interactions. After a careful critique of the studies, Arter and Jenkins concluded that the findings are remarkably consistent in that 14 found no interactions and only 1 (Bursuk, 1971) reported an interaction consistent with modality model predictions. Bursuk studied tenth graders and measured comprehension skills; the other 14 studies used elementary age subjects and focused on decoding outcome measures. The interaction Bursuk obtained was due to greater improvement in reading comprehension of auditory learners when they were also taught listening comprehension. Visual learners did not show a transfer from listening comprehension to reading comprehension. Arter and Jenkins concluded, as have other reviewers (e.g., Ysseldyke, 1973; Vellutino, Steger, Moyer, Harding, & Niles, 1974), that either the modality model is invalid or, given current limitations in educational assessment and programming techniques, it is not applicable at this time.

Other Interaction Investigations

Traits other than relative modality patterns have been studied in relation to different kinds of reading instruction. Among these are level of reading readiness (Stallings & Keepes, 1970, which also found a significant modality interaction but was not reviewed by Arter & Jenkins), reading achievement (Sabaroff, 1963), and introversion–extraversion (Whitehill & Jipson, 1970). [See Berliner & Cahen (1973) and Bracht (1970) for reviews of aptitude-treatment interaction studies, including those just cited.] At this time few specific, definitive answers are available as to interactions between such traits and beginning reading instruction. Teaching lore, if not hard data, supports the generalization that children of low ability benefit proportionately more than do children of high ability from tightly structured, systematic reading programs.

Reed, Rabe, and Mankinen (1970) reviewed studies of teaching reading to brain-injured children and found 42 articles written during the 1960s that dealt with educational and remedial methods for such children. Only 9 studies (covering 7 investigations) evaluated methods experimentally; the other 33 described or recommended teaching procedures without providing evidence of their merit. After analyzing the seven empirical studies, the reviewers (Reed et al., 1970) concluded: "Above all, there is no empirical basis for recommending certain pedagogical procedures . . . for brain-injured children as opposed to non-brain-injured children who also may have a learning disability [p. 396]." Although these studies were not designed as aptitude-treatment interaction studies, they indicate the absence of a data base for the claim that certain reading methods are better than others for brain-injured children.

Models for Further Aptitude-Treatment Interaction (ATI) Research

Salomon (1972) questioned whether ATI research can contribute very much to improving instruction because learners can be divided on the basis of innumerable, uncorrelated variables, but he said that ATI research can assist in developing better explanations and conceptualizations as to the nature of instruction. He proposed three models, all of which relate directly to the problem of whether learning disabled children should be taught to read differently from other children.

The Remedial Model. The remedial model is based on a task-analytic view of teaching and can predict ATIs only when (1) task-specific capabilities account for a large part of the variance in learning outcome, (2) the material to be taught is sequentially ordered, and (3) all subordinate objectives on the hierarchy are to be learned as a result of instruction. The model assumes that the learners will be changed, that is, they will be taught to do what they cannot yet do. This model would predict, for example, that given high and low "visualization" scorers and a task requiring attending to certain details to make spatial transformations, the high visualizers would perform better under an activation treatment that merely enables them to do what they already know how to do. The low visualizers would perform better under a modeling treatment that taught them skills they lack.

The Compensatory Model. The compensatory model does not assume that the learner will be changed. It assumes, instead, that the deficiency in the learner will be compensated for by the treatment. If one assumes that memory is unlikely to be changed by a treatment, then this model would predict that persons low in memory would perform better in a lecture treatment with quizzes interspersed every 5 minutes (to reduce the memory requirement), whereas those high in memory would do better in a standard lecture with note taking. If the "personalogical" variable can be changed, the remedial model would be preferred, according to Salomon (1972).

The Preferential Model. The preferential model is useful for personalogical variables that represent general mediating processes across a variety of tasks, and it capitalizes on style of information processing, type of motivation, and so on. The personalogical variables are not unlike those in the compensatory model, but the logic of the matching is different. The preferential model would predict that students high on achievement motivation would perform better with achievement-oriented feedback, whereas those high on affiliation motivation would do better with affiliation-oriented feedback. The unsuccessful efforts to match modality and reading instruction reviewed earlier may have been conceptualized as efforts to employ this model, although it could be argued that some investigators may have viewed their work as fitting the compensatory model.

Salomon's review of studies led him to conclude that (1) when treatments provide the mediators that low performers cannot (do not) provide for themselves, that treatment will depress the performance of those who do provide the mediators themselves; and (2) when treatments capitalize on stronger aptitudes, the high scorers benefit more.

Summary and Implications

The failure of modality-matched reading instruction to show the expected aptitude–treatment interactions need not yet preclude further investigation of other traits in relation to instruction. If learning disabled children do suffer, as Ross (1976) suggested, from selective attention deficits, Salomon (1972) would predict that they would benefit, where other children would not, from reading instruction that either compensates for that deficit or teachers selective attention directly. In the following section, an approach to reading instruction is proposed for learning disabled children that does as Salomon suggests and does so in the context of intensive, direct decoding instruction derived from a task analysis of reading.

THE FOURTH APPROACH

Much remains unknown about reading processes, learning disabled children, and reading programs. And yet enough is known, if only it can be implemented, to reduce greatly, if not totally eradicate, the severe reading problems now so rampant in American schools. What follows is this observer's perspective on what is known that bears directly on how reading should be taught to learning disabled children.

Learning disabled children are those who must be taught by the best reading methods available if they are to succeed. So taught, they can and do learn to read. Therefore, *teaching disabilities* is a more precise term than *learning disabilities* for the cause of reading failure. Near failure-proof methods for teaching all children to read are already available. Continued failure of schools to employ these programs is at best negligent and at worse malicious. Implementation of the best that is currently available would help mightily; further refinements in these programs would help slightly more.

Beginning Reading Processes

The first step in beginning reading is converting written symbols to their spoken equivalents, which may be done theoretically with any unit, from paragraph to single grapheme. Conventional beginning reading programs of the last 40 years have used the word as the initial unit to be converted. Both data and logic suggest that better reading achievement accrues from using smaller units. The word approach has been defended by inappropriate extrapolation from questionable analyses of proficient adult reading and by claims that it provides easy access to meaning in order to maintain children's interest. But how interesting are Dick and Jane's "ohs" and "looks," and how much more reinforcing is memorizing whole words versus "figuring out" new words? See Blumenfeld (1974) and M. Johnson (1970). Regardless of the merits of the whole-word or the meaning-emphasis approach for the majority of children who do seem to learn to read by osmosis and without intensive, systematic, or structured instruction, it is clear that this method is disastrous for learning disabled children. Systematic decoding must be the first step in reading and must be the direct focus of initial instruction for learning disabled children. Furthermore, it must be recognized that decoding, not comprehension, is the potential pitfall for learning disabled children.

Task analysis of decoding reveals that it contains certain subskills: (1) responding to graphemes or grapheme clusters with appropriate phonemes or phoneme clusters; (2) responding in the appropriate temporal sequence, derived from the spatial order of the written symbols; and (3) blending the phonemes or phoneme clusters into words. Adequate sound–symbol association learning allows the inference that its subskill of letter discrimination was performed, and that discrimination in turn allows the inference that the child's attention was selectively and appropriately focused on relevant stimulus dimensions.

Two skills are conspicuously absent from a task analysis of decoding: letter naming and picture of "context" reading.

Letter Naming. Correlations between knowledge of letter names (number known) at the beginning of first grade and reading level at the end of first grade have been reported by Bond and Dykstra (1967) to range between .51 and .60. However, in a well-designed study, Speer and Lamb (1976) have shown that fluency (rate) of letter naming correlated from .79 to .85 with reading achievement. Since it is logically evident and empirically established (Samuels, 1971) that letter names do not per se facilitate reading, the fluency factor becomes even more relevant. Speer and Lamb predictably found no relationship between gain scores in letter naming and reading achievement. Rate of accurate decoding is probably a more important factor in early reading proficiency than has been recognized in the past (Starlin, 1971). Unfortunately, the children for whom the initial associative learning of sound–symbol relationships is difficult are the children who obtain less practice and whose fluency is thus doubly hindered.

Picture and "Context" Reading. Pictures may be used to teach the concept that symbols on paper can signal us to say something. Programs using rebus writing do just that (e.g., Rozin & Gleitman, 1974; Woodcock & Clark, 1969). Many children do need systematic instruction in the concept that speech can be depicted in written form. However, there is no clear evidence that the concept is too difficult to teach by means of words and letters. Only if a learning disabled child does not acquire the concept, in spite of "clean" teaching using graphemes or words (a most unlikely event), would it seem appropriate to use pictures. Since learning disabled children, by definition, have more than their share of difficulty in reading, it is foolish to teach unnecessary steps.

The other use of pictures in beginning reading programs is as an aid to comprehension. The merit of this procedure must be weighed against the fact that humans seem to walk the paths of least effort. Pictures often enable the child falsely to appear to be decoding. Fluent, automatic decoding is a prerequisite to later holistic comprehension (LaBerge & Samuels, 1974), and for some learning disabled children pictures can significantly distract attention and energy from the essential task of decoding. The argument that decoding and comprehension initially use different cognitive processes and perhaps even different areas of the brain can be made, but for present purposes the need for focusing attention on decoding is a sufficiently strong argument against using pictures as a comprehension aid.

A related contention is that pictures are motivating or reinforcing. This is probably true, and therefore they should be used after successful decoding is achieved to provide informational closure and feedback (Gibson, 1970) or whatever other type of reinforcement they can. At least one program (*Distar*) uses pictures this way.

Other context clues often urged upon children inevitably lead the children to adopt guessing as a decoding tactic. That proficient adult readers do form hypotheses and expectations about what the next ideas will be is not disputed. The contention is that accurate decoding skills must be acquired before that stage and that, for learning disabled children, guessing strategies interfere with accurate decoding.

Reading Instruction for Learning Disabled Children

If learning disabled children differ as a group from other children in ways relevant to teaching reading, these differences might be described as need for (1) more systematic aid in attending to the relevant features (shape and position) of the graphemes to be discriminated (Ross, 1976), (2) greater than usual number of repetitions of correct grapheme–phoneme associations, and (3) more systematic reinforcement of new learning. (For closely related observations on unfamiliar learning, see Engelmann, 1976.)

As indicated earlier, special education efforts to find modality aptitude–treatment interactions have been notably unsuccessful. Literature from other disciplines (e.g., Berliner & Cahen, 1973; Cronback & Snow, 1969) is not as pessimistic. It is too early to dismiss the possibility that some techniques of reading instruction are particularly beneficial for some children. Learning disabled children, as currently labeled, are not a homogeneous group. However, to the extent that characteristics are shared, these characteristics may constitute appropriate personological variables for interactional investigation. The hypothesized lower performance on selective attention to graphemic features and more trials to mastery are characteristics that would be changed through successful intervention, and, therefore, Salomon's (1972) remedial ATI model would be appropriate. The model would predict that treatments including direct teaching of selective attention and numerous repetitions would deter the performance of children who are not learning disabled and who already discriminate symbols and need few repetitions. ATI literature seems to suggest the principle that the farther away a learner is from mastery of an objective, the more the learner benefits from structured, deductive, "ruleg" approaches. Conversely, the less that is yet to be learned, the greater the benefit derived from "egrule," or inductive approaches (Tobias, 1976). This principle is related to the often heard generalization that academically able youngsters can learn to read with any approach, whereas children who are difficult to teach need a structured phonics program.

It has been definitively established that all or even most learning disabled children have these particular deficits. A reasonable interpretation of available data suggests that they might. To the extent that they do, ATI models should be employed more carefully than in the past in an effort to match these learning characteristics successfully with suitably structured teaching techniques.

Attending to Relevant Phoneme Features. Learning disabled children should be taught the rule that letters and numbers point only one way. Everything children have learned about spatial orientation prior to encountering letters and numbers has suggested that an object's label is not affected by rotation and that one need not, therefore, attend to how it is "pointed" when naming it. It is hard to know whether to laugh or cry when "severe strephosymbolia" in a 10-year-old boy is instantly cured by teaching the "Pointy Rule." It is even harder to answer his somber, "Why didn't any of my teachers tell me that?" Admittedly, and remarkably, most children figure out the Pointy Rule even though they do not articulate it. They are masters of incidental learning; learning disabled children are not.

Learning disabled children need practice, to mastery, in discriminating all letters from one another—for example, *b* from *d*. As yet unresolved, but readily determinable, is whether children who require more practice reach mastery more readily by overlearning *b* before *d* is introduced or by initial confrontation with the pair. In either case, learning is made easier initially if other discriminable features (e.g., type style) are added to spatial orientation. Hyman and Cohen (1975) showed that decreasing the stimulus intensity of the vertical line aids in this discrimination. In short, reversal problems and other letter discrimination failures can be prevented by good pedagogy—even if those problems and failures do have their origin in minimal brain dysfunction, in the genes, or in a weak ego.

Greater Repetitions to Associative Mastery. Precise data are difficult to locate, but clinical lore suggests, probably quite accurately, that some learning disabled children require as many as 1,500 to 5,000 correct associations of initial sound–symbol correspondences before reliable retention will occur. After the first few symbols are learned (i.e., the correct sound response is invariably given to the letter stimulus), the number of required repetitions drops markedly and may approximate that of children who are not learning disabled. It is difficult to determine in ordinary teaching situations whether the repetitions are required because of difficulties in selectively attending, discriminating, or associating. The teacher should, therefore, give special care to each possibility. Commonly, teachers find it difficult to provide sufficient opportunity for monitored oral response to the first symbols taught before more are introduced. The child's confusion mounts, and uncorrected errors proliferate, further compounding the failure cycle. Teachers must be especially alert to the pitfalls of providing "off-target" practice. Circling a thousand worksheet pictures of things that start with /m/ provides no practice in looking at *m* and responding with /m/. It is only the latter skill that is part of decoding. The clear implication is that teachers must somehow provide sufficient and appropriate repetitions and must monitor progress very precisely. This is a large order, but anything less is not teaching and is not defensible. Letter names double the child's learning burden and do not contribute to reading skill. Therefore, they should be taught only after decoding skills are well established.

The Use of Reinforcement. Children can be taught to read, even though we have not resolved the complex and fascinating disputes between behaviorists and those of other persuasions over the nature of the acquisition of language skills. However, some learning disabled children will not be taught to read without careful use of well-established behavioral principles of reinforcement. The complexities of reinforcement schedules and the technicalities of differences between negative reinforcers and punishers need not be mastered by all teachers, but we do need to recognize that mastering decoding skills is not sufficiently intrinsically rewarding to all children to maintain the necessary effort. We might ardently wish it were or even believe it should be. Neither changes the fact that it is not. Reading programs should include procedures for appropriate reinforcement and for visibility and precise monitoring of children's progress. If these are not included, the teacher must provide them. A how-to presentation of reinforcement and recording is outside the scope of this discussion, and the interested reader will find ample information in a variety of sources such as Burdett and Fox (1973),

Haughton (1972), Lovitt (1973), and Starlin (1971) for recording techniques, and O'Leary and O'Leary (1972) and Becker, Engelmann, and Thomas (1971) for reinforcement and management techniques useful in classroom reading instruction.

Teacher Training

At the present time, the single greatest obstacle to successful reading instruction for learning disabled children is inadequate teacher training programs in the nation's colleges of education. Learning disabled children can learn, and reading programs adequate to teach them, in the hands of well-trained teachers, are already available. Those who would improve the abysmal state of reading instruction for learning disabled children have a twofold job—first, persuading the education world that improvement is currently possible and then, teaching that world the skills required to do it. The persuasion burden may be the heavier. Research has not been a potent aid; litigation may be (Abel, 1974; Bateman, 1975; Saretsky, 1973; Sugarman, 1974).

SUMMARY

Like other children, learning disabled children bring to school adequate auditory, visual, auditory-visual integrative, syntactic, and semantic skills for learning to read. Like other children, they do not need to learn letter names or picture reading to decode. Like other children, they do need to be taught the separate, or at least separable, skills of decoding sound–symbol correspondences, processing left-to-right, and blending sounds. Perhaps *unlike* other children, they need programs that and teachers who especially emphasize selective attention to relevant grapheme features, provide and require adequate repetitions of grapheme–phoneme correspondences to ensure mastery, and systematically use principles of reinforcement. And, finally, all our children need accountable schools committed to teaching them to read, even if that commitment requires, as it does, the relinquishment of excuses for failure and the acceptance of demonstrably effective reading programs and teaching techniques.

REFERENCES

Abel, D. Can a student sue the schools for educational malpractice? *Harvard Educational Review*, 1974, *44*, 416–436.
Abt Associates. *Education as experimentation: A planned variation model* (Vol. 3). Boston: Abt Associates, 1976.

Anderson, R. W. *Effects of neuro-psychological techniques on reading achievement.* Unpublished doctoral dissertation, Colorado State College (Greeley), 1965.

Anderson, W. F. The relative effects of the Frostig program, corrective reading instruction, and attention upon the reading skills of corrective readers with visual perceptual difficulties. *Journal of School Psychology,* 1972, *10,* 387–395.

Arter, J. A., & Jenkins, J. R. *Examining the benefits and prevalence of modality considerations in special education.* Unpublished manuscript, University of Illinois (Urbana–Champaign), 1975.

Artley, A. S. *The controversy: Reading problem or learning disability: What are the issues?* Paper presented at the meeting of the International Reading Association, New York, May 1975. (ERIC Document Reproduction Service No. ED 110 960)

Baker, R. D., & Gray, B. B. *Monterey reading program.* Monterey, Cal.: Behavioral Sciences Institute, 1972.

Balow, B. Perceptual activities in the treatment of severe reading disability. *Reading Teacher,* 1971, *24,* 513–525.

Bandura, A. *Principles of behavior modification.* New York: Holt, Rinehart, and Winston, 1969.

Bannatyne, A. A suggested classification of the causes of dyslexia. *Word Blind Bulletin,* 1966, *1*(5), 5–14.

Bannatyne, A. Research design and progress in remediating learning disabilities. *Journal of Learning Disabilities,* 1975, *8,* 345–348.

Bateman, B. D. *The Illinois test of psycholinguistic abilities in current research.* Urbana: University of Illinois, Institute for Research on Exceptional Children, 1965.

Bateman, B. D. Three approaches to diagnosis and educational planning for children with learning disabilities. *Academic Therapy,* 1967, *2,* 215–222.

Bateman, B. D. Educational implications of minimal brain dysfunction. In F. de la Cruz, B. Fox, & R. Roberts (Eds.), *Minimal brain dysfunction.* New York: Annals of the New York Academy of Sciences, 1973.

Bateman, B. D. Poor reading instruction and the law. *Reading Informer,* 1975, *3,* 17–19.

Becker, W. C., Engelmann, S. E., & Thomas, D. R. *Teaching: A course in applied psychology.* Chicago: Science Research Associates, 1971.

Becker, W. C., & Engelmann, S. E. *Technical report 1976-1.* Unpublished manuscript, University of Oregon, 1973. (a)

Becker, W. C., & Engelmann, S. E. *Technical report 73-2.* Unpublished manuscript, University of Oregon, 1973. (b)

Becker, W. C., Engelmann, S. E., & Thomas, D. R. *Teaching 2: Cognitive learning and instruction.* Palo Alto, Cal.: Science Research Associates, 1975.

Berliner, D. C., & Cahen, L. S. Trait-treatment interaction and learning. In F. N. Kerlinger (Ed.), *Review of research in education* (Vol. 1). Itesco, Ill.: Peacock Publishing, 1973.

Bijou, S. W. What psychology has to offer education—now. *Journal of Applied Behavior Analysis,* 1970, *3,* 65–71.

Birch, H. Dyslexia and maturation of visual function. In J. Money (Ed.), *Reading disability. Progress and research needs in dyslexia.* Baltimore: John Hopkins University Press, 1962.

Birch, H., & Belmont, L. Auditory-visual integration in normal and retarded readers. *American Journal of Orthopsychiatry,* 1964, *34,* 852–861.

Blank, M., & Bridger, W. Deficiencies in verbal labeling in retarded readers. *American Journal of Orthopsychiatry,* 1966, *36,* 840–847.

Blank, M., Weider, S., & Bridger, W. Verbal deficiencies in abstract thinking in early reading retardation. *American Journal of Orthopsychiatry,* 1968, *38,* 823–834.

Bliesmer, E. P., & Yarborough, B. H. A comparison of ten different beginning reading programs in first grade. *Phi Delta Kappan,* 1965, *46,* 500–504.

Blom, G. E., & Jones, A. W. Bases of classification of reading disorders. In E. O. Calkins (Ed.), *Reading Forum* (NINDS Monograph No. 11, U.S. Public Health Service Publication No.0–418–318). Washington, D.C.: U.S. Government Printing Office, 1971.

Blumenfeld, S. L. *The new illiterates—and how to keep your child from becoming one.* New Rochelle, N.Y.: Arlington House, 1974.

Bond, G. L., & Dykstra, R. The cooperative research program in first grade reading instruction. *Reading Research Quarterly*, 1967, *2*, 5–142.

Bracht, G. H. Experimental factors related to aptitude-treatment interactions. *Review of Educational Research*, 1970, *40*, 627–645.

Burdett, C. S., & Fox, W. L. *Measurement and evaluation of reading behaviors: Word recognition, oral reading, and comprehension.* Austin, Tex.: Austin Writers Group, 1973.

Bursuk, L. A. *Sensory model of lesson presentation as a factor in the reading comprehension improvement of adolescent retarded readers.* New York, 1971. (ERIC Document Reproduction Service No. ED 047 435)

Burton, E., & Glass, G. G. *Students' conception of their decoding skill.* Paper presented at the Educational Research Conference, 1968.

Calfee, R., Chapman, R., & Venezky, R. How a child needs to think to learn to read. In L. Gregg (Ed.), *Cognition in learning and memory.* New York: Wiley, 1972.

Caron, A. J. Conceptual transfer in preverbal children as a consequence of dimensional training. *Journal of Experimental Child Psychology*, 1968, *6*, 522–542.

Carroll, J. B. Review of the ITPA. In O. K. Buros (Ed.), *Seventh mental measurements yearbook* (Vol. 1), Highland Park, N.J.: Gryphon Press, 1972.

Chalfant, J. C., & Flathouse, V. E. Auditory and visual learning. In H. Myklebust (Ed.), *Progress in learning disabilities* (Vol. 2). New York: Grune & Stratton, 1971.

Chall, J. *Learning to read: The great debate.* New York: McGraw–Hill, 1967.

Chall, J. Recent research in reading and learning disabilities. *Journal of Learning Disabilities*, in press.

Clements, S. D. *Minimal brain dysfunction in children: Terminology and identification* (NINDS Monograh No. 3, U.S. Public Health Service Publication No. 1415). Washington, D.C.: U.S. Government Printing Office, 1966.

Cohen, S. A. Studies in visual perception and reading in disadvantaged children. *Journal of Learning Disabilities*, 1969, *2*, 498–507.

Cohen, S. A. Minimal brain dysfunction and practical matters such as teaching kids to read. In F. de la Cruz, B. Fox, & R. Roberts (Eds.), *Minimal brain dysfunction.* New York: Annals of the New York Academy of Sciences, 1973.

Cronbach, L. J., & Snow, R. E. Individual differences in learning ability as a function of instructional variables (Final Rep., U.S. Office of Education, Contract No. OEC-4-6-061269-1217). Stanford: Stanford University, School of Education, 1969.

de Hirsch, K., Jansky, J. J., & Langford, W. S. *Predicting reading failure.* New York: Harper & Row, 1966.

Delacato, C. H. *Neurological organization and reading.* Springfield, Ill.: Thomas, 1966.

Della-Piana, G. M., & Endo, G. T. Reading research. In R. M. W. Travers (Ed.), *Second handbook of research on teaching.* Chicago: Rand McNally, 1973.

Diehl, K. The workshops were wonderful. *Reading Informer*, 1975, *3*, 14–15; 24.

Drader, D. L. The role of verbal labeling in equivalence tasks as related to reading ability. *Journal of Learning Disabilities*, 1975, *8*, 154–157.

Dykstra, R. The effectiveness of code- and meaning-emphasis beginning reading programs. *Reading Teacher*, 1968, *22*, 17–23.

Eimas, P. D., Siqueland, E. R., Jusczyk, P., & Vigorito, J. Speech perception in infants. *Science*, 1971, *171*, 303–306.

Engelmann, S. E. Relationship between psychological theories and the act of teaching. *Journal of School Psychology*, 1967, *5*, 93–100. (a)

Engelmann, S. E. Teaching reading to childen with low mental ages. *Education and Training of the Mentally Retarded*, 1967, *2*, 193–201. (b)

Engelmann, S. E. *Conceptual learning*. Sioux Falls, S.D.: Adapt Press, 1969. (a)

Engelmann, S. E. *Preventing failure in the primary grades*. Chicago: Science Research Associates, 1969. (b)

Engelmann, S. E. *Tactual speech: A study in unfamiliar learning*. Unpublished manuscript, University of Oregon, 1976.

Engelmann, S. E., Becker, W. C., Carnine, L., Meyers, L., Becker, J., & Johnson, G. *Corrective reading program*. Chicago: Science Research Assoicates, 1975.

Engelmann, S., & Bruner, E. C. *Distar reading level I*. Chicago: Science Research Associates, 1974.

Engelmann, S. E., & Carnine, D. W. *A structured program's effect on the attitudes and achievement of average and above average second graders*. Unpublished manuscript, University of Oregon, 1975.

Fernald, G. *Remedial techniques in basic school subjects*. New York: McGraw–Hill, 1943.

Flesch, R. *Why Johnny can't read and what you can do about it*. New York: Harper & Row, 1955.

Frostig, M., & Horne, D. *The Frostig program for the development of visual perception*. Chicago: Follett, 1964.

Gibson, E. J. *Principles of perceptual learning and development*. Englewood Cliffs, N.J.: Prentice-Hall, 1969.

Gibson, E. J. The ontogeny of reading. *American Psychologist*, 1970, *25*, 136–143.

Gillingham, A., & Stillman, B. *Remedial training for children with specific disability in reading, spelling, and penmanship*. Cambridge, Mass.: Educators Publishing Service, 1966.

Glass, G. G. Perceptual conditioning for decoding: Rationale and method. In B. Bateman (Ed.), *Learning disorders: Reading* (Vol. 4). Seattle: Special Child Publications, 1971.

Gurren, L., & Hughes, A. Intensive phonics vs. gradual phonics in beginning reading: A review. *Journal of Educational Research*, 1965, *58*, 339–346.

Hallahan, D. P. Distractibility in the learning disabled child. In W. N. Cruickshank & D. P. Hallahan (Eds.), *Perceptual and learning disabilities in children* (Vol. 2), *Research and theory*. Syracuse, N.Y.: Syracuse University Press, 1975.

Hallahan, D. P., & Kauffman, J. M. *Introduction to learning disabilities: A psycho-behavioral approach*. Englewood Cliffs, N.J.: Prentice-hall, 1976.

Hallahan, D. P., Kaufman, J. M., & Ball, D. W. Selective attention and cognitive tempo of low achieving and high achieving sixth grade males. *Perceptual and Motor Skills*, 1973, *36*, 579–583.

Hammill, D. D., Goodman, L., & Wiederholt, J. L. Visual-motor processes; Can we train them? *Reading Teacher*, 1974, *27*, 469–478.

Hammill, D. D., & Larsen, S. C. The relationship of selected auditory perceptual skills and reading ability. *Journal of Learning Disabilities*, 1974, *27*, 429–435.

Haring, N., & Bateman, B. *Teaching the learning disabled child*. Englewood Cliffs, N.J.: Prentice-Hall, 1977. (Chapter with D. Carnine).

Haring, N. G., & Hauck, M. A. Improving learning conditions in the establishment of reading skills with disabled readers. *Exceptional Children*, 1969, *35*, 341–352.

Harrigan, J. E. Initial reading Instruction: Phonemes, syllables, or ideographs? *Journal of Learning Disabilities*, 1976, *9*, 74–80.

Harris, A. J. Practical applications of reading research. *Reading Teacher*, 1976, *29*, 559–565.

Haughton, E. Aims—growing and sharing. In J. B. Jordan & L. S. Robbins (Eds.), *Let's try doing something else kind of thing: Behavioral principles and the exceptional child*. Arlington, Va.: Council for Exceptional Children, 1972.

Hegge, T., Kirk, S. A., & Kirk, W. *Remedial reading drills*. Ann Arbor, Mich.: Wahr, 1936.

Heiman, J. R., Fischer, M. J., & Ross, A. O. A supplementary behavioral program to improve deficient reading performance. *Journal of Abnormal Child Psychology*, 1973, *1*, 390–399.

Hewett, F. M., with Forness, S. R. *Education of exceptional learners.* Boston: Allyn & Bacon, 1974.

Hively, W. A framework for the analysis of elementary reading behavior. *American Educational Research Journal*, 1966, *3*, 89–104.

Holmes, J. A. The substrata-factor theory of reading: Some experimental evidence. In H. Singer & R. B. Ruddell (Eds.), *Theoretical models and processes of reading.* Newark, Del.: International Reading Association, 1970.

Hyman, J., & Cohen, S. A. The effect of verticality as a stimulus property on the letter discrimination of young children. *Journal of Learning Disabilities*, 1975, *8*, 98–107.

Jacobs, J. N. Visual perceptual training programs. *Educational Leadership*, 1968, *25*, 332–340. (Research Supplement)

Johnson, D. J. Educational principles for children with learning disabilities. *Rehabilitation Literature*, 1967, *28*, 317–322.

Johnson, D. J., & Myklebust, H. R. *Learning disabilities, educational principles and practices.* New York: Grune & Stratton, 1967.

Johnson, M. *Programmed illiteracy in our schools.* Winnepeg: Clarity Books, 1970.

Kass, C. E. Psycholinguistic disabilities of children with reading problems. *Exceptional Children*, 1966, *32*, 533–539.

Keogh, B. K. Bender–Gestalt as a predictive and diagnostic test of reading performance. *Journal of Consulting Psychology*, 1965, *29*, 83–84.

Keogh, B. K. Optometric vision training programs for children with learning disabilities: Review of issues and research. *Journal of Learning Disabilities*, 1974, *7*, 219–231.

Kephart, N. C. *The slow learner in the classroom.* Columbus, Ohio: Merrill, 1960.

Kirk, S. A. *Educating exceptional children.* Boston: Houghton Mifflin, 1972.

Kirk, S. A. *Introduction to state of the art: Where are we in learning disabilities?* Los Angeles: Los Angeles Association for Children with Learning Disabilities and California Association for Neurologically Handicapped Children Publications, 1974.

Klesius, S. E. Perceptual-motor development and reading—A closer look. In R. Aukerman (Ed.), *Some persistent questions on beginning reading.* Newark, Del.: International Reading Association, 1972.

Koenigsberg, R. S. An evaluation of visual versus sensorimotor methods for improving orientation discrimination for letter reversal by preschool children. *Child Development*, 1973, *44*, 764–769.

Koppitz, E. M. Bender–Gestalt test, visual aural deficit span test and reading achievement. *Journal of Learning Disabilities*, 1975, *8*, 154–157.

Krippner, S. Research in visual training and reading disability. In B. Bateman (Ed.), *Reading performance and how to achieve it.* Seattle; Special Child Publications, 1973.

LaBerge, D., & Samuels, S. J. Toward a theory of automatic information processing in reading. *Cognitive Psychology*, 1974, *6*, 293–323.

Larsen, S. C., & Hammill, D. D. Relationship of selected visual perceptual abilities to school learning. *Journal of Special Education*, 1975, *9*, 281–291.

Larsen, S. C., Rogers, D., & Sowell, V. The use of selected perceptual tests in differentiating between normal and learning disabled children. *Journal of Learning Disabilities*, 1976, *9*, 85–90.

Lerner, J. W. *Children with learning disabilities.* New York: Houghton Mifflin, 1971.

Lerner, J. W. Remedial reading and learning disabilities: Are they the same or different? *Journal of Special Education*, 1975, *9*, 119–131.

Lerner, J. W. *Children with learning disabilities* (2nd ed.). Boston: Houghton Mifflin, 1976.

Lovell, K., & Gorton, A. A study of some differences between backward and normal readers of average intelligence. *British Journal of Educational Psychology*, 1968, *36*, 240–248.

Lovitt, T. C. Self-management projects with children with behavioral disabilities. *Journal of Learning Disabilities*, 1973, *6*, 15–28.

Lovitt, T. C., & Hurlburt, M. Using behavior-analysis techniques to assess the relationship between phonics instruction and oral reading. *Journal of Special Education*, 1974, *8*, 57–72.

Mann, L. Are we fractionating too much? *Academic Therapy*, 1970, *5*, 85–91.

Mann, L. Psychometric phrenology and the new faculty psychology: The case against ability assessment and training. *Journal of Special Education*, 1971, *5*, 3–14.

Matthews, M. *Teaching to read.* Chicago: University of Chicago Press, 1966.

McGrady, H. H., & Olson, D. A. Visual and auditory learning processes in normal children and children with specific learning disabilities. *Exceptional Children*, 1970, *36*, 581–589.

National Advisory Committee on Handicapped Children. *Special education for handicapped children* (First Annual Rep.). Washington, D.C.: U.S. Department of Health, Education and Welfare, 1968.

Newcomer, P., Hare, B., Hammill, D., & McGettigan, J. Construct validity of the ITPA. *Journal of Learning Disabilities*, 1975, *8*, 220–231.

O'Donnell, P. A. The effects of Delacato training on reading achievement and visual-motor integration (Doctoral dissertation, Stanford University, 1969). *Dissertation Abstracts International*, 1969, *30*, 1079A–1080A. (University Microfilms No. 69-14, 035).

O'Keefe, R. A. *STARTER/101: A structured beginning reading program for young children.* Morristown, N.J.: Silver Burdett, 1970.

O'Keefe, R. A. *STARTER/101*: A system for structuring the teaching of reading. In B. Bateman (Ed.), *Learning disorders: Reading* (Vol. 4). Seattle: Special Child Publications, 1971.

O'Leary, K. D., & O'Leary, S. G. *Classroom management: The successful use of behavior modification.* Elmsford, N.Y.: Pergamon, 1972.

Otto, W. Adequate reading instruction: Fact or fantasy? *Slow Learning Child*, 1972, *19*, 3–11.

Peter, L. J. *Prescriptive teaching.* New York: McGraw-Hill, 1965.

Reed, J. C., Rabe, E. F., & Mankinen, M. Teaching reading to brain-damaged children: A review. *Reading Research Quarterly*, 1970, *5*, 379–401.

Robbins, M. The Delacato interpretation of neurological organization. *Reading Research Quarterly*, 1966, *1*, 57–78.

Robinson, H. M. Perceptual training—does it result in reading improvement? In R. C. Aukerman, (Ed.), *Some persistent questions on beginning reading.* Newark, Del.: International Reading Association, 1972.

Ross, A. O. *Psychological aspects of learning disabilities and reading disorders.* New York: McGraw-Hill, 1976.

Rozin, P., & Gleitman, L. *Syllabary: An introductory reading curriculum.* Washington, D.C.: Curriculum Development Associates, 1974.

Rozin, P., & Gleitman, L. The reading process and the acquisition of the alphabetic principle. In A. Reber & D. Scarborough (Eds.), *Toward a psychology of reading: Proceedings of the CUNY conference.* Hillsdale, N.J.: Lawrence Erlbaum Associates, 1977.

Rozin, P., Poritsky, S., & Stotsky, R. American children with reading problems can easily learn to read English represented by Chinese characters. *Science*, 1971, *171*, 1264–1267.

Rupert, H. *A sequentially compiled list of instructional materials for remediational use with the ITPA.* Unpublished manuscript, Greeley, Col.: Rocky Mountain Special Education Instructional Materials Center, no date.

Sabaroff, R. A comparative investigation of two methods of teaching phonics in a modern reading program: A pilot study. *Journal of Experimental Education*, 1963, *31*, 249–256.

Sabatino, D. A. Auditory perception; Development, assessment, and intervention. In L. Mann & D. A. Sabatino (Eds.), *The first review of special education.* Philadelphia: Buttonwood Farms, 1973.

Salomon, G. Heuristic models for the generation of aptitude–treatment interaction hypotheses. *Review of Educational Research*, 1972, *42*, 327–343.

Samuels, S. J. Reading disability? *Reading Teacher*, 1970, *24*, 267, 271, 283.

Samuels, S. J. Letter–name versus letter–sound knowledge in learning to read. *Reading Teacher*, 1971, *24*, 604–608.

Saretsky, G. The strangely significant case of Peter Doe. *Phi Delta Kappan*, 1973, *54*, 589–592.

Senf, G. M. An information–integration theory and its application to normal reading acquisition and reading disability. In N. D. Bryant & C. E. Kass (Eds.), *Leadership training institute in learning disabilities: Final report* (Vol. 2). Tucson: University of Arizona Press, 1972.

Silver, A. A., & Hagin, R. A. Specific reading disability: An approach to diagnosis and treatment. *Journal of Special Education*, 1967, *1*, 109–118. (a)

Silver, A. A., & Hagin, R. A. Strategies of intervention in the spectrums of defects in specific reading disability. *Bulletin of the Orton Society*, 1967, *17*, 39–46. (b)

Speer, O. B., & Lamb, G. S. First grade reading ability and fluency in naming verbal symbols. *Reading Teacher*, 1976, *29*, 572–576.

Staats, A. W. *Learning, language, and cognition.* New York: Holt, Rinehart and Winston, 1968.

Staats, A. W., Brewer, B. A., & Gross, M. C. Learning and cognitive development: Representative samples, cumulative-hierarchial learning, and experimental-longitudinal methods. *Monographs of the Society for Research in Child Development*, 1970, *35*(8, Serial No. 141).

Staats, A. W., & Butterfield, W. H. Treatment of nonreading in a culturally deprived juvenile delinquent: An application of reinforcement principles. *Child Development*, 1965, *36*, 925–942.

Stallings, J. A., & Keepes, B. D. *Student aptitudes and methods of teaching beginning reading: A predictive instrument for determining interaction patterns* (Final Rep., U.S. Office of Education, Contract No. OEG-9-70-0005, Project No. 9-1-099). Washington, D.C.: U.S. Government Printing Office, 1970.

Starlin, C. Evaluating progress toward reading proficiency. In B. Bateman (Ed.), *Learning disorders: Reading* (Vol. 4). Seattle: Special Child Publications, 1971.

Steger, J. A., Vellutino, F. R., & Meshoulam, U. Visual-tactile and tactile-tactile paired associate learning in normal and poor readers. *Perceptual and Motor Skills*, 1972, *35*, 263–266.

Stewart, D. *Educational malpractices: The big gamble in our schools.* Westminster, Cal.: Slate Services, 1971.

Sugarman, S. D. Accountability through the courts. *School Review*, 1974, *82*, 233–259.

Tarver, S. G., & Hallahan, D. P. Attention deficits in children with learning disabilities: A review. *Journal of Learning Disabilities*, 1974, *9*, 560–569.

Tobias, S. Achievement treatment interactions. *Review of Educational Research*, 1976, *46*, 61–74.

Vail, E. *Formula phonics.* Los Angeles: Lawrence, 1969.

Vail, E. Formula phonics. A broad spectrum reading method. In B. Bateman (Ed.), *Learning disorders: Reading* (Vol. 4). Seattle: Special Child Publications, 1971.

Vellutino, F. R., Steger, J. A., & Kandel, G. Reading disability: An investigation of the perceptual deficit hypothesis. *Cortex*, 1972, *8*, 106–118.

Vellutino, F. R. *Psychological factors in reading disability.* Paper presented at the meeting of the American Educational Research Association, Chicago, April 1974.

Vellutino, F. R., Steger, B. M., Moyer, S. C., Harding, C. J., & Niles, J. A. *Has the perceptual deficit hypothesis led us astray? An examination of current conceptualizations in the assessment and treatment of exceptional children.* Paper presented at the meeting of the International Convention of the Council for Exceptional Children, New York, April 1974.

Venezky, R. L. *Prereading skills: Theoretical foundations and practical applications* (Theoretical Paper No. 54). Madison: University of Wisconsin, Wisconsin Research and Development Center for Cognitive Learning, 1975.

Wepman, J. M. The perceptual basis for learning. In H. A. Robinson (Ed.), *Meeting individual differences in reading.* Chicago: University of Chicago Press, 1964.

Wepman, J. M. Modalities and learning. In H. M. Robinson (Ed.), *Coordinating reading instruction.* Glenview, Ill.: Scott, Foresman, 1971.

Westman, J. C., Arthur, B., & Scheidler, E. P. Reading retardation: An overview. *American Journal of Diseases of Children*, 1965, *109*, 359–369.

Whitehill, R. P. & Jipson, J. A. Differential reading program performance of extroverts and introverts. *Journal of Experimental Education*, 1970, *38*(3), 93–96.

Wiederholt, J. L., & Hammill, D. D. Use of the Frostig–Horne visual perception program in the urban school. *Psychology in the Schools*, 1971, *8*, 268–274.

Woodcock, R. W., & Clark, C. R. *Peabody rebus reading program.* Circle Pines, Minn.: American Guidance Service, 1969.

Ysseldyke, J. E. Diagnostic-prescriptive teaching: The search for aptitude–treatment interactions. In L. Mann & D. Sabatino (Eds.), *The first review of special education* (Vol. 1). Philadelphia: Buttonwood Farms, 1973.

Ysseldyke, J. E., & Salvia, J. Diagnostic-prescriptive teaching: Two models. *Exceptional Children*, 1974, *41*, 181–195.

Zeaman, D., & House, B. J. The role of attention in retardate discrimination learning. In N. R. Ellis (Ed.), *Handbook of mental deficiency.* New York: McGraw–Hill, 1963.

Zurif, E. B., & Carson, G. Dyslexia in relation to cerebral dominance and temporal analysis. *Neuropsychologia*, 1970, *8*, 351–361.

10 Analysis of Behavior in Reading Instruction

James G. Holland
University of Pittsburgh

My aim in this chapter is to illustrate the usefulness of the experimental analysis of behavior for the design of reading instruction. From the perspective of the analysis of behavior, all instruction consists of arranging sequences of contingencies. Each contingency has three parts: (1) Some material is presented to the student; (2) the student interacts with the material; and (3) the interaction has a consequence, frequently a reinforcing consequence. By concentrating on this deceptively simple concept of contingency, I will demonstrate that it has far-reaching implications for contrasting the *modi operandi* of several approaches to teaching beginning reading.

When contingencies are effectively designed, the material presented is appropriate to the student's current level of achievement in the subject, the interaction is a behavior that takes the learner another step toward mastery, and the consequence reinforces the desired, newly emitted behavior. Among the ways that instructional materials can fail to establish effective contingencies are by the provision of inappropriate cues that allow the correct answers to be achieved by trivial student behaviors or by the elicitation of behaviors only superficially related to mastery. Both problems can be illustrated in relation to reading instruction.

INAPPROPRIATE RESPONSE CONTINGENCIES

Usually in an instructional situation only a small part of the student's activity is public and observable by the teacher—a question is answered about material the student has read, or an answer is written to a problem in the lesson material. The student's final public performance should depend on the correct execution of the private act—a correct answer should indicate that the material has been read or that the problem has been worked out. Overcuing or inappropriate cuing enables the student to respond correctly without having performed the task that the lesson was intended to evoke. For example, when a teacher has students "read" aloud together, some children will respond on the basis of cues provided by other students rather than on the basis of the printed text. Such responses are miscued. The importance of ensuring appropriate response contingencies is often underestimated because of the apparent improbability of controlling a child's behavior by very subtle, inappropriate cues. However, psychology's famous horse story is an illustration of how, given proper training conditions, behavior can be controlled by inappropriate stimuli so subtle that even the source of the cues, the horse's trainer, was not aware of giving them.

Many students of general psychology are familiar with the story of Clever Hans, the remarkably intelligent Russian trotting horse, who had (in the hands of an extremely skillful teacher) demonstrated an ability to count, perform arithmetic problems, comprehend complex questions, spell, and even read (Pfungst, 1911). Unfortunately, Hans could not talk, so he would manifest these skills by head pointing or by tapping out numerical answers with a hoof. In demonstrating his ability to read, a series of words was placed before him and he would point with his nose to the correct words. Han's teacher, the remarkable Herr von Osten, used friendly encouragement and rewards in the form of bread or carrots. He worked entirely without aversive consequences—and this in 1904 while Skinner was but an infant in rural eastern Pennsylvania!

The first group of scientists evaluating Hans was quite taken in. A second group discovered that Hans could solve problems only with an informed audience. For example, if persons asking the question did not themselves know the answer, Hans was unable to answer it, and, in a more revealing instance, if the audience and Hans were asked different questions, Hans answered the question put to the audience. Hans had learned to respond to subtle cues from the audience. To determine whether Hans could read correctly, the audience had to identify the position of the correct word and then watch Hans make his choice. In doing so, the audience gave Hans the cues he needed to get his carrots. Yet, Herr von Osten believed that he had trained Hans to perform on an intellectual level equal to that of normal 13- to 14-year-old children.

Indeed, Herr von Osten had used a careful training sequence. On the targeted skills, he began with an extremely simplified subject matter. For example, in teaching Hans to "read," he first taught Hans to indicate a single word, then one of a pair of words. He physically guided the earliest responses, then indicated them with gross physical motions, and then with more subtle signs. He was always ready with carrots and bread at the instant that his student followed his lead. Two progressions were present in this training procedure—the targeted tasks increased in complexity and, at the same time, the extraneous cue of physical guidance, gesturing, and so on decreased gradually until the trainer himself was unaware that he was still providing cues. Unfortunately, the targeted cue—the text itself—never gained control. The fading stimuli, which were not completely removed until the revealing experiments were performed, continued to control.

The lesson of Clever Hans has been difficult to learn. At the 1975 American Psychological Association meeting an experiment was described in which a severely retarded girl was taught a sight vocabulary of 54 words or phrases (see Rosenbaum & Breiling, 1976). The reading material appeared on individual cue cards and included such phrases as *Point to the car* or *Point to the man smiling.* The girl responded by pointing to one of several pictures on cards laid on the table before her. During training, if she was correct, she was praised and given candy. If she was incorrect, the experimenter read the instruction aloud and modeled the behavior for the girl. After a pause, the card was presented again and she was prompted to do what the card said. If necessary, she was physically guided through the behavior. Learning appeared to be amazingly rapid—after only eight 15- to 20-minute training sessions, the severely retarded girl was close to 100% correct.

The experimenters were mainly interested in identifying what reinforcing aspects of the situation were important. First, candy was eliminated, and various attempts were made to obscure the face of the experimenter. However, none of these efforts had more than a minor disruptive effect on performance until a projector was used to present the cues and the experimenter left the room to observe through a one-way mirror. Performance then disintegrated to between 10% and 35% correct in various sessions. It seems that the ghost of Clever Hans haunts this experiment.

When both Clever Hans and a severely retarded child can convince people especially attuned to the misuse of the cues that they are "reading," can we possibly be surprised by the wholesale failure in maintaining appropriate response contingencies in the traditional classroom? John Holt, a leading author in the educational protest literature, provided many examples from classrooms of children using inappropriate cues—cues that circumvent the skill to be learned. In one instance, he described a classroom in which the teacher was performing on the blackboard a drill designed to teach the identification of nouns, adjectives, and verbs. She arranged three columns on the blackboard, one for each category, and as she said each word, she asked a child in which column it belonged. As Holt (1964) described it, in that drill

   ... the percentage of hits was remarkably high, especially since it was clear to
   me from the way the children were talking and acting that they hadn't a notion

of what Nouns, Adjectives, and Verbs were. Finally one child said, "Miss————
————, you shouldn't point to the answer each time." The teacher was
surprised, and asked what she meant. The child said, "Well, you don't exactly
point, but you kind of stand next to the answer." This was no clearer, since the
teacher had been standing still. But after a while, as the class went on, I thought I
saw what the girl meant. Since the teacher wrote each word down in its proper
column, she was, in a way, getting herself ready to write, pointing herself at the
place where she would soon be writing. From the angle of her body to the
blackboard the children picked up a subtle clue to the correct answer [p. 15].

Furthermore, this teacher kept the three columns approximately equal in
length. Thus, the first word after the columns came into balance might be a
blind guess, but for the next word there would be one chance in two to get it
right, and for the final word the remaining unfilled column was a dead
giveaway.

Holt described many such failures to assure a contingent relation between
correct performance and actual mastery in the classroom. It is likely that most
of us can think of a host of examples from our own experience. The new
educational technology should help the teacher who is, frankly, faced with an
almost impossible task. Indeed it does help, but even with technology and
with theory-inspired design, there are problems of inappropriate contingencies.

O. K. Moore's Talking Typewriter

One technologically based effort in reading instruction received considerable
popular attention in the 1960s, spurred by a film report showing a few
children learing to read using a "talking typewriter" (Moore & Anderson,
1960). In the film, O. K. Moore's daughter and a few other children, under
careful adult guidance, use an electric typewriter. Early in training, as the
child strikes a key, the adult says its letter name. Later the adult approximates
the phonic sound as a key is struck. Next a projector presents letters, and the
child matches the letter by striking the appropriate key. The adult operates a
hand switch to cut off the power should the child begin to strike an
inappropriate key. When the appropriate key is struck, the adult pronounces
the phoneme. Later the projector presents whole words, and still later,
sentences. The adult continues to use the hand switch to cut off power before
inappropriate keys are struck and continues to pronounce the individual
phonemes and the completed word. The entertaining filmed report gives the
impression of well-designed contingencies in a progression of tasks that result
in reading.

Unfortunately, the film is not sufficiently detailed to permit one to
ascertain precisely what elements of the described procedures are effective or
whether there are other, perhaps unrecognized, roles played by the adult.

When the "talking typewriter" was fully automated, it became possible to examine carefully the effects of the procedures and contingencies. Automated equipment, prepared by Edison Responsive Environment, produces letter names or appropriate phonemes automatically as a key is struck. When the child is to match a projected letter, inappropriate keys are locked, permitting only the designated key to operate.

Using this automated equipment, Richardson and McSweeney (1970) experimentally evaluated the "talking typewriter" procedures and found the results most unimpressive. In analyzing the failure of these procedures, Richardson and McSweeney noted that in the initial free exploration days, when a press on any key produces the appropriate sound, there is, in fact, absolutely no contingent relationship between the keyboard letter and the spoken sound so far as the child is concerned. The child does not need to look at the letter or attend to the produced sound, even though this phase is supposed to teach letter–sound associations. Thus many children fail to learn these associations. In the later phase, when the child is shown words or letters and is to type corresponding letters, the automated keyboard locks all incorrect letters. The child needs merely to hunt among the keys to find the unlocked one and, in time, type a perfect message without attending to the visual display, the letters on the keys, or the sounds produced in striking the keys. If a child has completed the first phase without learning letter–sound associations, it is especially likely that he or she will continue to perform in this nonreading way. And that child will continue to succeed! Nothing in this "advanced" phase assures that the child will attend to any grapheme–phoneme association. Clever Hans lives in the age of technology.

TEACHING EARLY READING "ERRORLESSLY"

Thus far I have focused on problems of ensuring appropriate response contingencies. Yet one could design items whose correct solution indicated appropriate learner behavior but that the intended learners simply could not solve. Although such items ensure appropriate response contingencies for correct answers, they are inadequate as teaching items. By devising a careful progression in task complexity, good materials ensure that the children can successfully perform the required behaviors.

To devise appropriate progressions in task complexity, a behavioral analysis of the task to be learned and of the entry behavior of the learner must be undertaken. As a first step, reading might be anlyzed as follows. Competent readers recognize a large number of words and have vocal or subvocal behaviors under control of whole words or phrases so that their rate of reading is far too fast for single graphemes and phonemes to be serving functionally as stimuli. In contrast, nonreading children may have substantial speaking and listening vocabularies, but they do not have these reponses under the control of textual stimuli. Children learning to read are confronted, then, with clusters of visual forms highly similar to one another. Yet these almost identical forms were arranged by the writer of the material the children are reading in response to the sequence of sounds in which the individual units or characters are controlled by corresponding sound. For skilled readers, the resulting sequence controls their vocal (or subvocal) behavior so that they will say the word or phrase that the writer wrote. When confronting an unfamiliar cluster of characters, the reader can fall back on responding to a smaller unit than the total word by emitting the sounds controlled by groups of syllables or, on rare occasions, even by the individual graphemes. This skill (responding to a new combination of letter forms to produce the sounds similar to those produced by the writer of the material is so uniformly developed throughout the literate population that an author may generate a completely new word and have it quickly become a part of everyone's reading vocabulary. Consider, for example, the word *snafu*.

And "snafu" might be the response of the "hep" English-speaking child on first discovering that many identical printed letter forms, in the context of other letters, must control different sounds (such as long and short vowels) and that many different letters forms control the same sounds (*c* or *k* for /k/). The reading teacher, then, has the task of getting the nonreader both to read a large number of words without resorting to smaller unit decoding and to decipher new words despite the lack of a simple phoneme–grapheme correspondence in English. The early tasks must be manageable by the child and, at the same time, must progress toward the targeted behavior of the proficient reader. The hotly debated issues among the look–say, phonics, and linguistic approaches are fundamentally debates on what form of early steps are both manageable by the child and useful in progressing toward proficient reading. I propose at this point to describe some basic findings from the experimental analysis of behavior that bear on these issues with the hope of suggesting a theoretical rationale useful both in deciding among reading instructional approaches and in sharpening the execution of particular approaches. The first illustration involves a relatively minor matter in sequencing.

Why Begin with the Alphabet?

Chall (1967) concluded that teaching either letter names or phonic values is necessary before beginning instruction in reading. The basic operant conditioning literature provides a rationale for the usefulness of early alphabet training in one of the best known and most fundamental findings— the phenomenon of stimulus generalization. In the typical demonstration, a given point on a stimulus dimension (e.g., a particular wavelength of light) is the occasion on which a response is intermittently reinforced and, as a consequence, future presentations of that wavelength result in responding. During a later test phase, other points along the stimulus dimension are presented. These, too, result in some responding. For example, if the test color is fairly close in the spectrum to the original trained color, it evokes almost as much responding as the original stimulus. The frequency of responding decreases with the distance from the trained stimulus, but a sizable amount of responding is evoked by stimuli that are a considerable distance away. More precise differentiation of the stimulus dimension results when responding to one stimulus is reinforced while responses to other stimuli even quite close to it are unreinforced, or when each stimulus is trained to a particular response (Nevin, 1973).

Letter forms are quite similar to one another. In fact, we might say, "All letter forms look alike," until we have become personally acquainted with them by, as it were, being on a first-name basis. Until some differential response such as the letter name is learned, the child would be expected to show stimulus generalization for letter forms by responding to different letters as though they were the same. Although critics of teaching letter naming are correct in contending that the act of naming letters is not actually a part of reading, differentially responding to letter shapes is a basic part of mature reading.

"Errorless" Learning Research and a Comparison of Three Early Reading Instruction Techniques

The basic operant conditioning literature also has something to contribute by way of a rationale concerning some contrasting approaches to providing a suitable series of learning tasks that introduce the novice to reading. Skinner's (1954) earliest work emphasized the gradual shaping of a new skill and, hence, what has been called "errorless learning." Reading curriculum approaches have always had some form of progression; to start with the complete reading task of the mature reader would be folly. But what is asked of the beginner, and how do the early tasks relate to later proficiencies? These are the issues that divide contesting approaches, and I believe that basic research on errorless learing is relevant to these issues. This research has been attempting to determine the conditions necessary for errorlessly attaining new discrimnative control (Sidman & Stoddard, 1967; Terrace, 1963; Touchette, 1968). Errorless sequences are usually successful when the progression is from a prominent stimulus to a more sublte stimulus along the same dimension. In fact, a simple gradual progression on the same stimulus dimension can easily carry control to the limit of sensory capacity. For example, Clever Hans's trainer prominently signaled the correct response with gross gestures early in training and later, unknown to himself, he maintained very subtle physical signaling.

A problem arises when there is no means of establishing initial control on the relevant stimulus dimension. A common solution involves pairing the target stimulus with an irrelevant but highly prominent stimulus that can initially control the response. In Clever Hans's case, the physical gesturing cues were supposed to be faded out until Hans was under exclusive control of textual stimuli. As we have seen, when the fading stimuli were indeed completely removed, it was shown that textual stimuli had never gained control. This fading cue technique, common in the laboratory and in instructional design, is frequently called a *transfer of stimulus control*. Unfortunately, the technique is unpredictable—sometimes it works, other times it does not. Instructional designers often find that developing a successful fading series involves a tedious trial-and-error procedure. Occasionally, when formative evaluation of an instructional design is weak or absent, an unsuccessful fading series may survive to haunt users of the finished curriculum materials. Basic research on fading cues offers designers some guidelines for developing successful fading series and a rationale for choosing among several techniques of beginning reading instruction.

Doran (1975) reasoned that during a fading sequence the fading stimulus and the target stimulus comprise a compound similar to the compound stimulus often studied in selective attention. Initially, only the fading stimulus controls the response. Doran argued that the criterion stimulus will gain control at the end of training only if it begins to share control with the fading stimulus sometimes during the fading sequence. This shared control should happen consistently only when the target stimulus itself is sufficiently prominent for the subject to begin to use it early in the fading series. If both cues do not share control well before the fading stimulus has been completely removed, the sequence will essentially train finer and finer discriminations of the irrelevant cue stimulus.

In Doran's experiment, children acquired a size discrimination for circles projected successively on a single transilluminated key (see Fig. 10.1). The positive stimulus (S^+) was always a brightly illuminated 14 mm diameter circle. The child responded by pressing the illuminated key. On S^+ trials, responding was intermittently reinforced.

The negative stimulus (S^-) was a smaller circle. On S^- trials, responding was never reinforced. During training, a fading stimulus or irrelevant cue was superimposed on the S^- circle. In this instance, the fading series began with S^- being a completely dark key to which children did not respond, and gradually over a series of trials, the S^- was brought up to full brightness. Thus the prominent irrelevant cue was brightness, and the target discrimination was circle size.

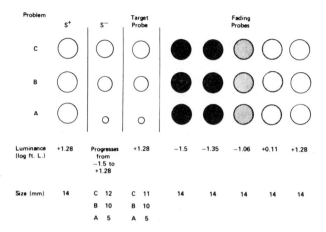

FIG. 10.1. Size and luminance of S^+, S^-, and probe stimuli. (From "Control by Stimulus Features During Fading" by M. J. Doran. *Dissertation Abstracts International*, 1975, *36*, 3642B. University Microfilms No. 76-344. Reprinted by permission of author.)

There were three different problem difficulties involving three negative stimuli (S^-) of different sizes. In all problems, the S^+ was a 14 mm diameter circle. In Problem A, the simplest problem, the S^- circle diameter was 5 mm, easily discriminable from S^+. In the intermediate Problem B, the S^- circle diameter was 10 mm, and in the difficult Problem C, 12 mm. Since S^+ and S^- were never present simultaneously, a 2 mm differemce in diameter was a very difficult discrimination.

After each block of 10 trials, 2 probe stimuli were used to identify which element of the compound stimulus controlled responding. One probe was the current S^- circle size, but at full brightness; the companion probe was the S^+ circle size, but at the brightness appropriate to that point in the S^- fading series. If the subject responded to the smaller, fully bright circle but not to the large, dimmer circle, responding was controlled by the irrelevant fading cue—brightness—alone. If the subject did not respond to either probe, dual control was indicated, since neither size nor brightness alone was sufficient to evoke a response. Responding to the large, dimmer circle but not to the small, bright circle indicated control by size alone. Finally, if the subject responded to both probes, neither stimulus was controlling the response, a condition that ordinarily prevailed when the subject was responding to all S^-'s in training as well.

Figure 10.2 shows data for five subjects on the most difficult of the size discriminations (Problem C) on four successive daily sessions (C_1 through C_4). The data are shown as individual records for each of the children in each

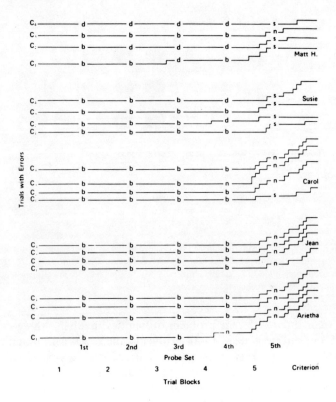

FIG. 10.2. Performance of five subjects given four size discrimination problems in the sequence CCCC. Each problem had five 10-trial program blocks, a 10-trial criterion, and five probe sets. For the program blocks and the criterion, each trial moves the data line one step to the right, and each errorful trial moves the line one step upward. Only the first response in each S^- trial is plotted. Performance on probe sets is coded as n (control by neither dimension), b (control for brightness), s (control by size), or d (dual control). (From "Control by Stimulus Features During Fading" by M. J. Doran. *Dissertation Abstracts International,* 1975, *36,* 3642B. University Microfilms No. 76-344. Reprinted by permission of author.)

of the sessions. They are plots of trials on which errors occurred. The horizontal lines in the first three or four blocks of trials indicate that performance was totally error free. The stairstep effect in the final blocks indicates that as the brightness cue became too difficult and finally impossible to use, errors occurred in the form of responding to the S^-. Typically, in the early trials consistent control by brightness is indicated by the first, second, and third probes, followed by control by neither for the fourth and fifth probes. In the final and criterion phase without a brightness cue there are extensive errors.

The conditions represented here are analogous to those seen in curriculum materials in which a prominent irrelevant cue is used to ensure initial correct responding, and the irrelevant cue is then gradually faded out. When there is no contingent relationship for attending to the target dimension and little likelihood that it will enter into a controlling relationship because of its relative lack of prominence, the fading sequence will frequently fail to ensure the desired final performance.

In the second condition in Doran's (1975) study, children first learned the easiest of the three discriminations (Problem A), then the intermediate one (Problem B), and finally the most difficult one (Problem C). This sequence involved a progression on the relevant target dimension—circle size. In each individual problem, however, the brightness fading series illustrated in Fig. 10.1 was used. It is apparent from the data presented in Fig. 10.3 that these five subjects collectively made very few errors in learning, and only one of the subjects, Ara, showed any errors in the criterion phase of the difficult problem. Typically, before the criterion phase of each problem was presented, probes indicated either control by size or, more often, dual control by size and brightness.

Because of the striking difference in size between S^+ and S^- in Problem A, brightness fading was successful. Having gotten size to control responding in one problem, it was easy to establish it in successively more difficult problems. Apparently, then, a progression on the target dimension maintains attention to the relevant stimulus and ensures success. Relying on fading an irrelevant cue dimension is a questionable practice that, when it must be used, should be paired with a particularly salient targeted stimulus that can then further progress toward an increasingly subtle criterion discrimination.

Stepping Stones to Reading. As I indicated earlier, approaches to establishing a useful progression in the teaching of reading differ in ways relevant to the Doran study. The unique feature in a reading curriculum called *Stepping Stones to Reading* (Kjeldergaard, Frankenstein, & Glaser, 1973) is its use of color to code the various graphemes. A given color is associated with a single phoneme, even though the phoneme is represented by various graphemes. For example, purple is used for the /i/ sound in *high kite* and *fly.* Moreover, when a given letter form is associated with different phonemes, the color coding functions to distinguish them. For example, in *kite, kit,* and *fir,* the letter *i* is printed in purple, red, and dark green, respectively. A total of 11 colors were used, but vocabulary was chosen so that no page had more than 5 colors. Here, then, is a reading program that has as its major feature the use of quite prominent fading stimuli that are irrelevant to the targeted stimuli of letter-form discriminations, spelling patterns, and context. Findings from the Doran study would predict some difficulty with this approach.

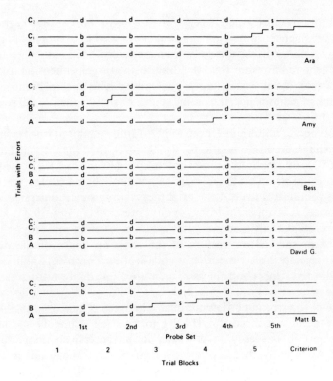

FIG. 10.3. Performance of five subjects given four size discrimination problems in the sequence of ABCC. Each problem had five 10-trial program blocks, a 10-trial criterion, and five probe sets. For the program blocks and the criterion, each trial moves the data line one step to the right, and each errorful trial moves the line one step upward. Only the first response in each S^- trial is plotted. Performance on probe sets is coded as n (control by neither dimension), b (control by brightness), s (control by size), or d (dual control). (From "Control by Stimulus Features During Fading" by M. J. Doran. *Dissertation Abstracts International*, 1975, *36*, 3642B. University Microfilms No. 76-344. Reprinted by permission of author.)

An experimental evaluation of *Stepping Stones to Reading* was carried out by Popp (1972), and I find some of her results compatible with the suggestion that this fading technique might be ineffective. Her study not only evaluated the standard version of the program but also had another group use a "reduced color version" that dropped the color coding more quickly. The version that dropped the color coding more quickly gave superior posttest results. This superiority of the faster fading also held for a "low readiness" group that the investigator had thought might need the most color prompting. They did not, possibly because the color prompting was not helpful. It is unfortunate that no version was tried that had no color coding. We cannot conclude from this study that color coding was no help at all, but the basic data from Doran's study raises this suspicion, and there is no evidence to dispel it.

Modified Alphabets.   Another way to attain consistent correspondence between graphemes and phonemes in early reading is to modify the alphabet so that the printed forms are in a (more or less) one-to-one relationship with English phonemes. Diacritical markings are among the most common and least extreme of these modifications, but the one that has received the most attention has been Pitman's (1973) *Initial Teaching Alphabet* (ITA), consisting of 44 characters, each having a single phonemic value. In the beginning stage of reading instruction, all materials are printed in the ITA characters illustrated in Fig. 10.4. After the children master reading this alphabet, they switch to the standard alphabet.

To translate Pitman's program into the language of the Doran experiment, the ITA is a set of initially controlling stimuli (fading stimuli), and the standard alphabet forms are target stimuli. Unlike the color-coding approach, the ITA bears some relevance to the targeted standard alphabet. First, the characters of the standard alphabet are included in the ITA, although there they represent only one phoneme. Many of the new forms

FIG. 10.4.   Sir James Pitman's Initial Teaching Alphabet. (From *Initial Teaching Alphabet* by J. Pitman. Copyright 1973 by Pitman Publishing Corp. Reprinted by permission.)

created for the ITA also bear a reasonable resemblance to the standard forms that must eventually control the child's responding, although other ITA forms are quite different. Since the child does start reading in ITA by discriminating forms, some of which are close approximations to the standard alphabet, the ITA approach should be less subject to problems of fading on an irrelavant dimension than would be a color-coding method. However, ITA does not seem to be an ideal fading series even so.

Here, as with experiments on the color-coding approach, one might wish for help from evaluation data, but unfortunately, here too the data are not sufficient to settle the point. Downing (1964a, 1964b) has shown that the ITA is more easily learned than the standard alphabet and has reported better word recognition a half year after transfer to the standard alphabet for ITA children than for children trained initially on the standard alphabet. However, Chall (1967) identified some problems with these data such as failing to report the makeup of the classes or to mention controlling for time spent in reading instruction. Most significantly, she pointed out that the ITA group started phonics work a good deal earlier than did the controls. Chall (1967) concluded:

> So far, the experimental evidence is still too limited to allow definite conclusions about the long-term advantages (and disadvantages) of using a modified alphabet. That ITA has its share of failures we know from a paper [of] Sir James Pitman...We also can infer some lack of success from Downing's report [1964b] revealing that after two years, 15 percent of ITA-trained children had not yet been transferred to [standard alphabet]...[p. 124].

This hint of difficulty in switching to a standard alphabet is suggestive of a deficiency in the fading series.

Bloomfield's Linguistic Approach. One early reading approach is exemplary in using a progression on a relevant dimension and thus in having the child perform from the beginning in terms of the stimuli that are to control final skilled performance. Bloomfield and Barnhart's (1961) *Let's Read* is an alphabetic approach to teaching reading. Bloomfield and Barnhart (1961) analyzed reading as "producing the phonemes of one's language when one sees written marks which conventionally represent these phonemes [p. 26]." However, early phoneme–grapheme correspondence is not taught by segmenting and subsequently synthesizing phonemes in what has been called the *systematic phonics approach.* Instead, only whole words are used from the very beginning. The progression in task complexity is from short words with completely regular spellings in which each letter has only one phonemic value (i.e., *get, got, gun,* but not *gem*) to more complex reading tasks, with the complexities grouped according to their spelling characteristics. Only in the fourth part of the five-part program are many irregularities introduced. By this time, the child is a veteran at handling the code.

A potential problem in Bloomfield's linguistic approach is that it is apparently difficult to get children to induce the sound values of letters. Nearly everyone who has modeled a reading program on Bloomfield has introduced some form of single-letter sound analysis. Given this additional prompting, the Bloomfield system seems to be an outstanding example of progression that maintains the desired behavior throughout.

The direct experimental data available on Bloomfield's approach is in the form of a comparison of a lingusitic program (*Let's Read*) a modified linguistic program (*Structural Reading Series*), and a basal reading program (*Ginn Basic Reading Series*) by Sheldon, Nichols, and Lashinger (1967). Although all three programs taught well and the differences in test results were minimal, the linguistic approach did yield better performance on the Gilmore Oral Reading Test, and the linguistic and modified linguistic groups were better than the basal in the Stanford Achievement Test subtests on word meaning and spelling. Unfortunately, experiments that would directly show the effect of progression along relevant target behaviors in the context of reading programs have yet to be done.

SUMMARY

A simple basic concept from the experimental analysis of behavior—the concept of contingency—has been shown to have important implications for classroom teaching practices, curriculum development, and the highly instrumented products of educational technology. For each, the failure to provide a contingent relationship between the given reading skill and student success in performing the exercise can lead to apparent repeated success without the student's performing the skill at all.

Frequently, errorless progressions first establish heavily cued or prompted behaviors different in kind from the desired terminal behavior. The cues or prompts are then gradually faded. Alternatively, a progression in complexity along the targeted behavior can be designed. Approaches to initial reading differ principally in the nature of the progression used. The color coding of different sounds is an extreme example of fading on an irrelvant dimension, the Bloomfield linguistic approach is a clear example of using almost exclusively the target behavior and the modified alphabet approach is intermediate between these. Basic research on errorless learning indicates that progression in the target behavior is usually the most effective approach. Hence, the basic research on errorless learning provides a framework for an informed judgment on the relative merits of the several approaches to beginning reading and for guidance for future development of beginning reading material.

Skinner (1954) long ago called attention to the implications of an experimental anlysis of behavior for educational practice. Given this descriptive approach to determining the variables controlling behavior, basic work leads naturally to application, and experience in practice leads equally naturally to basic and analytic research. Indeed, I have shown elsewhere (Holland, 1976) that basic work in errorless discrimination learning received its first impetus from common practice in the early days of programmed instruction.

The ease of application of the experimental analysis of behavior contrasts markedly with the generally meager practical yield of much cognitive research. This contrast is a direct result of the difference in objectives and methods of the two types of research. For the cognitive theorist, errors or latencies of responses are the data explained by theories involving physiological or mental events. The theoretical entity, "accessing of memory," is the object of study; the observed behavior, latencies in reading words, is an indirect index of the nonbehavioral entity. A systematic understanding of reading, or even of latencies in reading words, is not the direct object of the research. Application, if it is ever to occur, must await the eventual completion and verification of the theory.

In contrast, the analysis of behavior determines controlling relationships on the behavioral level. The "pure" laboratory study may use artificial stimuli, and the complexity of the world of practice may be reduced for analysis, but the laboratory and practical setting are not different in kind. Errorless learning is the same phenomenon, whether seen in reading natural materials or in artificially restricted laboratory materials. In the experimental analysis of behavior, the applied versus pure research distinction disappears. A thoroughgoing experimental analysis of reading instruction could improve our understanding of reading and solve many of the problems of reading instruction.

ACKNOWLEDGMENTS

This work was supported in part by funds from the National Institute of Education, United States Department of Health, Education, and Welfare. The positions expressed in this chapter do not necessarily reflect the position or policy of the sponsoring agency and no official endorsement should be inferred.

REFERENCES

Bloomfield, L., & Barnhart, C. L. *Let's read: A linguistic approach.* Detroit: Wayne State University Press, 1961.
Chall, J. *Learning to read: The great debate.* New York: McGraw-Hill, 1967.

Doran, M. J. Control by stimulus features during fading (Doctoral dissertation, University of Pittsburgh, 1975). *Dissertation Abstracts International,* 1975, *36,* 3642B. (University Microfilms No. 76-344)

Downing, J. A. The i.t.a. (initial teaching alphabet) reading experiment. *Reading Teacher.* 1964, *18,* 105–109. (a)

Downing, J. A. *The i.t.a. reading experiment: Three lectures on the research in infant schools with Sir James Pitman's initial teaching alphabet.* London: Evans Brothers, 1964. (b)

Holland, J. G. Reflections on the beginnings of behavior analysis in instruction. In L. E. Fraley & E. A. Vargas (Eds.), *Proceedings of the third national conference on behavior research and technology in higher education,* Atlanta, Ga.: Georgia State University, 1976.

Holt, J. *How children fail.* New York: Delta Publishing, 1964.

Kjeldergaard, P. M., Frankenstein, R., & Glaser, R. *Stepping stones to reading* Experimental ed.). New York: Appleton-Century-Crofts, 1973.

Moore, O. K., & Anderson, A. R. *Early reading and writing.* Pittsburgh: Basic Education, 1960. (Film)

Nevin, J. A. Stimulus control. In J. A. Nevin & G. S. Reynolds (Eds.), *The study of behavior: Learning, motivation and instinct.* Glenview, Ill.: Scott, Foresman, 1973.

Pfungst, O. *Clever Hans.* New York: Henry Holt, 1911.

Pitman, J. *Initial teaching alphabet.* New York: Pitman, 1973.

Popp, H. M. *Test project for the LRDC beginning reading program "Stepping Stones to Reading."* Pittsburgh: University of Pittsburgh, Learning Research and Development Center, 1972. (Publication No. 1972/8; ERIC Document Reproduction Service No. ED 070 040)

Richardson, E., & McSweeney, J. An analysis of the E. R. E. "Talking Typewriter" as a device for teaching beginning skills. *Educational Technology.* 1970, *10,* 81–88.

Rosenbaum, M. S., & Breiling, J. The development and functional control of reading–comprehension behavior. *Journal of Applied Behavior Analysis,* 1976, *9,* 323–335.

Sheldon, W. D., Nichols, N. J., & Lashinger, D. R. *Comparison of three methods of teaching reading in the second grade* (U.S. Office of Education Cooperative Research Project Rep. No. 3231). Syracuse, N.Y.: University of Syracuse Press, 1967.

Sidman, M., & Stoddard, L. T. The effectiveness of fading in programming a simultaneous form discrimination for retarded children. *Journal of the Experimental Analysis of Behavior,* 1967, *10,* 3–15.

Skinner, B. F. The science of learning and the art of teaching. *Harvard Educational Review,* 1954, *24,* 86–97.

Terrace, H. S. Discrimination learning with and without "errors." *Journal of the Experimental Analysis of Behavior,* 1963, *6,* 1–27.

Touchette, P. E. The effects of graduated stimulus change on the acquisition of a simple discrimination in severely retarded boys. *Journal of the Experimental Analysis of Behavior,* 1968, *11,* 38–48.

11 An Analysis of Two Beginning Reading Programs: Some Facts and Some Opinions

Isabel L. Beck
Karen K. Block
Learning Research and Development Center
University of Pittsburgh

Beginning reading programs, designed and developed by commercial publishers, have an important influence on both the chances that children will learn to read and the speed and ease of their learning to read. Although the implementation of these programs undoubtedly varies with individual teachers, there is evidence (Diederich, 1973) that the content sequence and instructional strategies specified in the teacher's manuals accompanying these programs heavily influence teachers' classroom behavior. Our personal experiences support this evidence and indicate that the type of basic program is an ingredient that strongly shapes the nature of classroom reading practices. Our analysis of two beginning reading programs is one way of documenting the form of that shaping. We are keenly aware, however, that data about programs are not data about actual teaching procedures in beginning reading classrooms.

In this chapter, we describe and analyze two beginning reading programs. We selected one program, Ginn's *Reading 720* (Clymer, Christenson, & Brown, 1976), on the basis of its potential widespread appeal. Its predecessor, Ginn's *Reading 360*, published in 1969, was used with over 15 million children, and the 720 program can be expected to become as popular as it becomes available for full scale implementation.[1] The 720 program is not

---

[1] Ginn stated in an undated document, *Reading 720 Materials and Learner Verification Statement,* that "reading 360 has been used since 1969 in about 2000 school districts. Over 15,000,000 pupils are estimated to have encountered Reading 360 as part or all of their reading program."

explicitly designed for pupils with learning difficulties or for meeting the needs of the "compensatory child." However, because of Ginn's predicted popularity, it will almost certainly be used with large numbers of children who have difficulty learning to read. Thus it is important to get some sense of the instruction it provides for these children.

A second reason for selecting the Ginn program was our interest in its phonics instruction. Since the pioneering work of Jeanne Chall (1967), the need for earlier, more systematic instruction in phonics has become widely accepted. Popp (1975) has noted that phonics instruction appears to be starting earlier in some of the newer basal reading programs, suggesting that publishers are trying to meet this need. There is also some evidence (Bliesmer & Yarborough, 1965) that pupils' reading achievement varies with type of phonics programs. We decided that an in-depth look at contemporary methods of phonics instruction was timely for documenting the directions taken and the changes made in this important area of reading instruction.

To provide a point of contrast with the Ginn 720 program, we have chosen to compare it with a code–emphasis program specifically designed for children who have difficulty learning to read. We selected *The Palo Alto Reading Program* (Glim, 1973) whose target population, as described in its promotional materials, includes children with "limited oral language development, children with below average learning abilities, those with perceptual difficulties." We suspected that, because each program does certain things well, any recommendations we might make about instruction for children who have difficulty learning to read would be on the basis of a synthesis of the positive aspects of both programs.

Another reason for comparing two quite different programs came from our interpretation of the task of program analysis. We interpreted this task broadly, with an eye to the eventual creation of methods for comparing programs. These comparisons would be made in terms of instructional variables that address important aspects of a program's design and reflect the quality of its suggested teaching strategies. To work out such procedures of analysis for beginning reading programs we began with clearly contrasting cases to capture the range of structural and instructional differences. We view our work here as a tentative start toward the development of such methods.

Reading programs, of course, can be analyzed and compared along a large number of structural and instructional dimensions. Our selection of program characteristics was influenced by several considerations. Since we believe that the primary objective of beginning reading instruction is the acquisition of decoding skills, we focused the major part of our analysis on variables that we believe, on the basis of research, theory, or practical experience, may make differences in the ease of acquiring and the eventual fluency of word attack and word recognition abilities. These variables fall into three general categories: what is taught (i.e., the subject matter—facts, rules, concepts, and so on), when it is taught (i.e., time and order variables—before, after, during, early, late, etc.), and how it is taught. Analyzing the how of teaching consisted of studying the instructional strategies (the directions, prompts, etc.) that are recommended for teachers to use when imparting new content. We also describe provisions made for maintenance, review, and application of previously learned content, and we note the provisions made for maintaining interest and motivation to read. However, we make no claim that our analysis is exhaustive in the sense of evaluating all the program variables that may have an important influence on learning to read.

After comparing the programs on each of the above variables, we state our preferences for a particular approach. Our preferences are based on concerns about aspects of learning to read that could lead to the development of habits of responding that can interfere with or enhance the acquisition of subsequent capabilities. Possible sources of difficulty associated with a given program characteristic are noted throughout the chapter when we make evaluative statements and voice preferences.

DEFINITION OF READING: PROGRAM SCOPE AND MATERIALS

Program developers' definitions of reading have important instructional consequences. Although a definition is only one consideration in the decisions made in designing a beginning reading program, it does affect some aspects of content, structure, and teaching procedures.

It is noteworthy that the two programs under consideration have different definitions of reading. The Ginn 720 definition recognizes that reading is multifaceted. According to it, reading is decoding, comprehending the author's message, critical evaluation, and using ideas (see Clymer et al., 1976, *Hello, Morning!*, Teacher's Ed., pp. T-9–10). In relation to the current array of definitions of reading, this is a very comprehensive, broadly inclusive definition. This definition is reflected in the seven strands, or categories, of content of the reading program that span kindergarten through sixth grade. These seven strands are further subdivided into three "Core" strands and four "Application/Enrichment" strands. The Ginn program calls its core strands Decoding, Comprehension, and Vocabulary.[2] The four Application/Enrichment strands are called Study Skills, Creativity, Language, and Literature. In this chapter, we have limited our study to the Core strands, since we have assumed the most basic implementation of each program and have confined our analysis to the first two grades.

---

[2]To avoid confusion between program labels for content components and the constructs of reading theory, we capitalize program component names.

The materials resources available for the Ginn program reflect its broad orientation, for they are numerous and varied. The materials, however, are divided into those considered essential ("Program Components") and those considered useful, but not necessary, for carrying out the program ("Other Materials Available"). In conducting our analysis of the core strands of Ginn, we examined all the materials considered essential and also several components from the Other Materials Available category that seemed relevant to core strategies. (Appendix A (page 309) contains a complete listing of the available Ginn materials. The materials that were included in this analysis are noted.)

Palo Alto provides a distinct contrast to Ginn's broad-based program. Although no definition is explicitly stated, it is claimed that the program adheres to a two-part definition of reading (see Glim, 1973, *Teachers' Guide, Books 1-2*, p. viii). Reading is decoding, that is, the translation of graphic symbols into a language the reader already knows—oral language. And reading is the "getting of meaning" when the reader deals with words in sentences and with the structures that bear meaning in discourse. In relation to the current array of definitions of reading, Palo Alto's is more restricted, with a "linguistic" orientation. Given this orientation, the major job of the program is the teaching of letter–sound relationships, relationships that enable the translation of print into (implicit) speech. This means that the program contains little in the way of activities to extend or further develop knowledge, except, perhaps, as it might be needed for a specific task. Instead, the focus is on deriving speech from print and on practicing this skill using information that is already known. The scope of the content taught in Palo Alto is roughly equivalent to the core version of Ginn, but Ginn intends to do much more in the long run through its Application/Enrichment strands.

The Palo Alto program spans kindergarten through third grade. Its narrower definition of reading is reflected in fewer available materials resources compared to the variety offered by the Ginn program. Most of Palo Alto's materials resources are required for everyday use, and, thus we have included nearly all the Palo Alto materials in our analysis. (Appendix A (page 309) contains a complete listing of the Palo Alto materials; resources not included in this analysis are noted.)

RELATIONSHIPS BETWEEN PROGRAM CONTENT UNITS AND SCHOOL GRADES

The largest unit of content in the Ginn program is called a *Level*, and there are 13 Levels available to provide instruction through the sixth grade. The largest unit of content in the Palo Alto program is called a *Book*, and there are 21 Books available to provide instruction through the third grade.

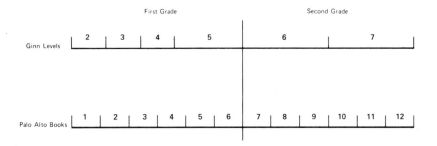

FIG. 11.1. The relationship among Ginn Levels, Palo Alto Books, and the first two school grades.

To make a variety of comparisons between the two programs, it was first necessary to determine the relationships among Ginn Levels, Palo Alto Books, and school grades. Establishing these relationships permitted us to compare programs at the same developmental level and to answer questions such as "In the middle of first grade, what Book of Palo Alto would students be using? What Level of Ginn would students be in?" (Appendix B (page 310) contains a description of the method for determining the relationships. The procedures described in Appendix B were adequate for our purposes. For other purposes, more precision in establishing the relationship between content units of different programs might be needed.)

Figure 11.1 illustrates the apportioning of the major content units of both programs according to their projected use in the first two school grades. The top portion of Fig. 11.1 shows that Ginn Levels 2, 3, 4, and 5 will probably be covered in first grade, and Levels 6 and 7 will be covered in second grade. The allocation of equal units of time to cover different numbers of Levels reflects the fact that the Ginn Levels are of different lengths. On the other hand, as shown in the bottom portion of Fig. 11.1, equal numbers of Palo Alto Books are used in first and second grades, reflecting the fact that individual Books are nearly equal in length.

FLOW OF INSTRUCTION

Within the Books and Levels of the programs is the more basic unit of content, the lesson. The flow of instructional events in a typical lesson of the Ginn 720 program is shown in Fig. 11.2. Figure 11.3 depicts the flow of instruction in a typical Palo Alto lesson. These diagrams were developed by studying the teacher's manuals of both programs to determine the instructional relationship and temporal order of story reading and skills

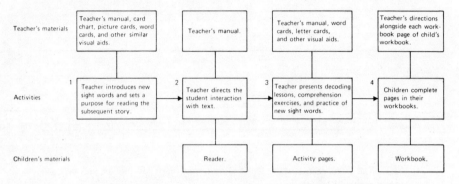

FIG. 11.2.   General flow of a typical lesson in the Ginn program.

development, the two commonly occurring instructional events in beginning reading.[3]

The numbered boxes in both diagrams represent the temporal order of different phases of instruction in the lesson. Referring to Box 1 of Fig. 11.2, a typical lesson in the Ginn program begins with the introduction of the new sight words that are to be encountered in the forthcoming story.[4] Following sight word instruction, the teacher sets a purpose for reading, often by telling children to read to find out why some event in the story took place. Next, children turn to their readers and the teacher guides the reading and discussion of the story, as shown in Box 2. Box 3 represents the third phase of the lesson, the Skills Development Activities. Skills Development consists of work in three skills areas: Vocabulary Development, Decoding, and Comprehension. Vocabulary Development consists of additional practice of sight words encountered in the story, some development of word meaning, and some review of "old" sight words. Instruction in Decoding consists of a teacher-led presentation of a phonemic or structural generalization, and Comprehension instruction consists of a teacher-led presentation of a concept considered important to comprehension. After the teacher introduces new content or leads review of the sight words, the children complete Activity pages that provide practice of the newly introduced or reviewed

---

[3]Ginn divides a lesson into four clearly stated steps: Preparation for reading, Reading and Discussing the selection, Interrelated Activities (Language Extension and Creativity), and Developing Reading Skills. By contrast, the Palo Alto program is not organized into clearly stated steps. Its objectives are often not stated and are frequently contained within descriptions of the lesson procedures themselves. Thus we had to read through many lessons to induce Palo Alto's basic procedures and then form categories of major lesson events before meaningful comparisons could be made with Ginn.

[4]Ginn refers to words that are taught as whole units as "basic words"; Palo Alto refers to them as "configuration words." We have chosen to refer to words that are taught as whole units as sight words. Our term encompasses both Ginn's basic words and Palo Alto's configuration words.

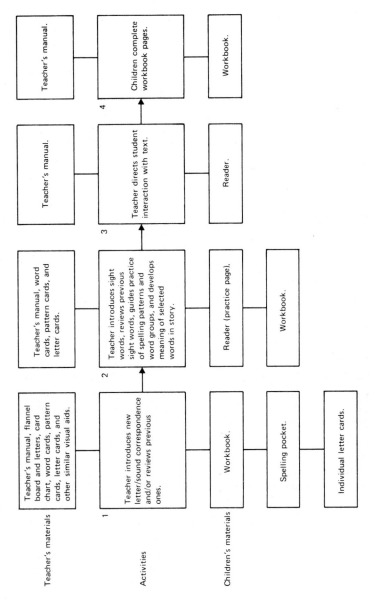

FIG. 11.3. General flow of a typical lesson in the Palo Alto program.

Teacher's materials

Teacher's manual, flannel board and letters, card chart, word cards, pattern cards, letter cards, and other similar visual aids.

Teacher's manual, word cards, pattern cards, and letter cards.

Teacher's manual.

Teacher's manual.

Activities

1
Teacher introduces new letter/sound correspondence and/or reviews previous ones.

2
Teacher introduces sight words, reviews previous sight words, guides practice of spelling patterns and word groups, and develops meaning of selected words in story.

3
Teacher directs student interaction with text.

4
Children complete workbook pages.

Children's materials

Workbook.

Spelling pocket.

Individual letter cards.

Reader (practice page).

Workbook.

Reader.

Workbook.

content. Children are then directed to additional practice pages in their workbooks (Box 4).[5] From this outline of the Ginn lesson, it can be seen that the major portion of reading skills development occurs after story reading.

A typical Palo Alto lesson, shown in Fig. 11.3, contains similarly functioning events. However, the instructional relationship between story reading and skills development is quite different from that in the Ginn program: The larger portion of skills development (Boxes 1 and 2) takes place prior to, rather than after, story reading (Box 3). The first event in a typical Palo Alto lesson is a teacher-led introduction to a new letter–sound correspondence, with review of previous correspondences. An important tool for correspondence learning, which is unique to the Palo Alto program, is the child's Spelling Pocket, a pocket into which each child's own store of individual letter cards can be placed to build words or to engage in word analysis activities. The second event in instruction (Box 2) consists of the introduction of new sight words, again mixed with a review of content previously taught. In the third event of the lesson, Box 3, the children read the story and the teacher guides the reading and discussion of the story. Then children complete pages in their workbooks that provide for practice of decoding skills or for the demonstration of story comprehension.

From these descriptions of each program, it should be clear that story reading and skills development have very different instructional relationships in the two programs. The instructional structures of the two programs are different because the program developers hold different views about the primary instructional function of the story. Palo Alto views the story primarily as an occasion for the child to apply learned correspondences to words in connected text. Ginn, on the other hand, views the story as the tool for enhancing word recognition through encountering new and old words in connected text. (In subsequent discussions, we make several points about the ways in which the different purposes of the story have influenced the quality of the stories themselves and their functioning in relation to correspondence learning.)

Two additional points related to instructional flow must also be made. The first is that we have assumed that teachers will probably follow the temporal order of lesson activities as laid out in the teacher's manuals and represented in the figures.[6] The second concerns the time requirements and distribution of

---

[5]In the two reading programs the consumable printed pages that students mark are described in a number of different ways. Palo Alto refers to these books as "Workpads" and to the pages contained in the books as "workpad pages." Ginn calls the books "Studybooks" and the pages contained in them "studybook pages." We have elected to call the books that students write in "workbooks" and the pages within these books "worksheets" or "workpages."

[6]Ginn's modular structure permits the teacher greater freedom in sequencing and combining lesson activities. For example, Skills Development need not follow story reading; it can be taught at another time. Palo Alto, on the other hand, is definitely not modular in design. All lesson activities are intermixed and purposefully designed to be quite interdependent.

the various activities within the reading "day." There is great variation from classroom to classroom and school to school in the amount of time devoted to reading instruction, so no standard time period can be assumed. We have, however, estimated that in the early Levels, sight words and story reading in Ginn could be accomplished in one 30-minute session, accompanied at times by some exercises from the Skills Development Modules (Box 3). However, there are enough materials included in the Skills Development exercises to enable them to be taught at another time. "Independent" work (Box 4) in both programs takes a negligible amount of time compared to the other activities. The first two activities in Palo Alto require more time than the first two activities in Ginn. They would probably require two to three sessions (60 minutes total). The third activity, story reading, would take one 20-minute session. These estimates are rough; we have not studied actual classroom implementation. It is, however, important to note that the boxes in Fig. 11.2 and 11.3 do not stand for equivalent amounts of lesson time.

In the forthcoming sections of this chapter, we analyze the way each program handles the major types of content taught and the major skill objectives typically contained in beginning reading instruction. Succeeding sections are concerned with letter–sound correspondences, relationships between story reading and correspondence learning, sight word instruction, and the development of comprehension. In our treatment of each topic we are concerned with program content variables, the selection and sequencing of content to be learned, and the quality of instruction as represented by the instructional strategy descriptions of the teacher's manuals. Throughout it will be necessary to refer back to the lesson flow descriptions, as they make apparent certain important differences between programs.

LETTER–SOUND CORRESPONDENCES

One of the important differences between Ginn and Palo Alto is in the basic units of lesson content. In the Ginn program, the primary content of a lesson is a set of words; in Palo Alto, the lesson is organized around a letter–sound relationship. However, Ginn also provides instruction in letter–sound relationships as part of its Skills Development component. Thus the programs may be compared in terms of their letter–sound correspondence instruction.

Letter–sound relationships are "taught" by all reading programs, including the older whole-word approaches, to the extent that millions of children who learned to read through the older whole-word programs sooner or later induced many of the letter–sound generalizations. Of course, the older programs did not make induction easy because the words they used did not maximize the regularities present in the coding system. Relative to such older programs, both programs under consideration here provide early and more systematic instruction in letter–sound generalizations. Thus both programs have established ordered sequences for introducing letter–sound correspondences.

The considerations involved in sequencing the letter–sound correspondences that are to be taught are both linguistic and pedagogic in nature. There are linguistic considerations because of the alphabetic nature of the English writing system. There are pedagogical considerations because correspondences differ in the ease with which they are learned. They differ in terms of their productivity and utility (when combined with others) for forming words that are both meaningful and vivid to children, and, depending on rates of introduction and relative placements, they differ in their effects on the child's developing concept of how the writing system works.

Developers of beginning reading programs are faced with the need to make decisions about rates of introduction, distribution, and sequencing of the correspondences that need to be taught. Although these decisions are not reported explicitly, they are, of course, implicit in the developer's product. To discern each program's position with regard to selected factors that appear to be important in the design of correspondence instruction, we performed several analyses. The purpose of these analyses was to try to define some ways of looking at the pedagogical factors of correspondence instruction, using the two quite different programs as raw data.

The first analysis involved identifying the actual correspondences taught by translating each program's labeling conventions and presenting correspondences in a common form. Then a sequence chart was constructed for each program. Table 11.1 contains the correspondence sequence chart for the Ginn program, and Table 11.2 contains the correspondence sequence chart for the Palo Alto program. The entries in the tables are the graphemic units taught followed by examples of words containing the phonemic elements with which they are related.[7] For example, entry 43 of Table 11.1 can be read as the correspondence of the letter pattern *qu* and its sound in queen and quilt. The target letter or letters are underlined in the word examples to show position treated in instruction; for example, entry 88 of Table 11.1 shows that *sk* is taught in both initial and final positions.

Pacing of Introduction

Through second grade, each program explicitly teaches nearly the same number of correspondences; there are 93 in Ginn and 91 in Palo Alto. There is, however, a difference between the programs in the number of correspondences taught per grade. Ginn covers 52 correspondences in first

---

[7]We did not include the sequence of morphemes in Tables 11.1 and 11.2. However, we make some comments in the text regarding the differences in morpheme distribution and sequencing in the two programs.

TABLE 11.1
Sequence of Letter/s–Sound Correspondences Through Second Grade for Ginn Program. Correspondence Number 53 Marks the Beginning of Second Grade

1.	b	ball	24.	k	fork	47.	th	thank path	70.	ow	snow
2.	l	look	25.	g	wig	48.	th	that	71.	ai	rain
3.	r	rose	26.	m	ham	49.	sh	ship	72.	cr	crown
4.	h	hide	27.	n	pen	50.	gr	grass	73.	ld	old
5.	j	jump	28.	i-e	ride	51.	fr	frown	74.	er	her
6.	c	cap	29.	s	us	52.	ff	stiff	75.	ear	learn
7.	f	fox	30.	ss	glass	53.	c	city face	76.	sl	sled
8.	y	yarn	31.	e	get	54.	oo	wood	77.	mb	lamb
9.	n	nose	32.	z	zoo	55.	pl	plane	78.	or	corn
10.	d	doll	33.	l	tail	56.	sm	smile	79.	or	work
11.	g	go	34.	ll	pill	57.	ch	chair peach	80.	ow	cow
12.	t	ten	35.	ee	knee	58.	u	bug	81.	fl	flag
13.	v	vase	36.	ea	seal	59.	o	top	82.	oa	boat
14.	m	mud	37.	e	be	60.	a	call	83.	ur	fur
15.	s	soap	38.	s	his	61.	aw	jaw	84.	ir	girl
16.	w	wagon	39.	a	apple	62.	nd	pond	85.	ou	out
17.	p	pig	40.	tr	tree	63.	nt	mint	86.	kn	knife
18.	i	hill	41.	ay	hay	64.	oo	moon	87.	br	brick
19.	b	tub	42.	a-e	cake	65.	o-e	rope	88.	sk	skate mask
20.	p	cup	43.	qu	queen quilt	66.	ar	car	89.	cl	cloud
21.	t	cat	44.	x	box	67.	o	go	90.	gl	glove
22.	d	bed	45.	st	stop fast	68.	bl	block	91.	dr	drum
23.	ck	duck	46.	wh	wheel	69.	tch	witch	92.	g	engine page
									93.	y	penny

289

TABLE 11.2

Sequence of Letter/s-Sound Correspondences Through Second Grade for Palo Alto Program. Correspondence Number 70 Marks the Beginning of Second Grade

#	Letter	Example	#	Letter	Example	#	Letter	Example	#	Letter	Example
1.	a	at man	24.	e	get	47.	spl	split	70.	e	be
2.	m	mom	25.	x	box	48.	str	strap	71.	ee	see seen
3.	r	ran	26.	qu	queen	49.	nd	hand	72.	a-e	made
4.	t	tan not	27.	bl	bled	50.	st	rust	73.	e-e	eve Pete
5.	s	sat	28.	cl	clam	51.	nt	plant	74.	i-e	like
6.	n	an not	29.	fl	flat	52.	mp	camp	75.	o-e	note
7.	l	lot	30.	gl	glad	53.	sk	desk	76.	u-e	mule
8.	f	fat	31.	pl	plan	54.	sp	crisp	77.	are	bare
9.	b	bat	32.	sl	slam	55.	ld	held	78.	ore	more
10.	o	not on	33.	br	brim	56.	lp	help	79.	sh	ship dish
11.	h	had	34.	cr	crib	57.	lk	milk	80.	o	go
12.	g	dog	35.	dr	drag	58.	lt	belt	81.	o	do
13.	v	van	36.	fr	frog	59.	ft	raft	82.	th	this father
14.	d	dad	37.	gr	grin	60.	pt	kept	83.	th	thin path
15.	i	it sit	38.	tr	trot	61.	ct	fact	84.	oo	moon
16.	z	zig	39.	sc	scab	62.	xt	next	85.	oo	book
17.	k	kit	40.	sm	smog	63.	ll	hill	86.	wh	when
18.	w	win	41.	sn	snap	64.	ss	pass	87.	ch	chair much
19.	p	pop	42.	sp	spin	65.	dd	add	88.	tch	catch
20.	u	up pup	43.	st	stem	66.	ff	muff	89.	ng	sing
21.	c	cat	44.	sw	swim	67.	gg	egg	90.	nk	bank
22.	y	yip	45.	tw	twig	68.	zz	buzz	91.	ck	back
23.	j	jig	46.	scr	scrap	69.	all	ball			

grade and 41 in second; Palo Alto covers 69 in first grade and 22 in second. Ginn's correspondence sequence is clearly more evenly divided between grades, whereas Palo Alto's presents 47 more correspondences in first grade than in the second. In these two programs, the number of correspondences introduced in each grade is partly a function of each program's schedule for introducing bound morphemes (i.e., units of meaning smaller than a word, such as -ly, -ed). Ginn distributes this morphemic content fairly evenly across the two grades, but Palo Alto prefers to introduce most of its bound morphemes in the second grade. The allocation of grapheme–phoneme correspondences to grades is thus affected. If we had to choose between the two, we would prefer Ginn's distribution of correspondence and morphemic content because bound morphemes are very important clues to meaning and they should be available to the child early in the acquisition of reading. A second reason for including bound morphemes early is that given their frequent appearance in speech, early inclusion increases the similarity of print (i.e., what the child reads) to naturally occurring spoken language.

Number Per Content Unit: Which Are Easy, Which Are Hard? Some classes of correspondences are harder to learn than others and require slower-paced introduction and more practice and review. As one reflection of the programs' conceptions of easy versus hard correspondences, we looked at the number introduced for each major content unit, the Book and the Level, and found that the number of correspondences introduced is not uniformly distributed in either program. A good example can be found in Table 11.2, the Palo Alto sequence chart. Correspondences 27 through 48 are initial consonant clusters, and they are taught within a single Palo Alto Book. In contrast, correspondences 70 through 73 are also taught in a single Palo Alto Book. These four correspondences are long vowel correspondences. This contrast in number introduced per content unit shows that the developers of the program were sensitive to the relative ease of learning certain correspondences, that is, Palo Alto reflects a pedagogical view that initial consonant clusters are more readily learned than are long vowels. Carrying this analysis further would enable one to make a judgment of the relative amount of agreement between programs regarding their conceptions of classes of easy as opposed to hard to teach correspondences.

The Nature of Correspondence Sequencing. Referring to Table 11.2, it can easily be seen that Palo Alto separates instruction of short and long vowels. For example, the short *i* appears at position 15, whereas the long *i* is introduced at position 74, a separation of 58 correspondences, or about a year of instructional time. In contrast, the sequence chart for Ginn (Table 11.1) shows that the short *i* is introduced at position 18 and the long *i* is introduced at position 28. Both programs separate the introduction of the long and short *i*, but the Palo Alto program separates them by about a year and the Ginn program by a few weeks.

Throughout the first grade, Palo Alto maintains a one-to-one correspondence between graphemes and phonemes; the long sounds of vowels are not introduced until the second grade. Ginn, on the other hand, introduces both long and short sounds of *i, e,* and *a* in the first grade. In relative terms, Palo Alto maintains a rather strong set for regularity with respect to vowel phonemes, whereas in Ginn the tendency is away from regularity toward diversity.[8] However, neither program introduces long and short vowels simultaneously, as might be suggested by the results of Levin and Watson (1963).

When considering the questions of a program's status with regard to a set for regularity or a set for diversity, it is important to note that this concept represents a difference in degree rather than in kind. However, in the case of the Palo Alto Program, we probably have found one of the endpoints of the range. As can be seen in Table 11.2, Palo Alto adheres rather strictly to a one-to-one mapping of vowel sounds to letters.

The introduction of variant spellings of a single phoneme (e.g., *out* and *cow*) is another facet of correspondence sequencing. Ginn introduces this concept in the first grade with examples such as *knee* and *seal* and *hay* and *cake*. Palo Alto, on the other hand, postpones introducing the concept until the second grade and attends to it then only with a very weak example (*be* and *see*). Palo Alto's one-to-one orientation is again apparent, this time in relation to variant spellings of a phoneme.

Another important aspect of correspondence sequencing is the introduction of digraphs, that is, pairs of letters that represent a single phoneme. Ginn introduces examples of both consonant and vowel digraphs in first grade (the *ea* in *seat* and the *sh* in *ship*). Palo Alto, on the other hand, does not introduce digraphs until the second grade.

It is important to note that if readers neglect to look ahead to detect the presence of a digraph (or diphthong) or a silent final *e,* they cannot correctly decode a word. Introducing digraphs and long and short vowels early and in close proximity are two ways to help establish the concept that a target letter must be considered in its environment with other letters before its sound can be determined. Ginn's early introduction (i.e., first grade) of examples of digraphs and long and short vowels may help to develop appropriate looking-

---

[8] A set for regularity implies that a one-to-one correspondence between a grapheme and a phoneme (e.g., the short *a* phoneme for the *a* grapheme) is established and kept that way for a long time, often many months, before another phoneme that can be represented by the original grapheme is introduced (e.g., the "long" sound of the grapheme *a*). A set for diversity suggests that multiple phonemes for the same grapheme (e.g., the short sound of *a* and the long sound of *a*) are introduced in close proximity.

ahead behaviors. We suspect that, on the other hand, Palo Alto's program may result in the child's developing a single letter, single sound misunderstanding.

Correspondence Selection and Productivity and Utility

The selection of correspondences that are productive, that is, those that are contained in many English words, is a vital aspect of program design. The learned correspondence should, in conjunction with previously introduced correspondences, be useful for the generation of words that are meaningful to children (the utility of a correspondence). Did the designers of these particular sequences consider productivity and utility? Ginn seems to have considered both. An example is the correspondences taught in Level 3 (numbers 18 through 30 of Table 11.1). At the end of the Level 3 reader, there is a listing of 64 words that the developers describe as words that "may be decoded independently by utilizing the skills [correspondences] learned in . . . [the Level 3 reader]" (Clymer et al., 1976, *A Duck Is a Duck,* p. 80). Many of these words are nouns and verbs whose meanings are familiar to most children (e.g., *bike, pin, kite, sit, rip, hit*).

It appears that Palo Alto's sequencing is not based on the same concern for productivity and utility. For example, when the *z* is introduced, the only words that can be generated at that point are *zig, zag,* and *zip.* When the *w* is introduced, the only words that can be generated are *wag, wig,* and *win.* In the cases of the *z* and *w* and a number of other correspondences, the developer's primary concern seems to be elaborating the concept of a class of single consonants, in that the 21 consonants are the focal content of a number of consecutive lessons. From the comparisons made here, we can clearly see the influence that correspondences have on the number and meaningfulness of words that can be generated for later reading.

In summary, we have considered a few important factors in sequencing correspondences in reading program design. We have attempted to characterize both programs in terms of some of these factors. We have considered only a few selected factors, and we are aware that there are other interesting linguistic and pedagogic issues in the area of correspondence sequencing.

Quality of Correspondence Instruction

We turn now from the content and sequencing of correspondences to considerations of how they are actually taught. The teacher's manuals of both programs contain definite suggestions to the teacher regarding strategies for presenting letter–sound correspondences.

To take a detailed look at the instructional strategy suggestions contained in both programs, we searched for identical content that would be taught at approximately the same time in the school year. We found that the short *i* is introduced near the end of Palo Alto's Book 2 and near the beginning of Ginn's Level 3 at approximately the same time in the school year (the latter can be seen in Fig. 11.1). In terms of placement in the correspondence sequence, the short *i* is the 18th correspondence in Ginn (see Table 11.1) and the 15th correspondence in Palo Alto (see Table 11.2); approximately the same number of correspondences are taught prior to the short *i* in both programs. In addition, the two programs provide about the same amount of instruction in the short *i*, as a count of the number of sentences in the teacher's manual of each program revealed (156 in Ginn, 142 in Palo Alto). The results of these analyses enabled us to compare the instructional strategies of the two programs, controlling for lesson content (it is the same, short *i*), prior content (it is at nearly the same point in the correspondence sequence), and for relative importance given by the program (amount of instruction in the content is nearly the same).

The basic data for the strategy analysis are abridged, abstracted versions of the instructional strategy descriptions for all lessons concerned with instruction in the short *i* in both programs. The abstracted versions of the strategy descriptions for the Ginn program and for the Palo Alto program are contained in Appendixes C (page 312) and D (page 315), respectively. It is important to note these appendixes because references are made to them in this text. The abstracted strategy descriptions are referred to by a system of notation in which the appendix, objective, main lesson event, and secondary lesson event are noted in turn. For example, *C.A.3.a* refers to Appendix C (the Ginn program), Objective A, Main Event 3, and Secondary Event a (i.e., the line beginning with *Manual notes: "Help children understand..."* in Appendix C).

The method for abstracting descriptions involved close reading of each description, identifying and including important instructional elements, and eliminating other less important discursive content. The instructional elements retained in these abstracted versions of the strategy descriptions are descriptions related to task directions (e.g., C.A.1.a), stimulus (C.A.1), student's response (C.A.1), prompts (C.A.4.a), and consequences and corrections (C.A.2.a). Also included were notations regarding the number and type of repetitions of a lesson event (C.A.2.a).

These abstracted strategy descriptions contain far more data than we are able to analyze here. However, there are a few major points about each program that we wish to make using the data contained in these descriptions.

The first obvious difference between the two programs can be thought of as a difference between analytic and synthetic phonics. Ginn clearly prefers analytic strategies (i.e., exploring a word for its parts), and Palo Alto prefers synthetic strategies (i.e., building a word from its parts).[9] The strong tendency that each program exhibits toward one phonics strategy accounts in part for the way the target phoneme is to be labeled by the teacher in each program. In Ginn any time the teacher refers to the sound of the short *i*, she or he refers to it as "the vowel sound heard in *fish*" or uses some other word that contains a short *i* phoneme. In Palo Alto the teacher produces the *i* phoneme and explicitly tells the children that a certain word "begins with the sound /i/" or that the "middle sound in a particular word is /i/."

The Ginn position regarding the production of phonemes in isolation clearly reflects the admonitions of Bloomfield (1942), Fries (1963), Gibson and Levin (1975), and many others, all of whom question the value, indeed even the possibility, of producing phonemes in isolation. It should be noted that in the Palo Alto program the teacher produces the sound in isolation, but at no point is the child requested to do so.[10]

A second difference between the two programs is reflected in Ginn's tendency to help the children "discover" a particular concept and Palo Alto's explicit statement of that concept. For instance, in Ginn the teacher asks the children "if they see anything about the words that is the same" (C.C.2.a).[11] On the other hand, in Palo Alto the teacher almost invariably tells the child what the particular concept under consideration is (D.A.1.a, D.E.1.a).

A third difference is that much more time is spent in "pure" auditory discrimination (attempting to help the child focus on a target phoneme in spoken words) in the Ginn program than in the Palo Alto program. For instance, 4 of the 10 Ginn lessons (i.e., Lessons A, B, F, and H) are mostly concerned with the child's "listening for the *i* phoneme in words." In the Palo Alto program, listening for the *i* phoneme appears to have a purpose different from that in Ginn. In Palo Alto it is likely that the activity is present because the developers wanted to start with what the child already knows, that is, words and the sounds in words. However, in Ginn work on auditory discrimination is required because the design of phonics instruction is such that good auditory analysis abilities are required prerequisite skills. The

---

[9]Ginn shows one instance of synthetic strategies (C.G.1), whereas Palo Alto shows a number of instances of analytic strategies, (e.g., D.E.6.b, D.E.6.d, D.E.7.b, D.E.7.d, D.E.9.b). Subsequent Ginn exercises show more instances of the kind of word building exemplified in C.G.1.

[10]Bloomfield, Fries, and Gibson and Levin argue against the child's producing isolated phonemes. We have not detected in their writings any direct statement against the teacher's producing phonemes, although given their theoretical positions, we assume that they would not recommend it.

[11]Two points regarding the notion of discovery in Ginn lessons should be explicated. The first is that the "discovery" tendency in Ginn comes through more strongly in the actual lessons than in Appendix C. The second is that Ginn does not confine their approach to a discovery method; indeed, Ginn does include a lot of "pointing out" and "telling" by the teacher.

phonics used in Ginn requires a step in which the child must extract the target phoneme from a spoken word. The emphasis on "pure" auditory tasks in Ginn and other similar programs probably represents an attempt to help the child develop auditory skills, for there is much evidence that many 5- and 6-year-old children have difficulty analyzing spoken words into phonemes and other speech segments (Bruce, 1964; Calfee, Chapman, & Venezky, 1972; Rosner, 1973).

A distinction is required here between "pure" auditory activities and activities that require auditory skills but are linked with the *i* grapheme. For example, activities for locating the position of the *i* phoneme in words are different in the two programs. Compare Ginn's C.A.7, where the teacher says 9 words (3 begin with *i*, 6 contain medial *i*'s) and children are asked to determine the position of the vowel, to Palo Alto's D.E.2, where the teacher says 13 words (5 begin with *i*, 8 contain medial *i*'s) and children demonstrate that they know where the *i* sound is—at the beginning or in the middle of the word—by placing their *i* letter cards at the beginning or middle of their Spelling Pockets. Both of the tasks require auditory analysis abilities, but one involves relating the phoneme to the grapheme, and the other does not. Ginn has many more "pure" auditory activities such as C.A.4, where the teacher says nine pairs of words (*sit/sat, hop/hit*) and the child is asked to repeat the word from each pair that "contains the same vowel sound that is heard in *fish.*" In our view, the kind of phonics instruction in Ginn requires very well-developed auditory abilities. In the Ginn program, in order for children to relate the phoneme with the grapheme, they must extract the target phoneme from a spoken word (*fish*) and hold it in memory long enough to link it to the appropriate grapheme—a very difficult task. On the other hand, in Palo Alto the teacher makes the phoneme available and spends more time linking it to the grapheme.

These differences in the "how" of phonics instruction make important differences for learning to read. First, the phonics instruction in the Ginn program has difficult task requirements; children who can do what Ginn requires will probably learn to read easily. Second, the auditory components of Ginn's phonics instruction are probably not adequate for developing the auditory abilities of children with poor entering skills. Palo Alto's phonics instruction, however, lessens the auditory demands of learning to read, and, furthermore, is more likely to foster the development of auditory abilities for several reasons. First, the target phoneme is made available explicitly. Second, it is more frequently associated with its grapheme. Third, through the use of the Spelling Pocket, both the phoneme–grapheme relationship itself and its temporal position in a word are made concrete; there is a physical referent for an auditory stimulus. This referent provides memory support and structure as the child's auditory image fades, a practice that supports the development of auditory perceptual skills. The letters used in conjunction with the Spelling Pocket also provide the opportunity to teach auditory skills explicitly because the visual prompts are helpful for establishing temporal positions of the sounds in words. Thus because of the considerations mentioned here, we suggest that Palo Alto's type of phonics instruction would better meet the needs of learners with whom we are concerned—those who have difficulty learning to read.

Another focus in our analysis of strategy descriptions is on graphemic base lessons in Ginn (C, D, E, G, I, and J in Appendix C) and the instructional value of the labels *CVC* and *unglided vowel sound.*

The Ginn lessons suggest that the teacher place the initials *CVC* above a list of words containing the consonant–vowel–consonant pattern. The value of this practice seems questionable. Although knowledge of the sound relationships of letter strings larger than graphemes is very important, it is not clear that introducing labels for these units helps either to develop or to organize that knowledge. We can think of no real reason for teaching the name of the pattern; sound–letter patterns can be taught without the use of a label. One defensible reason, in the Ginn program, is that the label is used frequently in subsequent lessons, and when consonant–vowel–consonant–silent-*e* words are introduced later, the label *CVCe* is used. Perhaps frequent use of the labels will help children to learn letter class memberhsip (vowels and consonants), but it seems that this is best taught directly within the specific tasks that may require this knowledge (i.e., for syllabication).

We also question whether the label *unglided vowel sound* will help children to learn the correspondence for *i.* Its use is written into the lessons, so that when the long vowel is introduced, it is called a "glided vowel" and compared to an "unglided vowel." Again, the labels seem to be unnecessary, and their use is difficult to defend pedagogically. (These same considerations apply to the old-fashioned labels *long* and *short* vowel.) In contrast to Ginn, the Palo Alto program does not use such labels. Instead, children are taught through examples provided by the teacher. As Carroll (1964) noted, "With regard to the actual use of phonics cues, the goal is not to have the learner acquire formally stated rules concerning letter–sound correspondences, but to teach habits of responding to letters and letter-combinations . . . [p. 343]."

A final consideration in evaluating the quality of correspondence instruction concerns the varied activities in the Ginn exercises and the repetitive nature of the activities in the Palo Alto program. In Ginn the variety of activities may overshadow the content. That is, so much is going on that it may be difficult for some children, especially compensatory children, to extract the relevant content. On the other hand, Palo Alto lessons are so predictable that they may be dull. A better mix would be some variations on the major themes in Palo Alto and a little less variation in Ginn.

Opportunities for Application and
Maintenance of Learned Correspondences

In the previous section we compared and contrasted the way correspondences are taught in the two programs. Our focus now is on their maintenance and use. It is one thing to be taught the letter–sound relationship for the short *i*; it is another to apply it to derive a pronunciation of a word. It is yet another thing to be so familiar with the correspondences that one does not have to stop and overtly apply it. Opportunities to use correspondences recently taught will heighten the chances that later application will become "automatic." Opportunities can be provided in the stories that the child reads. The degree to which these opportunities are provided is a variable that Chall (1967) has called "opportunities to transfer newly learned correspondences to sentences and story reading [p. 347]."

In an earlier section, we noted that the Palo Alto stories were specifically designed to function as occasions for the application of newly learned correspondences. Because of several factors, the Ginn stories function somewhat differently. As noted previously in Fig. 11.2, correspondence instruction in a Ginn lesson occurs after story reading, so there is no opportunity to apply newly acquired information to stories in the same Level. It is, however, reasonable to expect these opportunities to appear in stories at the next Level. For this to happen, of course, the correspondences taught at the prior Level must be used in the generation of words for the stories at the next Level. Our concern was to determine the degree to which Ginn provides, as does Palo Alto, opportunities to apply learned correspondences to connected text.

There are at least two ways that textual design could provide opportunities to apply letter–sound correspondences. The first is that some new words introduced in a Level could be selected so as to be decodable on the basis of correspondences taught in the previous Level. For example, Level 4 of Ginn introduces 46 new sight words, and 7 of those are labeled by the program as "decodable."[12] However, only 4 of those 7 decodable words are decodable on the basis of correspondences taught in Level 3.

The second way that design could provide opportunities to apply letter–sound correspondences is, for example, that the 64 words that are considered decodable at the end of Level 3 and that have not yet appeared in stories (see previous section "Correspondence Selection and Productivity and Utility") could be used in the Level 4 stories. An examination of these Level 4 stories revealed a number of places where some of the 64 decodable words

---

[12]We define decoding as the translation of print into meaningful speech. One is decoding when one recognizes words rapidly or when one sounds those words out. Ginn uses the term *decodable* to mean that all the correspondences in a word are known. We have adopted the term *decodable*, as Ginn uses it, because it was awkward not to.

could have been used without changing the theme or story line, but they were not. Ironically, Ginn suggests that the 64 words may be used by the teacher to develop additional decoding lessons. Why should the teacher develop additional word analysis exercises with a set of words that contains correspondences that have already been taught? Would it not be far better to include a number of those words—words learned through analysis exercises—in connected text? In our opinion the Ginn program missed a golden opportunity by its failure to include a good portion of the 64 decodable words available at the end of Level 3 in the Level 4 stories.

The importance of frequent opportunities to apply learned correspondences should not be underestimated. A newly learned correspondence is a tool for "unlocking" the pronunciation of a word in order to get to the meaning of the word and, thereby, the meaning of larger units (sentences and paragraphs). Newly learned correspondences should be encountered frequently in words, and those words should appear in connected text. This condition provides the means for moving the words themselves into the child's recognition vocabulary (i.e., the store of words the child recognizes rapidly), as well as enhancing facility with new correspondences.

Because we did not see much connection between correspondences learned and words used in the later Ginn stories, we sought to determine whether the correspondences learned in one Level were maintained through subsequent correspondence instruction. To determine this, we reviewed the treatment given Level 3 correspondences during Level 4 correspondence instruction. In reviewing the Level 4 content, we found that the major new Level 4 correspondences are the short *e* and the *ee* and *ea* digraphs. As we looked through the Level 4 teacher-led correspondences exercises and the child's workbook activities, we found that little attention was paid to the major correspondences (the short and long *i*) taught in the preceding Level. One can reasonably conclude that maintenance of correspondences is at best minimal and that the correspondence "tools" might well get "rusty" and be of little use when needed.

This analysis was not done for the Palo Alto program, for it is clear that there are a great number of opportunities to apply correspondences to connected text. The program was built with that specific purpose in mind. As evidence of this, and to provide direct contrast to Ginn, another analysis was conducted. The results of this analysis are contained in Table 11.3, which shows the percentage of decodable words that children encounter in the stories contained in each Ginn Level and each Palo Alto Book. The percentage decodable was obtained by dividing the total number of words a program considers "decodable" for each Book or Level by the total number of new words introduced in that content unit. The percentage decodable was easily calculated for the Ginn program from word lists in the readers. Palo Alto, on the other hand, does not provide this information in direct form, and the data had to be collected.

TABLE 11.3
Percentage of Decodable Words in Stories

Ginn Levels	Percentage	Palo Alto Books	Percentage
2	0	1	78
3	15	2	62
4	15	3	73
5	43	4	54
6	33	5	57
7	57	6	78
		7	63
		8	53
		9	48
		10	87
		11	64
		12	78

The beginning of each Palo Alto Book contains a list of sight words introduced in the Book, along with a list of words that are decodable on the basis of prior learning. These latter words are mixed with the new decodable words. The new decodable words were isolated from the total set by determining whether they contained a letter that was taught in the Book. Words that did contain such a letter were identified and counted, and a percentage decodable was calculated. The estimates of percentage decodable found in Table 11.3 for the Palo Alto program must be qualified by the fact that, in the later Books, words listed as sight words in early Books are retaught in the program as pattern words. Thus they are decodable in the story. This means that our estimates are really underestimates of the actual percentage decodable in the Palo Alto program. Despite this qualification, the percentage decodable is far lower in the Ginn program than in the Palo Alto program.

The data in Table 11.3 confirm the separateness of correspondences and text in the Ginn program and the interrelatedness of correspondences and text in the Palo Alto program. We think that the Ginn program could have raised its percentage decodable on the basis of considerations noted previously. It could have more fully implemented its early and more systematic phonics by increasing the opportunities to apply learned correspondences.

SIGHT WORD INSTRUCTION

In the Ginn program, as in similar basal programs, the sight words introduced are selected from high-frequency words and from words that are expected to be in the child's experiential and knowledge store. The order of the introduction of words is not constrained by the correspondences the child has learned. For instance, if the author of a Level 4 story wants to write a story about helicopters and airports, those two words become sight words for the lesson in which the story is used.

On the other hand, in the Palo Alto program, where the primary purpose for reading connected text is to apply learned correspondences, the selection of the majority of words used in the stories is constrained by the correspondences taught. In code-emphasis programs, a word is introduced as a sight word when all the correspondences in that word have not been taught. However, even in the strictest code-emphasis program, there are some English words, such as the word *one*, that must be taught as sight words. As it is, the Palo Alto program introduces a very large number of sight words for a code-emphasis program. Since both programs introduce words as sight words, it is interesting to compare them on selected factors concerned with sight word instruction.

The sight word teaching techniques in both programs are quite similar. The teacher displays the printed words, either by using word cards or by writing them on the chalkboard, and then uses each word in a phrase or sentence. After pairing the printed word with the spoken word, the teacher asks students to read the words as she or he points to them and asks children to use the words in original sentences.

From the teacher's manuals, we counted the number of pairings of the printed word and the spoken word implied in the instructional strategy descriptions. This was done to determine each program's assumptions about the number of pairings required for establishing recognition. A comparison of 10 randomly sampled lessons at each of two Levels of Ginn, Levels 3 and 5, with 10 randomly sampled lessons in two Books of Palo Alto, Books 2 and 6, revealed that at least two pairings is the lower bound for each new sight word. In Ginn the average is 4.2 pairings for each word (out of a 71-word sample), and in Palo Alto the average is 5.6 pairings (out of a 41-word sample). One of the pairings in Palo Alto comes from the reading of the sight words contained on the Practice Page, a page in the child's reader that precedes a set of stories.

It is interesting to note the techniques used to focus attention on the word to be taught. Although the sight word teaching techniques of the two programs are quite similar, the instructional strategy descriptions in the teacher's manuals are strikingly different. The Palo Alto program provides quite a detailed description of certain aspects of the instructional task. Directions to the teacher about the conduct of the lesson are stated in terms of what the teacher or the children are to say and do. Ginn's descriptions, on the other hand, are more discursive. To take an example from Palo Alto sight word teaching, the program directs the teacher as follows:

> Say: I shall say some sentences. What is the the word that comes after I in these sentences? I do want to go home early. I do like ice cream. Put the Word Card *do*

in the Pocket Chart, and tell pupils that it stands for the word *do*. As pupils make up similar sentences and say them point to *do* each time. (Glim, 1973, *Teacher's Guide*, Book 2, p. 103)

It is hard to know, of course, whether teachers follow these descriptions. The descriptions are of interest for their fine-grained programming of selected aspects of an instructional task.

Ginn and Palo Alto handle maintenance of sight words very differently. Ginn claims a schedule of at least three repetitions of each sight word in subsequent stories. Of more interest is the fact that except for important function words, Palo Alto does not claim to maintain sight words, nor does it expect mastery of sight words after they have been introduced. Instead, sight words are reanalyzed for the correspondences they contain at a point in the program where all these correspondences have been taught.

Palo Alto introduces a very large number of sight words for a code-emphasis program. Through the second grade, 534 sight words are introduced, compared to 613 introduced in Ginn. To a large extent, except for important verbs and other function words, Palo Alto introduces sight words before a story, uses them in the story, and does not maintain them as sight words. Had the program chosen to include fewer sight words and to select them more carefully from function words, irregular words, and useful story words, the words could have been easily maintained in subsequent lessons. With a total of 613 sight words, more suitably chosen for utility and meaningfulness, Ginn was able to produce far more interesting stories having more natural syntax than was Palo Alto with its comparably large number of sight words and its hundreds of additional words generated as subsequent correspondences were introduced. Our claim that Ginn's words are more useful for generating stories is based more on a general sense of the words selected and less on the several analyses of the story words that we conducted. One analysis did reflect differences in the story words, and it is reported in the next section.

THE DEVELOPMENT OF COMPREHENSION

Comprehension is developed in both programs through activities associated with story reading and through direct instruction in specific comprehension abilities (inferring main ideas from details, understanding cause and effect, distinguishing fact from fantasy, etc.). Comprehension of stories is shaped by events that occur prior to, during, and after reading.

Referring to the lesson flow diagrams, Figs. 11.2 and 11.3, it can be seen that some events prior to reading (Box 1 in Ginn, Boxes 1 and 2 in Palo Alto) are common to the two programs but that there are some differences. New sight words are taught in both, and they both provide some preteaching or discussion of concepts on which comprehension of the story depends.[13] Palo Alto, however, provides more extensive, specific preparation for reading through its review of words, word groups, and patterns that are to be encountered in the story. Palo Alto's assumption is that in order for decoding skills to be applied to connected text, content previously taught must be reviewed immediately prior to the story, presumably to enhance its availability. Students in the two programs thus begin the story with differently "primed" skills. Of pedagogical interest is the influence these different "readiness" states have on the development of comprehension of connected text.

Events shaping story comprehension during and after reading (Box 2 in Ginn; Boxes 3 and 4 in Palo Alto) are also somewhat different in the two programs. A major difference is in the forms of the teacher directions and questions about the story information that are recommended in the instructional strategy descriptions of the teacher's manual of each program.[14] An analysis of the suggested lesson strategies for the first five stories of Book 2 of Palo Alto and Level 3 of Ginn showed that after story reading, Palo Alto directs teachers to tell children to locate information in the text that contains an assertion ("Find the sentence that tells...") or supports a conclusion ("What in the story makes you think that...?"). By contrast, Ginn to a large degree suggests that teachers use more common question forms like *Wh* questions ("What is Bill doing? Where do you think the ducks come from?"). We think that the form of questioning may be an important pedagogical difference between the programs.

"Correct" answers to comprehension questions depend on the information contained in the story. At the time the question is asked, this information must be recalled and used in the formulation of an answer. The Palo Alto program, by virtue of its type of question format, leads the child back to the text after reading. This means that children might develop a set to return to, or recall, information given in the story as a first step in answering questions about it. If such a set does indeed develop, it can both help and interfere with the development of comprehension, depending on how relevant the question is to the information in the text. Ginn's more generally framed *Wh* questions seem less likely to develop this set, but there are disadvantages to exclusive reliance on *Wh* questions that are unaccompanied by directives to refer to the

---

[13]Ginn's "Setting a Purpose for Reading" (Box 1) offers suggestions to the teacher for concept review and development prior to the story. Palo Alto provides for preteaching the meaning of selected vocabulary words (Box 2) to be encountered in the story.

[14]Ginn notes that the questions and suggestions contained in the Guided Reading Section of its teacher's manual are optional and need not be followed. We have assumed they will be used here.

text to locate information that contains an assertion or supports a conclusion. Also, the two types of postreading activities ("Find ..." vs. *Wh* questions) differ in other ways, for example, response mode, and these additional differences may influence the comprehension processes developed.

An analysis was performed to check the extent to which the Ginn program makes explicit the role that information contained in the story plays as a basis for answering questions. This analysis consisted of counting the number of "challenge" questions (e.g., "Prove your answer." "Tell me how you know.") in the first five stories of Level 3. There is a total of 27 comprehension questions and 4 challenge questions, indicating that Ginn does attend to this important factor.

Revealing the information base for the answer to a question is only one step, however, in the question-answering process. There are other steps consisting of linking stated information to other information in the child's knowledge store through various kinds of language and reasoning processes. In addition to asking challenge questions, the teacher should take more steps to bring out and describe some of the basic concepts and find ways of relating concepts on which correct answers to questions depend. This information must be made explicit before it can be learned, and not all children, particularly those in our target population, already posses it. In other words, we are suggesting that comprehension (i.e., question answering) be explicitly taught, rather than left to children to induce as they try to answer questions and get corrective feedback.

Content of Stories

We have mentioned various aspects of a program's design and intent that influence the selection of words used in the stories. These words in turn influence the semantic content and phonological characteristics of the sentences. We performed an analysis that demonstrates the effect of different available word pools on the characteristics of the connected text children read. We sampled every word from every tenth sentence at comparable developmental levels of Ginn and Palo Alto—Levels 3 and 5 in Ginn and Books 2 and 6 in Palo Alto. Then we classified these words according to syllabic composition. Table 11.4 shows the results of this analysis.

The percentage of polysyllabic words in Ginn is much greater than that in Palo Alto. Palo Alto reflects excessive use of single syllables, typical of "linguistic" programs. The phonological characteristics of what children read are clearly different in the two programs, with the result, we think, that there is a more severe departure from natural patterns of spoken language in the Palo Alto program. This is another important pedagogical factor to consider in that it may interfere with the development of comprehension.

TABLE 11.4
Monosyllabic and Polysyllabic Words from Selected Portions of Each
Program

Program	Monosyllabic	Polysyllabic	Total	Percentage Polysyllabic
Ginn				
Level 3	114	7	121	5.8
Level 5	488	90	578	15.6
Totals	602	97	699	13.9
Palo Alto				
Book 2	151	2	153	1.3
Book 6	415	23	438	5.3
Totals	566	25	591	4.2

Although we did not systematically analyze the content of the stories, that is, the topics and concepts children read about, a quick look shows that Ginn covers a wide range, from realistic child-centered stories, with characters who represent various racial backgrounds, to fantasy stories. Palo Alto stories seem to be primarily realistic and child-centered, with some nature concepts included. There are a few characters whose race is other than Caucasian, but our sense was that in general, the characters are primarily middle class and white. In all respects, Ginn's stories are more interesting, varied, and of higher quality than Palo Alto's, and Ginn's provide a better picture of our pluralistic society.

Specific Comprehension Abilities

In addition to reading stories and answering questions about them, beginning reading programs provide for the development of comprehension through instruction in what might be called "specific comprehension abilities." A list of these abilities would include such skills as arranging events in sequence, distinguishing fact from fantasy, separating main ideas from supporting details, and so forth. These specific comprehension abilities are listed in the skills charts of both programs, indicating that each program contains activities to develop them.

An attempt was made to compare the instructional procedures recommended by both programs to develop these specific comprehension abilities. In the Ginn program the instruction and associated workbook activities are clearly labeled and are easily located in the program's Skills Development strand. This is not true of the Palo Alto program. The program does not list specific pages of the teacher's manuals where instruction in specific comprehension skills can be found; the program only lists the Books in which the instruction can be found. Furthermore, the instruction is not easily located in a given Book because it is not labeled by the name of the specific comprehension ability. Instead, it is labeled by other names. For example, in the class of fact versus fantasy, a listed topic is entitled "What Is It? What Can It Do?..." (Glim, 1973, *Teacher's Guide*, Book 5, p. 108). Finally, although the comprehension pages in the student's workbook that accompany the teacher-led lesson are clearly labeled as comprehension pages, the descriptions used often refer to the types of response formats (e.g., comprehension through answering questions and writing an original sentence) rather than to the comprehension abilities the instruction is supposed to develop.

A quick overview of the comprehension activities in both programs revealed some similarities in the types of exercises children are asked to do, even though these exercises are named differently. There appears to be some degree of difference in the relatedness of the specific comprehension activity to the content of the story. In the Palo Alto program, the teacher uses the story to develop skills such as retelling events in sequence (e.g., Glim, 1973, *Teacher's Guide*, Book 2, pp. 117–118). By contrast, because of its modular design, the Ginn program develops specific comprehension skills by frequently using text specifically written for the ability to be developed. These are only general impressions, however, and require more systematic analyses for verification.

Our analysis of the development of comprehension as found in two beginning reading programs has been brief. We do, however, have some general notions about factors to consider in a more complete analysis. First, one should look at the sequence of actual comprehension tasks children are asked to perform. The properties of these tasks should then be described, taking into account important variations in the nature of the stimuli presented, the instructional directions, and the responses requested. Neither program reviewed here provides descriptions that offer insight into the development of comprehension. Ginn merely labels its comprehension instruction according to the ability that is supposed to be learned; Palo Alto describes comprehension instruction in terms of test performances or response classes (e.g., comprehension through matching sentences and pictures). Neither program provides adequate descriptions of the instructional events associated with story comprehension. For example, the postreading questions have not been analyzed or described in terms of their linguistic structure or relationship to the text. Neither program fully describes the content of the comprehension instruction. Better descriptions are required, both for understanding what is taught and for teaching in a more explicit manner. These characteristics are quite important for children who have difficulty learning to read.

The problem of developing an adequate scheme of comprehension task description is a difficult one. To characterize the comprehension of connected text requires a description of the content of the text, with attention to semantic conent and linguistic structure; a description of the instructional directions (i.e., the purposes the teacher sets for reading); and a description of the response classes (i.e., what the reader is asked to do after reading— answer certain kinds of questions, retell a story in her or his own words, etc.). Care must be taken so that comprehension task descriptions reflect as much of the important variation as exists in task and content dimensions while still retaining qualitatively similar classes of tasks. To identify sources of variation in certain task dimensions, one could look at linguistic and psychological research to find out how a certain task dimension has been operationalized. For example, one could look at Kintsch's (1974) work to describe the content of connected text, Anderson's (1972) work to analyze and describe classes of questions and their relationships to the story text, Frase's (Frase & Kreitzberg, 1975) work to identify variations in learning directions, and so forth. Developing a system of comprehension task descriptions on the basis of variables created by research would have two advantages: It would lead to a more refined system of task description than we have at present, and it would tie instruction to research evidence, leading to an understanding of, or some hypotheses about, what existing comprehension instruction develops.

Of course, the development of a more adequate system of task description is only one component of an analysis of comprehension instruction. To be able to evaluate the quality of the instruction, the instructional strategies must be analyzed, with the capabilities of the learner in mind, as we have done with phonics instruction in this chapter. The situation may be more complex with comprehension instruction, however, because it is not clear that learning outcomes have, to date, been adequately specified. Nevertheless, future work that attempts systematically to describe current practices in comprehension instruction could provide a useful baseline for making informed recommendations for change.

SUMMARY AND CONCLUSIONS

In this chapter we have analyzed two beginning reading programs along several dimensions of instructional concern—correspondences and phonics instruction, sight word learning, and the development of comprehension. To compare programs, we focused on pedagogical aspects and attempted to describe the programs in those terms. Where our knowledge of theory and data or our experiences permitted, we made some evaluative statements. We made these statements keeping in mind the child who has difficulty learning to read.

With regard to the programs studied, our early thoughts that desirable conditions for learning to read would reflect a synthesis of the positive aspects of both programs were correct. Overall, we have preferred Ginn's correspondence sequencing, its corpus of sight words, and it stories. By introducing a relatively even amount of correspondences and morphemes across the first two grades, Ginn's program increases the probability that the language in the stories will resemble naturally occurring spoken language. Ginn's early introduction of digraphs and its presentation of long and short vowels in close proximity teaches the beginning reader to consider the target letter in its environment, precluding the "one letter, one sound" misunderstanding. Correspondence sequencing that early introduces morphemes, digraphs, and so on allows for the generation of useful nouns and verbs that are likely to be both familiar and productive to the child. Ginn's sight words and polysyllabic words, chosen for their utility, produce a wide variety of stories and a more natural syntax.

Palo Alto provides better designed phonics instruction and more opportunities to apply learned correspondences to connected text. Its program lessens the auditory demands on the child by having the teacher extract the phonemes and produce them in isolation and by frequently associating the phonemes with corresponding graphemes. The child, through use of the Spelling Pocket, is given a memory support for an auditory image as that image fades. Palo Alto also avoids labeling concepts—a practice that adds unnecessarily to the learning load in Ginn's materials. The order of lesson flow in Palo Alto's program provides the child with an immediate opportunity to apply learned correspondences to a related text. The interrelatedness of correspondences and text raises the percentage of decodable words and moves the words into the child's recognition vocabulary.

In this chapter we discussed at some length the nature of phonics instruction in these two programs. Concerning phonics, two points merit mention here: Both programs teach correspondences in the "backward" direction—they go from sound to letter (a spelling requirement) rather than from letter to sound (a reading requirement), and neither program requires the child to produce the sounds in isolation. The theoretical issues associated with these practices are complex, the evidence is incomplete, and it is not within the scope of this chapter to provide a full discussion of these points. Nevertheless, it is our belief that successful practices provide a framework for evaluating and questioning certain other practices and prescriptive positions. Is is our belief that letter to sound is the correct direction to teach correspondences, because it is the same as that of the terminal behavior and it thereby avoids the burden of having to reverse the process. It is also our experience that with a good training model for blending, a limited use of sounds in isolation in teaching beginning reading is not harmful, but facilitative, especially for our target population.[15] These beliefs, we think, should be integrated into any final statements on the advisability of certain practices in phonics.

With regard to methods for analyzing reading programs, our approach emphasizes our belief that analysis should be done considering, as a framework for judging programs' strengths and weaknesses, aspects of program design that can facilitate or impede learning. In our chapter we have given a brief outline of some of what we consider to be major instructional factors that merit attention in any program analysis. Program analysis, however, should not be the only consideration in studying how children are taught to read. The program itself is only one of many factors that influence how the child is being taught and the quality of the instruction received.

In our discussions of reading program design, we were able to show through specific examples the aspects of design that could have been better handled. Because of this, we have shown on an operational, rather than on a discursive level, how better "balance" in a reading program might be achieved. As a final note, we wish to add that because we believe program design is both a science and an art, the program analyst must go beyond the things that are easily counted and measured. A reading program is more than the sum of its parts, and the analyst must attempt to capture a program's intuitive bases and its appeal to the developing child.

APPENDIX A

MATERIAL RESOURCES IN THE GINN AND PALO ALTO PROGRAMS

Ginn

Ginn lists its materials resources under two headings: *Program Components,* which are essential for the conduct of the program and *Other Available Materials,* which are useful but not essential. The resources in each category appear in Table A.

Although we would have preferred to include the Decoding Sound Filmstrip and the Resource Activity Book in our inspection, we felt that we could limit our analysis to the components indicated since they are clearly the most essential materials. The other components are viewed as being enriching and supplementary rather than as being essential and integral. Indeed, from our experience, we know that when a publishing house divides materials into

---

[15]See Resnick and Beck (1976) for a description of a training model for blending and its rationale.

TABLE A
Essential and Supplementary Components in Ginn

Essential Program Components	Supplementary Materials
Kit of manipulatives to teach Level 1[a]	Skilpaks[a]
Teacher's editions[a]	Evaluation materials[a]
Pupil's texts[a]	Picture maps
Workbooks[a]	Basic card set I[a]
	Basic card set II[a]
	Decoding sound filmstrips
	Readalong recordings
	Resource activity book
	Magic circle books
	Decoding activity charts
	Supplementary materials bibliography

[a]Materials examined.

essential and supplementary categories, schools often purchase only the essential materials.

Palo Alto

Palo Alto's publisher does not specifically state which resources are essential and which are supplementary. Most of the materials are directly related to the decoding and meaning components of the program. The materials resources in the Palo Alto program are summarized as follows: Teacher's Guides, Pupil's Books, Workbooks, Pocket Chart and Cards, Skills Practice Kits, Tests, and Wall Charts. All the materials, with the exception of the Skills Practice Kits, were examined.

APPENDIX B

PROCEDURES USED TO TRANSFORM CONTENT UNITS TO RELATIVE PROPORTION OF TIME SPENT IN THOSE UNITS FOR THE FIRST TWO GRADES

The scope of our analysis involves the time span from the first through the second grade. Thus we determined the grade coverage of Levels and Books on the basis of information provided by the publishers. Ginn suggests that the majority of first graders will start with Level 2 and complete Level 5 by the end of the first grade. Some children are expected to complete Level 6.

Considering our target population, however, we used the more conservative estimate of coverage, Level 5.

Level 1 is Ginn's readiness component. It contains content designed for use in either kindergarten or the first year of instruction, and any letter–sound correspondences introduced in Level 1 are reviewed in Level 2. Since excluding Level 1 from our analysis omitted no important first-grade content, we have agreed with the publisher that Levels 2 through 5 are representative of first-grade content. According to Ginn, Levels 6 and 7, and perhaps 8, will be completed in the second grade.

In the first grade, the four Levels of Ginn are not of uniform length. To determine the relative proportion of time spent in each Level during the first grade, we counted the number of pages contained in the basic materials resources. Table B shows these data.

As can be seen from the table, the total number of pages in the Level 5 resources is approximately twice the number contained in each of the other Levels. Hence, Level 5 covers approximately twice as much content as Levels 2, 3, and 4. Levels 6 and 7, covered in the second grade, were the same length. The translation of Ginn Levels to proportion of instructional time in grades one and two can be seen in the top portion of Fig. 11.1 in the text.

As with Ginn, the content of Palo Alto's readiness component is covered elsewhere in the program, so it was excluded from Fig. 11.1. The publisher reports that an approximate first-grade coverage in the Palo Alto program is Books 1 through 6. These Books are nearly equivalent in length, and hence, they represent equivalent proportions of first-grade instructional time (as is shown in the bottom portion of Fig. 11.1). With reference to Book coverage in second grade, the publisher expects Books 7 through 13 to be completed. Considering our target population and our sense of their likely rates of progress through the Palo Alto Books, we believed Books 7 through 12 was a more realistic estimate of content covered in the second grade. Because these Books are of equal length, they represent equivalent proportions of time in the second grade (as is shown in Fig. 11.1 in the text).

TABLE B
Number of Pages in the Teacher's Manual, Child's Reader,
and Storybook in Levels 2, 3, 4, and 5

Resources	Levels of the Ginn Program			
	2	3	4	5
Teacher's manual	194	131	131	242
Reader	—	72	72	203
Studybook	92	47	47	95
Totals	286	250	250	540

APPENDIX C

AN ABSTRACTED DESCRIPTION OF THE
10 SHORT *i* EXERCISES IN
LEVEL 3 OF GINN

This appendix contains an abstracted description of the 10 short *i* exercises contained in Ginn's Level 3. The demarcation of the exercises is indicated by a letter (A through J), with the objective of the exercise quoted next to the letter. In Exercise A, the first short *i* exercise, each instructional strategy the teacher uses has been abstracted. In subsequent exercises, only those strategies that are new have been listed, with strategies used in preceding exercises referenced to those exercises.

It is important to point out that the 10 short *i* exercises do not occur one after the other. Instead, they are taught across five lessons, so that they are interspersed with five stories and other activities. The 10 exercises are sequenced in the teacher's manual as follows:

Exercises A and B after Story 1
Exercise C after Story 2
Exercises D, E, and F after Story 3
Exercises G and H after Story 4
Exercises I and J after Story 5

Although we attempted to abstract the material in the teacher's manual as much as possible, we were concerned that the language of the lesson be apparent to the reader, as that langauge will be an important part of our discussion concerning the quality of the instruction.

Following are the descriptions of the 10 Ginn short *i* exercises:[16]

A. "The pupil will identify words containing the unglided (short) vowel sound as in *hill*. (Introductory Activity)."
   1. Teacher shows picture of a fish and a witch and has children name them.
      a. Teacher asks children to "listen for the vowel sound in the middle of *fish* and *witch*."
   2. Above procedure repeated with *crib*. (For example, children see picture, name corresponding word; teacher asks children if "they can hear the same vowel sound in the middle of *crib* that they hear in middle of *fish* and *witch*.")
      a. Teacher confirms the above activity by having the group repeat the three words together.

---

[16] Adapted from Teacher's Edition of "A Duck Is a Duck" of the *Reading 720* series by Theodore Clymer and others, © copyright 1976, 1973, 1969, by Ginn and Company (Xerox Corporation). Used with permission.

3. Above words (*fish, crib, witch*) listed on board and read. Teacher underlines *i* in *fish*.
   a. Manual notes: "Help children understand that this (underlined letter) is a symbol for the vowel sound heard in the word *fish*."
   b. Volunteers underline the *i* in *crib* and *witch*.
   c. The three words are read.
4. Teacher says nine pairs of words (e.g., sit/sat, hop/hit). Children repeat the word from each pair that "contains the same vowel sound that is heard in *fish*."
   a. Teacher is cautioned to read the words slowly and distinctly for children who have trouble identifying the vowel.
5. Teacher writes *Bill* (known sight word) on board.
   a. Manual notes: "Help children locate the vowel sound in middle of... *Bill*, by sweeping your hand from left to right below the word as you read it," and "to call attention to the middle position of the vowel letter *i*."
6. Teacher says *is* (known sight word) and asks children if they can hear that the vowel sound at the beginning of *is*, is the same as the vowel sound in the middle of *Bill*.
   a. Teacher writes *is* on board.
   b. The procedure described above in (5a) is used to establish that the vowel is in the initial position.
7. Teacher says nine words (three begin with *i*, six contain medial *i*). Children are asked to determine the position of the vowel.
8. Children write letter *i* next to pictures on a worksheet whose names have the same vowel sound they heard in *fish*.
   a. Manual notes: "Refer to the vowel sound in the word *fish* as an unglided vowel sound. The children may make this term part of their speaking vocabulary."
B. "The pupil will identify words containing the unglided (short) vowel sound as in *hill*. (Practice 1)."
   This lesson uses the same instructional strategies described in A and the following new activity:
   1. The teacher's manual suggests preparing a "word box" for further practice of the short *i* sound.
      a. A word box contains objects whose names contain the /i/ sound as in *hill* (e.g., "a baby's bib, a lid to a pan, a paper clip"). These objects are placed in a box. Pupils select an object and name it.
      b. Manual notes: "If the pupil is familiar enough with the word, ask the pupil to write it on the chalkboard and circle the letter that represents the vowel sound. Lead to conclude that the words on the chalkboard have the unglided vowel sound as in *hill*."
C. "The pupil will decode words containing the graphemic base *id*. (Introductory Activity)."
   1. Teacher writes *hid* on board.
      a. Volunteer reads the word.
      b. Manual notes: "If help is needed, point to letter *i* and say, 'It stands for the same vowel sound that is heard in *fish*.' "

2. Teacher writes *did, lid, bid,* and *kid* in vertical column under *hid.*
    a. Teacher asks children "if they can see anything about the words that is the same."
    b. Teacher draws a vertical line separating *id* from beginning consonants "when the word part *id* is noticed."
    c. Manual notes: "Help children understand that knowing the graphemic base *id* can help them read these words."
3. Teacher sketches stick figure on board and writes name *Sid* beside it. Word *Sid* is read.
    a. Teacher writes four sentences about Sid on board (e.g., *Sid hid at the zoo.*)
    b. Teacher guides children through reading the sentences.
4. Children complete sentences on worksheet by choosing the correct word from two *id* words.

D. "The pupil will decode words with the graphemic base *it.* (Introductory Activity)."
This lesson uses the same strategies described in C for *id.*

E. "The pupil will decode words containing the two graphemic bases *id* and *it.* (Practice 1)."
1. Teacher writes *bit* and *sit* on board.
    a. Volunteer reads words and underlines the graphemic base *it.*
2. Above procedure repeated for *did* and *hid.*
3. Teacher writes *fit, hit, pit, kid, bid,* and *lid* in two columns.
    a. Volunteers underline the graphemic base in each list.
4. Teacher writes six *id* words and four *it* words on board and reads story that contains these words. (Children are told that the story contains a number of words that end with *id* or *it.*)
    a. Teacher rereads story slowly so the children have a chance to discover the *id* and *it* words and read them from the board.
5. Additional activity suggested:
    a. Teacher hangs a lid in a box and has each child throw three ping pong balls at it, scoring one point for every hit.
    b. Teacher gives each child who can find an *it* or *id* word from the words listed in E.4. a chance to hit the lid.

F. The strategies described in A and B are used to identify words with short *i* in a new lesson (Practice 2). The following new activities are introduced:
1. Teacher tells children a story and asks them questions about the story, with the direction that their answers should contain the unglided *i* as in *this.*
    a. Teacher reads: "One night a boy and girl went out exploring. Was the boy's name Dick Smith or John Jones? Was the girl's name Mary Jones or Cindy Smith?"
    b. Activity continues as above with four other questions.

G. "The pupils will decode words containing the graphemic base *im.* (Introductory Activity)."
This lesson uses strategies from C and E and the following new activity:
1. Teacher places graphemic base card *im* in card holder. Children select one consonant letter card from five cards (*d, h, j, k,* or *t*) and place it in front of the *im* and read the resulting word.

H. Students again practice identifying words containing the unglided vowel sound as in *hill* (Practice 3), using the strategies from A and B.

I. "Phonemic analysis: The pupil will decode words with the CVC pattern and unglided vowel sound as in *did*. (Introductory Activity)."

    1. Teacher writes *sit* on board. Word is read.

        a. Volunteer is asked to "name the vowel letter in *sit*."

        b. Manual notes: "Write a *V* above *i* in *sit* and explain that *V* stands for *vowel*."

        c. Follow a similar procedure with consonants in *sit*, completing the pattern *CVC* above the word *sit*.

        d. Teacher writes *fit, pit,* and *lit* below *sit*. Words are read.

    2. Teacher writes *did* on board.

        a. Same procedure described above (in 1) is followed.

    3. Same procedure is followed for *him* (as described above in 1).

    4. Teacher draws vertical lines between the first consonant and between the vowel and last consonant for words in each of three lists. Children read the lists of words.

        a. Manual notes: "Establish...that each word contains the unglided vowel sound represented by letter *i*."

        b. "Refer to the CVC pattern and explain that...when the vowel letter *i* is between two consonant letters, the corresponding vowel sound is usually unglided."

J. "The pupil will identify the CVC pattern with *i* as in *did*. (Practice 1)." This lesson uses strategies from G and I.

APPENDIX D

AN ABSTRACTED DESCRIPTION OF THE SEQUENCE FOR TEACHING SHORT *i* IN BOOK 2 OF PALO ALTO [17]

This appendix contains an abstracted description of the short *i* sequence as it is taught in Book 2 of Palo Alto. The sequence is continuous; it is not broken up into lessons with intervening activities. The material that follows would be done in order, although not necessarily completed in one day of instruction.

We have made a demarcation (as noted by the letters A through E) when the objective of the sequence changes. The objective is quoted after the letter.

Following is the description of the short *i* sequence:

A. "Listening to and saying beginning /i/ sound as in *it*."

    1. Teacher tells children to "listen to the sound that begins the words *in, imp, igloo*."

        a. Teacher tells children "they [above words] all begin with the sound of /i/ as in *it*."

    2. On worksheet children draw rings around pictures whose names begin with the /i/ sound as in *it*.--

[17] Adapted from *The Palo Alto Reading Program*, Teacher's Guide Books 1-2, Second Edition by Theodore E. Glim, © 1973 by Harcourt Brace Jovanovich, Inc. Reprinted by permission of the publisher.

B. "Introducing *i* as seen in print."
   1. Teacher places letter *i* card in pocket chart, says words beginning with /i/ sound, discusses shape of *i*.
   2. Children say appropriate letter name as teacher holds up letter cards *i, l, o, v*.
   3. Teacher gives children their own *i* cards and tells them to get their *a, t, s, n*, and *o* cards. (Every child gets each letter in both upper and lower case after it has been introduced.)
      a. Teacher says a word (e.g., *in*). Children locate from the six letter cards the letter with which the word begins. Fourteen words are suggested (six *i* words; other eight words begin with sounds represented by the other five letter cards above).
   4. On worksheet children draw rings around each *i* found in rows of single letters and ring the two and three letter words that begin with *i*.
C. "Introducing the writing of *i*."
   1. Teacher writes *i* on chalkboard and discusses its shape (e.g., straight line with a little dot on top).
   2. Children practice writing *i*'s on paper.
   3. On worksheet children trace broken line *i*'s, then write *i* under each *i* found in a row.
D. "Recognizing the writing of Capital *I*."
   (Same procedures described in C above for lower case *i* are followed for upper case *I*.)
E. "Listening to and saying the /i/ sound as in *sit*."
   1. Teacher asks children to listen for the middle sound as she or he says *sit, hit, lit, bit*.
      a. Teacher tells children that "the sound in the middle is /i/ and is spelled by the letter *i*."
   2. Teacher says a word containing /i/.
      a. Children demonstrate that they know whether the /i/ sound is at the beginning or in the middle of the word by placing their *i* card at the beginning or middle of their spelling pockets (five words begin with *i*, eight words contain medial *i*'s).
   3. Teacher places letter *s* and *t* in pocket chart and puts *a* between them. Students read *sat*.
      a. Teacher replaces *a* with *i*. Children read *sit*.
      b. Same procedure as above used with seven other word pairs (e.g., *ham/him, ram/rim*).
   4. Children place *h* and *m* (with a space between the consonants) in their spelling pockets.
      a. Teacher says *ham*, children place *a* in pocket.
      b. Teacher says *him*, children place *i* in pocket.
      c. Same procedure as above followed for six other *a/i* contrast pairs. Before each pair teacher tells children which beginning and ending consonants to place in chart (e.g., *b, t, f*).
   5. Children place *am* in spelling pockets. Teacher says, "I shall dictate some rhyming words. You put the beginning sound for each word in the spelling pocket as I say it." Teacher says *ram*. Children place *r* in front of *am*.
      a. Initial consonant substitution continues for five other words.

6. On a worksheet, children:
   a. Draw a ring around pictures whose names contain the /i/ sound (three medial *i* words, two distractors).
   b. Ring the word in a pair that has *i* in medial position (five pairs).
   c. Trace broken line *i*'s.
   d. Write *i* under words that have *i* in their medial position (three medial *i* words, two distractors).
7. On a worksheet evaluation page, "children ... discriminate among sounds represented by fifteen letters in beginning, ending, and medial positions" by completing the following activities:
   a. Chidren name, then copy letters.
   b. Teacher dictates six words and asks pupils to write letter that stands for the beginning sound of each word (one *i* word).
   c. Teacher dictates six words and children write letter that stands for ending sound of each word (no *i* words).
   d. Teacher dictates six words and children write letter that stands for middle sound they hear in each word (two *i* words).
8. Letter patterns *im, it, in, ig,* and *id* are placed on flannel board. Teacher puts consonant letter cards before pattern and asks children to read words. Twenty-two words suggested. Teacher is instructed to use both upper and lower case consonant letters.
9. Using the practice page in their readers (page preceding a set of stories that lists pattern words, sight words, and phrases that will be encountered in the story), children respond to the following:
   a. Teacher asks children to read various words and word groups.
   b. Teacher asks how many different words (from a given set of words) end in *it*? In *im*?
   c. Teacher discusses meanings of words children may not know and deals with multiple meanings (e.g., multiple meanings of *bit*: "It doesn't hurt a bit." "She bit me." "Just a little bit, please.").

REFERENCES

Anderson, R. C. How to construct achievement tests to assess comprehension. *Review of Educational Research,* 1972, *42,* 145–170.

Bliesmer, E. P., & Yarborough, B. H. A comparison of ten different beginning reading programs in first grade. *Phi Delta Kappan,* 1965, *46,* 500–504.

Bloomfield, L. Linguistics and reading. *Elementary English Review,* 1942, *19,* 125–130.

Bruce, D. J. Analysis of word sounds by young children. *British Journal of Educational Psychology,* 1964, *34,* 158–169.

Calfee, R. C., Chapman, R. S., & Venezky, R. L. How a child needs to think to learn to read. In L. W. Gregg (Ed.), *Cognition in learning and memory.* New York: Wiley, 1972.

Carroll, J. B. The analysis of reading instruction: Perspectives from psychology and linguistics. *The Sixty-third Yearbook of the National Society for the Study of Education* (Pt. 1), 1964, *63,* 336–353.

Chall, J. *Learning to read: The great debate.* New York: McGraw-Hill, 1967.

Clymer, T., Christenson, B., & Brown, V. *Reading 720.* Lexington, Mass.: Ginn, 1976.

Diederich, P. B. *Educating those who teach reading* (Educational Testing Service TM Rep. 23). Princeton: ERIC Clearinghouse on Tests, Measurement and Evaluation, 1973.

Frase, L. T., & Kreitzberg, V. S. Effect of topical and indirect learning directions on prose recall. *Journal of Educational Psychology,* 1975, *67,* 320–324.

Fries, C. C. *Linguistics and reading.* New York: Holt, Rinehart and Winston, 1963.

Gibson, E. J., & Levin, H. *The psychology of reading.* Cambridge, Mass.: MIT Press, 1975.

Glim, T. E. *The Palo Alto reading program: Sequential steps in reading* (2nd ed.). New York: Harcourt Brace Jovanovich, 1973.

Kintsch, W. *The representation of meaning in memory.* Hillsdale, N.J.: Lawrence Erlbaum Associates, 1974.

Levin, H., & Watson, J. *The learning of variable grapheme-to-phoneme correspondences.* In a basic research program on reading (U.S. Office of Education, Final Rep., Project No. 639). Ithaca, N.Y.: Cornell University, 1963.

Popp, H. M. Current practices in the teaching of beginning reading. In Carroll, J. B., & Chall, J. S. (Eds.), *Toward a literate society.* New York: McGraw-Hill, 1975.

Resnick, L. B., & Beck, I. L. Designing instruction in reading: Interaction of theory and practice. In J. T. Guthrie (Ed.), *Aspects of reading acquisition.* Baltimore: Johns Hopkins University Press, 1976.

Rosner, J. Language arts and arithmetic achievement and specifically related perceptual skills. *American Educational Research Journal,* 1973, *10,* 59–68.

IV DISCUSSION

12 Concerning the Marriage of Research and Practice in Beginning Reading Instruction

Walter Kintsch
University of Colorado

The invitation by the editors of this volume to write a discussion chapter took me by surprise. I accepted gladly, and I am not sorry that I did: This was quite an educational experience, and I think I have really learned something new. My first task was to figure out why I was invited, since I am certainly not an expert on reading. My guess is that the editors wanted me to provide the experimental psychologist's viewpoint. Therefore, I will respond to this implicit task demand and direct most of my comments to one issue: the problem of the unconsummated marriage of research and practice in reading instruction. I propose to inquire into the relation between research and application as discussed in the chapters in this volume. In other words, I will ask to what extent the art is a science. However, I cannot quite resist the temptation to step out of my role as an expert on something or other and say what I perceive the state of the art to be.

Let us take a look at the role basic research should play in the practice of reading instruction in an ideal world. First, we would want a theory of reading as a subtheory of cognitive processing, with an appropriate experimental data base to back it up. Second, we would have a body of applied research, including just plain experience, in order to arrive at guidelines for educational practice. How close are we to this state of affairs?

Note that I am not asking what is good or bad, or right or wrong. I am merely trying to characterize the relations among theory, basic research, and educational practice in the field of reading. It is necessary to have a clear idea about these relations as a prerequisite for a serious evaluation of the state of the art in reading instruction. The comments that follow are directed only toward this limited objective. I am not making a value judgment; I am not saying that every statement made that is not supported by basic research findings is no good. It is clear that reading instruction relies on several different sources: basic research, applied research (e.g., program evaluation), experience, speculation, and logical task analyses. I make no claim that one of these is necessarily superior to the others; I am merely interested in sorting out the roles of basic experimental research and general cognitive theory in this total picture.

RESEARCH OR INTUITION AND EXPERIENCE

The first point I want to establish is that basic research appears to play a relatively minor role in the practice of reading instruction, which is largely based on classroom experience and intuition. I do not think this is surprising, so I will be brief, discussing some examples of evaluative statements from some of the chapters in this book and looking at the basis of the evaluations given. For a start, I picked 10 such examples haphazardly from the Beck and Block chapter. [Eds. Note: These examples were taken from an earlier version of Beck and Block's chapter. In the revised version printed here the authors have deleted Points 1 and 5 and changed Point 9.] For three of the examples, data are cited:

1. The Ginn prereading program is criticized as being too broad, and Venezky's work is cited to the effect that prereading does not entail high cognitive loads.
2. Relevant research data are given in support of Ginn's position of avoiding the production of phonemes in isolation.
3. An emphasis on pure auditory discrimination is justified on the basis of research data showing that this is difficult for children.

In the fourth example, a recommendation is made where relevant research data could have been cited:

4. It is said to be important to give frequent opportunity to apply learned correspondences—which is supported by a large body of data on repetition and spacing effects in learning, encoding variability, and so on.

In the other six examples, the argument is made without recourse to research results:

5. When should morphemes be introduced? Is it true that "materials should be as meaningful as possible within the constraints of vocabulary control?"
6. Should the introduction of long and short vowels be separated by 1 week, 1 year—or perhaps not introduced at all?

7. Beck and Block "suspect that Palo Alto's program [of adhering to one-to-one mappings between sounds, and letters for one year] may result in the child's developing a 'single letter, single sound' misunderstanding."

8. It is claimed that Ginn's phonics instruction relies too much on already existing abilities.

9. For questions after reading, Ginn's WH–questions are said to be better than Palo Alto's questions about where in the text something is.

10. Both programs go from sound to letter (spelling) in teaching correspondences, but Beck and Block say that going from letter to sound is better "because it is the same as that of the terminal behavior."

The score is three (or four) to six for intuition. I am not saying these intuitions are bad, but note that all these questions could be answered by research.

Let's look at some similar examples from Bateman's chapter, paying a little more attention to the pitfalls that arise with this reliance on intuition. Venezky's program, the *Distar* program, and Bateman's own proposal all rely very heavily on logical task analyses of reading. Three components of reading are emphasized: (1) responding to a grapheme with a phoneme, (2) the appropriate temporal sequence, and (3) the blending of the phonemes. Are these supposed to be stages of information processing, or at least components thereof? If so, are they separable? Additive? Are they the right ones? As cognitive psychologists, we know from sad experience that we cannot simply assume that our logical analysis corresponds to how the head works! These are problems that cry out for research. Logical analysis says, for instance, that letter naming should not be included as a subskill of reading. However, as Holland points out in his chapter, although letter naming is not itself a part of reading, making discriminative responses to the letters certainly is. I find it very hard to trust these logical task analyses very far. Certainly, they are a good starting point, but what I have observed over and over again is that they are too often also a stopping point.

Distar's teaching to mastery is praised by Bateman for avoiding wasted practice. Again, there is no experimental evidence for this claim, so far as I can tell, and knowledge of the overlearning literature makes me doubt that it is correct.

Rozin and Gleitman claim that "semantics is easier to access than syntax, and syntax is easier than phonology," and "syllables are easier than phonemes." Some hard evidence would be nice. After all, children learn to talk very early and respond to phonemes while still in the crib (but not, I suppose, to noun phrases). [Eds. Note: Rozin and Gleitman's claims are not discussed in the revised version of Bateman's chapter.]

Some unsupported statements from Glass: "Meaning should be made irrelevant to decoding instruction." "Because successful decoders do not consciously use rules, rules should not be taught." Why? (Notice the beautiful counterexample later in Bateman's chapter when she talks about the Pointy Rule).

I do not want to belabor the point. Without questioning the uses of intuition, experience, and so on as a guide to reading instruction, I would suggest that research results could and should be used more widely and more effectively.

I would like to add supporting data from my own laboratory to two claims made by Sticht: First, Sticht's main thesis is that the language processes in (adult) reading and auding are the same. As part of a larger experiment, Kintsch, Kozminsky, Streby, McKoon, and Keenan (1975) compared immediate recall of 70-word paragraphs for listening and reading (with the reading time equated to the listening time). There were several experimental conditions, but the relevant observation here is merely that in all of them mean performance was within 1% for reading and listening. Indeed, when we did a very detailed analysis of exactly which propositions were recalled from the texts, the overall correlation over propositions was $r = .86$ between reading and listening. Clearly, there will be situations where reading–listening differences will be obtained, but at least for our college student subjects, it did not matter at all whether they read a text or listened to it. I would even go further than that. We have done considerable work on the nature of inferences that people make when reading simple stories (the work of Keenan, McKoon, & Kintsch, in Kintsch, 1974). We have replicated this work with cartoon sequences, that is, we let pictures rather than words tell the story (Baggett, 1975). In all crucial respects the similarities between the text and picture conditions are overwhelming. When it comes to cognitive processing, the precise nature of the perceptual input is less interesting than the content of the message being processed.

The second point concerns Sticht's observation that the content of a text is the main determinant of reading rates. We have shown that the time subjects take to read a text is an approximately linear function of the number of propositions expressed by that text, even when the number of words in the text is controlled (Kintsch & Keenan, in Kintsch, 1974). The number of propositions expressed by a text is an objective measure of what others have called "idea density." Our result implies that each proposition requires a certain comprehension time (of the order of 1 to 1.5 sec) and that increasing reading speed merely means that fewer propositions will be processed.

READING RESEARCH

Turning now from the applications to the experiments, again I will not ask whether these studies are good or bad as experiments but will ask what they tell us about the practice of reading instruction.

Sticht reports an experiment on reading "talk" in first grade that is informative with respect to the auding–reading issue: Children read only slightly better when they read their own talk than when they read the talk of other children. This is a negative but relevant result. On the other hand, the two experiments in the form of training programs that Sticht reports have little direct bearing on the issue at hand. The oracy training program provided ambiguous results that are of little use. The adult literacy program showed mainly that transfer needs to be specific rather than general, but it has no relevance to the auding–reading question. [Eds. Note: The section on the oracy training program is deleted in the revised version of Sticht's chapter.] In contrast, Sticht's test instrument to measure the auding–reading gap is an excellent example of how basic research can be fruitfully applied in reading instruction.

In their chapter Perfetti and Lesgold refer to a series of experiments designed to investigate whether good readers are better able to organize what they read than are poor readers. Their results are disappointing in that they failed repeatedly to find differences in organization between skilled and nonskilled readers. However, I suggest that they were looking in the wrong place. They are looking at syntactic chunking, as it is induced by the phrase structure of sentences. Such phrase structure chunking is important in sentence perception, however, only when the task is one of verbatim repetition of the sentence. Perfetti and Lesgold should have looked at the semantic organization of the text by skilled and nonskilled readers. How is the content of a text organized? Are skilled readers better able to form a notion of the gist of a passage than are poor readers? We have investigated problems of the overall organization of text, the formation of summaries, and so on for some time now, and a report on this work can be found in Kintsch (1977).

Perfetti and Lesgold continue with a number of interesting experiments on coding speed, memory interference effects, tachistoscopic recognition, matching and categorization tasks. However, only the first of these is used in their section "Implications for the Teaching of Reading," where coding speed measures are proposed for measuring coding efficiency. The two other implications they talk about are quite independent of the experiments that had gone before: What is good practice? Who needs practice? We are back to intuition here (although note that both questions are perfectly good research problems).

I conclude, therefore, that practice in reading instruction is largely intuitive, relying on "experience" and program evaluation studies, and only to a small extent on basic research findings. Basic research findings tend to be a bit removed from questions of practice. The reason for this undesirable state of affairs is, in my opinion, the lack of theory.

THE NEED FOR A THEORY

We have good experiments on various components of reading and reading programs, but the two are insufficiently interrelated because we do not have a theory of reading worth speaking of. Without theory to guide us, the many bits and pieces we now have refuse to fall in place. A number of authors in this volume discuss theory and theoretical ideas—primarily Chall, Frederiksen, the Goodmans, and Shuy. But these discussions are at a gross level, lacking specificity and detail. They constitute preliminary ideas aimed toward the formation of a theory of reading, rather than the well-worked-out theory that we need. We may have some good beginnings here but not more than that.

I find Frederiksen's ideas highly congenial, I think he makes some important points, and I would not quarrel with the general thrust of his chapter (and I do not think this is the place to argue over minor details). However, the level of his discussion is too general to be very useful. Such terms as *top-down* and *bottom-up* are merely catch words when they are used without further specification. Exactly what is meant when Frederiksen calls inference making a top-down process? Consider the sentence pair:

It is spring in Pittsburgh. The grass is green.

Readers will probably infer that there is some kind of connection between these two sentences, for example, a causal one. In what way does this top-down process of inference formation change when we provide readers with an explicit cue in the text as to the connection between the sentences, as in:

It is spring in Pittsburgh. Therefore, the grass is green.

What happens if, instead of an explicit cue, we merely give the readers a general indication that they are supposed to look for some kind of connection, as in:

It is spring in Pittsburgh, and the grass is green, too.

Do we change from top-down in the first example to bottom-up processing in the second, and to what in the third?

Similarly, what are we to make of Frederiksen's claim that people revert to bottom-up processing when they encounter "difficulty"? There seems to be a grain of truth here, but we are overwhelmed by vagueness.

The Goodmans' discussion of language functioning is excellent and important, but it suffers from the same lack of specificity. Shuy provides some detail in this respect, but he only outlines what needs to be done. What we really need to make this approach work is something like Shuy's Table 1 on a much grander scale, with special emphasis on how these various language functions are realized in speech and print.

Next, consider an example from Sticht. He talks about the "ability to comprehend," and "complete comprehension." One cannot stop with terms like these. They are merely broad, descriptive phrases behind which we hide our lack of understanding of the information processing involved, its stages, their interrelations, resource requirements, and so on—in other words, a precise model of "comprehension."

Chall's stage theory of reading is most interesting and will undoubtedly become very influential. She herself makes the point that the present work is merely preliminary, and I can only second her in stressing the need for greater specificity. In particular, the stages must be defined at the information-processing level. I will come back to this point later, but consider here Chall's characterization of Stage 2 learning. The child reads "for confirming what is already known" and learns "to use...the redundancies of the language." Perhaps this is so, but what we need is a step-by-step processing analysis of how such learning occurs. This is very important because Chall thinks that Stage 2 is a main failing point for many literacy campaigns!

I would also like to raise a voice of caution about the use of the concept "stages of reading." The term implies that something is changing qualitatively. As an example, consider the transition from Stage 2 to Stage 3. Chall argues that there are peculiarities in information processing in children's reading during Stage 2 that prevent the children from acquiring new information through reading. Therefore, children in this stage read and re-read things they already know—fairy tales, *Little House on the Prairie,* or, in the old days, religious tracts. Between Stages 2 and 3 the reading process changes, enabling children to learn new things by reading, at first in a limited way. Further changes in the characteristics of the reading process occur later, making reading more and more useful and flexible.

This is a nice analysis, but do we really need the concept of a stage? We can only teach what is already partly known. [Eds. Note: The following point is based on an earlier version of Chall's chapter, not on the revised version printed here.] New information can be successfully handled only if there exists an apperceptive mass to which it relates. The reason children must read fairy tales and *Little House on the Prairie* for so long is that this is all they can absorb. As they learn more, their horizons broaden and they are better able to learn from reading. They cannot learn from reading in Stage 2, not because of any peculiarities of their information processing, but simply because their knowledge base is too small. As their knowledge increases, it becomes easier and easier to add to it.

Chall would argue that children in Stage 2 learn orally, but not from reading. However, this might simply be a resource allocation problem. When reading is not yet fully automated, most of the reader's resources are used up by the decoding process, leaving insufficient resources for the comprehension process. When I read French, I encounter a similar problem: Most of my resources go into translating, so that at the end of a page I often find that I do not remember anything from it, although I had laboriously read it. Similarly, college students in laboratory experiments who are given mirror-reversed texts to read often remember very little of the content of what they had read.

I am not saying that Chall is wrong in talking about stages of reading. I am merely saying that I am not yet convinced that such a radical assumption is really necessary. One certainly should explore the alternative of describing reading development in terms of continuity of information processes. The things that change might be the type of material that can be read and the use people can make of the information, not necessarily the reading process itself.

The kind of model called for here is illustrated by the work of Venezky and Massaro. Before discussing it, let me remind you of some of the ground rules for the construction of information-processing models, as discussed in the chapter by Perfetti and Lesgold, who assume that (1) reading is a complex process with interrelated but isolable components, and (2) the relationship between skilled reading and beginning reading is not a straightforward one. (But I should add, neither is there no relationship, and there are researchers like the Goodmans, who specifically claim that there is only one kind of reading.)

Venezky and Massaro's chapter, as I said, is the kind of detailed work we need, but at the same time this particular work illustrates some of the dangers of this approach. Basically, they start with a perceptual analysis that transforms the visual stimulus into a possible letter list; here the orthographic regularity effects are important (see their Fig. 3.1). Further analysis constructs the visual representation of a word from the possibilities generated earlier. From there they go to the abstract representation of the word, at which point speech and reading merge and Venezky and Massaro stop.

The trouble is that Venezky and Massaro have separated components out of the total system and neglected feedback loops from higher cognitive processes (linguistic-syntactic, semantic, and pragmatic analyses of the message) that greatly influence not the visual analysis per se but the use that the system makes of its output. In other words, it is a fine model for word recognition but not for reading. The serial stages imply that a stage must be finished before the next one becomes operative. However, it is possible that output is continuously available and that lower level analyses are rarely completed to the point where they provide a "list of possible letters for each position in a word." Indeed, the full visual analysis of a letter takes considerable time (300 msec by some accounts), and higher order processes do not wait for them to be completed. Instead, decisions are made on the basis of partial visual analyses and context. Reading is not only decoding but also using context, and I think Venezky and Massaro tend to neglect the latter. They say that "the goal of beginning reading instruction is ... rapid word recognition, probably the only major skill unique to reading." It does not follow that beginning reading is best taught as word recognition. Our goal is reading, not word recognition.

Venezky and Massaro's criticism of the Johnson (1975) experiment is justified, and I would like to repeat it. When words are compared with words, if only one or two letters are perceived as being identical or as being different, the subject can make a "same" or "different" response, respectively. However, when a target letter is compared to the word, each letter of the word must be checked against it. The point Venezky and Massaro seem to miss is that reading is like word matching—it is a hypothesis-testing process with feedback loops so that there is no need to analyze all the letters of a word if you can make out the word from just a few. Reading is not like letter detection, which requires a more complete analysis.

Venezky and Massaro's conclusion is probably correct—that phonemic quality and word meaning do not "influence the initial visual resolution of letter strings"—but so what? The problem here is that a component process of reading is treated in isolation. The real question is: To what extent is reading (in the beginning reader, in the skilled reader) determined by visual factors, orthographic regularity, phonemic quality, whole-word features, syntax, semantics, the macrostructure of the message, and so on? Venezky and Massaro will say, of course, that they were not talking about reading in general but beginning reading. Obviously, decoding here is crucial. However, it does not follow that we can neglect everything else. Even if Venezky and Massaro suggest the perfect instructional program for word recognition (i.e., beginning reading), it still might be unsatisfactory as a reading program because it assumes that all other cognitive processes involved in the target behavior may safely be neglected in beginning instruction. Perhaps so, but we should not simply assume it.

In part, this weakness simply reflects the shortcomings of their chapter, because more complete descriptions of their model do take into account the factors whose omission I have criticized here (e.g., Massaro, 1975). In spite of this weakness of the model, the Venezky and Massaro approach is, I think, exemplary in this volume because it is the only one that is specific and detailed enough to be seriously criticized. (Just one nice example of the virtue of being specific: One can argue forever about the role of phonemic encoding in reading, without any hope of agreement, but in the present model, phonemic coding is specified in such a way that it becomes an empirically decidable issue.)

Perfetti and Lesgold's theoretical notions are much more vague in comparison. The bottleneck hypothesis they discuss is very general. What they call the by-product hypothesis is so vague and so implausible (does it really presume that there are no central processing limitations in the human organism?) that it is useless. Indeed, Perfetti and Lesgold propose to bypass the kind of cognitive psychology models that I am calling for here. They say we know about correlation, but we do not know about causation. (If there is a moral discernible in the chapters, it is certainly this: that we continually get ourselves into trouble because we do not know how to interpret correlational data.) They propose to bypass the hard task of determining causal chains and to go directly to the most educationally relevant problem: What should one do in terms of practice and instruction to improve reading? My preference would be to give an answer to this question based on a sound information-processing model of reading. It is the long way, but I do not see much reason to trust shortcuts.

What I have said so far can be summarized quite easily. Applied work on reading instruction appears to flourish (although the actual practice in the classroom seems to be another matter). Basic research in reading is going equally strong, especially insofar as it concerns decoding problems. However, the interaction between the two is insufficient: Applications rely more on intuition and experience than on laboratory research, and the laboratory research frequently bypasses the issues that are most important in reading instruction. I have tried to argue that the lack of a serious theory of reading is one of the main reasons for this state of affairs. Compared to the level of specificity that is found in some of the applied work (e.g., Beck & Block, Bateman) and the precision of the experimental research (e.g., Venezky & Massaro; Perfetti & Lesgold), the poorly articulated global analyses that pass for theories in the field of reading are disappointing indeed. I do not think that we can hope for an improvement in the relation between reading research and practice, and between basic and applied research in reading, until we have a good model of the reading process. As we have seen in this volume, there are some promising theoretical ideas from which such a model might evolve, and that is the point at which progress must occur if the whole area is to develop soundly.

STATUS OF READING RESEARCH

At the beginning of this discussion I set myself the task of exploring the relation between research and practice, as it is reflected in these chapters. This task done, I would like to look at the status of reading research in a more general way.

I am puzzled by two seemingly contradictory facts. First, I read in the newspapers almost continuous complaints that somewhere between 25% and 30% of our children "can't read." Second, I learn from these chapters that we have the reading programs now to teach all children (or at any rate, 98% of them) to read. This claim is made explicitly by Bateman, but it is implicit in many of the other chapters and discussions in this series.

To resolve this conflict, I borrow Shuy's very handy outline of the factors involved in reading. My adaptation of Shuy's Fig. 7.4 is shown below, and I want to make a single, rather simple point with it. The excellent programs for early reading instruction that we have available today rely primarily on the teaching of letter–sound correspondences (decoding, in teacher talk), as shown by point *A* in my Fig. 12.1. Semantic and pragmatic factors play a minor role when children learn to read in this way. When we say that we have reading programs available today that, if they were actually used properly in our schools, would assure that practically all children could read, we mean that we know how to get a child to read in the manner designated by point *A*. Skilled reading, on the other hand, is a different matter, as shown by *B*. Although, with our best instructional procedures today, we can get children to *A*, we do not know how to get them from *A* to *B*. Most of the time they will, of course, make that transition (and be helped by our teaching), but we do not have the same degree of control over this phase of learning to read that we have in getting the beginning reader to *A*.

Indeed, the experts disagree at this point. The majority of contributors to this volume see the problem as one of phasing *A* out and *B* in. This viewpoint is best articulated in Chall's stage analysis. We know how to get to *A*; the problem is to keep up our advantage and prevent the transition problems that often occur in the second and third grades. What happens in the later grades is not really a reading problem but a general cognitive problem. Even if we could close the auding–reading gap quite early, most of those 25% to 30% "who can't read" would still not be able to perform at the eighth-grade level. The minority opinion, ably represented here by the Goodmans, believes that starting at *A* interferes with the later achievement of *B* and that a better procedure would be to teach the beginning reader to use pretty much the same cues of a semantic-functional type that support skilled reading. It might be harder to start that way, but it avoids problems later.

It would appear that the decoding party would need to show us how to solve the transition problem in Figure 1, and the advocates of reading for meaning would have to develop beginning reading instruction programs that would be as successful as the decoding-oriented programs. I certainly cannot

FIG. 12.1. A graph after Shuy, showing the dependence of early reading on letter–sound correspondences, with semantic-functional cues playing a minor role, and the ascendance of the latter as the reader becomes skilled.

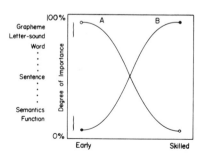

tell you which of these alternatives will eventually be the best, but if the analysis that I have given here is correct, it has sharpened the issues a little.

REFERENCES

Baggett, P. Memory for explicit and implicit information in picture stories. *Journal of Verbal Learning and Verbal Behavior,* 1975, *14,* 538–548.

Johnson, N. F. On the function of letters in word identification: Some data and a preliminary model. *Journal of Verbal Learning and Verbal Behavior,* 1975, *14,* 17–29.

Kintsch, W. *The representation of meaning in memory.* Hillsdale, N.J.: Lawrence Erlbaum Associates, 1974.

Kintsch, W. On comprehending stories. In P. Carpenter & M. Just (Eds.), *Cognitive processes in comprehension: Twelfth annual Carnegie symposium on cognition.* Hillsdale, N.J.: Lawrence Erlbaum Associates, 1977.

Kintsch, W., Kozminsky, E., Streby, W. J., McKoon, G., & Keenan, J. M. Comprehension and recall of text as a function of content variables. *Journal of Verbal Learning and Verbal Behavior,* 1975, *14,* 196–214.

Massaro, D. W. (Ed.). *Understanding language: An information-processing analysis of speech perception, reading and psycholinguistics.* New York: Academic Press, 1975.

13

Applying Theories and Theorizing about Applications

Michael I. Posner
University of Oregon

A VIEW OF APPLICATION AND THEORY

The conventional wisdom about the relation between application and theory goes something like this: Basic scientists work out a detailed theory of how a process such as reading takes place. The theory specifies the role of different variables governing the process. After basic scientists have developed their theory, practitioners can apply it—preferably with the requirement for a little creativity of their own in adapting it to young minds in large classrooms rather than college students working in individual laboratories. It is that conventional wisdom which Venezky and Massaro[1] seemed to have in mind when they lamented the difficulty of developing a really detailed account of the reading process when we are manipulating only one or two variables at a time in the laboratory. That would indeed be a staggering task when literally dozens of decisions about the contents and order of aspects of lessons need be made, as discussed in the chapter by Beck and Block.

It hardly needs to be said in the home city of Simon (1969) that the difference between natural science and artificial science is larger than the conventional wisdom supposes. It is hopeless to expect that basic scientists will produce the kind of theory of reading that will render routine the efforts of curriculum designers to produce programs that teach efficiently and motivate the children who use them. However, this does not mean that basic science is irrelevant to the job of application. Instead, the basic science serves both as a lens and as blinders that practitioners may wear when they perform

---

[1]Citations without specific reference dates are to contributors to this volume.

the complex psychological search process involved in seeking a satisfactory design.[2] Basic science theory serves to amplify those aspects of the problem on which experimental psychologists have labored. It also tends to reduce attention to other problems that may be important in design but that lack status within basic psychology.

Chall referred to these blinders when she discussed the pioneering views that Orton (1925) brought to the attention of psychologists as he sought to explain why normally intelligent children were unable to learn to read. The psychologists of the time, dominated by behaviorists, Gestalt theorists, and psychometricians, were simply unable to assimilate to their language the observations of Orton. Thus, according to Critchley (1964), the illiterate or barely literate population was looked on as having the mildest form of imbecility. Psychology could hardly view deficit in any way other than as a generalized imperfection in mind or brain that would show up in reading as in any other task. Psychology had no language in which to discuss the difficult problems of dyslexia, and thus Orton turned to neurology for a more receptive viewpoint.

I believe that the language used in this volume is much richer in its ability to aid the practitioner to think about and to search for the important variables in the design of curricula. However, we should be aware of the lenses and of the blinders that the kinds of theoretical presuppositions represented in this volume are providing to the analysis of reading.

DEVELOPMENTAL AND PROCESSING STAGES

Two major theoretical predispositions are presented in this volume. The first is developed by Chall who outlines a stage approach to the processes in reading (see the upper panel of Fig. 13.1). To my way of thinking, it is an important idea because it brings some unity to the set of problems faced by a designer in the development of a reading curriculum. For example, the fact that decoding is only the very first phase in Chall's set of stages suggests that a volume such as this one, which is focused on elementary education, must also face the smooth transitions necessary to allow what is learned in decoding to serve as the basis of later fluency. If one viewed this volume without Chall's chapter, one might suppose that the problem of reading was solved with decoding, whereas in fact only the initial stage can be solved by decoding.

The developmental stage view helps us to focus on a demand that will be of increasing importance as practitioners attempt to design new curricula. What kinds of tests will tell us whether students have mastered some level? It is fairly

---

[2]For a description of the psychology involved in this kind of problem-solving task see Simon (1969).

CHALL'S STAGES

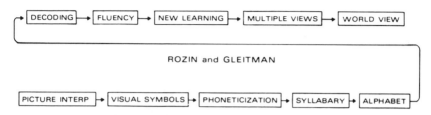

FIG. 13.1. Development stages in reading. Upper panel extracted from Chall's contribution to this volume; lower panel extracted from Rozin and Gleitman (1977).

easy to determine whether students have mastered decoding because they can read aloud. How can we tell if reading is fluent, if it is fostering new learning, if it is leading to new views of the world, or if it is fostering the student's own world view? These are issues that will require new and subtle forms of diagnosis.

The Chall view is not without its blinders. One of them is most critical in understanding the controversy between Chall's position and that of the Goodmans.[3] I believe that the stage view of Chall begins too late. In Fig. 13.1 (lower panel) I have included a set of stages from recent work by Rozin and Gleitman (1977). Rozin and Gleitman, like the Goodmans, recognize that children come into the reading situation not only with a well-developed auditory language (which has been stressed in this volume) but also with highly developed visual routines that allow them to interact appropriately with objects in their environment. It should be no surprise that, as the Goodmans point out, children who do not know how to read and have never had any instruction can react quite appropriately to cans of soup and candy bars. Rozin and Gleitman indicate that the visual routines we have learned about objects lead naturally to an understanding of written language in its logographic sense. Children need no instruction to understand that visual symbols have meaning. Rozin and Gleitman also point out that the difficult problem of reading is mastery of the peculiar alphabetic principle at the basis of a phonetic writing system such as ours. I believe that the Chall stages start too late and thereby make it seem that reading as a whole is unnatural, a difficulty that is probably true of the alphabetic principle rather than of reading as a whole.

Moreover, Chall's stage view might lead us to suppose that decoding is completed in the first stage. After all, there is a decoding stage followed by a

---

[3]The critique of Chall's contribution was based on an earlier version of her chapter and not on the revised version that appears in this volume.

fluency stage. I am sure that she does not intend to imply this, but unfortunately one of the problems of basic science theory is that the theorist never accompanies the theory to explain its full meaning. Stage views are often conceived of by readers as consisting of sets of discrete processes. A reader might very well think that the decoding process ends as fluency and reading for new learning begins. However, if Venezky and Massaro are right, one of the most important aspects of fluent reading does not lie in its phonetics but in its orthography. It may be that important kinds of decoding skills are being learned during and beyond the stages at which fluency is being obtained. Stage views need to be seen as involving shifts of emphasis but not as meaning that one stage ends before the next begins.

I hope to have used the Chall view to illustrate how each basic science theory provides both lenses for the examination of issues and blinders that divert attention from some problems.

In contrast to the developmental stage view of reading, one can examine another theoretical predisposition that is emphasized in this volume—the information-processing view. The power of viewing reading in terms of information flow is that it forces one to view reading as a skill with much in common with other skilled performance. For example, Perfetti and Lesgold found that higher-level strategies did not distinguish between good and poor readers. What did distinguish them were the processes involved in perceiving a single word. This result is reminiscent of the points made by DeGroot (1965) and Chase and Simon (1974) in the study of chess. Chess masters did not differ from others in the protocols they produced describing the reasons for their choice of moves, but they did differ in their ability to see almost immediately the organization of the chess board. A similar effect was found by Reicher and Haller (1971) to distinguish very good from mediocre sight readers of music. Although this view of reading may need to be supplemented at later developmental stages by something like Frederiksen's notion that higher-level strategies also differ between good and poor readers, the Perfetti and Lesgold view suggests that in the early stages reading may be viewed like other skills. If so, one should be able to look to selection, training, and human engineering of the task as means of improving the skill. These are the methods by which psychologists have attempted to improve other types of skilled performance (Posner & Keele, 1972).

An extremely important aspect of the problem of reading instruction is that we are no longer able to use selection to choose only the people best able to learn to read. This is very unlike almost all other training that goes on in our society. Nearly any other program of skill training can select those people who are most interested or most able to learn the skill. Imagine the national crisis if all Americans had to learn to draw, run the 6-minute mile, or speak Italian. Reading instruction is unique in that we expect every person to learn the skill. With selection out, we naturally focus, as this volume does, on training methods in an attempt to improve the skill. I will comment on these suggestions in later sections.

A third way in which other skills have been improved is to redesign the task. For example, skiing instruction has been greatly aided by the use of the short ski, with transitions being made to longer and longer skis as the skill develops. Efforts in this direction in reading, for example, the Initial Teaching Alphabet (ITA) or the fading methods discussed by Holland have not been particularly successful. I think the reason for the failure of human engineering to improve the decoding skill is due to a failure to recognize the importance of orthographic and visual familiarity as part of the skill of reading. Although ITA aids children in sounding out words, it may inhibit their learning the orthographic and visual codes that are going to be an important part of the later fluency stage. A similar criticism can be made of the color coding schemes discussed by Holland.

In the later stages of reading development there will be, it seems to me, greater opportunity for human engineering of the task. For example, legibility studies have already done a great deal to help us choose better column widths and type fonts. The type of work in which Frederiksen and others are engaged should also lead to new summarizing devices that could aid readers in grasping the organization of a chapter they are about to read.

Perhaps the most important benefit in viewing reading as a skill is that the flow diagrams that have developed from the general information-processing approach have become available as tools to examine reading. Both Venezky and Massaro and LaBerge and Samuels (1974) have proposed such models. I prefer the LaBerge and Samuels model because it can be modified slightly, as in Fig. 13.2, to emphasize the parallel organization of the visual and phonetic codes and because it strongly impresses on us the importance of cognitive

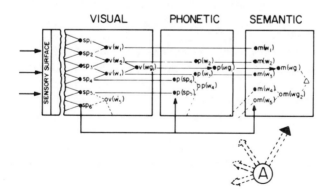

FIG. 13.2. Adaptation of the reading model developed by LaBerge and Samuels (1974).

control by separating the attentional mechanisms from the passive abstraction of information. Cognitive control by attention has been stressed in this volume by Frederiksen and Bateman among others. It is clearly important that issues involved in cognitive control of information flow be represented to the practitioner involved in designing reading curricula.

Although the information flow diagrams are useful in conceptualizing the reading task, they also have problems. For example, they tend to ignore the developmental stage issues that are so nicely emphasized by Chall's model. Even if it is the case that the skilled reader will rely primarily on orthographic or visual codes of stimuli rather than on phonetic recoding, it still may be important, if only for reasons of motivation and independence, to start off with an emphasis on the phonetic representation. Flow diagrams, based as they are on the skilled readers, give us a language for talking about the internal processes involved in reading, but they may cause us to ignore the unique problems involved in how one gets to be a skilled reader in the first place.

NATURE OF CODES

I have already alluded to the importance of the visual configuration of the stimulus in reading, which is most clear when words are dealt with in logographic form. However, one of the most important points made in this volume is the view expressed by Venezky and Massaro that it is now possible to separate experimentally the visual code of a stimulus from its phonetic recoding. It is quite surprising that a word is perceived as a unit in the visual system independently of its being pronounced. This unit depends in part on the rules that provide the orthographic regularity of the English language. It may also depend in part on the visual familiarity individuals have with particular combinations, even combinations that are not orthographically regular, such as "FBI" or "IBM." This point, eloquently discussed by Venezky and Massaro, means that one cannot limit the decoding skill to the transformation of the visual array into its phonetic representation. Instead, one needs to build up skills in seeing complex visual arrays as units. Venezky and Massaro give us no specific means for so doing, but it is clear that some methods that might be excellent for teaching phonetic representation, for example ITA, probably interfere with our ability to develop visual units. Brooks (1977) in particular has discussed methods by which orthographic regularity might be stressed in visual presentation. Indeed, even *Distar,* which places great emphasis on phonetic recoding, also teaches certain subroutines, such as scanning words visually, that might be successful ways of teaching the orthographic code.

Clearly we must find out whether learning to pronounce is a good basis for teaching orthographic codes or whether it interferes with our ability to learn the visual regularity of our language. This is important because, as Baron (1973) has pointed out by showing subjects phrases such as *Tie the not*, we make semantic judgments not only from phonetic codes of the stimuli but from our sense of their visual correctness.

The idea of an organized visual code and its relation to semantics was one basis for the look–say method. That method rested on an implicit assumption that visual familiarity of a letter string was the most important basis for the visual code. Recent research has suggested that orthographic regularity, even of visually unfamiliar material (e.g., *GaRbAgE*), is of equal or greater importance. Unfortunately, we do not know the best means for teaching this code.

Although it is important to emphasize the visual code of written language, it is still important to recognize that much initial comprehension rests on the already developed relationship between auditory input and meaning. More than anyone else in this volume, Sticht has stressed this close relationship in suggesting that we ought to look at the limits of comprehension of children in terms of their ability to deal with auditory language. I believe that Sticht's methods are clever and ought to be used, as perhaps they already are. However, I do not believe that they will turn out to be useful in the later stages of reading. Materials that can be conveyed best in the spoken language differ quite a bit from what can be best understood in the written language. Even if it turns out that in the early decoding stages of reading Sticht is correct and we can use auditory comprehension as an upper limit for the child's ability to comprehend reading, I doubt this will be true in the later stages. Instead, we will need to focus on the kinds of information that are most appropriately conveyed in the written language, as Shuy suggests.

COGNITIVE CONTROL

One reason to prefer the flow diagrams presented by LaBerge and Samuels (1974) is that they explicitly recognize the importance of cognitive control by freeing the attentional mechanisms from a particular place in the sequence of processing and by making them available to work on information in any of the codes. More than anyone else in this volume, Frederiksen outlines the importance of such an assumption. His two hypotheses emphasize the role of the reader in exercising cognitive control by developing hypotheses and inferences about what is being read. (Obviously, cognitive control is increasingly important as one reaches the later stages in Chall's developmental scheme.)

Frederiksen proposes first that control from higher-level cognitive mechanisms and from formation of hypotheses is an essential characteristic of skilled reading. This hypothesis is certainly confirmed by studies that show the importance of set, even on the most primitive aspects of the reading process. For example, Schindler, Well, and Pollatsek (1974) have shown that when subjects are set to expect words, they perform physical matching more efficiently for words than when they are not set to perceive words. Moreover, Hawkins, Reicher, Rogers, and Peterson (1976) have also shown that when subjects have a large number of homophones in a list such that the phonetic recoding of the visual information will not be an effective strategy, they seem to adopt a visual representation rather than a phonetic one. These experimental demonstrations fit with the long-standing anecdote about the man who picked up a telephone expecting to hear Russian, a language he did not speak, and was consequently unable to understand the English that was actually spoken. There is ample evidence that even the most automatic characteristics of the reading process are influenced by cognitive control, as Frederiksen's first hypothesis would suggest.

What is less well understood is the difficulty in bringing to awareness some of the automatic components involved in recognizing patterns. Experimental efforts have generally been directed to showing that some process is automatic, rather than to understanding the difficulty we have in bringing to awareness some aspects of processes that are automatic. This notion has been emphasized by Gleitman and Rozin (1977), who proposed a general principle to relate awareness and automatic processing:

> The child's natural history of explicit language knowledge proceeds in a sequence similar to the evolution of writing. The young child first becomes explicitly aware of meaning units, and only later becomes aware of the syntactic and phonological substrata of language. Thus it is easy for the young child to learn the principles of a script that tracks meanings directly and hard for him to acquire a script that tracks the sound system. These parallels suggest an approach to teaching reading.... It might be useful for the child to be introduced to visual language as a logography. Thereafter we suggest that the syllabic unit, which maintains its shape and sequential integrity in speech perception and production, may be useful for introducing the learner of an alphabet to the general class of phonographic scripts. In this approach, the abstract phonemic (alphabetic) concepts would be introduced to the learner relatively later. Summarizing, we propose that an initial reading curriculum that essentially recapitulates the historical evolution of writing will mirror the metalinguistic development of the child [p. 50].

These challenging concepts propose that it is useful in the learning process to bring to awareness the automatic characteristics that combine individual phonemes into a complete word in the listener's awareness. In their reading curriculum, Rozin and Gleitman (1977) use the general principle that decoding is best taught by taking advantage of the level of processing of which the child is aware, rather than at first attempting to teach the alphabetic principle. Unfortunately, little evidence is yet available that producing awareness of a process is a good means of producing learning. This question raises a fundamental issue in the important and complex relationship between cognitive control and automatic processing. I believe this is one place where intensive experimental analysis of the relation between awareness and learning should be developed.

Frederiksen's work also points to important literature that is emerging in the area of semantic memory (Kintsch, 1972; Norman, 1973), which I mentioned previously as perhaps leading to an ability to apply the principles of human engineering to the design of reading materials appropriate for the later stages of development. These studies point to the types of structures that subjects produce from complex stories and other written materials. Semantic memory research shows clearly that the cognitive structures bear a complex relation to the surface stream of words actually presented. There is much room for the development of diagrams, outlining, and other techniques that will help us to relate the surface stream of words in reading to the underlying semantic codes of our own long-term memory systems. The work done so far only scratches the surface of what should be a major contribution of cognitive psychology to the design of educational materials. This work relates less to the early stages of elementary school reading, which are emphasized in this volume, than to the later stages of the developed reading skill at which one attempts to build the multiple and world views outlined in the Chall stages.

INDIVIDUAL DIFFERENCES

There is relatively little discussion in this volume of differences among individuals. Perhaps the data reported by Bateman indicating that nearly any individual can learn to read given the proper teaching program seems at first to overcome any necessity for examining individual differences. Surely one would not wish the examination of individual differences to be used as an excuse to avoid accountability for providing the very best teaching possible to every person. Nonetheless, from both a basic research and an applied viewpoint, it is important to recognize differences among individuals. Fisher's discussion of central nervous system dysfunction as a possible cause of reading disability, although only preliminary, may raise difficult ethical problems in people's minds in the fear that such discussion could be used as an excuse to avoid accountability. However, we must recognize that the flow diagrams produced by information-processing psychologists are, however preliminary, diagrams about how the brain is organized. We should expect that as the human goes through different developmental stages and learns new things, brain organization changes. We should not get in the habit of thinking that the organization of the brain is something innate and fixed in time. Teaching does reprogram the brain. It provides new organization, information flow, and temporal patterns. The fact that individuals differ in brain processes should not necessarily be thought to imply that such differences are immutable.

With this caution in mind, we should recognize, as Fisher points out, that some dyslexics have specific information-processing problems that might arise from a variety of different systems. Work with dyslexics by Marshall and Newcombe (1973), Shallice and Warrington (1975), and Sasanuma (1974) has shown that brain damage yields different syndromes and specific disorganizations of the reading process. Indeed, Sasanuma has shown that one sort of brain damage can interfere with reading of the *kana,* or phonetic characters, of the Japanese language, whereas another kind disturbs the *kanji,* or logographic, characters. These findings are consistent with the different systems pointed out in the flow diagrams illustrated in Fig. 13.2. We should expect, and indeed data suggest, that in the normal range there are vast differences in the way in which individuals orient to language. Recently Baron and Strawson (1976) pointed out a distinction between subjects who have great difficulty in detecting spelling mistakes but who do very well in decoding words that sound like familiar English (who are called "Phoenicians") and subjects who detect spelling errors easily but are not good at sound tasks (who are called "Chinese"). Work by Hawkins, Reicher, Rogers, and Peterson (1976) suggests that the same subject can switch strategies between different codes of the stimulus from time to time. These findings are important because they suggest that reading may be done in fundamentally different ways. Thus we might find both individual differences and intraindividual differences to be important in the codings involved in reading.

We need to use our knowledge of individual differences to develop tests that will be appropriate to the particular coding complementing an individual's style of learning. Some ideas concerning appropriate tests were mentioned briefly by Sticht, Perfetti and Lesgold, and Frederiksen. All of them suggest probes that might help the teacher understand what is going on in the mind of students as they proceed through various aspects of the curriculum.

PROGRAM DESIGN

In these remarks I have viewed theory as a lens and also as a blinder which, when worn by programmers or curriculum designers, helps them to make the many decisions necessary to develop a curriculum. Obviously, basic researchers need to provide programmers with cues to the directions in which they should search in trying to make the complex decisions necessary to produce a full curricular design. Both stage theories and information flow theories provide some direction for programmers about the crucial decisions they might make in any particular curriculum.

Second, theory should provide teachers with a language in which to discuss problems of reading. It does little good to say that people cannot read because they are deficient. However, when one starts to talk about the specific difficulty of a given person, one can begin to find ways around that difficulty. Many of the chapters in this volume may be seen as providing languages for the teachers to talk more completely about the complex problems individual children have in finding their way through a curriculum.

Finally, a most important role of theory may eventually be to provide students with more control over their own learning. One of the most important facts uncovered by psychology is the difficulty in gaining insight into one's own mental structures and information-processing activities. Although introspection provides powerful entry into some aspects of our own internal mental lives, we cannot produce by introspection the analyses presented in this volume. Perhaps one of the most important roles for psychology in the teaching of reading is for children themselves to learn something more about what is going on inside their heads as they learn the skill. This new insight may provide both motivation and some degree of self-direction over the course of a child's reading. This self-control is obviously more important in the later of the Chall stages than in the earlier, but it is a direction toward which psychologists should aspire as more becomes known about the internal processes involved in cognition. Self-control is undoubtedly the most important control mechanism that can be used to ensure the learning of reading. For, after all, it is not easy or perhaps even possible to teach people what they do not wish to learn.

ACKNOWLEDGMENTS

This commentary was supported in part by the National Science Foundation through Grant No. BMS73-00963-A02 to the University of Oregon. The author is grateful to Brian Davidson and John Lloyd, who were helpful in the development of this analysis.

REFERENCES

Baron, J. Phonemic stage not necessary for reading. *Quarterly Journal of Experimental Psychology,* 1973, *25,* 241–246.

Baron, J., & Strawson, C. Use of orthographic and word specific knowledge in reading words aloud. *Journal of Experimental Psychology: Human Perception and Performance,* 1976, *2,* 386–393.

Brooks, L.   Visual patterns in fluency word identification. In A. Reber & D. Scarborough (Eds.), *Toward a psychology of reading: Proceedings of the CUNY conference.* Hillsdale, N.J.: Lawrence Erlbaum Associates, 1977.

Chase, W., & Simon, H. A.   Perception in chess. *Cognitive Psychology,* 1974, *4,* 55–81.

Critchley, M.   *Developmental dyslexia.* London: Heinemann, 1964.

DeGroot, A.   *Thought and choice in chess.* The Hague: Mouton, 1965.

Gleitman, L., & Rozin, P.   The structure and acquisition of reading I: Relations between orthographies and the structure of language. In A. Reber & D. Scarborough (Eds.), *Toward a psychology of reading: Proceedings of the CUNY conference.* Hillsdale, N.J.: Lawrence Erlbaum Associates, 1977.

Hawkins H. L., Reicher, G. M., Rogers, M., & Peterson, L.   Flexible coding in word recognition. *Journal of Experimental Psychology: Human Perception and Performance,* 1976, *2,* 380–385.

Kintsch, W.   Notes on the structure of semantic memory. In E. E. Tulving & W. Donaldson (Eds.), *Organization of memory.* New York: Academic Press, 1972.

LaBerge, D., & Samuels, J.   Toward a theory of automatic information processing in reading. *Cognitive Psychology,* 1974, *2,* 293–323.

Marshall, J. C., & Newcombe, F.   Patterns of paralexia: A psycholinguistic approach. *Journal of Psycholinguistic Research,* 1973, *2,* 175–198.

Norman, D. A.   Memory, knowledge and the answering of questions. In R. Solso (Ed.), *Contemporary issues in cognitive psychology.* Washington, D.C.: Winston, 1973.

Orton, S. T.   Word-blindness in school-children. *Archives of Neurology and Psychiatry,* 1925, *14,* 581–615.

Posner, M. I., & Keele, S. W.   Skill learning. In R. Travers (Ed.), *Handbook of research in teaching.* New York: Rand McNally, 1972.

Reicher, G. R., & Haller, R.   *Further studies of the masters eye.* Unpublished manuscript, University of Oregon, 1971.

Rozin, P., & Gleitman, L.   The reading process and the acquisition of the alphabetic principle. In A. Reber & D. Scarborough (Eds.), *Toward a psychology of reading: Proceedings of the CUNY conference.* Hillsdale, N.J.: Lawrence Erlbaum Associates, 1977.

Sasanuma, S.   Impairment of written language in Japanese aphasics: Kana vs. Kanji processing. *Journal of Chinese Linguistics,* 1974, 141–158.

Schindler, R. M., Well, A., & Pollatsek, A.   Effects of segmentation and matching and expectancy on matching time for words and nonwords. *Journal of Experimental Psychology,* 1974, *103,* 107–111.

Shallice, T., & Warrington, E.   Word recognition in a phonemic dyslexic patient. *Quarterly Journal of Experimental Psychology,* 1975, *27,* 187–199.

Simon, H. A.   *The sciences of the artificial.* Cambridge, Mass.: MIT Press, 1969.

14

How the Mind Works When Reading: Describing Elephants No One Has Ever Seen

S. J. Samuels
Center for Research in Human Learning,
University of Minnesota

It is refreshing that in this first of three volumes on reading, one cannot find evidence of a sharp demarcation between pure and applied research. Even in the more theoretically oriented chapters, considerable effort is taken to indicate the relevance of the pure research to applied problems of reading. According to Garner (1972), there is a mistaken belief that the scientist accomplishes most when completely isolated from the applied problems of everyday life. To the contrary, Garner argued, the research scientist interested in the acquisition of knowledge may be helped immeasurably by attempting to find solutions to the important problems emerging from the practical arena of everyday life. Problems associated with reading acquisition present a rich area of inquiry for both the theoretical and applied scientist.

IS THERE A READING PROBLEM?

Before discussing the chapters contributed to this volume, I would like to present some information relevant to several questions raised here. The first question is whether there is a reading problem in the United States today. If there is not a serious reading problem, then the considerable amount of time, effort, and money spent on overcoming a supposed problem may well be wasted. The answer to this question depends on how one defines reading. If one uses the United Nations' definition of literacy, which is that a person is literate if that person can read a simple, everyday paragraph with understanding, then we do not have a reading problem. Using that definition, the 1960 census found that only 2.4% of the American population was illiterate. Although the percentage was low, it did represent 2,619,000 persons. The great majority of these persons, however, were over the age of 45. In the very youngest age bracket, 14–24, the national illiteracy rate was about 1 in 170 (Wattenberg & Scammon, 1967).

Another way to answer the question is to use the term *functional illiteracy*. The concept of functional illiteracy had its beginnings in America in the 1930s when men were recruited into the Civilian Conservation Corp (CCC) and it was found that those individuals with less than a third-grade education were frequently unable to follow written directions. Administrators in the CCC program began to classify men with less than a third-grade education as functional illiterates. During World War II the U.S. Army discovered that when a soldier had less than a fourth-grade education, he was often unable to comprehend written directions. The 1950 census divided the population into those with 5 or more years of schooling and those with less than 5 years of schooling, and those with the lesser amount of education were classified as functional illiterates. In the 1960s, when the statistical work on the poverty program was being reviewed, it was decided that all Americans with less than 6 years of schooling were to be designated as functional illiterates. By that standard, there were 8.3 million adult functional illiterates in the United States in 1960.

It is important to point out that the term *functional illiterate* may be used in two ways. It may be used to denote an arbitrary line in an educational attainment distribution. The 8.3 million Americans so labeled included well over 100,000 who earned over $10,000 a year in 1959, and in former years this category would have included men such as Abraham Lincoln. The second way in which the term *functional illiterate* may be used is to indicate an arbitrary point on a reading achievement grade-level distribution below which the individual is designated as being illiterate. If one defines illiteracy in a third, somewhat different fashion, such as the inability to read or write on a level necessary to deal with everyday practical situations, a different picture begins to emerge. It is assumed that 8 years of schooling is sufficient to allow an individual to deal satisfactorily with these everyday reading situations. By this standard, about 13% of the population aged 25 years and over is functionally illiterate (Bureau of the Census, 1972).

One may inquire as to how realistic an eighth-grade designation may be in terms of preparation for reading the mass of material that must be processed. Analysis of readability levels indicates that much of what we must process in everyday life, such as instructions, exceeds this eight-grade level. The Harris study (1971) assessed functional illiteracy by testing Americans' ability to comprehend written information in materials such as employment ads, telephone dialing instructions, and application forms. This survey found that at least 4% of the adult population was unable to handle these materials satisfactorily.

It should be pointed out that a mismatch between the readability level of the written materials and the reading ability of the individual does not necessarily mean that the individual will not be able to comprehend those materials. An important factor to consider is the motivation of the individual who wishes to comprehend the materials. Prisoners with a relatively low level of reading attainment have been known to read with understanding the legal books relevant to their particular criminal cases. With sufficient motivation, an individual may read and re-read the materials a sufficient number of times in order to comprehend them. Mismatches may have more important consequences for individuals who are not highly motivated or who do not have a great deal of time to spend with those materials.

One way to increase the functional literacy of individuals may very well be to decrease the difficulty of the materials with which they will have to come in contact. In keeping with this view, the Chicago Continental Bank has simplified its customer account agreements. Checking account agreements, for example, read, "If you write a check for more money than you have in your account, you will be overdrawn and we will return the check. Because this means extra work for us, we charge $5 for each check returned." Several life and accident insurance companies have rewritten their agreements into understandable English. In our public schools, one can find textbooks in which the readability level exceeds the reading ability of the students by 6 years. It would seem to be a good idea for school systems to try to match the readability level of the texts they use with the known reading level of their students prior to purchasing the texts. If this practice were followed on a national scale, it would force publishers to be very careful about making their books readable by the intended school populations.

Another concept of literacy has been propounded by Bormuth (1975), whose concept of literacy does not represent a particular level of reading attainment but is task related. According to Bormuth, a person is literate if that individual is able to read with understanding the materials encountered in any aspect of his or her life, job related or otherwise. Thus it would be possible for a person to be literate when engaged in one type of reading activity and illiterate when engaged in a different type of activity. College professors, for example, may be literate when reading a professional journal in their areas of expertise but be considered illiterate when trying to comprehend an income tax form. Similarly, one may be literate when reading material in one's own field and be illiterate in an unrelated discipline.

Before leaving the question of the extent of the reading problem in the United States today, it is important to present the data provided by the National Center for Health Statistics (Vogt, 1973). In this study youths 12- to 17-years-old were given a basic test of literacy. Findings indicated that among this age group the illiteracy rate was 4.8%. However, when a stepwise regression analysis was done, it was found that illiteracy rate among low-income, black males living in small urban areas was 38%. Among low-income, white males whose parents were relatively uneducated the illiteracy rate was 46%.

The answer to the question regarding the extent of the reading problem in the United States is not easily answered. Part of the problem relates to how one defines literacy. If the Bormuth definition is used, then all of us are illiterate, at least with respect to some kinds of materials. If the data provided by the National Center for Health Statistics are used, then the illiteracy problem is related to factors of social class such as income, and to demographic factors. Contrary to the sanguine opinion voiced by Wattenberg and Scammon (1967) to the effect that illiteracy tended to be clustered among older Americans, the National Center for Health Statistics indicated that illiteracy is to be found among our youth as well. As we will see later, the solution to the problem is not simply one of increasing the decoding ability of those people termed illiterate. Sticht (this volume) has pointed out that among the illiterate group there are those whose reading and listening comprehension both are low. Increasing the decoding ability of this particular group will probably do little to increase their literacy since the problem is not essentially one of decoding.

TEACHING READING

Another question is related to whether we can do a better job in teaching reading. Even when reading instruction is less than ideal, many children learn to read. Silberman (1964) reported on an experimental program used to teach beginning reading, finding that the brighter children acquired the necessary reading skill he wanted them to learn, but that the less bright seemed unable to transfer their knowledge to words not specifically taught. Classroom teachers brought in to evaluate the program discovered that a necessary subskill had been omitted. Only after the necessary subskill had been included in the program were all the children able to master the transfer to untaught words. What is interesting is that even with an important subskill missing, the brigher children were able to overcome this obstacle. Silberman's study suggests that brighter children may be able to overcome an inadequate program, but the less bright have great difficulty.

Another example of how children were able to overcome a less than adequate teaching program is reported by Feitelson (1973). Prior to the 1950s, reading pedagogy in Israel was dominated by an official viewpoint indicating that the child's own interest was the major factor to consider in constructing a reading program, and it was assumed that as long as the child was motivated, the child would acquire necessary reading skills. According to this viewpoint, to maintain motivation it was necessary for the child to read in units larger than the word, mostly in phrase units. This holistic approach assumed that beginning readers were not at all interested in analyzing words into their component parts. Teaching letter–sound correspondences was not an acceptable practice at that time. Feitelson said that until the 1950s this way of teaching reading was widely used, and the results in general were satisfactory.

Subsequent to the 1950s, there was large scale immigration into Israel from Arab countries, and schools began to report failure rates from 50% at the end of the first grade. It would have been easy enough to attribute the cause of failure to the new influx of a different group into Israel. However, a study was sponsored to find out what the possible causes of failure might be. One of the more startling findings emerging from this study was that failure to acquire reading was not evenly dispersed. An entire classroom would either be successful in acquiring reading skills or unsuccessful. The successful classrooms were found to have teachers who did not use a holistic approach and who devoted a great deal of time to systematic phonics drill and to breaking words into smaller components. A second finding of interest was that parents were very helpful in overcoming the harmful effects of the holistic teaching practices of the day by teaching phonics. What the child was not offered in school, the parents were teaching at home. Many teachers taught in holistic units, but at home the parents were drilling the children on the components of words so that the children could attack new words based on letter–sound correspondences and blending. A less than adequate program was overcome and the teacher and parent behavior that was effective happened to be the teaching of essential decoding skills.

We have just seen how some children are able to overcome the shortcomings of certain reading programs, either because of high intelligence, teacher skill, or parental intervention. The reading problem in the United States today is generally with children at risk—the lowest 15% of the children in the IQ distribution. There is evidence, however, that there are exemplary reading programs that are successful even with high-risk children. Weber (1971) reported on the program characteristics of four highly successful inner-city schools where a major emphasis was placed on building positive student and teacher interaction, building pride in one's background and group, extensive use of positive reinforcement, extensive pupil evaluation, specialized teacher-training programs to promote positive interaction between the teaching staff and the administration, a belief that high achievement is an obtainable goal, use of teacher aides who participated actively in the reading program, availability of a reading specialist in the school, and the use of open records of student progress so that everyone was aware of students' progress. Although Weber acknowledged that nonschool factors can and do contribute to success or failure in beginning reading, he argued that a great difference in reading achievement can result from instruction, depending on the school's effectiveness in teaching beginning reading. Weber found that strong leadership, higher expectations for the students, an orderly, pleasant, happy atmosphere, a strong emphasis on reading, use of additional personnel, use of phonics, individualization, and careful day-by-day evaluation of pupil progress contributed strongly to the success of the reading programs. Other studies of exemplary reading programs have identified program character-istics similar to the ones set forth by Weber.

Two other program characteristics appear to be associated with success in reading. Guthrie (1976) found that the amount of time allocated to reading is positively associated with reading achievement. Other studies have found that time on task is also related to reading achievement (Lahaderne, 1968; Samuels & Turnure, 1974). In general, these findings tend to support the notion that one can build exemplary programs in reading and that the total amount of time devoted to reading, as well as the amount of time on task, are factors that must be taken into consideration in engineering a successful reading program.

I had an opportunity to discuss what was needed to improve the teaching of reading with Tom Sticht, John Guthrie, Harry Singer, and Dennis Fisher. There was consensus that at the present time a sufficient amount is known about practical aspects of reading so that all children, even those at risk, can be taught to read. The problem then, is not lack of knowledge about how to teach reading. The problem is one of dissemination, transfer, and use of this information. Overcoming these problems, in the opinion of this group, represented the major thrust that reading work should take in the years to come. These problems are not very different from the problems of changing the smoking habits of the American public. Presently we know that smoking is dangerous to health. Despite this knowledge, many people are unable to change their smoking habits, and many others take up this harmful habit. The task of changing smoking habits is probably more formidable than changing the reading practices of school systems. Increasingly, the constraints of limited resources coupled with the desire for excellence have generated a demand for a result-oriented teaching system and for accountability. With the clamor of public interest groups for information about their schools and with the recognition by taxpayers and educators alike that the school must be accountable in some sense for the products of its system, we may well be moving toward an era in which schools will be doing a more efficient job of teaching reading.

DISCUSSION OF CHAPTERS

Jeanne Chall

Chall's chapter traces what has happened in reading pedagogy since the publication of her book, *Learning to Read: The Great Debate,* a decade ago. One of the changes is the added importance given to a code emphasis for beginning reading. The importance of a code emphasis is made manifest by

Goldberg (1973), who conducted a large-scale study of the beginning reading of disadvantaged children. Goldberg speculated that, although teachers may be stressing comprehension, children may be busy devising ways of breaking the sound–symbol code and trying to figure out what the printed material says rather than what it means. This speculation is particularly relevant to the current debate in educational circles as to whether reading should begin with a meaning emphasis or a code-breaking emphasis.

A decade ago Chall (Chall, 1967) concluded that a code emphasis was justified, and subsequent research has supported her contentions. Dykstra (1967), who evaluated the first-grade studies, concluded that those programs emphasizing decoding produced students who were superior in word recognition. More recently, Katz and Singer (1976) re-evaluated the data from the first-grade studies and found that those programs emphasizing a decoding approach produced students superior in those subskills necessary for recognizing words that had not been previously taught. Studies by Bishop (1964) and Jeffrey and Samuels (1967) found that students who were given training in letter–sound correspondences, as well as training in blending, were able to decode words that they had not previously encountered. These skills are important first steps in learning to read. A behavioral task analysis of reading would strongly suggest that accuracy in decoding skills and automaticity are important prerequisites for skilled reading.

The second part of Chall's chapter presents "a modest proposal for reading stages," a section that begins with a passing reference to the Coleman findings which indicate that it is difficult, if not impossible, to find evidence of school input variables associated with academic achievement. Most of the variability in school achievement, according to Coleman, is associated with socio-economic status factors over which the schools have no control. Critics of the Coleman report have pointed out that such factors as school facilities, books in the library, per-pupil expenditures, the presence of science facilities, and related measures used by Coleman do not begin to reflect the essence of an organization. One must also understand that *socioeconomic status* is merely a descriptive term and by itself has no causative impact. New analyses of schooling effects (Bidwell & Kasarda, 1975; Brown & Saks, 1975) indicate that, contrary to the Coleman report, schools have a significant impact on academic achievement.

Chall's stage approach to reading includes a prereading stage, a decoding stage, development of fluency, reading for learning, multiple viewpoints, and finally a world view. The value of this stage theory is that it recognizes the concept of reading as a developmental skill and specifies the stages. Several comments are in order regarding the stage theory. Simply labeling a stage as the decoding stage implies that this is all that is going on. However, although the child may be wrestling with problems of decoding, nevertheless he or she is able to comprehend the text. Following the decoding stage is the fluency development period. Chall is correct in noting that decoding skill may be separated into two stages. The first stage is what may be termed an "accuracy stage," whereas the next stage goes beyond accuracy to automaticity (the Perfetti–Lesgold chapter discusses this more deeply). During the accuracy stage, the child is able to recognize words, but attention is used in the process. One of the characteristics of the accuracy stage is that the response is laborious and quite slow. It is only during the automaticity stage that attention to decoding is not required and word recognition takes place at a very rapid rate.

In the third stage, the reading-for-learning period, the assumption is made that word recognition skill is at the automatic level and the student is able to use written materials for gaining new information. The final two stages in this model represent levels of comprehension that extend far beyond what we may ordinarily think of as literal comprehension or beginning reading.

One important topic Chall takes up has to do with the development of reading fluency. As Chall points out, the development of fluency generally comes about through practice. For some strange reason, *practice* has become a dirty word in some educational circles, and practice is labeled by an acrimonious term, namely, *drill*. Recent work by Chomsky (1978) and Samuels (1979) indicate the value of what may be termed "drill on developing reading fluency." Using a method that may be called "repeated readings," Samuels (1979) had mentally retarded children read short passages (50 to 250 words) from very simple stories over and over until a criterion rate of 70 words per minute in oral reading was achieved. Then the children selected the next part of the story and repeated the procedure. This simple adjunct to the regular reading program produced noticeable improvement in the reading skills of the children. In fact, it was noticed that the children were using this repeated reading method even when it was not required. The Chomsky method is similar. Stories were recorded on audiotape, and the child listened to the auditory input while silently reading stories. When the child was sufficiently familiar with the story, the audio input was discontinued.

To get beyond the accuracy stage in word recognition, that Chall refers to as the "decoding stage," a great deal of practice with simple materials would be helpful. Practice can be provided through repeated readings or through reading materials that most researchers would consider to be easy for the child. Ordinarily this level is called "the recreational reading level." With sufficient practice, the student should reach the fluency stage, where decoding can be done automatically and attention may then be paid to deriving meaning from the material being processed.

Thomas Sticht

Sticht's chapter in this volume represents an application of the Audread model to reading evaluation and instruction. Sticht has a number of interesting hypotheses. For example, Sticht feels that auding surpasses reading ability in early school years and that this gap should close as reading ability becomes more fluent. In a sense, this hypothesis represents what might be called a "stage theory of reading." The first stage in reading is the transfer from the auditory signals one has mastered to the written signals. When the student can respond as quickly and as easily to written signals as to auditory signals, the transfer stage is complete. Using the concepts of Perfetti and Lesgold (this volume), one might think of these stages as the preaccuracy stage, the accuracy stage, and the automaticity stage. When the student is automatic in decoding, then the transfer is complete and reading is as efficient as auding.

Another hypothesis presented by Sticht is that auding ability is predictive of reading ability. This hypothesis assumes that decoding is essentially at the same degree of automaticity as is auding. Consequently, auding ability would then represent what one's general level of comprehension might be. As Sticht points out, there are many people who can read as well as they can aud, but they cannot and very well, which implies deficits or difficulty in both reading and auding comprehension. If one assumes that comprehension is a multicomponent process, then one can easily understand why an individual may have difficulty in both auding and reading comprehension. An individual may have decoding skill at the automatic level but still have difficulty in comprehension because of possible deficits in a component of comprehension such as background knowledge. Thus if one wishes to increase comprehension for those who decode well but who comprehend poorly, the remedy lies in improving aspects of comprehension other than decoding.

Another important idea found in Sticht's chapter is that reading comprehension may be improved by improving auding comprehension. Too often reading educators make the mistake of trying to improve reading comprehension directly through the reading act when it may be more efficient to do so through auding.

There is a critical need for a test that will indicate if a person is automatic in decoding. Sticht has developed just such a test based on the idea that by holding the rate of input constant, when comprehension during reading is equal to comprehension while auding, the decoding is at the automatic level. Although this is an important start, we need additional work to measure the automaticity of what may be considered the subskills in reading.

Charles Perfetti and Alan Lesgold

The chapter by Perfetti and Lesgold suggests that one of the limitations to comprehension is found in short-term memory. In light of its restricted capacity and the limited longevity of items placed in it, their "bottleneck hypothesis" seems reasonable. However, it should be pointed out that the rate of input into long-term memory is relatively slow, so that actually there are two bottlenecks to comprehension. In addition to the limitations of long- and short-term memory, there are other obstacles to comprehension, and these may be conceptualized as the components of comprehension, including word knowledge or vocabulary, prior knowledge of the concepts being discussed, and ability to decode the text without the use of attention. These components of comprehension influence the load on short-term memory.

An important question raised by Perfetti and Lesgold has to do with why fast decoding is associated with high comprehension. Fast decoding in and of itself does not seem to be the critical factor, but it serves as an indicator of automaticity. When we find the relation between speed of decoding and comprehension, what we are really seeing is a response that seems to be both fast and automatic. Automatic decoding is viewed as being an important factor in comprehension, because when decoding is automatic, attention may be focused on deriving meaning.

Another concern of the Perfetti–Lesgold chapter is how one might help poor readers. The point is made that although drill is boring, there is need for extended practice. As mentioned earlier, there is need for educators to overcome the tendency to associate extended practice with boring drill. As Perfetti and Lesgold state, practice on recognizing words in isolation does not seem to have the transfer effects to fluent reading that one might desire. Instead, the student must be given extended practice on reading materials at the recreational level. The recreational level is considered to be a level at which the student can read the materials with relative ease and with a low rate of word recognition errors.

The final section of the Perfetti–Lesgold chapter deals with measuring verbal coding efficiency, and a recommendation is made that reading tests be designed to distinguish among three types of performance: inaccurate, slow but accurate, and automatic. This seems to be an excellent way to distinguish various degrees of reading fluency. Reading tests are presently designed to differentiate accurate from inaccurate performance, but they are not designed to identify what might be called "automatic" and "nonautomatic" levels of decoding. Consequently, indicators of automaticity are needed as a next step in the development of reading tests. An individual is not either automatic or nonautomatic in reading. The reader can be automatic at identifying letters but be nonautomatic with words. The fluent reader may be automatic on nearly all the words encountered but require attention for the decoding of some words. What is needed, then, are indicators of automaticity for different types of important subskills considered to be important in reading. Although we are able at the present time to measure the automaticity of a response in the laboratory, the critical need is for the development of paper-and-pencil tests of automaticity that can be easily administered in the classroom.

Richard Venezky and Dominic Massaro

The chapter by Venezky and Massaro is about the orthographic structure of a word and its effect on word recognition. Orthographic regularity is thought of as those features of a word that reduce the uncertainty of what letters might be present. Consequently, these features would consist of letter groupings that correspond to the rules of English spelling. Orthographic structure is thought to be important because rapid word recognition depends on strategies using orthographic regularity.

For some time now, since the first decade of this century, researchers have recognized that there is something about the spelling pattern and structure of an English word that facilitates its recognition. We have known that recognition of a short common word proceeds about as fast as one can recognize a single letter and that arrays of letters are recognized faster when they are arranged to form a word rather than in some totally random way. In fact, when children who are just beginning to read are asked to perform a matching task on pairs of simultaneously presented letter sequences that are either words or nonwords, they do so faster for the words than the nonwords, strongly suggesting that even beginning readers abstract something about the pattern of English spelling to enable them to make judgments about English words faster than the anagrams of the words.

A word may be thought of as a higher order unit with rule-governed relations within it. When synthetic words are constructed to correspond to these rules and are given to students of different grade levels and different degrees of reading skill, one finds that accuracy of pronunciation increases over time and that good readers are more accurate than poor readers in pronouncing these synthetic words (Calfee, Venezky, & Chapman, 1969).

Additional evidence indicates that children seem to abstract that which we may call "intraword redundancy" or orthographic structure. For example, Gibson, Osser, and Pick (1963) had first- and third-grade children read and spell three-letter strings of words presented with a tachistoscope (*ran, nar, rna*). First graders were most accurate with the familiar three-letter words and also read the pronounceable trigrams significantly better than the unpronounceable ones. Other work by Rosinski and Wheeler (1972) compared children in first, third, and fifth grades on sets of nonsense words varying from three to six letters in length. The task for the child was to indicate which of the set of words typed on a card most resembled a real word. One of each pair was pronounceable and the other was not. First-grade children were at a chance level, although it should be kept in mind that they had extraordinarily little reading instruction. The other two groups performed significantly better than chance on the task.

Work done at our Minnesota laboratory (Terry, Samuels, & LaBerge, 1976) on the relationship between word length and response latency throws some light on how orthographic structure is used by a skilled reader. When shown high frequency words in mirror image text varying in length from three letters to six letters, we found an increase in response latency for each additional letter up to the fifth but then no increase after the fifth letter, implying that the skilled reader gathers letter information over the first few letters but then is able to predict what the next letters will be through internalized knowledge of higher order units of spelling pattern. This finding supports the notion of Venezky and Massaro that one of the aids provided to the skilled reader by knowledge of orthographic structure is that less visual information is needed in word recognition. Whether spelling patterns and their pronunciation are learned implicitly or intentionally is a question that needs to be researched.

Roger Shuy

Shuy's chapter states that past research attempting to find the basis for poor reading in the mismatch of child language and school language was a misguided attempt. According to Shuy, ascribing poor reading performance to the mismatch of child language and school language is a thesis which at the present time is not seriously held by anyone. Shuy, having the advantages of 20–20 hindsight, can make this claim, but if one looks at the research studies done to test this idea, as well as at the large-scale curriculum projects designed to reduce this mismatch, one can see that the language mismatch thesis was widely held at one time.

The study of language mismatch has produced some positive results for reading pedagogy. Teachers are more aware today of the fact that language variation does not represent inferior speech; teachers are far more willing today to accept deviations from standard English; the language of reading primers is far more believable and part of regular speaking patterns; and in teachers' guides and teacher-training institutions a great deal of emphasis is being given to the fact that we have a number of dialects in the United States and that these simply reflect regional speaking patterns. Teachers are also being told today that as long as the child makes a reasonable approximation of the word that is in the text, the teacher should not correct the child.

Past attempts to ascribe poor reading performance to language mismatch were probably wrong for a number of reasons. First, the groups which were extensively examined were low on the socioeconomic status scale. These were the groups that had what were called "language mismatches." However, in addition to their language variation, these groups may also have been characterized by lower income, lower education, fewer books in the home, and generally poorer health and prenatal environment, as well as by differences in cultural outlook and motivations. All these factors, not only language mismatch, are correlated with reading achievement. We must be cautious about ascribing cause-and-effect relationships to variables that are merely correlated. One can argue that some of the other factors, such as economic deprivation, health, and nutrition, may be as important as the language mismatch. The second factor to keep in mind is that it is highly unlikely that a single variable such as language mismatch will account for any large proportion of variance in reading comprehension. To pin all of one's efforts on this one factor is probably a misguided effort. In retrospect, however, Shuy is right in contending that today the mismatch is not seen as the significant variable in the lower reading performance of certain groups in our population.

Shuy is now calling for a new type of research. What is needed now, according to Shuy, is the study of occupational and institutional dialects. For example, what does it mean to talk like a teacher? According to Shuy, this, is where future payoffs in research may come. However, it is not clear precisely how this knowledge will be useful in reading.

It seems that the relevance of studying functional language use would be to show possible mismatches between the child's uses of language, the use of language in the textbook, the use of language by the characters in the reading textbook, and the use of language by people in the real world. Although this study of functional language mismatch may be worthy in its own right, it is not at all clear how this would change the reading accomplishments of children at risk. On the positive side, however, it might indeed be refreshing for children's books to reflect in a realistic manner the social status and power of the people portrayed in the text.

Isabel Beck and Karen Block

The Beck and Block chapter consists of an analysis of the Ginn 720 and the Palo Alto programs and provides a perceptive view into the state of the art of curriculum design and material development. In designing reading materials numerous decisions must be made. What technological base is available to aid in the decision-making process? A start in this direction has been provided by Coleman's (1970) tables that scale common words for ease of learning, the graphemes for ease of learning their sounds, the English sounds for ease of blending, and the letters for ease of printing. The reading literature is filled with experimental data that provide additional information for decision making, but unfortunately much of the research is not definitive or there are counterfindings.

A second factor to consider when appraising curriculum products is their value. Unfortunately, curriculum materials frequently are used without any prior testing. Some states, such as California, now require some evidence of the value of the curriculum products prior to their adoption. An exception to the general rule that reading materials are usually not tested prior to their introduction may be found in the federally funded research and development laboratories, such as the one in Wisconsin, and the regional laboratories, such as CEMREL. Products from these laboratories, such as the *Wisconsin Design for Reading Skill Development* and CEMREL's *Language and Thinking Program*, have been tested and revisions have been made based on the test evaluations.

One area of controversy and decision making in curriculum design relates to the definition of the reading process. The Ginn program assumes that reading consists of getting meaning from the printed page, whereas the Palo Alto program assumes that reading consists of first decoding from print to sound and subsequently deriving meaning from that mediated sound production. This difference in definition is not mere academic hairsplitting, because different types of reading programs emerge from different viewpoints regarding the nature of the reading process. One type of program places an early emphasis on deriving meaning, whereas the other program emphasizes decoding.

Another curriculum decision concerns the type of student for whom the materials are planned. The materials may be planned for either high- or low-IQ children, middle or low socioeconomic status children, or normal learners as opposed to the learning disabled. As mentioned earlier, it is generally the lowest 15% of the children in the IQ distribution, or those children at risk, for whom reading is most difficult and the excellence of the materials most important. Although it may be possible to overcome the shortcomings of a poor program with a bright, highly motivated child whose parents can provide tutorial help, it is far less likely that the child's disadvantaged classmate will be able to overcome the shortcomings of a poor program.

Curriculum developers must also consider the placement of skill instruction in the instructional sequence. In some reading programs, such as the Ginn, the instructional sequence is discussion, reading, and then skill instruction. In the Palo Alto series, on the other hand, it is assumed that skill instruction will be introduced prior to story reading so that the child may be helped to read the story.

Yet another decision pertains to the types of words introduced. Words may be introduced primarily to build interest in the story or primarily to correspond to some phonic rule. These decisions involve a tradeoff between words selected to enhance a story line and words selected for decoding. In the Ginn program, where the emphasis is on meaning, words are selected to enhance the story line. However, as Goldberg (1973) pointed out, the teacher may be assuming that students are reading for meaning, but the students in fact may be busily attempting to decode words prior to getting that meaning.

Beck and Block are critical of both the Ginn and Palo Alto programs for teaching correspondences in a backward direction—going from sound to letter (a spelling requirement) rather than from letter to sound (a reading requirement). This seems to be a simple enough question to be answered by empirical research. As we know, many associations, although taught in one direction, are also learned in the reverse direction. It is probably the case that although correspondences are learned from sound to letter, they are learned in the reverse direction as well. Whether this holds for the low-IQ child remains to be seen, and a simple empirical study can answer this question. Should this research indicate that children of the educable IQ range and higher learn letter–sound association in both directions, then the question is resolved. If the learning is only in the direction taught in the programs, curriculum designers should have this information so that suitable teaching decisions can be made.

The Ginn program teaches letter–sound correspondences in the context of words. In Beck's (1977) reading program, letter–sound correspondences are taught in isolation. Linguists point out that phonemes do not exist in isolation, and consequently they believe phonemes should be taught in the context of a word. On the other hand, there is evidence that children tend to learn these correspondences best when they are presented in isolation.

There are a number of ways in which letter–sound correspondences may be learned. One way could be called the "discovery method," in which a number of different words containing the same letter–sound correspondence (*money, monkey, merry*) are introduced. The child then searches for the common element. There is also the guided discovery method, in which the teacher points out specifically what these words have in common. A third way is to present the sound in isolation, just the letter followed by its sound. It is highly probable that the successful teacher uses all these methods in combination to make the point for the child. Beck and Block believe that letter-to-sound is the right direction in which to teach correspondences because it goes in the same direction as the decoding behavior required in reading. It is also their belief that the child should be taught to blend sounds, as well as to produce a limited number of sounds in isolation. It is their contention that teaching children to blend sounds in isolation has good transfer value to reading.

Both the Palo Alto and the Ginn program use phonics, but the Ginn program uses analytic phonics whereas the Palo Alto program uses synthetic phonics. These procedures grow directly out of the manner in which letter–sound correspondences are taught. As mentioned previously, in the Ginn program letter–sound correspondences are not produced in isolation but within the context of a word. Consequently, a whole word is introduced and then each of the correspondences within the word is sounded out, a procedure we call "analytic" phonics. Conversely, the Palo Alto program does have sounds produced in isolation by the teacher. Consequently, a synthetic type of phonics with blending is used to teach word analysis skills.

Still another curriculum decision that must be made is related to where and when digraphs and blends will be introduced. Digraphs such as *ph, th, oi,* and *wh* must be seen as a single perceptual unit to which a sound is to be attached. It is not at all clear when is the best time to introduce digraphs. If the introduction of digraphs is delayed until fairly late in a teaching sequence, the limited selection of words may have a serious effect on the child's interest in a story line.

These are just some of the vexing problems touched on by Beck and Block in their analysis of the Palo Alto and Ginn reading programs. These decisions have to be made by curriculum developers, and presently there are no clear guidelines to use in making these decisions.

Another important decision that must be made by curriculum developers has to do with the subskills that are to be taught in a program. Presently, although we know that there are subskills in reading, we do not know what all of them may be, and new ones are recognized from time to time. For example, it is now thought to be important to introduce the beginning reader to "the language of instruction" and to introduce reading through the use of rebus reading materials. It is thought that these are important skills and approaches to reading and that they should have transfer effects to make the acquisition of reading easier.

Kenneth Goodman and Yetta Goodman

The Goodmans' chapter presents a number of provocative ideas. An important point made is the differentiation between that which is natural and that which is innate. The two are not mutually exclusive categories. For example, language acquisition has an important component of that which may be called "innate," and in most cases, it is acquired naturally. The oral communication skill is acquired in a natural manner when the child is motivated, and the skill has functional importance in that child's life. According to the Goodmans, an important indicator of a naturally occurring behavior is that the behavior is performed because there is reason and need to perform it. This is what should occur in reading.

Although the Goodmans present one reason for the child to engage in reading, children read for a variety of reasons, one of which is intrinsic motivation. For about a decade, psychologists have accepted the idea that there is an innate human will to learn, a desire to know, to find things out. These intrinsic motives do not depend on reinforcement from the world that lies outside the organism but derive instead from the satisfaction derived by the organism from mastering an element of its environment.

Another reason children read is what might be termed "achievement motivation." In some societies, mastery over aspects of one's environment is an important motive. In our society there are certain developmental tasks that are viewed as part of the growing-up process. These tasks include toilet training, learning to dress appropriately, acquiring social skills, learning to read and write, learning to drive and being able to go about in one's city, and learning job-related skills. One of the motivations for learning to read is that it is an important developmental task in the growing-up process.

Still another reason that children engage in reading is that important role models in the child's environment have reading skills. When a child can identify with the model who commands respect, the child may adopt the motives of the model. Parents, teachers, or older siblings may serve to implant in the child the importance of acquiring reading skill.

Children may also engage in reading through the use of external reinforcers. The operant conditioning literature and the behavioral management literature are explicit about how the child may be induced to engage in reading. There are a number of people who are critical of the use of extrinsic reinforcers for inducing reading. However, a sound argument may be made that what is really being attempted is to get the child to practice reading to the point where natural reinforcers such as the pleasure of reading will finally be sufficient and the external reinforcers may be withdrawn.

A point made by the Goodmans is that if learning to read could be made as natural as learning to listen and speak, all children would acquire literacy skills. This hypothesis is indeed interesting but almost untestable. According to this view, whenever children have difficulty in acquiring literacy skills, one can always say that the reason is that the social environment for learning was unnatural.

The Goodmans are on safe ground regarding the need to provide relevant reasons for reading. Too often teachers forget this and simply want the child to read because the child is in school and reading is part of the curriculum. Consequently, some children may be turned away from acquiring complex reading skills. To the extent that we can build an environment in which children are motivated to read we will be that far ahead in teaching literacy skills. However, assuming that we can provide an environment in which children will be highly motivated to read, will that be sufficient to guarantee success in teaching reading? Since research on characteristics of successful reading programs indicates that reading method is only one element in a complex system, it appears to be an oversimplification to believe, as the Goodmans do, that "children are in no more need of being taught to read than they are of being taught to listen."

The Goodmans claim that beginning readers keep their minds on meaning. This does not seem to correspond to the facts. The learner must decode prior to acquiring meaning, and it is important that we give children these decoding skills so that they can then derive meaning from what is on the page.

The Goodmans claim that if literacy skills were acquired in as natural a way as speaking and listening, we might possibly have as much success with literacy as we do with speaking and listening. It should be recognized, however, that the learning of a first language, with its speaking and listening components, is uniquely human and different in important ways from other kinds of learning, such as learning to read. There are a number of arguments to support the belief that learning a language involves innate, genetically determined mechanisms that operate on information about the structure of language that a child gets from listening to speech. There is support for the notion that language potential is genetically encoded: First, we have evidence for the fact that language is universal and common to all humans. Second, historical investigations of languages reveal that although spoken languages change, at no time does one find evidence of speech that can be described as being aphonemic or ungrammatical. Although an individual's speech may be ungrammatical in terms of some standard, as in "He don't know better," we do find that the patterning of words is rule governed. Third, specific language disability characterized by delayed speech onset, poor articulation, and marked reading disability, with general intelligence remaining unaffected, appears to be inherited. Fourth, the developmental schedule of language acquisition tends to follow a fixed sequence so that even if the entire schedule is retarded, the order of the attainment of skills remains constant. Finally, comparisons of children learning a language other than an Indo-European language with children learning English indicate a high degree of concordance between the milestones of speech and motor development.

Although it is true that speech acquisition appears to proceed easily and naturally, it is not at all certain that learning to read need necessarily proceed in as easy a manner. The primary reason for this difference is that whereas speech acquisition appears to be natural to humans, much like walking, reading is not a natural behavior indigenous to our species. All humans have developed language systems, but not all societies are literate. Generally, learning to speak is accomplished with little difficulty, whereas learning to read requires considerably more effort. The process of speech acquisition is gradual, beginning at infancy and extending for a considerably period of time; the introduction of reading is much more abrupt and less gradual. There are strong sources of reinforcement involved with speech acquisition, whereas sources of reinforcement for reading may be much less forceful. Those strong reinforcers that are applied in speech acquisition are applied almost immediately following appropriate speech behaviors. In the process of learning to read, the reinforcers, usually much weaker, are often delayed. It is accurate to say that for nearly all people, acquisition of their first language is easily mastered. However, for a sizeable number of people, literacy is achieved only with difficulty, if at all. It is apparent that by providing an environment that is more conducive to motivating children to read, we can help children to acquire reading skills. This is no magic panacea for reading fluency problems but merely an important component of pedagogy.

Carl Frederiksen

Frederiksen's chapter is concerned with the process of converting discourse into meaning. Two ways this process may take place are described. These are referred to as top-down and bottom-up processing. *Bottom-up processing* refers to a procedure in which lower level processing occurs before higher level processing. To put it in Frederiksen's terms, "in the bottom-up conception, the processes by which a person understands a discourse are controlled by the textual input, that is, there is a more or less automatic parsing of each sentence in an input text followed by semantic interpretation based on sentence syntax." The top-down version "represents an opposite extreme in which the syntactic and interpretive components are presumed to be always under the control of high-level inferential processes." The latter view holds that we bring our experiences and knowledge to bear on a verbal input and use our semantic generative capacities, as well as the verbal input, to gather meaning. This latter view suggests that we use text input as needed. According to Frederiksen, top-down and bottom-up processing are not mutually exclusive.

Top-down processing seems to be more economical, at least in terms of the load imposed on short-term memory. There may be times when bottom-up processing occurs, such as when an individual is at a relatively beginning stage in acquiring a verbal process, or when the individual encounters difficulty in processing texts at a higher level. Frederiksen suggests that an individual who encounters difficulty in processing at a higher level will drop down to a lower level to process material. The LaBerge–Samuels automaticity model suggests precisely the same thing with regard to perceptual processing. According to the LaBerge–Samuels model of visual memory, an individual who is using bottom-up processing would start at the feature level and combine these features to form letters. Letters are then combined to form letter clusters, which then are formed into words. The words themselves are then concatenated to form word groupings. The model assumes, however, that an individual will work at the highest level possible and drop down to lower levels when processing at the higher level becomes ineffective. Empirical evidence from our laboratory with regard to visual processing has provided support for this model (Terry, Samuels, & LaBerge, 1976). We have found that in processing common words in regular orthography, the individual may be working at the whole-word level, but when these same words are presented in mirror image, the individual drops down to either a feature or letter level. Similar operations may be at work in processing at the semantic level.

Since top-down processing of discourse seems to be more economical, Frederiksen is concerned that emphasis in reading instruction on subskills and decoding may be counterproductive in that it may encourage the child to process in an ineffective direction. However, using a behavioral analysis of reading, one may argue that decoding precedes comprehension. Once the decoding skills become automatic, the child will then be able to process meaning in a top-down direction. What we must be careful of is trying to instill the processing strategies of highly skilled readers in beginning readers, thus denying them developmental trends in skill development.

Dennis Fisher

Fisher's chapter has two parts—a theory section, in which a model of reading based on the ideas of Hochberg and LaBerge and Samuels is presented, and a section dealing with applications to disabled readers. Fisher states that he finds the LaBerge–Samuels model of memory acceptable but that any model of reading that fails to include peripheral and foveal involvement in the recognition process is inadequate. Considering our current state of development in model building, perhaps all we should be doing is creating partial models rather than full comprehensive models of the reading process (cf. Gregg & Farnham-Diggory, Volume 3, this series). Some of our comprehensive models of the reading process are so poorly described as to be nearly incomprehensible, even to highly trained psychologists. An additional weakness of some of these comprehensive models is that they fail to generate testable hypotheses. The LaBerge–Samuels' automaticity model makes no claim about being a comprehensive model and focuses instead on the role of selective attention as it relates to reading.

Before describing the educational implication section of Fisher's chapter, a few comments about theory section are in order. Fisher notes that when spaces between words are removed, the reading fluency of fifth and sixth graders was affected but not that of first and second graders. This finding fits well with the data we collected at the Minnesota Reading Research Project. In comparing the size of the visual unit used in word recognition, the Minnesota studies found that beginning readers tended to use a letter-by-letter serial processing, whereas more highly skilled readers tended to use a much larger unit of perception—often the whole word. Eliminating spaces between words by filling them in with X's would not interfere with the beginning reader since the beginning reader is simply using a single letter in the word recognition process. The adult, however, who is using a unit as large as a word, needs to have the space between words in order to set off the word boundaries. Consequently, eliminating the cue for the word boundary interferes with the processing of a more highly skilled reader.

Much of what Fisher has to say about application is highly acceptable to reading researchers and teachers. For example, Fisher claims that the problem in reading disability seems not to be perceptual and that there is great need for practice on grapheme–phoneme correspondences until some level of automaticity is reached. Poor readers have also been found to have short saccadic eye movements, which implies letter-by-letter processing. These readers have also been found to have eye fixations of some fairly long duration, which implies long central processing time.

However, there are other statements by Fisher that probably would evoke disagreement among a segment of those people who are concerned about the reading process. These statements have to do with the disabled reader. The disabled reader is defined as one who has the necessary intelligence for reading, has no perceptual defects, has normal motivation, has had adequate instruction, but who does not profit by that instruction. If this child reads at a level sufficiently below his or her potential, then he or she is defined as a disabled reader. This type of diagnosis is of the weakest type, because it is what might be called "diagnosis by elimination." All other sources of possible causes of failure are ruled out, and the only thing left is that the reader is disabled.

One aspect of the problem of diagnosis in reading failure has to do with what might be called "attribution theory." The problem we are dealing with concerns ascriptions of causality. In diagnosing a child as "dyslexic" we are ascribing reading failure to forces within the child rather than to forces that may be external to the child. In this case, Fisher attributes the cause of reading disability to an area within the brain, known neurologically as Broca's or Wernicke's area. It is important for us to distinguish between those individuals who have acquired literacy skills and subsequently lose them through brain injury, which we may call "alexia" (an acquired failure produced by a cerebral lesion to comprehend written words), and those individuals who have an inherent incapacity to learn or comprehend written material and in whom there is no evidence of a brain lesion (*dyslexia*). There is adequate empirical evidence for alexia, but at the present time, there seems not to be an adequate amount of evidence for the support of dyslexia, at least to the point where we are able to ascribe difficulty in learning the written code to particular areas of the brain.

Statements by Fisher such as "the truly dyslexic or reading disabled ... will never learn to read ..." and "It must be understood that dyslexia can't be cured—the brain will not stand for that" are statements that will surprise many, given our current state of knowledge regarding why children have difficulty in reading. These statements are so definitive that they seem to be out of keeping with the state of the art in reading pedagogy. In fact, many children who have been labeled as dyslexic have learned to read, although their rate of progress may be slow, and some of these children have gone on to occupations demanding a high level of reading. One can argue, then, that in a large proportion of cases, reading instruction is less than adequate and we should look to our failures in instruction before labeling a child as disabled.

Barbara Bateman

The chapter by Barbara Bateman presents a critical overview of efforts to solve the reading problems of a group of students labeled as "learning disabled." There are a host of reasons that a child may experience difficulty in reading. These reasons or factors may include variables external to the child such as poor materials, poor teaching practices, or poor reinforcing contingencies. On the other hand, there may be factors internal to the child such as unusually low intelligence or perhaps some (hypothesized but yet unproven) neurological problem.

Bateman's chapter is provocative in many ways. Instead of being cautious, Bateman makes her statements in a very strong form, inviting either criticism or agreement. One of the major points of Bateman's chapter is that we already know enough about how to teach reading to make a significant difference. The problem then is not lack of knowledge about teaching but one of implementation. Another strong point Bateman makes is that an early emphasis on reading for meaning without proper emphasis on decoding skills is disastrous and may well explain why we have reading failure.

Bateman proposes that a reasonable approach to overcoming some of the reading problems includes using task-analytic programming and applied behavioral analysis, and reducing attention deficits, implying that detailed analyses of terminal reading behaviors must be done in order to extract the subskills involved in reaching these desired behaviors. Such an approach has not been carried out sufficiently well in reading. For example, numerous nonessential skills are taught in reading, and we presently lack sufficient information on what the necessary skills might be and their order of introduction. Most researchers would agree that a complex behavior such as reading is comprised of subskills, but the exact type of hierarchy one might build from these subskills is unclear at the present. Much research needs to be done on the problems relating to hierarchical subskills in reading before this question can be answered.

Bateman emphasizes the important role of attention in reading. There are two aspects of attention, an overt and a covert component, and we should be clear in differentiating between the two. Overt attention is related to factors that are generally observable, such as the direction of gaze, compliance with task demands, eyes in book when requested, listening to the speaker, and general alertness. Research on overt attention and its correlation with reading achievement indicates that the two are substantially correlated. It has been known for some time that, at least in the early stages of reading, girls are superior to boys. This has been attributed to sex-linked genetic factors. However, recent research by Samuels and Turnure (1974) found that girls were significantly more attentive in class and also read better. It may well be that the superiority of girls in the early stages of reading is environmentally produced through greater compliance with teacher task demands, rather than being genetic in origin.

The nonobservable aspect of attention is also important. This internal component of attention is important because the reader's attention can be directed either to decoding or to getting meaning, but not to the two processes simultaneously. Beginning readers tend to focus attention on decoding, and consequently, comprehension suffers. On the other hand, skilled readers decode automatically. One important developmental aspect of reading is growth in decoding skill to the point where it can be done automatically, freeing attention to be deployed primarily on getting meaning.

Another point Bateman makes is that method does make a difference. As mentioned earlier, Bateman believes that an early emphasis on meaning in which decoding is not emphasized is disastrous. Since decoding is important, according to Bateman, programs focusing on it should be selected. In working on decoding skills, teachers should make every effort to provide adequate opportunity for working on meaning. It is entirely possible to have a good reading program that teaches decoding subskills and at the same time gives the child adequate experience with meaningful reading material.

Perhaps the most interesting part of the Bateman chapter is the suggestion that courts of law may be used as a means to achieve a measure of educational accountability and to remedy the poor teaching that may be going on in our schools. Where teaching is found to be inadequate, one approach may be to change the pedagogical practices of either the teacher or the school system. Bateman claims this course has been tried and found to be ineffective. Instead, Bateman would sue in the expectation that the teachers and administration would be so highly motivated to change behavior that forces from within the school would merge and look for alternative and better ways to do the teaching job. In a sense, we are dealing with what might be called "educational malpractice." However, whereas in medicine physicians may agree on which therapies are acceptable and which courses of action are unacceptable, it is not at all clear that this type of agreement can be found in the realm of educational practice.

James Holland

Holland's chapter shows how behavioral analysis can be applied to reading by examining environmental stimuli controlling a behavior that we may label as reading behavior. This analysis extends to those stimuli that appear on the printed page, as well as to those stimuli that follow responses having reinforcing potential. One of the points Holland makes is that behavior resembling reading may merely be an example of a child's responding to extraneous cues on the printed page.

Early in the process of learning to read it is not unusual to find children who identify words on the basis of irrelevant cues such as word length, word configuration, or some unusual characteristic. As an example, I recall a child who was able to identify a word on a flash card but was unable to do so when that word appeared in context. Since it is usually easier to identify a word in context, I asked the child why he was able to identify the flash card word but not the word in his reading book. The child's answer was that the flash card contained an ink spot in the corner and he knew that whenever the ink spot appeared the response was the one he gave. Chidlren sometimes learn to identify words on the basis of irrelevant cues, such as first or last letters. When given the sentence *The boy fell down,* the student may use the first letters of the words to identify them. Then, when new words are introduced containing the same letters, such as *bats* and *far,* the child calls these words *boy* and *fell* simply because the student is using first letter cues to identify the words. As many teachers who introduce children to reading through a sight-word approach have found, there is generally rapid learing of a sight vocabulary for about the first 25 to 30 words, followed by a period in which there is virtually no increase in sight-word acquisition. The explanation for this common finding is that chidlren use irrelevant cues such as the ones previously mentioned in order to learn the response, but then as new words get introduced that have the same letters, length, and contour, the strategy breaks down and learning stops until the children acquire a more appropriate set of skills for recognizing the words.

There are still other types of extraneous cues that children may use during reading. One of the more ubiquitous examples occurs when pictures and print are presented together. Assume that a picture of a plane and the word *plane* appear together on a card. For the beginning reader the picture more readily illicits the appropriate response, and the learner, using what might be called "the principle of least effort," will focus attention on the picture rather than on the word. The correct response is given, but it is to the wrong cue. The problem is one of transfer of stimulus control. It is important to get the child to focus attention on the printed word rather than on the picture.

Still another example of the problems we must be alert to occurs when we superimpose color on a word, as is done in some reading programs when each color is associated with a particular sound value. The child learns which sounds are associated with which particular colors. The problem arises when the color cues are removed. Generally, one finds that when the color cues are removed, the response can no longer be given because the child was using color as the cue rather than the particular letters of the word. Generally speaking, those reading programs that have used color cues as aids to reading have not evaluated the systems for transfer when color cues are removed. Holland is quite correct in claiming that color coding is not doing a useful job. Holland points out that when evaluations have been done for reading programs using color coding, these evaluations have indicated that the transfer to traditional orthography is relatively ineffective.

CONCLUSION

Having discussed a number of views regarding theories and practices in reading, I am reminded of John Godfrey Saxe's poem "The Blind Men and the Elephant." Curious about the appearance of an elephant, the six blind men decided to study the elephant by direct examination. The first touched the elephant's sturdy side and likened it to a wall. The second felt the tusk and thought the elephant resembled a spear. The third touched the squirming trunk and though the elephant was much like a snake, while the fourth touched the elephant's knee and though the elephant was like a tree. The fifth chanced to touch the ear, and to him, the elephant was like a fan; and the sixth, having touched the tail, thought the elephant was like a snake. Saxe concluded his poem with this thought:

> And so these men of Indostan
> Disputed loud and long,
> Each in his own opinion
> Exceeding still and strong,
> Though each was partly in the right,
> And all were in the wrong!
> The Morale:
> So oft in theologic wars
> The disputants, I ween,
> Rail on in utter ignorance
> Of what each other mean,
> And prate about an elephant
> Not one of them has seen!

Perhaps we who study the reading process are like the blind men. Our views of the process, colored by the discipline orientations within which we work and by the procedures we use to study the process, give each of us but a limited perspective of the process, and so all our views of reading process are partly in the right and all are in the wrong.

REFERENCES

Beck, I. Comprehension during the acquisition of decoding skills. In J. T. Guthrie (Ed.), *Cognition, curriculum, and comprehension.* Newark, Del.: International Reading Association, 1977.
Bidwell, C. E., & Kasarda, J. D. School district organization and student achievement. *American Sociological Review,* 1975, *40,* 55–70.
Bishop, C. H. Transfer effects of word and letter training. *Journal of Verbal Learning and Verbal Behavior,* 1964, *3,* 215–221.
Bormuth, J. R. Reading literacy: Its definition and assessment. In J. B. Carroll & J. S. Chall (Eds.), *Toward a literate society.* New York: McGraw–Hill, 1975.
Brown, B. W., & Saks, D. H. Proper data aggregation for economic analysis of school effectiveness. *Review of Public Data Use,* 1975, *3,* 13–18.

Bureau of the Census, Department of Commerce. Educational attainment: March 1972. *Current Population Reports,* No. 243, November 1972.

Calfee, R. C., Venezky, R. L., & Chapman, R. S. *Pronunciation of synthetic words with predictable and unpredictable letter-sound correspondences* (Tech. Rep. 71). Madison: Wisconsin Research and Development Center for Cognitive Learning, 1969.

Chall, J. S. *Learning to read: The great debate.* New York: McGraw-Hill, 1967.

Chomsky, C. When you still can't read in 3rd grade: After decoding what? In S. J. Samuels (Ed.), *Research implications for teaching reading.* Newark, Del.: International Reading Association, 1978.

Coleman, E. B. Collecting a data base for a reading technology. *Journal of Educational Psychology,* 1970, *61,* 1–23.

Dykstra, R. *Continuation of the coordinating center for first-grade reading instruction programs* (Office of Education, Final Rep. No. 6-1651). Washington, D.C.: U.S. Government Printing Office, 1967.

Feitelson, D. I. In J. Downing (Ed.), *Comparative reading.* New York: Macmillan, 1973.

Garner, W. R. The acquisition and application of knowledge: A symbiotic relation. *American Psychologist,* 1972, *27,* 941–946.

Gibson, E. J., Osser, H., & Pick, A. A study in the development of grapheme–phoneme correspondences. *Journal of Verbal Learning and Verbal Behavior,* 1963, *2,* 142–146.

Goldberg, M. L. *The effects of various approaches to beginning reading* (Final Rep., Beginning Reading Project). New York: Columbia University, Teachers College, 1973.

Guthrie, J. T. *A study of the locus and nature of reading problems in the elementary school* (Final Rep., National Institute of Education). Washington, D.C.: U. S. Government Printing Office, 1976.

Harris, L., and Associates. *The 1971 national reading difficulty index.* New York: National Reading Center, 1971. (ERIC Document Reproduction Service No. ED 057 312)

Jeffrey, W. E., & Samuels, S. J. The effect of method of reading training on initial learning and transfer. *Journal of Verbal Learning and Verbal Behavior,* 1967, *6,* 354–358.

Katz, I., & Singer, H. *Effects of instructional methods on reading acquisition systems: A reanalysis of the first-grade study data.* Paper presented at the meeting of the International Reading Association, Anaheim, Cal.: 1976.

Lahaderne, H. Attitudinal and intellectual correlates of attention: A study of four sixth-grade classrooms. *Journal of Educational Psychology,* 1968, *59,* 320–324.

Rosinski, R. R., & Wheeler, K. E. Children's use of orthographic structure in word discrimination. *Psychonomic Science,* 1972, *26,* 97–98.

Samuels, S. J. The method of repeated readings *The Reading Teacher,* 1979, *32,* 403–408.

Samuels, S. J., & Turnure, J. E. Attention and reading achievement in first-grade boys and girls. *Journal of Educational Psychology,* 1974, *66,* 29–32.

Silberman, H. F. Exploratory research on a beginning reading program. Santa Monica, Cal.: System Development Corp., 1964.

Terry, P. R., Samuels, S. J., & LaBerge, D. The effects of letter degradation and letter spacing on word recognition. *Journal of Verbal Learning and Verbal Behavior,* 1976, *15,* 577–585.

Vogt, D. K. *Literacy among youths 12–17 years* (National Center for Health Statistics, DHEW Publication No. HRA 74-1613). Washington, D.C.: U. S. Government Printing Office, 1973.

Wattenberg, B. J., & Scammon, R. M. *This USA.* New York: Pocket Books, 1967.

Weber, G. *Inner-city children can be taught to read: Four successful schools.* Washington, D.C.: Council for Basic Education, 1971.

15 Theories and Practice of Beginning Reading: A View From the Back of the Bus

Edmund W. Gordon
Teachers College, Columbia University
and
Educational Testing Service

I have subtitled my remarks "A View from the Back of the Bus," because I do not know whether I should be flattered by being given the opportunity to have the last word or whether I should be protesting about being placed at the end of the line. Nevertheless, there is one advantage to being last—at least those who disagree with me do not have a chance for rebuttal. The disadvantage is that I miss the benefits of discussions of my reflections. However, you may benefit in that I may make my remarks somewhat more brief.

I have been asked to do two things: to present a general reaction to the chapters and to comment on two reading programs, both of which have been developed in a culture-specific context. I attend to the latter task only briefly, as a more thorough analysis than was possible in the time available would be necessary to do these programs justice. Let me simply indicate, however, that both of these programs, one developed by Cureton (1973) and the other by Simms-Macharia and Simms (1972) working with Preston Wilcox, proceed from the assumption that there are content and stylistic characteristics peculiar to the black community. They assume further that when these characteristics are appropriately represented in the reading materials and reading instructional practices to which black children are exposed, they result in more active involvement in the learning task by these children and ultimately in more effective learning. I do not have access to evaluation data on those programs and can only report that the programs have been received rather enthusiastically in some black communities.

A report on one of the programs, the Cureton program, did reach the newspapers a few years ago when George Cureton and Kenneth Clark (the latter is a strong supporter of Cureton's work) were called to task for some alleged irregularities in the evaluation procedure. Cureton argued that it was a political move: I think Clark supported him on that claim. What seems to have been in dispute was whether the supplementary strategies used in connection with the instructional procedures were so specific to the evaluation measures as to have influenced the evaluation outcomes. Available data indicated significant gains in reading achievement associated with the use of the Cureton materials and procedures. Both of these programs stress motivation, active rather than passive participation, directive structure in the learning experience, and reinforcement of appropriate involvement and responses on the part of the pupil.

It is my judgment that the assumptions underlying the development of the materials are probably too simplistic to address all the broad problems in reading achievement among black children. However, I do not at all doubt that these materials can effectively facilitate the learning of reading by some children. The assumptions seem sound. The materials and procedures are well conceived. The content of the material is culture sensitive. They are a welcome addition to the instructional resource pool.

THEORETICAL NEEDS

Let me turn to my other assignment. A number of problems have been raised by several of the authors. I will identify a few and share some of my biases. There are the problems that relate to the search for a theory or theories of reading, theories of instruction, theories of reading dysfunction, and theories of reading instructional dysfunction. There are problems that relate to the understanding of reading as a developmental process, to the social context of reading and reading instruction, and to the characteristics of the persons who are learning to read.

In our search for theories, it is interesting that almost all of us have conceptions of what reading is, of what makes for reading dysfunction, or of how one should go about teaching reading. This may be a reflection of the complex nature of the reading process itself and of the complexities of the circumstances that influence it. Because of these complexities, each of us looks at a part of the process; or at the whole process from a particular perspective; and comes up with a slant that makes sense under certain conditions. Certainly, a search for multiple theories makes more sense, given the present state of our knowledge, than looking for a single theory. We remember, of course, that theories are not facts; they are constructs that enable us to work more effectively on a problem. It is in the very nature of theories that they are to be tested and discarded or tested and reformulated, and they are the basis for organizing experiences, information, or practice until they are disconfirmed.

I find the stage theory advanced by Chall quite interesting and particularly useful in understanding one of the problems to which I have devoted a good bit of my work. Her identification of the decoding stage as being different from the confirmation and fluency stage and her description of the characteristics of the confirmation stage permit us and her to explain a possible source of difficulty for low-status children as they learn to read. It may be that the social conditions and characteristics of life for low-status people in our society do not permit richness of literacy experiences essential to the confirmation of decoding skills and the development of fluency in their use.

The attention to process in Frederiksen's chapter is novel for trying to understand the functional tasks of reading, but his top-down or bottom-up scheme probably is not presented in a sufficiently dialectical form. [Eds. Note: These remarks are based on an earlier version of Frederiksen's chapter, not on the present version.] What seems to be missing is attention to the dynamic— even protean—nature of the process. The functional demands and situational characteristics of the immediate task, or even subtask, have their influences on the process. The characteristics of one aspect of the process can influence—even determine—the direction of other aspects of the process. Reading, like any other complex process, is likely to be dialectical and interactive rather than unidirectional and nonvariant.

Venezky and Massaro's concept of orthographic regularity and its critical function at several stages of reading provides a useful reference point for trying to understand reading dysfunction in a variety of learners. In addition, as they point out, the concept provides additional rationale for phonics instruction. It is not only essential to learning to decode, but in concert with habit formation it is a central feature of anticipation and prediction in rapid word recognition.

Additional contributions to theory are made in other chapters, which I will not cite. The problem is that none of these theories is complete. Some address reading as a process, some address instruction, and some address dysfunctions in both. Not only do we need to continue this theoretical work to fill in the gaps; we also very greatly need more synergistic formulations, building on complementarities between postulates. Fisher speaks of the synthesis of models as an alternative to the development of additional competing models. One of the outcomes of this series of volumes might well be the generation of more complete micro- and macro-theoretical systems from the many contributions to theory produced by our collective efforts.

READING AS A DEVELOPMENTAL PROCESS

Several of the chapters introduce, suggest, or at least imply that reading is a developmental process. Chall describes the stages through which the process passes. Perfetti and Lesgold, Sticht, and Frederiksen are among those who discuss discrete processes or process sequences involved in the development of reading proficiency. All this is useful work. However, the neglected problem, as I see it, has to do with the relation of skill to competence. What is the role of skill acquisition in the development of competence? What is the relation of skill training to the facilitation of competence? And, maybe of even more importance, what is the relation of skill development to the functional and satisfying expression of competence?

I think Beck and Block approach that issue, but they do not fully engage it. It appears that the Goodmans also speak to this issue. In their chapter, which beautifully reflects the humanistic traditions of education, they set forth an approach to teaching which, when it works, should result in learning being a joyful experience and, in my logical scheme, should result in enthusiastic expression and use of what is learned. Even more important, the approach seems to be concerned with making what is learned an extension of one's self and a reflection of that which is natural to human societies. The Goodmans see themselves as facilitating the development of linguistic competence without necessarily stressing skill mastery. Their question to Holland would be, I believe, "Is there something about language that makes the behavioral approach particularly appropriate?" This would not be simply an expression of the Goodmans' impatience with behaviorists; it would also be an expression of concern that the way in which skills are developed and the excess (and even sometimes destructive) baggage accompanying that development may get in the way of the development and satisfying expression of competence.

All of us no doubt agree that we have to learn how to do things before we develop facility for doing them, and certainly before we derive joy from the expression of them. Yet in our approach to this developmental problem we seem to be giving very little attention to the possibility that efficient mastery training may be counterproductive to satisfying competence expression. As we try to facilitate, develop, or train for skill mastery in these children, what do we know about the relation of such skill mastery and the way it is developed to their ultimate achievement of competence and the satisfying expression of that competence? If we recognize reading to be a developmental process, then we must worry more about the dialectical relation of skill mastery at one stage to the development and expression of competence at the next stage.

Another problem relating to viewing reading as a developmental process involves the development of automaticity as an expression of skill or as the foundation for competence. Several of the authors of these chapters refer to automaticity. It is generally treated as if it were a naturally occurring phenomenon. We have not yet determined how automaticity is developed, of what it is composed, and the fate of these component elements. I suggest that this is an important unsolved problem, not so much for understanding those who develop automatic reading behaviors but for understanding those who do not. We certainly cannot look only at skilled automatic behavior in order to determine how it develops or what remedial steps should be taken to facilitate it.

I often recall an experience that Stella Chess (1969), a child psychiatrist who supervised my training in psychotherapy, recounted about a little girl whom she was treating who had a number of phobias associated with some physical handicaps she had. The little girl had cerebral palsy and had some residual weakness in her left arm. Chess was including among her evidence of phobic behavior the youngster's great difficulty and unwillingness to learn a simple activity that children perform—to bounce a ball and throw one's right foot over it. Chess simply thought that this was another expression of this young girl's general anxieties until one day, when she was on a playground watching some younger children playing, she noted that some of them were learning how to perform this activity. She noted that to learn it, you hold on to a support with your left hand before starting to effect mastery with your right hand and right foot. Once the behavior was mastered, that support was no longer necessary. What Chess realized was that in the process of learning this task, her patient, whose failure to master the task she had attributed to phobic reactions, was actually unable to master it because of the real physical handicap on her left side.

If one looks at only the terminal behavior, one misses the subbehaviors that are a part of the developmental process. I ask, then, with respect to reading, what are the developmental micro-components of a macro-process we recognize as automaticity? And what is the relation of mastery or failure to master those micro-components to the spontaneous or directed development of automaticity?

SOCIAL CONTEXT OF READING

There are problems related to the social context of reading and reading instruction. Except for the chapter by Shuy, in which differential language systems are discussed in their relation to reading instruction, and the Frederiksen chapter, where reference is made to possible sources of inference interference, we have given little attention to the social context of reading. As important as our more technical anaylses of the reading process are, I must mention in passing that reading instruction, learning to read, and reading behavior all occur in situations that support, interfere with, or are neutral to the phenomenon. I have no hard data to support the observations, but as I travel around the country looking at school programs, children do seem to learn to read in institutions where it is clear that they are expected to learn and where there is support for the behaviors that underlie reading competence. In some schools reading is the thing to do; in other schools you "dare not be caught dead" reading. These situational differences are important.

It is my view that the approach to the facilitation of learning that the Goodmans discuss will probably be effective for many children who come to school prepared and ready for academic reinforcement and the academic socialization process begun at home. I do not mean to demean their work, but many of these children cannot help but learn as long as the efforts of the school are positive, or at least benign. Nevertheless, we are worried about reading in part because there are too many children who are not adequately taught to read. They come disproportionately from low-status families that, with a high degree of regularity, send them to school poorly prepared and lacking in readiness for traditional approaches to academic reinforcement. They need academic habilitation if mainstream academic and social competence is to be our goal for them.

One of my students, studying reading in mildly retarded subjects, has generated data that show relatively low relationships between intelligence test scores and scores on the Bender Gestalt Test, and scores on tests of reading achievement. His data show, on the other hand, a considerably higher relationship between the degree of support in the home for reading and reading achievement. In other words, the test scores did not predict reading achievement, but the home environment ratings did so quite well.

When Birch (1967) studied all the 10-year-old children in Aberdeen, Scotland, he found a better correspondence between reading achievement and support for reading in the home than between neurologic and health cnditions and reading achievement. Ogbu (1974), an anthropologist, reported low-level involvement and achievement in reading and other academic subjects among pupils who view the postschool opportunity structure as stacked against them. Labov (1973) reported that indigenous decoding skills demonstrated in natural settings were superior to decoding skills demonstrated in school among black youth in Harlem and Bedford Stuyvesant. Williams (1975) reported that black children's performance was superior to that of white children when the decoding task involved a symbol system specific to the black community.

Wallace (1968) discussed the relation between the purposes of schooling and what actually happens in schooling in different phases of societal development. Seeing the purposes of schooling as involving the development of intellect, the develolpment of morality, and the development of skill, he described three developmental stages through which societies pass: the revolutionary phase, the conservation phase, and the reactionary phase. Priority with respect to educational purpose is given in relation to that phase which is dominant in the society. In the revolutionary phase, highest priority is given to morality, with intellect and skill following thereafter. In the conservation phase, skill is most emphasized, followed by morality and intellectual development. Wallace suggested that in socieities in the reactionary phase morality, which by that time has become primarily concerned with the maintenance of law and order, is given top priority. There is some attention given to skill and relatively no attention given to intellect. What Wallace did not discuss, though, is that in any society, different segments of that society may be in different phases of development so that there may be some segments in the revolutionary phase, some in the conservation phase, and some in the reactionary phase. If there are children in school whose phase of development is different from the phase of society, and if, therefore, the purposes for which they use the school are different from the purposes for which the society maintains the school, there is the kind of disjunction that interferes with the nature of the involvement of the children in the educative process. There may be a misfit between the institutional purposes and the personal purposes of the children our schools serve so poorly. In its reactionary phase, the dominant society may be more concerned with socializing its pupils to be compliant and orderly than with developing skill and intellect. To ignore the problems of social context may be counterproductive to our goals of educational improvement.

It is not only the behavior of learners that is influenced by context; the behavior of teachers is also situationally influenced. Samuels mentions that there is a vast amount of information and technique available to us that we do not use. There is no question but that intrinsic and extrinsic factors combine to reduce our tendency to use the knowledge and material resources available to us. Whether the aim is to limit the consumption of tobacco and drugs or food and fuel, or to expand the use of new techniques and ideas, our attitudes and behavior require as much attention as do research and technological development.

In our work with and discussion of reading and its improvement, we seem to forget or simply neglect the empirical and theoretical work of Lewin (1938). Little of our work is directed toward the ways in which we manipulate or control situational or attributional variables to influence what teachers do with what they know and the available resources. It is in the examination of the social context of teaching and learning transactions that we may find the levers by which power is given to our theories and techniques of reading instruction.

I must add to this list of social contextual problems the recent intrusion into education of labor union tactics. If you think they do not influence what teachers are able to do, the way in which parents relate to schools, and the ways in which youngsters relate to schools and teachers, go to New York and observe the struggle there.

CHARACTERISTICS OF LEARNERS

The chapters by Bateman, Beck and Block, Fisher, Frederiksen, and Shuy are particularly relevant to issues related to the characteristics of those who are learning to read. We must be careful to avoid the political problems involved as we group children who are handicapped by naturally occurring conditions, such as physical and mental defects, and those who are handicapped by deprived conditions, such as social disadvantage or opportunity denial. However, the problems are associated with the characteristics and the conditions of children who are trying to learn to read. I must express my appreciation to Bateman for reintroducing into this discussion a concern for attribute treatment interaction. I completely agree with her that we prematurely wrote off that concept and that it deserves additional attention and reconceptualization. I must also call attention to Fisher's efforts at introducing idiosyncratic response tendencies into the discussion—I wish he had discussed it more—and to Holland's discussion of behavioral analysis, particularly if he is willing to include behavior settings as phenomena of importance equal to that of behavior itself and equally in need of analysis. (I assume that as a behaviorist Holland does in practice attend to settings, despite the lack of an explicit reference in his text.) These authors are striking at what I consider to be the heart of the problems of learning dysfunction. There is no question but that learners vary along a broad continuum and in a variety of ways. Some of the variance exceeds the limits of what we call "normal." Whether normal or abnormal, the relevant variance in the characteristics of schooling seems to be too narrow to accommodate the variance in our pupils. It is in the achievement of a higher degree of complementarity between learners' functional characteristics and the resources supportive of learning and available in schools that I place my hopes for making schooling more effective.

I want to refer to the work of some of our "psychoeducational optimists" and then go on to another issue. I refer to Bruner (1966), who asserted that almost anything can be taught to almost anyone if the learning experience is appropriately designed. I refer to Carroll (1963) and to Bloom (1974), who asserted that aptitude is a function of time spent in a set of behaviors or encounters appropriate to the task to be learned. I refer, of course, to Hunt (1972), who asserted that the problem of pedagogy is the problem of the appropriate match between the characteristics of the learner and the characteristics of the learning experience. There are others, of course, but let us move on.

I really do not want to apologize for having no data, but I should admit that what I say from here on is based completely on speculation. Most of the chapters in this volume are based on data. According to our tradition, that makes them more respectable. However, it may be that this heavy emphasis on data and validation limits our work. Quantification and validation, at some stages of the generation of knowledge and understanding, may be dysfunctional. I had the experience not so long ago of sitting with a group of scholars who were trying to draw inferences from the massive review that White, Day, Freeman, Hantman, and Messenger (1973) did of the research and evaluation studies of early intervention in the development of children. After about three days of work, we concluded, among other things, that the problems we were confronted with were too complex to depend on available quantitative data to inform public policy. We agreed reluctantly that the honest judgment of wise people may be a better basis. We also agreed that too heavy a dependence on quantification may blind us to the great value of the use of the clinical analysis of one or a few cases and the analytic and synergistic use of the human brain as research tools. Without detailing our argument, I simply want to suggest that in our current stage of development, a careful application of selected aspects of that knowledge to individual cases of developing readers and to the contexts in which their reading develops and their reading instruction occurs may produce promising hypotheses that can then be subjected to validation.

I believe that the variance we find in learners, in treatments, and in situations is so great as to make individual and small-scale clinical work essential. Furthermore, I believe that the existing and traditional ways of grouping learners for study are dysfunctional. We group them by race, sex, social class, age, IQ, et cetera, and view all these status indicators as being symbolic of some functional processes we assume to be peculiar to these groups. If we must group, why not group by the functional characteristics determined to exist and thought to be important? Among these are cognitive style, rate of information processing, rate of habituation, nature of motivation, direction and strength of interest and aspiration, presence or absence of functional operations related to reading or whatever is to be taught, and something I call "affective response tendencies." Thomas, Chess, Birch, Hertzig, and Korn (1971) called the latter "aspects of temperament"— all things such as activity level, approach–withdrawal, adaptability, intensity of reaction, and so forth. I am simply mentioning that these functional aspects of behavior may be more informative with respect to design of educational experience than are the status variables we have used to group youngsters. Such groupings, or more important, the treatments applied on the basis of such groupings, require not an assessment of the status but an assessment of the function or the process. This function or process data should have greater capacity for informing instruction than do the usual status data.

We cannot talk about the analysis of process adequately without the concurrent analysis of the context—that is, the situation of which the behavioral process is a part. In this analysis, what the teacher does, what the class requires, what the situation permits, what the conditions support, and what the climate expects are important parts of the analysis of the way in which the individual is functioning. When a learning experience is prescribed on the basis of this kind of analysis, a contradiction between the Goodmans and some of the other authors in this volume subsides, since data on some children will indicate that the Goodmans' approach to their education is appropriate. I hope that they are willing to accept that some other children may need other approaches.

In this volume we have examined what we know about reading and reading instruction. Some authors naturally focused on the children who have been served less well, but the problem of reading, reading dysfunction, reading instruction, and reading instructional dysfunction must be understood before that knowledge can be applied to compensatory education. However, understanding that those problems are related to the characteristics of learners and to the contexts of learning enables us to grasp the two concerns. I believe that the problem of equality of educational opportunity in this country is a problem that involves the nurturance of diversity and the achievement of social justice. We may be failing to educate large numbers of low-status children because we have not sufficiently achieved the "match" that Hunt (1972) discussed, the match between the functional characteristics and needs of these youngsters and the educational treatments available to them. The task imposed on nurturance by the diversity of human characteristics is the diversification of treatments. We may not yet know completely how to do that. Yet I see the raw materials with which to work in the diversity of conceptions and strategies reflected in the excellent chapters of this volume. If each of us no longer has to prove that he or she has the universal or generic treatment, if we realize that in our collectivity we have a diversified armarmentarium that now needs to be specified to the needs and characteristics of specific types of learners and to specific situations, we may begin to move closer to the improvement of reading and to the development of social justice.

REFERENCES

Birch, H. Unpublished personal papers, 1967.

Bloom, B. S. Time and learning. *American Psychologist,* 1974, *29*, 682–688.

Bruner, J. *Toward a theory of instruction.* Cambridge, Mass.: Belknap Press of Harvard University, 1966.

Carroll, J. B. A model of school learning. *Teachers College Record,* 1963, *64*, 723–733.

Chess, S. *An introduction to child psychiatry.* New York: Grune & Stratton, 1969.

Cureton, G. O. *Action-reading: The participatory approach.* Boston: Allyn & Bacon, 1973.

Hunt, J. *Human intelligence.* New Brunswick, N.J.: Transaction Books, 1972.

Labov, W. *Language in the inner city: Studies in Black English vernacular.* Philadelphia: University of Pennsylvania Press, 1973.

Lewin. K. *The conceptual representation and the measurement of psychological forces.* Durham, N.C. Duke University Press, 1938.

Ogbu, J. U. *The next generation: An ethnography of education in an urban neighborhood.* New York: Academic Press, 1974.

Simms-Macharia, G., & Simms, P. *The new approach method.* Trenton, N.J.: NAM, P.O. Box 1303, 1972.

Thomas, A., Chess, S., Birch, H., Hertzig, M., & Korn, A. *Behavioral individuality in early childhood.* New York: New York University Press, 1971.

Wallace, A. Schools in revolutionary and conservative societies. In E. Lloyd-Jones & N. Rosenau (Eds.). *Social and cultural foundations of guidance.* New York: Holt, Rinehart, & Winston, 1968.

White, S., Day, M. C., Freeman, P. K., Hantman, S. A., & Messenger, K. P. *Federal programs for young children: Review and recommendations* (Vols. 1–4; HEW Rep. No. DHEW-05-74-101). Washington, D.C.: U.S. Government Printing Office, 1973.

Williams, R. L. The BITCH-100: A culture specific test. *Journal of Afro-American Issues,* 1975, *3,* 103–116.

Author Index

Subject Index